Immigrants & Intellectuals

IMMIGRANTS & INTELLECTUALS

May '68 & the Rise of Anti-Racism in France

Daniel A. Gordon

MERLIN PRESS

© Daniel A. Gordon, 2012

First published in the UK in 2012
by The Merlin Press
6 Crane Street Chambers
Crane Street
Pontypool
NP4 6ND
Wales

www.merlinpress.co.uk

ISBN. 978-0-85036-664-8

British Library Cataloguing in Publication Data is available
from the British Library

Cover photo: French Communist Party's Fête du
Château, Nice, June 2002 (author)

Printed in the UK by Imprint Digital, Exeter

Contents

Acknowledgements

This book was made possible through the Alistair Horne Visiting Fellowship at St Antony's College, Oxford. I am very grateful to the Fellows of St Antony's, to its then Warden the late Marack Goulding, and to Alistair Horne himself, for awarding me the Fellowship. Funding was also received from the Arts and Humanities Research Board, the University of Sussex Graduate Research Centre in the Humanities, and the Research Development Fund at Edge Hill University. Thanks are due to Tony Zurbrugg and Adrian Howe at Merlin Press, and to the staff of the libraries and archives I used, especially Laurent Cantat of the Mouvement contre le Racisme et pour l'Amitié entre les Peuples, Annie Kuhnmuch and Pascal Clerc of the Confédération Française Démocratique du Travail's Archives Confédérales, Phillipe Malpertu of the Archives Départmentales de la Seine-Saint-Denis and Christine Pelloquin of the Centre d'Information et d'Etudes sur les Migrations Internationales in Paris, and Ramzi Tadros of the Centre d'Information et de Documentation sur l'Immigration et le Maghreb in Marseilles, who all went out of their way to provide me with primary sources. I am grateful to the Confédération Française Démocratique du Travail, the Direction des Archives de France and the Jeunesse Ouvrière Chrétienne, for permission to consult restricted access material from their archives.

I am very grateful to audiences at seminars and conferences at the Universities of Sussex, Oxford, Manchester, London, Nice, Princeton, Cambridge, Loughborough, Liverpool, Edge Hill, Greenwich, St Andrews, Paris 8-Saint-Denis, Portsmouth and the Open University, and to an anonymous referee, for the opportunity to try out my arguments on them. For advice on a much earlier version of Chapters 2 and 3, I am very grateful to Rod Kedward and examiners Julian Jackson and Paul Betts, as well as Ian Birchall, Stephen Castles, Máire Cross, Adrian Favell, Ralph Grillo, Alec Hargreaves and Mark Mazower. I would like to thank everyone who helped me in my subsequent Oxford interlude, including Gilles Bertrand, Chris Brooke, Martin Conway, Niall Ferguson, Robert Gildea, Felicity Heal, Cathie Lloyd and James McDougall. For welcoming me with good humour, I would like to thank students and colleagues at Edge Hill University, and former colleagues from the 'Ethandune years' there, during which much of this was written, including John Doran, Rosaria Franco, John Grundy, Tina Hadlow, Roger Ryan, Lee Sartain, Tony Webster and the late Len McDonald. When I was a student protester, 'Higher Education for Everyone, not just the rich' was a slogan on placards: the History team at Edge Hill continue to turn it into a daily reality. Comradeship and intellectual exchange were also provided in recent years by the Association for the Study of Modern and Contemporary France, and the Chester Philosophers Forum.

This book would not have been possible without the support and encouragement of friends and family. For welcoming me during an unforgettable postdoctoral year in Nice I owe much to Omar Djabri, Hassan Hammi, Mouss Mella, Djamal Nouri, Alain Romey, Eric Warembourg and everyone else who used to meet in the cafeteria at the Faculté de Lettres, from whom I learnt a great deal about being an immigrant in France. For their hospitality on my many visits to Paris, I am very grateful to Hiroshi Hirayama, Sudip Kar-Gupta, my cousin Christiane Saxonoff, and especially Angela Zhou and her son Alex Ladurie. I hope that the France in which Alex is growing up is a better place than it would have been but for the events described here. I would also like to thank my father, Jeffrey Gordon, who first awakened my curiosity for political debate and contemporary history, my sister, Sarah Mendez, for our memories of summers spent in France, and my sister-in-law, Kate Horbury, who has shared my enthusiasm for obscure films about 1968. My mother-in-law, Katharine Horbury, proof-read more than one complete draft. My wife, Mary Horbury, encouraged me to begin in the first place, has been very influential in shaping the arguments of this book, and continues the present-day struggle for justice for migrants. Our daughter Diana, who was born some way into the writing of the book, brings great happiness and a passion for telling stories. Thinking over the longer term, I would like to remember my mother Diana Gordon, who was definitely not a 68er, but whose love of France was an inspiration, and her parents Nat and Vera Clyne, who first led me to think about what it is to be an immigrant.

Finally, I would like to thank those for whom 1968 is not just an abstract discussion, but part of their own history, for sharing their memories with me, including Neal Ascherson, Sue Beigel, Rica Bird, Faouzia Bouziri, Rachael Clyne, Anne Couteau, Malcolm Crook, William Feaver, Barbara Furst, Pierre Gineste, Anne Guérin, William Horbury, Selma James, Irene Jones, John Joseet, Jean-Jacques Lebel, Jill Lovecy, Paul Oriol, Guy Phillippon, Sam Semoff, Paul Werner and the late Peter Lennon. Among them, this book is dedicated to the memory of the late Saïd Bouziri, who was at the centre of the story told here, and inspired so many with his generosity in the struggle for human rights.

Any errors of fact or judgement are, of course, entirely my own responsibility.

Daniel A. Gordon
Chester, September 2011

Glossary

Action Directe – Ultra-leftist group, carried out terrorist actions 1979-87.

AAE (Friendly Association of Algerians in Europe) – Immigrant organisation linked to FLN government of Algeria, founded 1962.

Arenc – Immigration detention centre in Marseilles, secret until exposed 1975.

Arrondissements – 20 administrative districts of city of Paris.

AMF (Association of Moroccans in France) / ATMF (Association of Moroccan Workers in France / Association of Maghrebi Workers in France) – Immigrant association opposed to Moroccan government and loosely linked to New Left, founded 1961, renamed 1982 and 2000.

Al Assifa – Newspaper, 1972-75 and theatre troupe, mid-to-late 1970s, both associated with MTA.

ATD-Quart Monde (Aid to All Distress-Fourth World) – Anti-poverty campaigning Catholic-humanitarian group, founded 1957.

Aubervilliers – Northern working-class suburb of Paris, site of deaths of five African workers in fire, 1970.

Autogestion – Workers' self-management.

Banlieue – Suburbs, applied especially to those with large working-class and immigrant populations.

Belleville – Working-class district of eastern Paris, with large North African Jewish and Muslim populations.

Beur – Second-generation French people of North African origin, 1980s.

Bidonville – Shanty town.

Black September – Massacre of Palestinian guerrillas in Jordan, 1970.

Blousons noirs – Leather-jacketed working-class youth, 1960s.

Bobigny – North-eastern working-class suburb of Paris.

Boulevard Barbès – Main North/South thoroughfare adjoining La Goutte D'Or.

Boulevard Saint-Germain – Main East/West thoroughfare of Left Bank Paris.

Boulevard Saint-Michel – Main North/South thoroughfare of Left Bank Paris.

Boulogne-Billancourt – Western suburb of Paris, site of Renault works, largest car factory in France.

Bulldozer affair – Controversy over bulldozing of hostel for Malian workers by Communist municipality in Vitry, 1980-81.

CATE (Worker-Student Action Committee) – Mainly anarchist group seeking to bring immigrant workers into May '68 movement.

La Cause du Peuple – Maoist newspaper affiliated to UJCML and GP.

CDVDTI (Committee to Defend the Lives and Rights of Immigrant Workers) – Principal organiser of *sans-papiers* hunger strikes, 1972-73, originally formed to defend Saïd and Faouzia Bouziri.

CEDETIM (Centre of Anti-Imperialist Studies) – Thirdworldist thinktank founded 1965, loosely associated with PSU.

Censier – Annexe of Paris University.

CFDT (French Democratic Labour Confederation) – Second largest trade union confederation in France, founded 1964, influenced by New Left ideas from PSU.

CFTC (French Confederation of Christian Workers) – Catholic forerunner of CFDT, founded 1919.

CGIL (General Italian Labour Confederation) – Largest trade union confederation in Italy, founded 1906, linked to Communist Party.

CGT (General Labour Confederation) – Largest trade union confederation in France, founded 1895, linked to Communist Party.

Champigny – Eastern suburb of Paris, with large Portuguese population.

Charonne – Metro station in eastern Paris, where nine Communist anti-war demonstrators killed by police, 8 February 1962.

Châtenay-Malabry – South-western suburb of Paris.

CIMADE (Intermovement Committee for Evacuated Persons) – Refugee solidarity organisation, linked to Protestant churches, founded 1939.

Cité Universitaire – International student halls of residence in southern Paris, occupied 1968.

CNHI (National Hall for the History of Immigration) – Immigration museum, opened 2007.

CNPF (National Confederation of French Employers) – Big business pressure group, headquarters occupied after Aubervilliers fire, 1970.

CNRS (National Centre for Scientific Research) – State-funded academic research organisation.

CNT (National Confederation of Labour) – Spanish anarcho-syndicalists, in exile in France 1939-77.

Common Programme – Agreement between PS and PCF, 1972.

Comités Palestine – Pro-Palestinian and immigrant committees, 1969-72.

Conseil d'Etat – State Council, constitutional appeal body.

Coopérants – French international development workers in Africa.

Coopérants rouges – 'Red', ie leftist, coopérants, 1960s.

Crèche sauvage – Unauthorised crèche at Nanterre University, 1970.

CRS (Republican Security Companies) – French riot police.

DOM-TOM (Overseas Departments-Overseas Territories) – French colonies that did not become independent.

Double peine – Double punishment of foreign nationals (prison plus deportation).

DST (Management of Surveillance over the Territory) – French state counter-intelligence agency.

Ecole des Beaux-Arts – Fine Arts School, where many 1968 posters produced.

Ecole Normale Supérieure – Elite Latin Quarter humanities college, where many UJCMLF and GP activists based.

EEC (European Economic Community) – Forerunner of European Union.

ENA (North African Star) – Algerian nationalist faction dominant in early phase of nationalist movement, 1926-37.

Esprit – Left-Catholic monthly intellectual journal, founded 1932.

Etablis – Far Left ex-students who 'established' themselves as factory workers to foster workers' revolt, 1967-c.1980.

FASTI (Federation of Associations of Solidarity with Immigrant Workers) – Pro-immigrant pressure group, founded 1966.

FEANF (Federation of Black African Students in France) – Thirdworldist student union, 1950-80.

FETRANI (Federation of Black African Students and Workers) – Autonomist group, mid-1970s.

Fedaï – Palestinian guerrilla, 1970s.

Flins – Renault car factory to west of Paris, site of battle between pickets and police, 7-8 June 1968.

FLN (National Liberation Front) – Dominant Algerian left-nationalist faction during and after war of independence, 1954-62.

FN (National Front) – Far Right party, founded 1972.

France Observateur / Le Nouvel Observateur – Mainstream left-of-centre weekly magazine, founded 1954, renamed 1964.

Gare de Lyon – Main railway terminus in eastern Paris.

Gare Montparnasse – Main railway terminus in southern Paris.

Gare Saint-Lazare – Main railway terminus in western Paris.

Gaullist – Supporter of right-wing governments of Charles de Gaulle and Georges Pompidou.

GP (Proletarian Left) – Prominent Maoists, successors to UJCML, 1968-73.

Gauchiste – Generic term for 1968-era far leftists, widely used by contemporaries, sometimes with derogatory implication.

GISTI (Group for Information and Support to Immigrant Workers) – Pro-immigrant pressure group, founded 1972.

GOP (Workers' and Peasants' Left) – Maoist-leaning faction within PSU.

La Goutte d'Or – Working-class district of northern Paris, with large North African population.

Groupuscule – 'Very small group', generic term for any far Left mini-party, originated as derogatory term, May 1968.

Harkis – Algerian soldiers fighting in French army against Algerian nationalists, 1954-62.

L'Humanité – Daily newspaper of PCF.

Ivry – South-eastern suburb of Paris, site of immigrant hostel dispute, 1969-70.

JCR (Revolutionary Communist Youth) – Forerunner of LCR, 1966-68.

JOC (Christian Workers Youth) – Left-Catholic youth group, held many meetings regarding immigrant members' participation in 1968.

Latin Quarter – University district of Paris, located on Left Bank.

LC/LCR (Communist League/Revolutionary Communist League) – Trotskyist/Guevarist party, founded 1969, banned 1973, renamed 1974, wound up 2009.

Le Figaro – Rightwing daily newspaper.

Legion of Honour – Prestigious state honour.

Libération – Daily left-of-centre national newspaper founded 1973 by 68ers.

Ligue des Droits de l'Homme (League of the Rights of Man) – Civil liberties pressure group, founded 1898.

Lip – Watch manufacturer in eastern France, prominent example of workers' self-management, 1973.

Loi anti-casseur – 'Anti-vandal law', enacted 1970 with intention of criminalising organisers of leftist demonstrations.

Lutte Ouvrière (Workers' Struggle) – Trotskyist party and newspaper, founded 1968 after banning of Voix Ouvrière.

Manouchian Group / MOI (Immigrant Labour Force) – Cell of foreigners active in French Resistance, affiliated to, but often acting independently of, PCF.

Marche des Beurs – Term applied by media to March for Equality And Against Racism, by French people of North African origin, 1983.

Maspero – New Left publishing house owned by François Maspero, 1959-82.

Le Mèridional – Right-wing daily local newspaper in Marseilles.

Midi – South of France.

Les Minguettes – Estate in suburbs of Lyons, site of rioting, 1981.

Le Monde – Daily centre-left newspaper of record.

MIB (Immigration and Suburbs Movement) – Radical anti-racist association in banlieue, 1995 to date.

MRAP (Movement Against Racism and for Friendship Between Peoples) – Anti-racist pressure group, loosely associated with PCF, founded 1949.

MTA (Movement of Arab Workers) – Prominent North African immigrant leftist group, loosely associated with New Left, 1972-76.

Mutualité – Left Bank meeting hall, site of riot by anti-fascist demonstrators, 1973.

Neuilly – Western suburb of Paris, wealthiest town in France.

Night of the Barricades – 10-11 May 1968, height of street-fighting in Latin Quarter.

OAS (Secret Army Organisation) – Far Right pro-French Algeria group, carried out terrorist actions 1961-63.

OCI (Internationalist Communist Organisation) – Trotskyist party, 1953-91, known for entryism into PS.

Odéon – Latin Quarter theatre, occupied 1968.

Ordre Nouveau – Far Right group.

Ouvrièriste – Workerist, often applied to PCF to designate overwhelming focus on manual workers.

Partisans – Far Left/thirdworldist periodical published by Maspero, 1961-73.

Penarroya – Lead manufacturer in Saint-Denis and Lyons, site of strikes by Moroccan workers, 1971-72.

PCE (Spanish Communist Party) – Official but Eurocommunist-leaning Communists, exiled in France 1939-77.

PCF (French Communist Party) – Official pro-Soviet Communists, founded 1920, principal party of Left in France, 1940s-70s.

PCMLF (Marxist-Leninist Communist Party of France) – Pro-Chinese Maoists, 1967-85.

Périphérique – Busy highway encircling Paris, dividing more middle-class city from more working-class suburbs.

Pied-noirs – Europeans from Algeria.

Place de la République – Square in eastern Paris, traditional site of left-wing marches.

Popular Front – Broad Left coalition government elected 1936, accompanied by strike wave.

Porteurs de valises – French activists who aided Algerian struggle for independence by carrying suitcases of money out of France.

PS (Socialist Party) – Mainstream socialist/social-democrat party, formed 1969.

PSU (Unified Socialist Party) – New Left party of several factions, formed 1960 in protest at SFIO's support for Algerian War, wound up 1990.

Renseignements Généraux (General Information) – Branch of French police concerned with gathering political intelligence.

Revisionist – Derogatory term for PCF, used by Maoists.

Révolution Afrique! – Group of ex-JCR militants involved in activism with African immigrants, 1969-1980.

Rive gauche – Left Bank, portion of Paris to south of River Seine.

RAP (Rock Against Police) – Association organising anti-racist concerts in banlieue, early 1980s.

Saint-Bruno – Annexe to Saint-Bernard church in La Goutte d'Or, site of hunger strikes from 1972.

Saint-Denis – Northern working-class suburb of Paris.

Sans Frontière – Weekly immigrant newspaper founded by former MTA members, 1979-86.

Sans-papiers – Immigrants 'without papers' seeking by own activism to obtain regularisation of status or prevent deportation.

SDS (Socialist German Student Confederation) – Principal student New Left group in West Germany, 1961-70.

Secours Rouge (Red Assistance) – Cross-party New Left humanitarian group, founded 1970.

SFIO (French Section of the Workers' International) – Mainstream socialist/social-democrat party, forerunner of PS, 1905-69.

Service d'ordre – Political party's security force.

Situationists – Ultra-leftist avant-garde intellectual movement, often held influential on slogans of 1968.

SNESUP (National Higher Education Union) – Lecturers' union, founded 1956.

Socialisme ou Barbarie – Small-circulation journal of ex-Trotskyists, known for analysis of bureaucratisation of pre-1968 society.

Soixante-huitard – 68er.

SONACOTRA (National Company for the Construction of Housing for Workers) – Provider of immigrant hostel accommodation, on rent strike 1975-80.

Les Temps Modernes – Monthly Left intellectual periodical, founded 1945.

Tiersmondiste – Thirdworldist.

Tout! – Newspaper of VLR.

Travailleur immigré – Immigrant worker.

La Tribune Socialiste – Weekly newspaper of PSU.

Tricontinental Congress – Thirdworldist gathering in Havana, 1966.

UGTSF (General Union of Senegalese Workers in France) – Radical union, loosely linked to New Left, founded 1964.

UJCML (Union of Marxist-Leninist Communist Youth) – Maoist students, forerunners of GP, founded 1966, banned 1968.

UNEF (National Union of Students of France) – Main student union, active during Algerian War and in 1968.

Vitry – Communist-run municipality in south-eastern suburbs of Paris, noted for controversy over bulldozing of hostel for Malian workers, 1980-81.

VLC/VLR (Long Live Communism/Long Live Revolution) – Libertarian group originating from Maoism, founded 1968, renamed 1969, wound up 1971.

La Voie Communiste – Far Left group of ex-Communists, late 1950s.

Zaâma d'Banlieue – Feminist/left-libertarian group in Lyons banlieue, early 1980s.

Introduction

The Shanty Town and the University

In the spring of 1968, student unrest at a university campus just outside Paris sparked off a chain of events that led to one of the world's leading industrial economies poised on what looked like the brink of revolution. That campus was Nanterre, a concrete brutalist design built next to one of the largest shanty towns in France. In those shanty towns thousands of immigrant workers lived with their families in muddy Third World conditions just a few kilometres to the west of the Champs-Elysées. Today the university still thrives, though challenged for dominance of the western suburban skyline by the grandiose business development at La Défense, more banal tower blocks of social housing (designed for, amongst others, those who once lived in the shanty towns), and even a barracks for members of the CRS riot police (the traditional foe of student and immigrant alike). This is the *banlieue*, the high-rise suburbs that have become globally synonymous with the controversies without end that swirl around the lived reality of immigration in France and beyond. As for the shanty towns, however, the casual visitor to Nanterre can see no visible sign that they ever existed.

If the visitor took a book from the library shelf and tried to find out more about Nanterre's turbulent past, they would discover much about the students, but little about the people who lived in the shanty town. It was while reading David Caute's otherwise comprehensive account of 1968 that the idea of this book first came to me. Caute mentioned in passing that the university was built next to an Algerian shanty town, but left it at that.[1] What, I wondered, did the Algerians think about the campus revolt that became a general strike? As they had little to lose, did they join in with enthusiasm, or did they wonder with incomprehension what middle-class students had to revolt about? How did 1968 look from the shanty town? For that matter how did the shanty town look to the 68ers? This book is the product of my search to uncover this meeting of two different worlds. The exploitation of immigration as a political issue by the Right in Europe over the last three decades is well known, and a familiar theme of reportage on France by the English-language media. Yet for twenty years previously, this issue had already been raised in a very different, anti-racist, way, by a broad collection of movements known internationally as the New Left, in France as *gauchistes*[2] – as part of their critique of capitalism during the years of social upheaval defined by the revolt of 1968. This book recounts the rise and fall, between 1961 and 1983, of a cycle of protest movements for the rights of immigrant workers in France. It debunks the myth that 1968 was solely an affair of French or European students. Neither glorifying nor demonising these movements, this book tells the fascinating but today largely forgotten story of the encounter of two worlds, the immigrant and the intellectual. It goes on to explain the legacy of this encounter for how the politics of migration, and the politics of protest, came to be as they are in France and beyond today.

Putting Immigration Back into the History of 1968

The conventional narrative of May '68 has been told many times before. Exactly ten years after President Charles de Gaulle had come out of retirement to establish the seemingly stable Fifth Republic, 'France was bored'. Suddenly a revolt broke out: apparently from nowhere, geographically from Nanterre. The campus became a centre of agitation as its predominantly middle-class students protested over the lack of facilities and outdated regulations, politicised by the young Dany Cohn-Bendit and his ideologically motivated libertarian friends into a wider revolt against the paternalist authoritarianism that characterised the regime of the aged general. On 3 May, Nanterre was shut, bringing the student revolt into the heart of Paris' Latin Quarter, where truncheon-wielding riot police invaded the Sorbonne and students retaliated by ripping up the area's legendary paving stones. By the night of 10 May, barricades had gone up, leading cynics to see the revolt as a kitsch pastiche of the revolutions of the nineteenth century. The trade unions protested at police brutality, with what was intended as a one-day strike and march on 13 May. But one by one, workers seized control of their workplaces and went on all-out strike. For a few short weeks, it seemed as if imagination was in power and all authority was breaking down ... until de Gaulle did one of his famous disappearing acts. He left for the French army's headquarters at Baden-Baden in West Germany on 29 May, only to return with one of his equally legendary radio broadcasts. A mass counter-demonstration reclaimed the streets for the government. Elections were called for June. Order was restored. The ephemeral, utopian dream of student-worker unity died, the French people went off on their holidays.

A 'return to normal'. The Right triumphed in the short term, only for the libertarian values often associated with 1968 to transform and liberalise a previously 'blocked society' in the decades that followed and make France what it is today. This national narrative depicts a quintessentially French example of how long-term change was brought about by short-term conflict. But it also, in common with many internationally dominant representations of the period, tends to concentrate on the softer cultural aspects of this change. As Cohn-Bendit put it four decades on, 'We won culturally and socially. But we lost politically. Thank God!'[3]. Or in the words of the historian Niall Ferguson, 'the 1968 revolution was all about clothes'.[4] A typical tale of the Sixties?

By contrast, this book aims to put immigrant workers back into the story. The events of May came at the height of the largest wave of immigration in post-war France, between 1954 and 1974. Some three million immigrants had arrived, with little fanfare or controversy, mostly from the underdeveloped economies of southern Europe and northern Africa. They came to fill the gaps in France's labour market – the dirty, tiring manual jobs in heavy industry that the French were decreasingly willing to do. The 'Thirty Glorious Years' of economic expansion after the Second World War were made by the labour of these migrants who built cars and homes which they could not afford to buy. Many were living in some of the worst housing in Western Europe, in shacks and shanty towns, hostels and cellars. Yet this features little in how 1968 is remembered today. So much effort has gone into portraying 1968 as a 'modernising' moment that it is easy to forget that it was closer in time and, arguably, in spirit to the France of the Popular Front government of 1936 than it was to the France of today. The consumer society now taken for granted in the West was, where it existed at all, a recent innovation. May '68 was – in contrast to say, the Eastern European upheavals of 1989, or even the American version of 1968 – among the last revolutions of the pre-television age, not only because the television journalists were on strike but because set ownership was not quite yet the norm. As recently as 1945, the majority of the French population had worked in agriculture. Industry was still expanding, deindustrialisation not yet on the horizon. While the notion that prosperity had eliminated old social conflicts was becoming more widespread, perceptive observers saw this as something of a myth. Writing in Jean-Paul Sartre's journal Les Temps Modernes in 1962, the key New Left thinker André Gorz refuted the notion that the class struggle was over. Poverty, exploitation and domination were still the reality for many. Though the prosperous hailed cars, washing machines and motorways as heralding the new age of comfort, those who walked, took public transport and had to ration their food intake were hidden from the dominant image of society.[5] If some of the issues raised by May '68 were characteristic of what would come to be described as a post-industrial society, this was a patchy early development, and the immigrant worker question was not really one of them. France's industrial working class was still growing, largely by recruiting from the children of peasants elsewhere in the Mediterranean basin. The experience of many inhabitants of suburbs like Nanterre was that of entry into an industrial society, not a post-industrial one: leaving a shanty town, going on foot, by bus or by train to work long shifts in a factory or building site.

Nor should it be forgotten that France had been virtually continuously at war, first at home, then in Indochina, then in Algeria, from 1939 to 1962: in two of the three cases, there had been a significant component of civil war. A relatively stable, dull liberal democracy of the type too often assumed to be the norm in the West since 1945 scarcely existed. The apparent stability of the five years immediately before 1968 probably seemed an anomaly, since in the five years before those there had been three serious attempts at military coups in France, one of them successful. Politics was, rather, still structured around the ideological clash of Left and Right. All of this and more informed the ideology of 1968, which owed more to Marx and Lenin, Mao and Che than it did to the structuralists and post-structuralists anachronistically packaged in the 1980s as '68 Thought'.[6] So to talk of 1968 in terms of trivial postmodernist symbols is terribly far from the reality. To anyone who remembered hearing of the Battle of Algiers in 1957 – or at least had seen the 1965 film about it – or perhaps had helped defend Paris against an expected airborne invasion by paratroopers in April 1961, the sight of de Gaulle seeking solace in Baden-Baden in the company of the paras' former commander General Massu was truly terrifying. In 1968 itself, contrary to the oft-repeated assertion that 'nobody died', real peoples' lives were at stake, with at least seven killed.[7]

If this was the case for French citizens, this was all the more so for immigrants from societies whose politics was even less stable or liberal-democratic. Of the eight foreign communities numbering over 50,000 at the time of the 1968 census, only two, the 570,000 Italians and the 65,000 Belgians, came from multi-party democracies, in the former case a less than secure one. They were collectively far outnumbered by the 605,000 Spanish and 300,000 Portuguese from the remnants of Europe's pre-war right-wing dictatorships, the 475,000 Algerians, 130,000 Poles and 60,000 Tunisians from one-party socialist states and the 85,000 from the absolute monarchy in Morocco. The underdeveloped world was in ferment, the liberation from colonial rule still fresh – in the case of the Portuguese empire, from whose wars thousands of young conscripts had deserted to France, still to be achieved. In 1968, the year that its dictator Antonio Salazar suffered a brain haemorrhage from falling off his deckchair, Portugal had been crushed by authoritarian rule for some thirty-six years, and its future social democratic leader Mario Soares was a political prisoner on the island of São Tomé off the coast of Africa. The colonial wars would drag on into the 1970s.[8] None of these backgrounds necessarily predisposed immigrants to collective leftist protest. But they indicate just how far their experience of 1968 differed from the hackneyed accounts of carefree students so dominant in Anglo-American narratives of the Sixties.

As observers as far apart politically as the L'Express journalist Eric Conan and the American academic Kristin Ross have noted, the single biggest omission from latter-day memorialisation of '68 is that it was carried out in the name of the working class.[9] The downgrading of the role of the traditional proletariat in the thought of the 'New' as opposed to 'Old' Left was only a matter of degree, and was not especially apparent in France. Most student radicals there – indeed, much of French intellectual life – remained committed to some variant of Marxism until the mid-1970s. Considerable stress, therefore, needs to be placed on the fact that for the France of '68, immigrants were workers first. The French New Left was interested in migrant workers because they were both nationally marginal and proletarians. Contrary to what is sometimes believed today, the events of 1968 and particularly the general strike in France reinforced for many the idea that the working class was a key force for change: ten years later, for example, sociologists entitled a book The Resurgence of Class Conflict in Western Europe since 1968. It was only with the economic crises of the late 1970s and early 1980s that the time came to bid Farewell to the Proletariat,[10] with severe consequences for how questions of migration came to be framed. 'Immigrant workers' powering the French economy were later relabelled as 'immigrants', supposedly posing an existential threat to the cohesion of French values, as in the numerous 'headscarf affairs' since 1989.

So to re-enter the earlier period requires a certain leap of the imagination. In 2006, much rose-tinted nostalgia surrounded the tenth anniversary of the death of President François Mitterrand, standard-bearer of the opposition to Gaullism, who had finally brought Socialists and Communists back into government on 10 May 1981. Yet this nostalgia was not so much for his actual 14 years in office, as for the hopes he, and the Left more widely, had inspired on coming to power. Awkward questions about Mitterrand's record in office were avoided: the presenters of one late night radio phone-in brushed aside two callers who brought up respectively his roles in the guillotining of Algerian Communists as Minister of Justice in the 1950s and as President during the Rwandan genocide of 1994 with a familiar litany of excuses and relativisations. Attention instead focused either on his very first measures as President, such as the abolition of the death penalty and the introduction of a wealth tax, or on his role as leader of the opposition in the 1970s. The general feeling was that whether you liked him personally or not, Mitterrand incarnated 'a certain hope for change' in the period leading up to 1981 – a period in which the backroom wheeler-dealer suddenly found himself being acclaimed by massive crowds at rallies singing the *Internationale*. Again in 2011 on the thirtieth anniversary of May 1981, commentators waxed lyrical: 'It was at the time when the Left sang. It was at the time of hope, the time of victory. At that time, the Left was winning. It was last century...'[11]

It was, after all, the last time when anyone came to power in Western Europe promising anything so radical as a 'break with capitalism' and to 'change life'. By contrast, anti-capitalist sentiments have again become widespread in recent years, yet – in Europe at least – frustratingly impotent against powerful forces in the opposite direction.[12] There is an understandable longing for a period still dominated by the aftermath of 1968, the 'in between two Mays' from May '68 to May '81, when society was impatient for change. This was an era in which the Left sought to challenge at last the inequalities of French society. It was a time when famous intellectuals from Jean-Paul Sartre to Michel Foucault marched in the street alongside immigrant workers. It makes sense, therefore, to re-examine that period as a unity. The period will be examined on its own terms rather than measuring it up against the bitter disappointments that followed when the Left returned to office, and against which it will inevitably be found wanting. Though not a general history of that era, the focus on one important issue will illuminate wider debates. Such debates are not simply a matter of historical interest. They are directly linked to both the inequalities that produced the *banlieue* riots of 2005 and the ongoing and repeated failure of the Left after Mitterrand, in 1995, 2002 and 2007, to attract the votes of enough workers to win a presidential election – or recreate the fervour of the 'between two Mays'. As once again a Left grown used to opposition attempts to muster its strength for the elusive possibility of dislodging a right-wing president in 2012, on a terrain where immigration is even more prominent, and protest enjoys something of an international revival, this history is of renewed current relevance.

Yet these burning issues of social inequality feature little or not at all in many subsequent depictions of '68. For a long time, these were dominated by the rival polemics of former student radicals, with sharply partisan agendas of either keeping the flame of 1968 alive or exorcising the ghosts of their youthful follies.[13] The results were impressive in their theoretical pyrotechnics but curiously weak in adding to our knowledge of what actually happened. Despite a welcome recent shift in priorities towards serious historical study based on primary research, especially beyond the Parisian student milieu, to workers, to the regions,[14] one important group remains particularly neglected. While issues of migration and ethnicity have loomed large in accounts of the Anglo-American experience of 1968, they have been conspicuous by their absence in the historiography of the French May. In one of the few cases where they have been mentioned at all, the American historian Michael Seidman asserts that immigrants were 'somewhat marginal' to 1968. Rushing to generalise about the behaviour of particular groups, he suggests that North African workers 'had not yet assimilated through the labor movement, as had previous generations of immigrants', explaining this with reference to highly dubious notions of a 'clash of civilisations' borrowed from Fernand Braudel.[15] The few French historians who have touched on immigrants and 1968 have provided useful but partial factual information, tending to emphasise passivity and fear, even panic, as the only or main response of immigrant workers to the events. 'A feeling of panic among foreigners' is how one of the most extensive accounts to date, ten pages by Yvan Gastaut, summarises the main reaction to the events of the mass of immigrants; Geneviève Dreyfus-Armand takes a similar view.[16] Such judgements are based on insufficient evidence for how far the mass of immigrants participated – leading to a problematic dichotomy between a small politicised minority and a mass of passive and fearful non-participants. Xavier Vigna has provided some corrective to that view,[17] but he concentrates on workplaces alone as part of a wider project on industrial unrest, continuing the tendency to over-claim about immigrants based on too few sources.

'68 has been romanticised – it was just a load of white people'. This opinion, expressed by one contributor to a BBC Radio travel programme about Paris, is thus a succinct summary of the prevailing view.[18] The historian of ideas Richard Wolin, for example, claims that 'it was no longer Algerian immigrants whom the Paris police were brutalizing. It was the sons and daughters of the French middle classes.'[19] Similarly, the 2004 film *Code 68* depicts a twenty-first century young woman's frustrated attempts to make a historical documentary about May '68. Whereas the Paris of markets, bars and shops that serves as a present day backdrop to her explorations is clearly a multicultural one, her interviewees mainly consist of rather self-important elite white French men. On seeing this, the viewer may be tempted to agree with the conclusion of Anne, the protagonist of *Code 68*, that '68 is a little mafia of forty people'.[20]

But the historical record reveals a far richer texture to the radicalism of that era. There was a '68 depicted either not at all or inadequately in the standard family-saga account of what one influential survey of post-war Europe terms the 'attractive and articulate young men leading the youth of France through the historical boulevards of Left Bank Paris'.[21] This book aims to show how '68 and its sequels also happened both in the *banlieues* and in poor working-class immigrant areas of the capital like La Goutte d'Or, not to mention their equivalents in other parts of France like the Porte d'Aix in Marseilles. Moreover, what happened there was deemed of great importance by what we more conventionally think of as the '68ers, the more privileged world of the Latin Quarter. It is in the syntheses, ironies and contradictions between these two worlds that lies much of the interest of this tale. France in the 1960s was undoubtedly a golden age of Intellectuals with a capital 'I', now familiar to students across a range of academic disciplines but often presented to them in something of a historical vacuum, like gods dispensing timeless wisdom from Mount Olympus. Rather, in this book they appear as all too human products of their specific place and time. I also hope to show that you do not have to be famous, or French, to be an intellectual – and that intellectuals are not necessarily professionally employed in that capacity. This book seeks to widen our understanding of what it meant to be a left-wing intellectual after 1968, by examining the roles both of rank-and-file French anti-racists, and of the marginal ex-students from the Maghreb who provided much of the political leadership of the immigrant workers' movements of the Seventies.

Given that writers have so often stressed the international dimension of the wider movements of 1968, it is odd that the international nature of France's own population has been neglected. After all, the thirdworldist orientation of '68 culture' is well known. Historians take for granted that the insurgents of 1968 drew inspiration from the far-away anti-colonial struggles of the peoples of the former French empire in the period culminating with Algerian independence in 1962. But what was the reaction of the *soixante-huitards* to real people from such countries arriving on their doorstep? One might get the impression from some of what has been written about the period that it was composed solely of French leftists looking outside France for inspiration. One profile of a Lebanese writer who studied in France in the early 1970s asserts that 'he had missed nothing by arriving in

Paris late in the day. In Lebanon, unlike Paris, the rhetoric and imagery of the radical 1960s were visible alongside the very conditions to which they had referred'.[22] Similarly, the British historian Tony Judt wrote with some justification 'The French intellectuals' preference for concerning themselves with the interests of Africans, Arabs, Asians and Latin-Americans was not wholly disinterested. It was the product of a search for the historical subject that would succeed where the French workers' movement had ostensibly failed.'[23]

It is true that for much of the Sixties the gaze was turned elsewhere, to Algeria, to Cuba, to China. Yet to argue that this 'served only to accentuate still further an unconcern with daily local politics and to widen the distance between Marxist discourse and the real needs and concerns of workers'[24] was to overlook that there was a third option for intellectuals looking for a historical subject, that appeared both exotic *and* close at hand. Mass labour migration to the metropole meant that there was a group of people straddling the divide between anti-colonial militant and French worker. The newly re-radicalised intelligentsia saw outsider, marginal elements including immigrant workers as among the key possible agents of social change. From the point of view of the New Left, this was just as well. The mass migration of the 1960s intervened at a time when the classic French proletariat, forged in the Resistance and the old 1940s school of Communism, was showing definite signs of *embourgeoisement*. What better way to sidestep the debates that emerged about 'the new working class', the 'affluent worker' integrated into bourgeois society by consumer goods, than to discover a new tranche of workers who were distinctly lacking in such accoutrements, resembling more the desperate proletariat of nineteenth-century France? It was increasingly apparent that many of the troops in the latest battle of an old war were from groups marginal to old-style trade unionism. By 1975 the Centre d'Etudes Anti-Impérialistes (CEDETIM) was arguing that immigrants represented the vital link between anti-imperialist struggles in the developing world and the class struggle in France.[25] There was, albeit very imperfectly, a real engagement through an extended period after 1968 with the needs and concerns of immigrant workers, and what their presence revealed about French society, and it is that story which this book seeks to tell.

Overlooking the impact of migration on the French '68 is also a curious omission given it is generally accepted for some of the other national examples of dramatic upheaval, notably the United States and Italy.[26] The suburbs of Paris were comparable to Detroit and Turin, two other centres of rebellion in what Arthur Marwick termed the 'High Sixties', with car factories as one of their principal industries and southern migrants as a key source of labour. In the US, Detroit's Dodge Revolutionary Union Movement aside, a major issue even in the student revolt at Columbia University was its status as a white enclave in the African-American community of Harlem.[27] In Italy, the key worker participants in the 'long hot autumn' of 1969 were southern migrants to the factories of the industrialised North. Yet Judt, for example, cited 'extensive migration from south to north' as what ensured that 'the social background to Italy's conflicts was quite distinctive' and hence 'very different' from France.[28] But the industrial Paris region, just like Milan and Turin, also received an extensive migration from the south. It was simply that unlike in Italy, France's 'south' lay largely outside the borders of its own nation state. To fully understand the migrations that supplied Europe's post-war boom, we need to escape nationally centred models of foreigners as opposed to citizens. Rather, the central contrast was between worker-exporting peripheral regions of underdevelopment and worker-importing core regions of economic growth. An Andalucian in Barcelona, an emigrant from the *mezzogiorno* to northern Italy or a Portuguese worker in Paris, like a Breton or an Auvergnat in 19th century Paris, was an immigrant and an excluded outsider in ways that differed only in degree from the classic (post-) colonial migrant from North Africa to France. So unskilled and semi-skilled workers, excluded from the benefits of the post-war consensus and making different demands from traditionally unionised skilled workers, were also numerous in France. From 1968 onwards, through strikes and anti-racist struggles to resist deportation and maintain and expand their rights, they would make their voices heard.

Putting 1968 Back into the History of Immigration

In 1981, the philosopher Etienne Balibar was expelled from the French Communist Party for writing 'From Charonne to Vitry', an influential critique of Communist attitudes towards immigration and colonialism. During the dying days of the Algerian War in 1962, a million people marched in Paris at the funerals of nine Communist anti-war demonstrators killed on the steps of Charonne metro station by ultra-violent café-table-throwing police. Yet in 1981, the *Communist* suburban municipality of Vitry-sur-Seine, shamefully, was demolishing the homes of Malian workers. What, Balibar wanted to know, had gone wrong between those two dates?[29] The history of the intervening two decades is vital, therefore, to any understanding of what has happened since to the politics of racism and antiracism in France. It is that period, characterised by the rise and fall of a cross-fertilisation between immigrants and the French Left, that represents the vital 'missing link' in the history of antiracism in France: after the end of the Algerian war of national liberation half a century ago – or at least after the war came to Paris with the brutally suppressed Algerian demonstrations of 17 October 1961 – but before the eruption of the 'second generation' into public consciousness with the so-called 'Marche des Beurs' of 1983.[30] A whole series of mobilisations, around fires in shanty towns, racist killings and deportations, including the first *sans-papiers* movement, was intimately related to the 68-era Left. So as well as putting immigration back into the history of 1968, this book puts 1968 back into the history of immigration, by providing a complete account of that 'missing link'. My work fits into a recent trend by historians to understand 1968 within a much broader chronology than used to be the case: thus the most comprehensive French book takes 1962 and 1981 as the beginning and end of the '68 years',[31] when visions of a better society were at their height. But here, it will be shown how the '68 years' were also the 'immigrant years'.[32]

Today, however, this is a largely forgotten story. Such neglect has allowed mutually contradictory ideas to flourish. On the one hand, where the literature on immigration does mention this earlier period, it contains many brief, vague and insufficiently substantiated references to 1968 as a positive turning point.[33] On the other hand, commentary on public protest and civil disturbance in France since the 1980s has tended to infer from the multi-ethnic character of the present, that the past had to be mono-ethnic, using 1968 purely as a negative foil. In 1989, for example, Jean-Marc Terrasse contrasted what he perceived as the white faces in 1968 demonstrations to the 'Black, Blanc, Beur' multiracial composition of a recent protest: 'In 68, the people in the street were white.'[34] Though we shall see many counterexamples to such generalisations, there is a grain of truth in them, for the simple reason that the majority of foreigners resident in France in 1968 were Europeans. Three of the four largest national groups were the Spanish, the Italians and the Portuguese. Algerians were also one of the largest groups, but there were then many fewer Moroccans and Tunisians, and even less from sub-Saharan Africa, though the numbers from both North and West Africa were to increase in the following years.

But skin colour is not the most crucial factor. During this period, in contrast to that since the 1980s, immigrants tended to be defined less by their ethnic origin, let alone their religion, than by their situation in the workplace as semi-skilled or unskilled workers. If, as Martin O'Shaughnessy argues, 'one facet of contemporary consensus politics is a privileging of claims based on the sexual or ethnic identities of different groups to the exclusion of claims based on other criteria, notably class or economic exploitation',[35] this was not yet the case in the 1960s. Of course no writer on this issue can afford to ignore the very real and specific legacies of colonial racism. But nor can any satisfactory history of migration to France exclude Europeans. The lazy stereotype equating 'immigrant' with 'non-white', 'Arab' or 'Muslim' is so widespread, that in casual conversations many people have enquired which nationality I am writing about – expecting an answer such as 'Algerians' and seeming surprised to hear instead the response 'All of them'. For the debate about immigration in France, and the position of migrant labour in continental Europe more generally, did not then necessarily share the Anglo-American obsession with 'race' and its binary polarisation between 'white' and 'black'. Europe actually had its own Southern Question, as Roberto Dainotto has written:

> If so much has been done already by the subaltern historiography
> of the new Fridays and Calibans, even more, arguably, remains
> to be done from at least another subaltern position – that of
> Europe's own PIGS (Portugal, Italy, Greece and Spain in Brussels'
> diplomacy's quite cynical acronym).[36]

This evocation of a derogatory shorthand that has became widespread during the current European financial crisis should remind us of some relevant historical facts. To take the largest intra-European migration to France of the Sixties, at the time Portuguese gross national product was only $600 a head, less than a quarter of that of France. Most migrants were recent arrivals from the poorest areas of rural Northern Portugal, where meat, butter and fruit were considered luxuries. They were illiterate and – unlike many North Africans – unable to speak any French on arrival. Many lived in shanty towns in conditions as bad as their North African contemporaries, working in similar positions as unskilled labourers. Admittedly Portuguese workers have subsequently found it easier than North Africans to move upwards into the petite-bourgeoisie, through their subsequent legitimisation as 'good' immigrants, as a result of cultural racism including them as allegedly more easily assimilable Latin Europeans. But this should not obscure the very real racism to which they were subject as recently as the 1960s (just as Italians, Poles and Belgians had faced when they first arrived).[37] Most people's understanding of who was an 'immigrant' at the time was as likely to be Southern European as North African, and both were in a similar socio-economic boat on first arrival. So in contrast to a certain tendency for the historiography of immigration to become merely a collection of separate histories of different national groups,[38] I use the term 'immigrant' in its simplest and broadest sense, to mean anyone born outside metropolitan France who subsequently moved there. Contemporaries also widely understood the term to be synonymous with 'immigrant worker',[39] but we shall see that a pivotal role was played too by people who were in the ambiguous position of being immigrants but not manual workers. Unlike much commentary on immigration on France, this book does not focus exclusively on the Algerian case which tends to dominate popular preconceptions. Rather it takes a broad and inclusive transnational scope reflecting the diversity of modern France, by also discussing migration from many other countries.

When they first arrived in France, immigrants had tended to live quite isolated lives. Because of this isolation, the French public remained largely ignorant of the lives of immigrant workers in the 1960s. Such indifference later gave way to a situation where immigration and 'integration' became a major if not the major political issue in France. Since the early 1980s, France has experienced an intense interest, bordering on obsession, with such issues. At first, this understandably focused on contemporary concerns, leading to a certain amnesia in which all sides to debates too often behaved as if France's history of immigration had begun with the emergence of the 'second generation' in about 1983. But from the late 1990s, the shanty town era re-entered public memories, in television documentaries, travelling exhibitions, and feature films.[40] These evocatively portrayed the social realities of the 1960s, but what was missing was politics, at least for the period after the end of the Algerian War. The film version of *Vivre au paradis* ['Living In Paradise'] for example, based on Brahim Benaïcha's autobiographical account of growing up in a Nanterre shanty town, ended with Algerian independence in 1962, even though the book had included material on 1968.[41] Activists with immigrant parents sometimes gave the impression that their parents had been passive, emphasising their distinctiveness by caricaturing their parents' generation as having suffered in silence.[42] So when I first began work in this area in 1998, there was very little known about the impact of 1968 on immigration: it remained the elusive, missing dimension.

More recently, however, several researchers have considerably advanced our understanding by investigating certain aspects of the previously little known immigration / politics crossover of this period, and this book is indebted to them. They concentrate on the pre-history of later anti-racist movements, or one particularly important factory or city, one important incident such as the now notorious massacre of 17 October 1961, the discourse of one leftist group, or representations in certain films.[43] There have, therefore, been the beginnings of a welcome move away from what Abdellali Hajjat, one of the historians to recently add to our knowledge of the subject, calls a 'miserabilist vision of history according to which immigrants cannot be historical subjects'.[44] There is still a tendency, though, to downplay the participation of immigrants in 1968 itself, in favour of their role as mere subjects of sloganising, followed by their entry into active struggle a few years later. This was the dominant view of speakers such as Aïssa Kadri at the only public event during the 40th anniversary of 1968 devoted to immigration. A poorly attended seminar in a squat in eastern Paris, it showed how relatively marginalised this subject remains within the wider memory of 1968 – despite immigration being in other respects so central to debates about contemporary French society.[45] Laure Pitti, who has carried out some of the most extensive recent studies of workers during this period, notes the importance of their having already experienced active struggle in 1968 itself, but her evidence for this point is essentially limited to the one example of Renault.[46] Rabah Aissaoui's study of the 1970s Mouvement des Travailleurs Arabes notes that they considered 1968 important, but without supplying details of what its members had done during the events.[47] The existing literature thus remains very dispersed and fragmentary in nature, reflecting a wider tendency for the history of immigration to be a 'history of fragments'.[48] There has been no overarching telling of the whole story of the immigrant / Left crossover of those years, with the result that attempts to summarise it have been less than fully accurate. Thus one otherwise suggestive recent survey of two centuries by France's leading historian of immigration does mention the post-68 period, but makes factual errors, including on the nationality of a leading activist.[49] One of the very few publications in English, a chapter by Maud Bracke, suggests a new interpretation, but no new primary evidence, and chooses to privilege Algerians in the title, even though many of the examples featured in it were not Algerian.[50] In short, as Pitti puts it, the history of immigrant mobilisations 'still largely remains to be written'.[51]

This book aims to plug the gap by providing a broad narrative of the rise and fall of these movements. It is the result of more than a decade of primary research[52] in France, including the mainstream and militant press, interviews, memoirs, films, sifting through thousands of leaflets and publications in search of clues about the presence of immigrants, and extensive archival research. This quest has taken me to a dedicated immigration movement archive in the back streets of Marseilles; to a demonstration in Nice the night Jean-Marie Le Pen came second in the presidential election; on many walks and bus journeys through Paris and the *banlieue*; to modernist municipal archives in the kinds of Paris suburbs where streets are still named after Lenin or Salvador Allende; to the musty basement of an anti-racist pressure group near the Gare Du Nord; to a trade union headquarters on a hill overlooking eastern Paris; to Nanterre University, where it all began; to the grandiose national library with forest inside that bears the name François Mitterrand; and even to the former headquarters of NATO in Fontainebleau, now a government archive – thanks to the special permission I was granted by the Interior Ministry to consult normally closed archives, including those of the Renseignements Généraux, the branch of the French police concerned with political surveillance. I hope therefore to have conveyed a little of this sense of place, in which historians in the era of Richard Cobb used to revel, but which is under threat in today's deskbound cult of the illusion that all knowledge is instantly electronically accessible. I have also been able to draw on the recent secondary work, mainly scattered in French periodicals and edited collections, and synthesise their findings for an English-speaking readership.

Together, this book tells for the first time in any language the whole story of the immigrant / Left crossover of the '68 years'. Chapter One is about how France became home to a massive force of cheap labour during the Sixties: exploited at work and home, kept without rights, yet saving and preparing for a return that, for many, never happened. Asking whether French responses to the massacre of 17 October 1961 constituted collaboration or resistance, the chapter is also about how the student radicals of the Latin Quarter dreamed revolution, looking across to the other side of the tracks to see in migrant workers a potential force for radical change. Chapter Two tells how this situation exploded, when the events of May-June 1968 made France 'discover' the three million immigrant workers in its midst, turning them into both a political issue and political actors in their own right. It uncovers the hidden story of how immigrants participated in the rebellion as strikers, as participants in debates and sometimes as street protesters. Chapter Three is about a time when everything seemed possible, between 1968 and 1971. It tells of how, in order to draw attention to the exploitation of immigrants, leftists both staged 'commando' raids and built crèches in places like Nanterre. The chapter delves into the ironies and contradictions involved in this meeting of two worlds, asking not only how the intellectuals viewed the shanty town, but how the residents of the shanty town viewed the intellectuals. Chapter Four is about the birth of an autonomous immigrant movement between 1971 and 1973. It recounts how the murder of the Algerian teenager Djellali Ben Ali, and a hunger strike by the Tunisian activist Saïd Bouziri, led to a movement that mobilised onto the streets of

Paris some of France's best-known intellectuals, from Sartre to Foucault, and opened up a whole cycle of immigrant activism. The chapter surveys the movement at its height, and examines the difficulty of creating solidarities between it and French workers.

Chapter Five shows how this movement started to enter the mainstream of French politics. Between 1973 and 1976, a generation of activists began to see their future as lying in France, and their boundary-crossing movement created a context for mainstream parties and thinkers of the Left to take up immigration as a positive issue. It also deals with the international impact, examining the 'French Connection' behind the end of the dictatorships in Spain and Portugal. Chapter Six is about the death of the Sixties. It analyses the transition away from the dreams of '68, both in the lived experience of immigrants and their families, and in the politics surrounding the issue. It examines how between 1976 and 1983 the sons and daughters of immigrants in the *banlieues* questioned the leftist culture of first generation activists in the inner cities. The Epilogue surveys the legacies of 1968 for the politics of migration and protest in twenty-first France and beyond. While the 68ers' dream of universal emancipation and liberation gave way to more modest and fragmented campaigns, many of those anti-racist campaigns are even today the work of the 68ers. The book ends by exploring continuities between past and present, up to the 'Arab Spring' of 2011.

To tell this story entails certain problems of interpretation. As Eric Hobsbawm has written:

> For all of us there is a twilight zone between history and memory ...
> It is by far the hardest part of history for historians, or for anyone
> else, to grasp ... For it is still part of us but no longer quite within
> our personal reach.[53]

A period during which the historian himself did not live, but so many of the people that shaped and continue to shape his own age did, presents particular challenges: long enough ago to appear quaint, yet too recent to qualify, especially in the eyes of those who lived through it, as 'proper' history. The 68ers and their enemies have handed down to us so many stereotypes and received ideas about the Sixties, both positive and negative, that to tackle it as dispassionate history is still difficult. My own approach to the subject is both distant and close. Born in 1975, I have no direct personal investment in the memory of '68. In general I have sought, as far as this is possible, to avoid the polemics that surround the memory of '68, approaching it instead with the perspective of the professional historian.

As the British historian Sheila Rowbotham, herself a 68er, put it: 'It is very important to be able to say "I don't know" and "Nobody knows, we need to find out" without being dismissed as stupid.'[54] We need to be surer of the facts about what really happened before reaching for the final moral judgements which contemporaries were perhaps too quick to reach with their myriad mutual accusations of betrayal and extremism. This relative detachment is an approach shared by many of the growing number of historians of '68 too young to have been participants, and it may be easier to fulfil when writing the history of a country other than one's own.

Yet at the same time the reader is entitled to know that my reasons for choosing the subject in the first place were connected to support for the struggle against racism and xenophobia in the present and a broad sympathy for the inspiration given by '68 – even a sense of disappointment that the more selfish and depoliticised era in which I grew up lacked something by comparison. But I have not been disappointed entirely, having had the good fortune during the first two decades of my adult life to associate with 68ers at close hand, as a result of playing very marginal roles on the fringes of a variety of single-issue protest campaigns, and of entering academic life not long before the relevant age cohort reached retirement. Earlier in my research I concentrated on written primary sources from the period, out of both timidity and a keenness to dig down to the empirical truth, beneath certain overly dominant narratives laid down by contemporaries. But as my research has proceeded, so I have had the chance to make my picture of the past more human by interviewing and getting to know some of those involved in the story that follows (as well as by reading the many 68er autobiographical reminiscences and interviews published over the past decade). While not set up in any formal anthropological sense as participant-observation, this element reflects the fact that an important part of being a historian is, as Hobsbawm puts it, keeping your eyes and ears open. In the manner of 'historian of the present' Timothy Garton Ash during the revolutions of 1989, I cannot attend a gathering of 68ers without feeling the obligation to posterity to take notes, for if I don't, who will?[55] This far down the line, I can now spot a 68er a mile off, and there is much that attracts me to them. It has become clear to me how much of the impetus of present campaigns, from the defence of refugee rights to the global justice movement, has derived from the idealism and campaigning energy of those 68ers who are still politically active, and it will be evident in what follows that I see this as a positive legacy. These have been opportunities which the passing of time will eventually mean that future generations will not have.

Nevertheless, the historian's first duty is to tell the truth, even if it is politically inconvenient – something at which leftists have not always excelled. Self-righteousness has sometimes been one of the less attractive characteristics of the 68er mentality. I have therefore not hesitated to document the many occasions on which leftists behaved in a foolish, naïve or arrogant way, and some of the significant weaknesses of their politics will emerge in the analysis that follows. At some level my wish to find out more about this subject was related to my personal disillusion as a protester with certain styles of protest and vanguard politics. Another early influence was the Subaltern Studies school of South Asian historiography – which emphasised the power relations *within* popular movements.[56] But nor do I wish to endorse an overly cynical view of '68, to pretend that nothing of significance happened, or that it was confined only to students, or to erase from history the genuinely liberating dimensions of the movements it spawned. To neither idealise nor belittle '68, but seek to understand how it was experienced by people at the time, requires a certain humility on the part of the historian. Loosely influenced by the empirically-based 'history from below' approach pioneered by E.P. Thompson, I have, perhaps unfashionably, sought to find out what happened and why, rather than slot it neatly and unproblematically into my own perspective – the 'enormous condescension of posterity'.[57] This is a warts and all story, but it is also a story of genuine hopes for a better future.

Chapter One

Dreaming Revolution:
Between Apathy and Activism, 1961-1967

'In our France, there is nothing but darkness.'
Kabyle emigrant interviewed by Abdelmalek Sayad[1]

The Cosmopolitanism of the New Left

The encounter between immigrants and the New Left was a meeting of two different worlds. The widespread idea that 1968 was a revolution of spoiled students contains, like many stereotypes, an element of truth beneath the encrusted layers of myth. Many Sixties teenagers – *les babyboomers* as the historian Jean-François Sirinelli puts it – did experience, compared to what previous generations had been through, and even to their own early childhood in the more austere post-war years, a golden age of prosperity and peace after 1962. Unlike their parents, or their elder brothers who had served as conscripts in Algeria, they had generally not experienced war at first hand. The retrospective film *Mourir à trente ans* ['To Die At Thirty'] made by and about members of the Trotskyist Jeunesse Communiste Révolutionnaire, suggests that political involvement, deadly serious though it was to become, could at first be an outgrowth of youthful exuberance and boisterousness, a hobby alongside others like cinema, rather than a dramatic life or death struggle.[2] As the British journalists Patrick Seale and Maureen McConville found: 'Politics has conquered the young in France, absorbing energies which in other countries go into model aircraft building, ham radio, the pursuit of pop idols, cricket.'[3] So while for the tiny remnants of the old Trotskyist far Left formed in the 1930s and 1940s, the pre-1968 period was a barren 'crossing of the desert',[4] it was amongst the young that the future seemed on the march. As they entered the expanding universities, middle-class youth were free to dream, to experience what one dominant account labels *Les années de rêve* ['The Dream Years'], and to take their political models from outside their immediate experience. There was no doubt that the Latin Quarter in the mid-Sixties was an exciting time and place to be a student.[5]

For the university milieu in which the radical ideas of the period swam was a profoundly cosmopolitan one. The Third World appeared accessible to French students, who could rub shoulders with international militants without leaving the Left Bank of the Seine. The famous boulevards of the Latin Quarter belonged, in the words of the old saying about Paris, not to the French but to the world. French leftist radicalism had often owed much, perhaps more than it gave credit for, to the presence in Paris of sections of the intelligentsia from France's colonies. From Ho Chi Minh after the First World War to Algerian nationalist students like Mohammed Harbi in the 1950s, many colonial militants had planned liberation for their homeland from within the imperialist citadel, often maintaining a dialogue with the 'other France'[6] of revolutionary universalism. The leaders of the Algerian Front de Libération Nationale (FLN) in France, for example, lived 'only a stone's throw from the existentialist cafés of the Boulevard St Germain'.[7] Institutions such as the Présence Africaine bookshop and journal gave anti-colonialists high visibility in the heart of student Paris. The period of anti-colonial struggle had left a legacy of militant expectations among student elites from former colonies. Thus the Fédération des Etudiants d'Afrique Noire en France (FEANF) had emerged in the 1950s, influenced by a synthesis of revolutionary socialism and Pan-Africanism. FEANF had an influence out of proportion to the relatively small number of African students in Paris, stretching forward into the post-independence period. This mix of Marxism and messianic thirdworldism, critical of the bourgeois nationalism of postcolonial elites, in many ways set the tone for the movements of the 1960s.[8] After independence, post-colonial governments were denounced for authoritarianism and insufficient emancipation from French tutelage. *Perspectives*, for example, the most important and most internationalist current of the student far Left in Tunisia, was founded in Paris in 1963. In 1966 and 1967, Tunisians associated with the review held meetings at 115 Boulevard Saint-Michel, a club at the centre of North African student life, to denounce repression in their home country. This was a very international crowd: associations representing not only North African and Middle Eastern but also Madagascan, Vietnamese, and French students supported their meetings, while Tunisian government supporters tried to disrupt them. It was also a milieu in which men and women mixed quite freely.[9]

The Latin Quarter in the Sixties was fortunate to experience an overlap between this postcolonial presence and its established tradition as a beacon for intellectuals from across Europe. The New Left, quite apart from the flow of ideas across national boundaries, was also richly cosmopolitan within national cultures. The considerable capacity of the French intelligentsia to absorb and assimilate those who learn to think like it disguises the fact that some of its leading figures were themselves immigrants. Gisèle Halimi, president of the Russell Tribunal on American war crimes in Vietnam and an important figure in the early French feminist movement, was born into a Jewish family in Tunisia. So was Albert Memmi, the writer whose *Portrait du colonisé* was a key influence on anti-racists. The Situationists' famous pamphlet *Sur la misère en milieu étudiante* ['On Student Poverty'] which caused a scandal in 1966 when students at Strasbourg University proceeded to bankrupt their students union by printing large quantities of it, was also written by a Tunisian, Mustapha Khayati.[10] And as a host country for exiled leftists, France was a rear base from which to plot revolution even within Europe. The urban theorist Manuel Castells, for example, was an exiled student activist from Barcelona, 'part feisty Catalan militant, part budding French *maître penseur*'.[11] Cornelius Castoriadis, the economist whose writings for the *Socialisme ou Barbarie* journal between 1949 and 1966 are considered a key influence on May '68, first came to France as a refugee from the Greek civil war. Greece supplied many other intellectuals to France, like the filmmaker Costa-Gavras, director of the much-watched political thriller *Z*; Nicos Poulantzas, influential Marxist theorist of the state; and Kostas Axelos, who played a role in introducing the ideas of the Frankfurt School social critic Herbert Marcuse.[12] André Gorz, cofounder of *Le Nouvel Observateur* and a key figure in debates within the French Left, particularly in his proto-ecologist critique of paid work, was born in Vienna and married an Englishwoman – but often wrote under the French pseudonym Michel Bousquet.[13]

Other figures, though relatively unknown at the time, may appear of at least retrospective significance, notably Boris Fraenkel, a translator of Marcuse and Trotsky and propagator of libertarian ideas about sexuality. A stateless person, born to Russian Menshevik refugee parents in interwar Danzig, Fraenkel should merit a footnote in the history of France, since in the run-up to the 2002 presidential election he caused some embarrassment to Lionel Jospin's centre-left campaign by revealing that in 1960 he had recruited Jospin to the Organisation Communiste Internationaliste, a Trotskyist outfit with a reputation for cloak-and-dagger secrecy. Meanwhile the curious young of the early Sixties, eager to escape from repressive conservatism at home in countries such as Spain or Ireland where Sartre's books were banned, naturally saw Sartre's old stomping ground as their escape route, their pole of liberty. The Irish journalist Peter Lennon, for example, seized the opportunity to settle in the Odéon quarter of the Left Bank just as the Sixties were commencing, interviewing for the *Guardian* everyone from Algerian FLN men to the Romanian-born playwright Eugène Ionesco. In 1967 Lennon teamed up with the New Wave filmmaker Raoul Coutard to make a very critical documentary about his native land, that could only have been made after a period exiled in a country with a vibrant film culture and which was used to people criticising their own country without being labelled unpatriotic.[14] The British socialist feminist Sheila Rowbotham has described the clientele she mixed with in one Odéon café at this time:

> exiles from the Spanish civil war, a lingering Mau Mau fugitive from the Kikuyu resistance to British rule in Kenya during the late fifties with a deeply lined, stretched face who stood staring out at the passersby and never smiled, a despairing Portuguese revolutionary who drank far too much and became morose and self-destructive.[15]

There were thus good reasons for the internationalism of the Parisian students. In many cases, their family background already predisposed them to an openness to other cultures. Many French-born activists had – not surprisingly, given the scale of immigration to France in the mid-twentieth century – parents or grandparents from Central or Eastern Europe, North Africa, Spain or Greece. Dany Cohn-Bendit, born to two Holocaust survivors in south-western France in 1945, is only the most famous example. The historian Yaïr Auron has shown, in the case of Jewish *soixante-huitards* like the leading Trotskyists Alain Krivine or Daniel Bensaïd, how family histories of persecution could lead them to seek radical solutions. The iconic rebel Pierre Goldman, for example, called himself in his autobiography 'A Polish Jew Born in France'.[16] While for the future historian Benjamin Stora, 'repatriated' from Algeria to the Paris *banlieue* with his Jewish family at the age of eleven, 1968 was a moment of liberation, allowing Stora to escape what he experienced as the shame of association with the European colonists of Algeria, take pride in his southern working-class origins – and finally be on the right side of history.[17] Auron's point could equally be extended to the children of refugees from the Armenian genocide or the Spanish Civil War. The student movement in Toulouse in particular bore a perceptible imprint of Spanish anarchist émigré culture.[18] Nevertheless, we should beware of this argument slipping into ethnic determinism.

Gaby Ceroni, a worker expelled from the Communist-led Confédération Générale du Travail (CGT) for excessive militancy in 1968, though the son of an Italian immigrant, attributed his anti-racism not to this, but to his mother's friendship with black American soldiers in France.[19] Indeed, it was possible to overcompensate for an immigrant background with an exaggerated French nationalism. Take the young Nicolas Sarkozy, whose self-perception as a second-generation son of immigrants was quite the opposite of a Cohn-Bendit or a Goldman:

> All my childhood, perched on my grandfather's shoulders, I never stopped watching, fascinated and moved, the 11 November and 14 July parades. The very idea of criticising France would never have entered our minds.[20]

Tiersmondisme: Founding Dates of an Ideology

As Kristin Ross has argued, May '68 was largely about a 'flight from social determination'[21] – an argument with implications for our understanding of the relationship between immigrants and the New Left. 68-ers of all backgrounds were intensely interested in the experiences of parts of the world with which they had few or no personal links, frequenting the bookshops of François Maspero or Présence Africaine with a real thirst for knowledge about distant countries. The case of Jewish 68ers who became propagandists for some of the most militant Palestinian guerilla factions such as the Popular Front for the Liberation of Palestine is only the most striking example of the *soixante-huitard* quest to understand the Other.[22] Whatever their national background, internationalism was a defining feature of the New Left. This was the first generation for whom international travel to attend demonstrations in another country – such as the Europe-wide anti-Vietnam War demonstration in Berlin in February 1968, was a realistic possibility.

Their internationalism spread far and wide, for if a wind was, as in the title of the Jean-Luc Godard film, blowing from the East, at a time of widespread idealisation of Maoist China, it was also blowing from the South. The colonial context was certainly important in defining how the New Left responded to immigration. While differing sharply in their interpretations of 1968, historians are agreed on the importance of *tiermondisme* in the origins of the movement. There had since the 1920s often been a symbiotic relationship between anti-colonial nationalists and the French far Left. Messali Hadj, founder of the Etoile Nord Africaine (ENA), who has been described as the Trotsky of the Algerian revolution, enjoyed good relations with the eternal revolutionary's disciples in France. But this became more sharply defined with the rise of a generation in France who had seen Third World independence not just as a distant dream, but as a realistic, and then realised, objective. As the FLN eclipsed the ENA's successor organisations, it enjoyed intellectual and logistical support from clandestine networks in France, which often overlapped with far Left currents like La Voie Communiste. In 1960-61, an embryonic mass student anti-colonialist movement formed in Paris and other cities. Unlike the Communist Party, it took a clear position not simply for peace and against the pro-French Algeria terrorists Organisation de l'Armée Secrète (OAS), but for the FLN's revolutionary struggle for independence. Many a *soixante-huitard* cut their political teeth in this struggle.[23] The age of *tiersmondisme* had arrived, and it looked like the future. The coming battles, so it seemed, would be between imperialists and anti-imperialists as much as between bourgeoisie and proletariat. From Frantz Fanon's *Les damnés de la terre* ('The Wretched of the Earth') in 1960,[24] through the FLN's triumphant entry into Algiers in 1962 to the Tricontinental Congress of 1966 and Che Guevara's rallying cry for the creation of 'two, three, many Vietnams', the mood in *tiersmondiste* circles was one of euphoric expectation.

Thirdworldism was an ideology with a long prehistory, the product of multiple encounters in both directions between global North and South.[25] But on the part of radicalised youth in France, *tiersmondisme* represented a catching up with lost time. In part this was old wine in new bottles: a 1960s version of the classic revolutionary dream, a compensation for having grown up in more peaceful times and thereby missing out on the heroism and glory of the European civil war of 1914-1945: 'I belong to a grade-B generation, condemned by a blank space in History to a pastiche of the one-off destinies that came before us.'[26] And in part *tiersmondisme* was an attempt to make up for the more recent failures of their elders. There was a widespread perception that the absence of a mass anti-war movement until the last stages of the Algerian War showed that the French Left, and especially its largest component the Communist Party, had failed this most vital of tests. Preoccupied with the sectional interests of the French working class, the party had been ambiguous in its relationship to French colonialism, failing to make a clear stand in support of Algerian independence until it was too late. This critique of Communist assimilationism had a distinguished history: as the poet Aimé Césaire, for example, had suggested in 1956, the main aim of the people of Martinique was not necessarily the liberation of the French proletariat.[27] Solidarity with the FLN had therefore been left to small groups of dissidents further to the Left. One important date in the birth of *tiersmondisme* was 27 October 1960. This was a day of risky, violent and controversial anti-war demonstrations in Paris called by the student union UNEF, remembered as the first major initiative carried out autonomously from the 'official' Left. For the historian Jean-Pierre Rioux, 27 October 1960 was the 'fracture from which all leftisms up to and including May 1968 rushed'.[28]

17 October 1961: Collaboration or Resistance?

Another defining moment was 17 October 1961, date of the now notorious massacre of Algerian demonstrators – clubbed to death, shot, or drowned, the culmination of two months of repression during which the police killed at least 120 people[29] in what Simone de Beauvoir described as 'this Paris full of autumn leaves and blood'.[30] That evening was the first time that thirty thousand Algerians – men, women and children – had marched out of the shanty towns and into the heart of tourist Paris, in direct defiance of a discriminatory night time curfew which applied only to them. But the march against the curfew was violently suppressed under the orders of Prefect of Police Maurice Papon, a highly successful career civil servant later convicted of complicity in crimes against humanity for his previous role in the deportation of Jews from Bordeaux to Auschwitz.[31] At location after location across Paris, from the Pont de Neuilly leading in from Nanterre, to the Pont Saint-Michel that joins the Left Bank to the Ile de la Cité, police intercepted the different columns of Algerian marchers as they tried to converge on the city centre. The result was, in the words of the normally sober London *Economist*: 'men and women beaten up in cold blood; broken limbs left unattended for days; victims strangled in the woods around Paris; half-dead people dropped into the Seine for the river to finish them off.'[32]

For 17 October 1961 saw a terrible conflict of expectations between peaceful protestors, believing they were making a reasonable point in a restrained manner, setting out in their best suits and ties, under strict orders from the march's FLN organisers not to carry anything that could be construed as a weapon – and an utterly combative Papon, prepared to deal with them as if they were an invading army. No better illustration of this could be found than the man who, approaching the police in an attempt to reason with them, was beaten to a pulp.[33] According to eyewitnesses, some of the killings even took place in the courtyard of the Prefecture of Police,[34] just behind where today thousands of tourists queue daily to see Notre Dame Cathedral.

In some respects, this brutal tragedy – what Jean-Luc Einaudi, author of the most important exposé of the truth about what happened that night, calls the 'Battle of Paris' – can be seen as the last, climactic stage of a colonial war, as colonial repression imported into the metropole.[35] But another interpretation would be as a foundational event of the postcolonial politics of immigration in France. For what many ordinary Algerians taking part on the march wanted was simply to be able to live a normal life in France: 'Never does a European say a word to us outside work and, however, I'd really like sometimes to speak with some, but they don't even look at us.'[36] Many took the opportunity to express themselves about the poor quality of their existence: 'About thirty women and young girls, with children, in despair, yelled in Arabic or French. They yelled about their intolerable life.'[37] The masses were not simply blindly following the FLN: some gatherings of Algerian demonstrators on and after 17 October took place in locations unauthorised by the leadership, who described the impromptu demonstrations as 'spontaneous' and themselves as 'overtaken'.[38]

Moreover, the autumn of 1961 saw protests by French leftists as well as Algerians. In retrospect, this was a crucial stage in the relationship between the two, the nature of which has caused great controversy on the Left ever since. The widespread idea that there was little or no reaction by French people to the killings is in fact something of a myth.[39] It contains a grain of truth, though, since one of the main aims of the demonstration was to draw the plight of Algerians under curfew to the attention of what the FLN considered an indifferent or hostile French public, as well as to wider international opinion. Only a handful of trusted French sympathisers were allowed on the demonstration as observers, since in a prior context of mutual suspicion between the FLN and the French Left, the FLN appears to have rejected last-minute Communist offers of more substantial French participation.[40] But the most heated polemics concern what happened, or did not happen, afterwards. Writing in the Tunisian weekly *Afrique-Action*, Jacques Lanzmann compared the French public's failure to react to the killings to the German villagers who ignored the black smoke rising from Nazi extermination camps. In her memoirs, de Beauvoir drew the same shocking parallel.[41] By contrast, the CGT later claimed that 'These events ... deeply moved French consciences'.[42] So who was right: the intellectuals or the trade unionists? Was the public response one of collaboration or resistance?

One can find anecdotal evidence to support both these arguments, and points between. If you were going to, as it were, do a Daniel Goldhagen, and argue that ordinary Parisians were 'Papon's willing executioners',[43] then you would seize on the limited evidence that there is of direct or indirect civilian participation. According to the *New York Times*, at one roundabout,

'French motorists jumped out of their cars and, seizing whatever was handy as a weapon, attacked the Moslem demonstrators.'[44]

FLN propaganda also suggested that passers-by assisted in arrests, while one Algerian witness recalls a café owner suggesting to the police that they round up the Algerians in his café and burn them alive.[45] On the other hand, if you were going to do something akin to the East German historians who made out that the German working class heroically resisted the Nazis throughout, you could make much of the various signs of resistance on the part of the public. Some shouted 'Murderers' from their windows. Practical aid was given to the victims, including in the Left Bank: a pharmacy on Boulevard Saint-Michel was turned into a makeshift hospital. Those attempting to giving such help were abused and obstructed by the police: one pamphlet singled out as the most revolting incident that night, police stopping passers-by from aiding two badly wounded Algerians, who remained in agony on the pavement all night. A few days later, Algerian women detained in a psychiatric hospital were helped by French nurses to escape.[46] And if you were going to take a middle view, stressing ambiguity, you could find evidence for that too: indeed, observers more often cited sins of omission rather than commission. According to testimony by French FLN sympathisers, there was indifference, though conditioned by an atmosphere of fear.[47]

But even before 17 October, beatings and killings of Algerians had not gone entirely unnoticed, attracting condemnation by, amongst others, the taxi-drivers' union, the Seine region of the CGT, and the Parti Socialiste Unifié (PSU), the largest of the New Left groups.[48] In the immediate aftermath, debate and overt political protest broke out, for there was no monolithic cover-up. It was to the office of Claude Bourdet and Gilles Martinet, the PSU-supporting editors of the weekly news magazine *France Observateur*, that a small group of dissident policemen came that night to testify to the horrific scene which they had witnessed in the Prefecture of Police. Eyewitness accounts of atrocities began to appear even in unlikely places like the right-wing daily *Le Figaro*: indeed a film about the massacre, though officially censored, was shown on the fringes of the 1962 Cannes Film Festival and made it onto the front cover of *Variety* magazine. Denunciations and protests – some 189, by the calculations of the historian Jim House – had already multiplied in the first three weeks after 17 October. Some commentators, for example *Socialisme ou Barbarie*, peremptorily dismissed these as empty and purely verbal. Ironically the same point was made by none other than Maurice Papon, who in his memoirs accused cowardly intellectuals, lacking the courage of their convictions, of making armchair protests instead of demonstrating in the street.[49]

Yet there were street demonstrations, in spite of the fact that all demonstrations were illegal. Contrary to what has sometimes been claimed,[50] not all of them were by students or intellectuals.[51] Nevertheless, these were the most visible protests in central Paris. Some two thousand students and staff met in the courtyard of the Sorbonne on 21 October. Student demonstrations followed in the Latin Quarter in the next two days. A protest meeting was organised by PSU students at the Mutualité for the evening of 27 October, only to be banned by the authorities. Denunciations also followed in semi-clandestine journals like *Vérité Liberté* which had long opposed the war. An appeal was signed by many prominent intellectuals, including de Beauvoir, André Breton, Aime Césaire, Marguerite Duras, Claude Lanzmann, Jean-Paul Sartre and Pierre Vidal-Naquet. On 1 November, two demonstrations took place, one attracting some attention for a speech by Sartre and for a plastic bomb going off as people were dispersing. Catholic, Jewish and Protestant groups all took an active part in solidarity. The Protestant CIMADE organisation also managed to visit detainees at the Vincennes detention centre (an example of what might be termed 'benevolent collaboration'). And many French women were at the forefront of protests on 20 October and 9 November against the imprisonment of their Algerian husbands and sons.[52]

As for trade unions and political parties, the CGT later claimed that 'Faced with the intolerable, the barriers of division fell'.[53] In reality, however, the Left's responses were fragmented, often along sectarian Cold War lines. The Communist CGT and the Catholic Confédération Française des Travailleurs Chrétiens (CFTC) engaged in mutual recriminations, failing to agree on what form protest should take. In the provinces, though, joint declarations were made more readily, for example at Mâcon in Burgundy on 21 October. The Trotskyist magazine *Quatrième Internationale* accused the Parti Communiste Français (PCF) of climbing onto the bandwagon of an approaching Algerian victory, supposedly in an attempt to divert attention from the messy goings-on at the 22nd Congress of the Communist Party of the Soviet Union. (In fact the Communist daily *L'Humanité*'s coverage of the Congress dwarfed that of the repression.)[54] Different organisations subsequently claimed to have had a monopoly on protests, such as the PSU for what was in fact one of two different demonstrations held on 1 November. It must be admitted that even the relatively large PSU demonstration, which mustered between one and three thousand from a secret rendezvous in a cinema queue, was small in absolute terms. Yet it was to enter into party mythology as proof of the PSU's uniquely unshakeable anti-colonialist principles.[55] Half a century later, at a conference I attended to mark the fiftieth anniversary of the foundation of the party, controversy erupted amongst veteran activists over the origins of the 1 November demonstration. Jean Baumgarten (aka Verger), member of a far Left tendency within the PSU, claimed that his motion at the party's Paris regional bureau proposing such a demonstration was opposed by a majority who feared the consequences, but that this was overridden a week later by the party's national bureau as a result of pressure from Algerian organisations. Others in the hall took issue with this account, with one dismissing it as a settling of scores.[56] This incident was symptomatic, arguably, of the moral weight of history still haunting French leftists over who exactly had or had not protested about 17 October.

Above all, many writers have rhetorically contrasted the low level of mobilisation for the Algerian dead with the massive turnout of up to one million people at the funerals of nine French Communist demonstrators, who on 8 February 1962 were crushed to death on the steps of Charonne metro station while attempting to flee a police baton charge on an anti-OAS demonstration.[57] The implication is that there was a racist double standard at work: the state kills French people, and the Left jumps up and down and screams blue murder; the state kills Algerian people, and the Left shrugs its shoulders. But as House argues, the 17 October-Charonne contrast is 'highly politically charged',[58] because it is a polemical point about the Communist Party's lukewarmness on opposing racism and colonialism. Indeed the memory of 17 October was an important point of crystallisation of a current orientated towards the Third World rather than the French proletariat – the ultimate confirmation that the party cared only about white French workers, and that the latter were racist. A key source for it was Georges Mattéi, one of the small group of French people who provided direct support to the FLN, often referred to as *porteurs de valises* because one of their chief tasks was the smuggling out of the country of suitcases of cash donated voluntarily or involuntarily to the FLN by Algerian migrant workers. According to the biography of Mattéi by his friend Einaudi, Mattéi's reaction to 17 October was one of disgust at the French public: 'He felt hatred, disgust at being French.'[59] In a 1980 article, Mattéi was to describe his impressions of the French public's response to the massacre in essentially collaborationist terms. He described how on 19 October, Mohammed Sadek, one of the key organisers of the 17 October demonstration, asked Mattéi: 'Did you see the workers of France? Did you see them? And the Left, did you see it?' and Mattéi had no reply. Therefore when he saw the enormous crowd mourning the killings at Charonne, Mattéi's response was to contrast it to

17 October.[60]

A main source for the 17 October-Charonne contrast, then, was an extreme anti-colonialist, who with good reason, having heard the screams of people being tortured, returned from military service as an enraged outsider, repelled and enraged by French society to the extent that he went off to link up with guerrillas in Latin America. This is not a neutral source. One does not have to agree with the startlingly McCarthyite line of the historian Jean-Paul Brunet, who attacks Einaudi for having been a member of the Parti Communiste Marxiste-Léniniste de France (PCMLF) and therefore an apologist for Pol Pot and Kim Il-Sung, to try and situate the Mattéi-Einaudi ultra-left viewpoint historically, rather than accepting it at face value. Although the same point was also made by slightly more moderate voices, such as the ancient historian Pierre Vidal-Naquet, accepting it too uncritically may suggest that only this small minority of hardcore resisters were concerned about what France was doing to the Algerians. This would be to downplay the protest of larger forces. That the clear, uncompromising anti-colonialist stance which may have been vindicated by posterity, was at the time the property of a small minority, does not mean that everyone else was uniformly wicked and colonialist. The roll-call of those who denounced the 17 October killings at the time contains some surprising names. They include – admittedly not the strongest worded or the promptest – statements by two men who on the far Left became bywords for treachery: Guy Mollet, the former Socialist prime minister who had sent the paratroopers to Algiers and Suez, and François Mitterrand. In addition, the historian Alain Dewerpe has challenged the idea that the memory of 17 October 1961 was entirely buried by Charonne: the Communist Party did in fact commemorate the two together in the years immediately following.[61]

We also has to ask: what would have counted as a good response to 17 October? Is the comparison with Charonne comparing like with like? Charonne happened after the antiwar campaign had had a crucial few extra months to transform itself into a mass movement, a development which 17 October itself fed into, with demonstrations of ten thousand-plus emerging from 18 November onwards.[62] Even Etienne Balibar, a leading critic of Communist indifference, did not claim there was *no* reaction to 17 October, suggesting in fact that without 17 October and 'the shock which it produced in public opinion, the French working class and its organisations would not have been shaken'.[63] A more appropriate comparison therefore might be with anti-war demonstrations prior to 17 October, which had been small. At by far the biggest one, on 27 October 1960, there were ten to fifteen thousand demonstrators. By those standards, the one to three thousand of 1 November 1961 was clearly disappointing, but not as miniscule as it looks compared to the million-odd of 12 February 1962. Though reasons of self-interest and racism did play a part in the relatively weak response to 17 October, no monocausal explanation will suffice. We need to bear in mind that, unlike at Charonne, there was no one single massacre, but many killings in small groups in different locations. The one really large-scale massacre was in the Prefecture of Police – behind closed doors, where the public could not have seen. Given the spread of disinformation by the authorities, the public did not have access to the clear picture that we have now, so it may be overhasty to morally judge them as if they did. The highest figure claimed in public in the immediate aftermath was fifty dead. Accustomed to hearing lies and propaganda, the public might well have assumed that the true figure lay somewhere between this and the official figure of two or three. In a context of war, this would seem bad, but not completely out of the ordinary. For example, people would have learnt about the demonstrations concurrently with the news of 48 plastic bombings in one day in Algiers, and several Muslims killed by rioting European civilians in Oran. Even in Paris, over the previous seven weeks, the FLN had killed some 13 policemen.[64]

Moreover, the summer and early autumn of 1961 saw a pronounced hardening of the authoritarianism of the Gaullist state, with many French antiwar activists having their homes raided by police. Under emergency powers, all demonstrations were illegal, and it was accepted as par for the course that demonstrators would be beaten in the street. An implicit acknowledgement of this was a curious badge scheme introduced to distinguish journalists from demonstrators, in response to embarrassing incidents in which journalists had been beaten.[65] It was not unknown for fatalities to occur on demonstrations even in metropolitan France, particularly in the early Cold War period when the police had become instruments of severe anti-communist repression, as in the strikes of 1947-1948. So French people who chose to protest in 1961 were running a risk: considerably lower than that run by the Algerians, but considerably higher than citizens of liberal democracies might expect in 'normal' times. In comparative context, can we say that the French public's behaviour was unusual? Indifference to the fate of people outside one's community of belonging – what the philosopher Norman Geras calls 'the contract of mutual indifference'[66] – is not, sadly, unusual in the *anomie* of modern existence, particularly if those people have been targets of sustained demonisation. Mass anti-imperialist movements in imperialist countries are the exception, not the rule, especially in situations of armed conflict with atrocities on both sides. One might respond that the difference was that in this case the violence was happening not only at the colonial periphery, but also at the very heart of the metropolis. House and MacMaster describe 17 October as 'the bloodiest act of state repression of street protest in Western Europe in modern history'.[67] While this statement is true for Western Europe since 1945, if the frame within which we view it is Europe as a whole in the twentieth century, or indeed the whole history of violence carried out by Europeans to non-Europeans, it does not appear quite so extraordinary. What is so shocking is that this kind of thing is not meant to intrude into our zone of postwar comfort and peace in the West, as it did on 17 October 1961.

There may, though, be delicate questions to ask about the form that resistance to the massacre took. Often this was not directly trying to stop it, but more indirectly in the form of speaking out: policemen leaking reports of atrocities to the press; the photographer Elie Kagan going around Paris on his Vespa taking photos, and so on. Telling the truth in a sea of lies was an important motivation, but not without moral ambiguities. In the 1992 British Channel Four documentary on 17 October, an eyewitness described the killing of an Algerian on a bridge over the Seine, declaring 'It was the first time I had seen a man die'. A sceptical viewer might respond, 'But you didn't do anything to stop it'. Similarly, when Kagan was confronted by an American journalist in Nanterre for taking photos while an Algerian lay badly injured on the ground, Kagan replied that he was just doing his job, and suggested to the American that if he was so charitable, they should take the Algerian to hospital together.[68] Resistance and collaboration may prove to historians to have been more complex matters in the Paris of 1961 – as we already know for the Paris of 1942 – than immediate posterity liked to admit. Todd Shepard is right to urge historians today to get beyond a simple 'rehearsal of "*tiers mondiste*" claims'.[69] But the lesson drawn at the time by the militant anti-colonialists, self-conscious of being a minority vanguard, was one about the indifference of the rest of French society to the Third World. Some of the protests after 17 October were not just protests against the killings, but also protests against a perceived lack of protests. Graffiti appeared on the banks of the Seine reading 'THEY DROWN ALGERIANS HERE'. Similar sentiments seem to have motivated *porteurs de valises* like Francis Jeanson to aid the FLN directly.[70] For the New Left journalist K.S.Karol, 'the West as a whole will ultimately have to pay the price for the Paris Pogrom'.[71]

Where Is the Third World?

The years immediately following the end of the Algerian War looked as if they might be, in France at any rate, much quieter, with some suggestions of a 'silence of the intellectuals'.[72] But many leading activists were busy in the newly decolonised countries themselves. Not surprisingly, so soon after the anti-colonialist euphoria of 1960-62, the developing world, rather than immigrants from it to France, was the primary focus of French *tiersmondistes*. The struggle against imperialism, rather than completed, seemed to be intensifying. There were anti-imperialist solidarity demonstrations to be organised, whether about still colonised French territories like Guadeloupe, where as many as fifty people were killed by security forces in the suppression of a revolt in May 1967, or about Vietnam, a major focus of activism in the run-up to 1968. It was Algeria, though, that occupied the most special place in the hearts of francophone revolutionaries. Under the presidency of Ahmed Ben Bella (1962-1965), the country was at the epicentre of Third World revolution, with close relations to Cuba. Where else in the world could French Trotskyists such as the mysterious 'Pablo' – himself a Greek immigrant – find themselves in demand as government advisers? Revolutionary migrants like 'Pablo' were known as the *pied-rouges* in an ironic twist on *pied-noirs*, the one million European settlers who had fled Algeria just as they were arriving. The small band of *pied-rouges* rubbed shoulders with rebels from across the world, including Nelson Mandela and Che Guevara. Algiers was not just important for its own sake but as a symbolic capital of Third World revolution. When Black Panther leaders Eldridge and Kathleen Cleaver fled the United States in 1969, what more appropriate place to claim asylum: had not the Panthers poured over the works of Fanon? In a villa overlooking the Mediterranean, the Panthers' international office remained in Algiers for three years.[73]

So when young French militants did take the plunge to leave the Latin Quarter, their first destination could well be Algeria or Bolivia, rather than Aubervilliers or Bobigny – suburbs of their own city. This could take a constructive form. Tiennot Grumbach, for example, spent 1962-1965 in Algeria, organising festivals and building up the tourist industry. Another later prominent Maoist, Robert Linhart, who subsequently worked alongside immigrant workers at Citroën, spent the summer of 1964 there. PSU members Paul Oriol and Anne Couteau, who would play an important role in supporting migrant workers in Paris from the 1970s onwards, left France to work in Algeria in 1963 and 1965 respectively: in many ways they remember their Algerian years as the best period of their life.[74] In 1965, the PSU activist Manuel Bridier founded the CEDETIM,[75] a centre of research and activism on Third World issues. Many of the CEDETIM militants, active since the anti-colonial struggles of the late 1950s and early 1960s, spent part of the Sixties as *coopérants rouges* in former French colonies, attempting to find a means of promoting Third World development consistent with their anti-colonial principles. It was not until the Seventies that the group moved to focus on immigration in France: more typical of CEDETIM debates circa 1967 were titles like 'What is the Third World?' and 'Where are Guinea and Mali headed?'[76] In a few cases *tiersmondisme* could take the more destructive form of armed struggle, notably with Régis Debray who quit the Left Bank to become a *compañero* of Che Guevara, at one point actually facing a Bolivian army firing squad. For Debray, the mundane political banalities of the France he abandoned at the end of 1965 were boring by comparison:

> For it was elsewhere – no longer in the West – that *it was all happening*. My compatriots were mere benighted Zulus, shaking their ballot-boxes like fetishes, unaware that serious things were going on behind their backs. Encirclement from the South, that was the important thing.[77]

In this context, the presence of Third World migrant workers in France itself was easy to overlook. As a guide to what the intellectual New Left was thinking in this period, we might take the rough French equivalents of the *New Left Review* – Sartre's *Les Temps Modernes*, and the publisher François Maspero's militantly confrontational *Partisans*. Between 1962 and 1968, *Les Temps Modernes* only carried one article specifically on migrant workers in France: tellingly, more favoured areas of interest were French students, Cuba, Vietnam and African-Americans. Similarly, even *Partisans* only carried three articles on the subject prior to 1968, preferring such themes as Algeria, China, Vietnam, Palestine, education, sexuality and youth. Maspero, son of a Sinologist, grandson of an Egyptologist, was fascinated by the wider world – but only got to know the *banlieue* in depth when, decades later, he wrote a travel book about it.[78] *La Tribune Socialiste*, the weekly paper of the PSU, also rarely featured immigration as an issue before 1968. In the whole of 1967, for example, it devoted just one article to the subject. Immigrant workers were mentioned in only one paragraph at the end of a very long and detailed 24 page party programme of January 1967, and not at all in a special supplement of *La Tribune Socialiste* for the parliamentary elections of March 1967. There was the odd exception – the Catholic-humanist *Esprit*, which had played a prominent and early role in the opposition to the Algerian War, did a special issue in 1966, and the review *Hommes et Migrations* provided probably the greatest continuity. But in precisely those leftist places where we would expect to find an interest in immigrant workers, that interest was absent.[79]

The Class Divide

How, then, are we to explain this absence? For one thing, in terms of the barriers of class. However cosmopolitan the pre-1968 New Left milieu, it was not one into which actual proletarians, whether French or foreign, often intruded. Writing in the late 1970s, the British writer R.W.Johnson sardonically contrasted the 'extraordinary international resonance' of the Latin Quarter Left, 'cloaked in revolutionary rhetoric and theorising' to

> another, more mundane French Left, one that is not glimpsed in the Fifth *arrondissement*. Just as the Right may talk of a '*pays réel*', so there is, too, a *gauche réelle*. It is the Left one sees if one wanders further out into the industrial wasteland of the Paris *banlieue*, where the great blocks of cheap multi-storey housing, the *habitations à loyer modéré* (HLM), march like some gaunt column of soldiers through the even less salubrious bidonvilles[80] of immigrant workers and the great fortress-like factories of French industrial life. Out here, beyond the Metro's reach, no one much has heard of Althusser and no one at all about Poulantzas. What matters here is *saisis* and *expulsions* (rent-evictions) and *coupures* (electricity and gas cut-offs for unpaid bills).[81]

There is good reason to suppose this segregation between middle- and working-class Lefts was if anything more marked prior to 1968. What was distinctive about what Anglo-Saxons called the 'New' as opposed to the 'Old' Left was not only its ideology but, to call a spade a spade, its social base. The proletariat no longer had a monopoly of revolutionary agency, which could now also be sought from colonial militants or people on the margins of metropolitan society – but always in alliance with a newly expanded intelligentsia.

Most revealing of this pre-1968 class segregation were the diverse reactions on these two Lefts to 17 October 1961, which were perceived as weak largely because they were dispersed and utterly separate from each other. Students and intellectuals protested in central Paris, workers protested in the *banlieue*. Little seen by the former, some 71 protests were held in the Communist-dominated working-class suburbs. In September, the PCF mayor of Nanterre had already spoken up for the Algerians living in shanty towns, demanding the withdrawal of *harki* forces[82] and the introduction of decent housing. On 18 October, work stoppages of between 15 minutes and an hour, sanctioned by the CGT, took place in many workplaces, including the famous Renault factory at Boulogne-Billancourt, from where several hundred workers marched to the town hall to deliver a petition. On 20 October, a crowd of between a few hundred and a thousand workers met in Gennevilliers, to the north-west of the capital, shouting 'Murderers!' at and badly shaking a police car – though despite official CGT support for the demonstration, dissident Marxist militants handing out leaflets for it were harassed. On 25 October, work was stopped for 15 minutes at a factory in the southern suburb of Malakoff in solidarity with an Algerian employee who had returned from police detention with reports of brutalities.[83] Meanwhile one of the few press conferences to denounce the massacre was given by, of all people, Jacques Duclos, one of the most senior figures in the PCF, who also asked questions in parliament about it. The point here is that Duclos, whose bombastic rhetorical style typified the Party's self-consciously proletarian approach, was as Old Left as they came: a veteran of the Battle of Verdun, and a Stalinist so loyal that he had once been falsely charged with sending carrier pigeons to Moscow to coordinate demonstrations in Paris against an American general accused of using biological warfare in the Korean War. The Secours Populaire Français, a Communist satellite organisation active in suburbs like Nanterre, visited and gave out money, food and even blood to the wounded and their families, claiming to have distributed over 3 million francs, 1200 tins of milk and 150 kilos of couscous.[84] So one vision of the Communist Party was of proletarian solidarity between French and immigrant workers. Indeed, for Etienne Balibar, the great tragedy was that a real unity between French and immigrant workers, had it not been for various opportunities missed by the PCF, *could* have occurred during the Algerian War, and made subsequent history very different.[85]

This vision of solidarity was not, however, what the New Left was most likely to see from its vantage point in central Paris. Far more symbolic for young dissidents like Alain Krivine (and slightly less young ones like Maspero), was the shocking sight of dead and wounded Algerians piled up in front of the closed shutters of the offices of *L'Humanité* on the night of 17 October. It is a sight that Krivine says he will never forget.[86] But to organise separately from the Communist Party, with its overwhelming hegemony over the working class, was an adventure into the unknown. For the fifty-odd ex-activists in the PCF's youth wing who, gathered in a café in 1966, undertook precisely this step to form the Jeunesse Communiste Révolutionnaire (JCR), it must have required considerable confidence on their part. As one of them, the future philosopher Daniel Bensaïd, put it: 'Next to the great party of the proletarians, of its legendary trade unionists, of its heroic Resistance fighters, of its poets covered with laurels, our juvenile conspiracy was very microscopic.'[87] The young rebels were led by the eldest amongst them, the 25 year old Krivine who, as hostile sources liked to emphasise,[88] was the son of a dentist and the son-in-law of Gilles Martinet. As Krivine himself admits, the JCR 'had few contacts with the working class'.[89] Symbolically, the Party congress they had walked out from was in Nanterre, a workers' suburb; the café they gathered in was in bourgeois Paris in the Place Saint-Sulpice. For the teenage Bensaïd, though inoculated against the 'religious cult of the red proletarian' by his years working behind the bar in a rather different café – his parents' one in a working-class district of Toulouse – his radicalisation occurred along with subtle social barriers opening up between him and the café's Communist customers as he entered university. Nevertheless, what the JCR lacked in proletarian authenticity, it could make up for as an avant-garde of anti-racism, steeped as its members were personally in the Holocaust and the Algerian War. Bensaïd senior kept his yellow star in the café till, while, having narrowly avoided deportation to the Nazi death camps, Krivine's parents later had to put up with the OAS trying to bomb their son's bedroom.[90] As Philippe Raynaud suggests:

> There remained from all that an exacerbated anti-racist and anti-fascist sensibility, combined with a profound refusal of French national myths, which had no difficulty finding echoes in later mobilisations[91]

The Other Side of the Tracks: Shanty Towns and Cellars

So what then, was happening on the other side of the *Périphérique*, the orbital highway then under construction that marks the physical, and class, boundary between Paris and the *banlieue*?[92] The 1960s were the peak period of immigration in post-war France. Two million people left their homes to fill the many vacancies in the French building and car industries at this height of the post-war boom. It was largely a movement of people from around the Mediterranean basin, conditioned as much by poverty at home as by opportunity in the North. Algerian peasants were forced off the land by rural impoverishment and war, driving them into shanty towns first in Algerian cities, then in France. Many Portuguese peasants made, in the title of a 1967 film *O Salto*, 'the leap', the dangerous clandestine journey up over the Pyrenees and down into France. Many of them were seeking to avoid conscription to fight in the colonial wars in Angola and Mozambique.

And though the Spanish economy was expanding by this time, it was a case of uneven development, with many in the South escaping the poverty of Andalucia for the opportunities sometimes of Barcelona, but sometimes of Toulouse or Paris. Smaller numbers of people also came from Yugoslavia, Morocco, Tunisia and francophone West Africa. So while France had been a recipient of transnational migrant labour since the nineteenth century, the migration of the 1960s was a new wave, transforming existing communities. Encouraged by French employers and governments, this was a chaotic and disorganised migration, in the rush for what was seen as temporary, cheap labour.[93]

Descriptions from the period tend to emphasise the scandalous conditions in which immigrants had to live, reduced to their physical labour alone as victims of dispossession, exploitation and squalor – isolated, depersonalised, uprooted and alienated.[94] Immigrants suffered from severe social problems, notably in housing, of which France had some of the worst examples in Western Europe. Even today, it is still possible to get some sense of the atmosphere of mid-twentieth century immigrant slum housing in the Petite Espagne district of the northern Paris suburb of Saint-Denis. In La Petite Espagne, the poverty can appear strangely Mediterranean in spite of the northerly setting. The old dilapidated buildings, some almost falling down, contrast sharply to the nearby modern blocks of flats now in the shadow of the Stade de France sports stadium. According to local historian Natacha Lillo, leading in the hot summer of 2010 an incongruous group of international academics round on a tour of immigration history, the last inhabitants of La Petite Espagne cannot afford the rents in the new flats, but are reluctant to be rehoused far away on the other side of town. As the name alludes, the district hosts a Spanish community centre, today hosting flamenco lessons, immigrant theatre and an older peoples' day centre. But as Lillo explained, standing in the centre's bar surrounded by unmistakeably Spanish murals, until 1976 the centre's main feature was a Catholic chapel, a focus of conflict between Spain's politically divided post-Civil War emigrants. Since the late 1950s, they had been joined locally by a mass of new migrant workers from Extremadura, a poor region of western Spain. While the Francoist-controlled centre sought to use the chapel as a means of social control over migrants, Republicans would refuse to let their children even enter the premises. Yet the centre was frequented by other local inhabitants including North Africans: one of them, Achour Boubeker, recalls the neighbourhood as a poor but 'rather joyful melting pot' where everyone played together.[95]

But the most dramatic indications of the uneven development of 1960s

France were the Third World-style shanty towns that had mushroomed on the outskirts of Paris and other towns and cities. In 1966, even a very conservative official estimate gave the number of people living in them as 75,000. The largest, at 14,000, was in the eastern Paris suburb of Champigny, while nearly 10,000 lived in shanty towns in Nanterre and nearly 5,000 in Saint-Denis. The majority of shanty town dwellers were either North African, as in Nanterre, or Portuguese, as in Champigny, though the housing shortage was such that even some French families lived in them. Life in the shanty towns, despite a certain conviviality compared to the high-rise apartment blocks that replaced them, was harsh – households had no running water, no sewers and no mains electricity – and sometimes dangerous. In one shanty town in the northern suburb of La Courneuve, 205 families and 230 lone men had to share one tap and one perilously infected sewerage channel. In this world, upward mobility did not mean the 'fast cars, clean bodies'[96] of consumerist imagery. It meant moving home from a horse-drawn caravan to a wooden shack, to a breezeblock construction, then to a 'better' shanty town, perhaps eventually to build a house – unless the police put paid to this by demolishing houses under construction, forcing the cycle to start all over again. Tuberculosis was a menace, as was hostility between the several different nationalities living there. Fires often broke out in the ramshackle buildings, as at Nanterre in March 1966, when three children were killed. In contrast to fires after May '68, such as in Aubervilliers in January 1970, shanty town fires in this earlier period attracted only passing attention from French public opinion. A few noises were heard from politicians about the need to replace the shanty towns. But little happened before 1968. Indeed in March 1968, just as unrest was spreading at Nanterre University, Bilani Lay Ben Lachen, a Moroccan father of three children, slid to his death from a dangerous building site on campus. Yet outside the shanty town his death went unnoticed and forgotten.[97]

The situation in many areas inside city boundaries was little better. As one Portuguese worker explained:

> I live in a cellar with two other friends. Before I lived in a shack, but I had to leave because of building work on the land. It's not much fun to live inside it but I really need to because I send a third of my salary to my wife who stayed in Portugal with our little boy. Here you need to pay a lot to have something, and even our compatriots exploit us.[98]

Whereas increasing numbers of North Africans were at least joined by their families, lone migrants from sub-Saharan Africa faced many of the very worst conditions, vulnerable to the 'sleep merchants' renting out insalubrious rooms, shacks and cellars. In the 11th arrondissement of eastern Paris, hundreds of Africans were reported to be sleeping in overcrowded cellars. In one privately owned hostel in the suburb of Ivry, it was claimed that as many as 541 people were living in just 11 rooms. Little wonder, then, that recruiters were fighting over each other in the African cafés of Marseilles to tap this lowest cost labour force yet. On streets in the centre of the port city, Africans could be seen in small groups, waiting patiently for a bed they took turns to sleep in. At times, some migrant workers found no alternative but to sleep underneath bridges in cardboard boxes.[99]

The tragic paradox, though, was that despite the overcrowding, for many immigrants, the dominant sensation experienced in France was an overwhelming feeling of loneliness. The majority were still men who came alone – but typically they were not 'single': many had a wife and children back home, who they had had to leave far away for long stretches of time in order to earn money to support them. On arrival, the more individualist mode of living characteristic of modern north-western European cities was a shock for those used to societies where even strangers would casually talk to one another. A Tunisian worker later interviewed for Yamina Benguigui's documentary *Mémoires d'immigrés* recalled, with considerable emotion, having got off the boat in Marseilles, walking through crowds of people ignoring him, sitting down on a bench and weeping.[100] One Algerian vividly described to the sociologist Abdelmalek Sayad this lived reality of *elghorba*, ['exile']:

> I will always remember this image of my arrival in France, it is the first thing I saw, the first thing I heard: you knock at a door, it opens on to a little room that smells of a mixture of things, the damp, the closed atmosphere, the sweat of sleeping men. Such sadness! Such misery in their eyes, their voices – they spoke softly – in their words. That gave me an insight into what loneliness is, what sadness is: the darkness of the room, the darkness in the room ... the darkness in the streets – the darkness of the whole of France, because, in our France, there is nothing but darkness.[101]

Such alienation indicated that the very people who worked hardest to sustain what was for others a period of prosperity had been reduced to the status of economic instruments. Marcuse's phrase 'one dimensional man' might come to mind.[102]

Economic Man: An Impossible Politicisation?

For it is important to remember that immigration was at this time considered an economic, rather than political issue, in total contrast to the situation that has prevailed since the early 1980s. Immigration was seen primarily as a temporary phenomenon of economic expediency, rather than as any kind of threat to French cultural identity. The main public arguments were not about mosques and headscarves, but about factory gradings and housing provision. Fitting with the 'guest-worker' paradigm dominant across western Europe, migrants were described as 'immigrant workers', rather than 'immigrants' *tout court*. The term 'immigrant worker' suited both the Marxist Left, because of its class implications, and the governing Right, which viewed immigrants in instrumental terms as mere economic units. As the then Prime Minister – later President – Georges Pompidou declared in 1963: 'Immigration is a means of creating a certain *détente* on the labour market and of resisting social pressure.' Still more blatantly, Jean-Marcel Jeanneney, Minister for Social Affairs, stated in an unguarded moment in 1966: 'Illegal immigration has its uses, for if we adhered rigidly to the regulations and international agreements we would perhaps be short of labour.'[103] Most immigrants entered France either clandestinely or as tourists and regularized their situation only after they found a job, if at all. So what would subsequently be demonised as 'illegal immigration' was actually encouraged by the authorities.

Pompidou and Jeanneney could not have expressed more succinctly the paradoxical politics of immigration in France prior to 1968. Any vulgar Marxist, or cynical capitalist, could tell you that economically, the Right represented the interests of the *patronat* – the bosses, who above all wanted cheap labour. The balance sheet calculations were clear: since it was estimated that Algerians in France produced ten times as much as they consumed, French capitalists had much to gain from their presence. One 1967 study calculated that migration represented a net subsidy from Algeria to France of a billion francs a year. Hence even the future president Valéry Giscard d'Estaing, in later years an outspoken critic of immigration, actively encouraged immigration as Finance Minister in this period. Yet not all ministers agreed with Giscard: the Right was also meant ideologically to represent French nationalism, for which the presence of minorities might pose a challenge. De Gaulle had himself let slip that a good argument for Algerian independence was so that his home village of Colombey-les-deux-Eglises would not become Colombey-les-deux-Mosquées.[104] Whereas the Left was meant to stand for the workers, who on the face of it hardly had much interest in being undercut by cheap foreign competition – quite the contrary. And yet, the Left was also meant to show solidarity with oppressed migrant workers, according to its ideological allegiances to proletarian internationalism. These were the central contradictions that were never resolved. Over the next decade, when governments began to try and restrict immigration, *gauchistes* would often throw back Pompidou's words at the French state.[105]

In 1963, representatives of metalworkers in Nantes declared that the Third World question was 'the number one issue which we will have to face up to in the years to come'. They belonged to the CFTC, the historically Catholic trade union confederation that on deconfessionalisation in 1964 became the Confédération Française Démocratique du Travail. The CFDT was the union confederation closest aligned with New Left thinking, under the influence of the innovative ideas of the PSU. CFDT militants were urged to educate workers about Third World issues and to struggle against what was considered their spontaneous self-interestedness.[106] But if the unions were aware of global inequality in broad ideological terms, what was their response to workers from these countries arriving in France itself?[107] Much of what was written on the Left about immigrants before 1968 focused on the negatives – the intense exploitation, the barriers to uniting them with French workers – not the positives. Writing in *Partisans* in 1966, Guy Desolre painted a dismal portrait of the unions' and Left parties' record in this area. They saw their duties towards foreign workers as limited largely to helping those who were already supporters of the same political tendency as themselves: 'Apart from these forms of collaboration, little real support. In France since the Popular Front, the tradition of internationalist solidarity ... has been lost'[108] Trade unionists were failing to confront racism from French workers, and urgently needed to work more with immigrants. The only glimmers of hope, considered Desolre, were the historically Catholic unions and the youth movement Jeunesse Ouvrière Chrétienne.

Desolre's argument was typical of a New Left position in implying the principal failure was that of the strongest part of the French labour movement – the Communist Party and its satellite union confederation, the CGT. There was some polemical exaggeration to this argument. The CGT did publish several foreign-language newspapers: *Unidad* ['Unity'] for the Spanish, *Lavoro* ['Labour'] for Italians (in addition to *L'Emigrante*, produced by the PCF, historically well implanted among this group) and from 1966 *La Tribune du Travailleur Algérien*, as well as later titles for Yugoslavs and Turks. Laure Pitti has shown that relations between Algerian workers and the CGT, though coming under strain during the Algerian War, had historically been good at the union bastion of Renault – although this was true only to a lesser extent for the PCF itself. During the 1960s, the PCF's language groups were revived, and campaigned for better housing for immigrants. The party was formally committed to uniting French and foreign workers together against capitalism, and the CGT had since the early Sixties abandoned outright opposition to further immigration.[109] Nevertheless, the Communist position, as set out in a Central Committee policy statement of 1963, was beset with a flagrant contradiction. On the one hand, it loftily declared: 'For us, the proletarians of all countries are brothers and workers who live and work on our soil, whatever their nationality, are brothers in poverty, brothers in struggle and hope.' Yet on the same page it condemned the government's use of cheap migrant labour as being 'against the national interest of our people', undermining workers' struggles in both France and the sending countries. The implication was that immigrant workers should be shown solidarity ... but also that they should not have come in the first place. It should be little wonder, therefore, if the claims of the PCF to be the 'guide, educator and organiser of the struggles of immigrants'[110] looked hollow to the party's critics.

The CFDT also developed its structures for immigrant workers, holding a national conference of migrant workers in March 1966 and setting up a national secretariat for them. Like the CGT, the CFDT moved during the course of the Sixties away from separate, ideologically inspired sections for different national groups towards integrating them into the life of the union. Nevertheless, its achievements remained modest. The CFDT had in 1967 just five members out of 7,155 immigrant workers at Renault's Boulogne-Billancourt factory, forty out of 1,384 at Renault-Flins, and 33 out of 24,000 at Citroën. When a Cameroonian worker wrote a letter to the CFDT in 1967 concerning a difficulty with his landlord, the union advised him that the best solution to his problems was to return to Cameroon. While the CGT, reflecting its overall dominant position in the labour movement, did have larger structures for immigrants than the other confederations, the numbers involved were still quite small. French unions organised a smaller percentage of the workforce than in many other industrial countries, and it is likely that the level of unionisation was lower for foreign than French workers. Given that as late as 1973, after a considerable upturn in strike activity by migrants, it was estimated that the unionisation rate among migrant workers was less than 10 per cent, we can assume the figure was lower than this in the more unpromising period before 1968.[111]

Since unions sometimes sought to maintain wage differentials in the interest of highly skilled workers, the egalitarian demands of those lower down pay scales, such as migrant workers, were not always stressed in practice. When, unusually, the CGT and CFDT agreed on a joint day of action for 17 May 1966, the 'underprivileged' categories that the CFDT insisted must feature prominently included those on the minimum wage, families, the elderly and disabled, but not immigrants as such. Those who participated on the day of action were less obviously multinational than those who would do so in the general strike of 1968: while some Italians participated, they belonged more to the 'old' working class of the 1940s than the latest wave of migration. There were occasional exceptions: for example, Moroccans participated in the miners' strike of 1963. Some 'early warnings' might be detected in the very immediate run-up to May 1968, just as historians have retrospectively detected a new combativity in other labour disputes of 1967-68. At the end of 1967, the CGT issued warnings to Algerian workers about Trotskyists and Maoists attempting to infiltrate them. In the early spring of 1968, Portuguese workers on a building site in Champigny went on strike for three days over pay.[112] But for the most part, the pre-1968 story is one of an absence of encounter between unions and migrant workers.

Explaining an Absence

Why, structurally, was there this absence? At the time, some New Left thinkers argued that the recourse to migrant labour was designed precisely in order to stabilise capitalism. André Gorz, himself an immigrant, was a proponent of this pessimistic view in which the whole point of using disenfranchised foreign labour was 'to diminish sharply the political and electoral weight of the working class, to diminish more sharply yet its ideological weight and coherence'.[113] It also saved governments of wealthy countries large sums on education and social services bills because workers now came ready prepared as adults, with the costs of their upbringing born instead by poor peasant families in the sending countries:

> So far as the economy of the metropolitan country is concerned, migrant workers are immortal: immortal because continually interchangeable. They are not born: they are not brought up: they do not age: they do not get tired: they do not die. They have a single function – to work. All other functions of their lives are the responsibility of the country they came from.[114]

Moreover, the New Left argument went on, the use of foreign workers in the least desirable jobs permitted French workers a degree of upward mobility. As they travelled Western Europe in a van writing an influential survey of the issue, the sociologists Stephen Castles and Godula Kosack therefore identified an objective split within the working class. Borrowing from Marx, Engels and Lenin, they suggested immigrants constituted a new 'industrial reserve army' that had become a permanent structural feature of capitalism. This 'divide and rule' strategy created a split within the working class, with hostility towards immigrants among indigenous workers based not so much on the colour of their skin as on their subordinate position in the workplace.[115]

For the moment at least, there were signs that such theorists might be right. While French organised labour was relatively strong and united in the aftermath of the Liberation, the divisions brought into sharp focus by the Algerian War were already undermining this force and coherence. Even a member of the PCF's own Politburo, Laurent Casanova, was reported in 1958 as having told the anti-war activist Francis Jeanson, 'But don't you realise the French working class is racist, colonialist, imperialist!'.[116] In 1966, the Maoist *L'Humanité Nouvelle* noted the existence of

> a certain chauvinism in various French proletarian milieux, a worrying feeling of their superiority, a lack of knowledge of the mass problems faced by our North African, Spanish, Portuguese or even Italian comrades. To initiate large actions of pure protest is becoming more difficult insofar as the spontaneous conscience of the proletariat is not managing to get beyond these separations, these divisions into groups, these apparent conflicts of interest to attain the profound unity of the working class.[117]

The same year, *Esprit* also detected a 'plebeian chauvinism and petit-bourgeois protectionism'[118] in popular French attitudes. It is true that such feelings lacked politically coherent expression. Organised political campaigns against immigration were weak: there was in the 1960s no French Enoch Powell, and no dockers marching in his support. Jean-Marie Le Pen, the future founder of the Front National, was in his 'wilderness years', an utterly marginal has-been. Uncharacteristically reduced to the role of passive spectator, Le Pen spent May '68 strolling around the Latin Quarter to watch the riots, before returning home stinking of tear gas – much to the annoyance of his wife, then pregnant with the future FN leader Marine Le Pen.[119] At this time, Jean-Marie Le Pen's comrades on the far Right were hopelessly divided, not especially interested in immigration (having more pressing matters to grapple with such as the defence of the Western world against Communism) and, most importantly, without the slightest sign of a mass audience. Whereas since the 1980s France has grown used to a National Front well into double figures in its share of the popular vote, at none of the five national elections held between 1967 and 1978 did the far Right receive even 1 per cent of the vote.[120] Indeed, it was possible for some observers, such as the British journalist John Ardagh, to take what appears in retrospect an excessively optimistic view of the level of racism in France, judging that 'hardly anywhere in France is colour any kind of social problem' and there was 'virtually no friction' between migrant workers and the French.[121] African-Americans still viewed France, a country where the President of the Senate, Gaston Monerville, was a black man from Guiana, as a relative haven of racial toleration. Nevertheless, this apparent tolerance could conceal more disturbing attitudes beneath the surface. The popular press, not only the far right *Minute* but more also more mainstream papers like *Le Parisien Libéré*, encouraged chauvinism by attempting to scapegoat immigrant workers for French social problems, depicting especially North Africans as dirty, lazy, violent and criminal.[122] Many people in France assumed that since the colonial issue had now been settled with the granting of independence to former colonies, culminating with Algeria in 1962, there was no reason for them to come to France. French workers sometimes asked: 'We've given them independence, they only have to manage by themselves'[123]– an example of working class racism that worked, because its seductively misleading logic suggested a clean break was possible, with no unpleasant imperial hangover: people from the former colonies were now 'foreigners' who had nothing to do with 'us'.

The French public were not, however, uniformly indifferent to the situation of immigrants. During the very severe winter of 1963, for example, there was a spontaneous movement to collect warm clothes for African workers, though the public largely forgot about them afterwards. The situation of immigrant workers was the object of more sustained concern by a few dedicated individuals, such as the social worker Monique Hervo and the priest François Lefort, who both spent long periods in the shanty towns. Lefort, who from the early Sixties organised outings for children from Nanterre, came from a very different social milieu to those he worked for. He was from the suburb of Neuilly, renowned as the wealthiest town in France (later its mayor was one N. Sarkozy), yet not far from the shanty towns of Nanterre. Similarly Josée Frouin, the daughter of a Spanish Republican and a French worker, in 1965 abandoned a career as a specialist on seventeenth century stamps to set up a support committee for the inhabitants of a shanty town in the southern suburb of L'Hay-les-Roses. Similar groups were often formed after some incident such as a fire which highlighted scandalous conditions locally, for example at Châtenay-

Malabry in 1961. They came together in 1966 to form the Fédération des Associations de Solidarité avec les Travailleurs Immigrés (FASTI). The Aide à Toute Détresse-Quart Monde movement had taken an interest in the lives of shanty town dwellers since its foundation by a Catholic priest in 1957. Embryonic versions of the New Left-immigrant crossover that flourished after 1968 could already be found beforehand, as in the case of Belkacem Boussouar. The son of an Algerian migrant, and later president of the French goat farmers' union, Boussouar frequented CFDT and PSU types in a village in Burgundy. And quite a few people were alerted to the situation of Portuguese migrants in particular by the film *O Salto* ['The Leap'].[124] There was also an 'old', institutionalised anti-racism existing as a heritage from previous rounds of anti-racist activity since the Dreyfus Affair. The Mouvement contre le Racisme et pour l'Amitié entre les Peuples (MRAP) for example, had been founded by Jewish Communist members of the French Resistance. During the Sixties, it campaigned energetically and relentlessly against racial discrimination, such as a bar near Paris' Gare du Nord that refused to serve black customers, or a swimming pool that refused entry to Algerians without a medical certificate. Nevertheless, the increasingly bureaucratised MRAP might be accused of a kind of well-intended but naive liberal anti-racism: 'Racism is a very grave sin.'[125] This approach of seeking to wipe out irrational prejudice had its limits.[126] The sum total of these various initiatives suggested that French interest in migrants as human beings, rather than cheap labour, was restricted before 1968 to such limited exceptions.

This may have been connected to a more general depoliticisation during this period. One sociological study of young entrants to the labour force in the late Fifties found them retrenched in private life and reluctant to participate politically. A third did not know what a union was and just 2 per cent considered themselves part of the working class. It was precisely this 'privatisation' of social life that led *Socialisme ou Barbarie* to disband itself in pessimistic despair just a year before May '68.[127] Even for French citizens, the pre-1968 Fifth Republic was characterised by a low degree of popular input into decision making. The perception of an out-of-touch authoritarian state in which ordinary peoples' voices were not heard is an important factor in explaining the origins of the mass participation of May. In this context, the new immigrant proletariat was not wholly exceptional. But the problem of lacking a voice was all the more acute for them. Their situation was not a major topic of public debate, and when it was discussed it was usually in the technocratic language of economics and statistics. The very last people who would have been consulted about it were the immigrants themselves.

Not surprisingly, then, the migrant proletariat was far from being immediately able to realise what Marxists would have viewed as its historic destiny, of coming to self-consciousness and struggle against capital. Being so heavily exploited and often quite bewildered on first arrival, lacking the basic tools for how they might change their situation, the development of organisation among migrant workers before 1968 was patchy, to say the least. Many arrived in France unable to read and write: estimates of illiteracy for West African migrants ranged as high as 98 per cent, and it was also very high among the Portuguese. Literacy teaching was limited mostly to *ad hoc* initiatives by individuals and associations.[128] Sally N'Dongo, a key figure in the immigrant worker-New Left crossover after 1968, first arrived in France from Senegal as an illiterate domestic servant in 1956. Many of his contemporaries in Senegal had been apathetic even during the nationalist struggles of the 1950s. He later recalled that it was common to see newly arrived Africans wandering the streets of Paris, completely lost, unable to speak a word of French. In such conditions politicisation was necessarily very slow, but first began around the issue of living conditions. N'Dongo formed an association, initially through official channels, which in 1964 became the Union Générale des Travailleurs Sénégalais en France (UGTSF). The union increasingly came into conflict with the French and Senegalese governments after N'Dongo was sacked from his job at the Senegalese embassy, accusing the Senegalese government of siding with its French counterpart to minimise Senegalese workers' rights in France. With two thousand members at its height, the UGTSF campaigned on housing and working conditions and racism, and set up literacy classes. It also lobbied for more training to be provided, which led to a polemic between N'Dongo and French far Left *groupuscules* for whom this was merely serving the needs of capitalism.[129]

Largely segregated from mainstream French society, the lives of lone male migrants were dominated by work. Sheer lack of time was one of the most important reasons for the absence of political activity: 'There was no life, only work.'[130] Indeed, the notorious curfew of 1961 had actually included an exemption for those Algerians whose work required them to be out during curfew hours.[131] The implication, that the only legitimate activity for an immigrant was work, speaks volumes about official attitudes towards their place in France. This was a balkanised, reserve army of labour, portrayed by some contemporary observers as a modern day form of slavery.[132] At one factory, cleaning shifts were organised so that the cleaners never got to meet each other. Some people worked for up to thirty years in such places.[133] Good illustration of the difficulties of organising the workforce could be found in the Citroën car factories, which were renowned for two reasons. First, for heavy-handed management and lack of union recognition. Citroën's owner, Pierre Bercot, was particularly notorious for his old-fashioned secrecy and arrogance, refusing to have any dealings with unions. Workers' bags were said to be searched for subversive material at the factory gate. Secondly, for the large number of Spanish and North African workers: estimates range from one third to 60 per cent. An observer on the eve of May '68 might well have concluded that the two phenomena were not unrelated. Recruits had to show their travel tickets as proof they had only recently arrived in the country and so were, it was presumed, politically unaware. Workers of different nationalities were placed next to each other on the production line, so that they were unable to speak to each other. Threats were made to remove the work permits of any troublemakers.[134]

The Myth of Return

We also need to bear in mind that the new wave of migration was at an early stage: many workers had only recently arrived. Historical comparison would suggest that peasants take some time to become proletarians, and organisation takes time to develop. Even if this was not their first experience of urban life – migration to France could be an extension of urban migration in home countries – traditional values and group solidarity sometimes took precedence over integration into the class struggle. At this stage it was assumed both by migrants themselves, and by French society, that this would be a temporary migration: the so-called 'myth of return'. Many immigrants were working in France simply or mainly in order to save up for their return to their home village, typically to build a house, or perhaps buy farm machinery or start a small business. This was characteristic of groups ranging from the Soninké people of the Senegal river valley in West Africa – some of those who the Parisian bourgeoisie looked down on as humble street sweepers, and leftists viewed as victims of 'neocolonial dependency', were in fact the heirs to a successful trading diaspora, planning to return to the village with money and land[135] – to the peasants of northern Portugal: 'The emigrant is a *travailleur* in France to be *petit-bourgeois* in Portugal.'[136] At the end of the month, immigrant workers could often be seen queuing up in the post office, waiting to send money home.[137] Such workers actively sought to work long hours, in diametric opposition to the French labour movement's traditional emphasis on the 'right to be lazy'.[138] With the future in mind, they were content to endure temporarily what many French viewed as an intolerably spartan and frugal existence, symbolised to many minds by the mud that surrounded the slums and shanty towns. Interviewed for the taboo-breaking television programme *Seize Millions de Jeunes* ['16 Million Young People'] as he waded through the mud outside his home in 1964, one Algerian responded to a question about the mud by expressing this sense of resignation:

> Well ... it's the rain that made that, but we can't do anything about it, it's a destiny which we are stuck with, to live in this mud for the moment... Because the French authorities don't want to help us. How do you want that they do something? So we live in it, we walk and we say this evening we will squeeze out our feet. Look, my feet have all sunk, and I can't do anything.[139]

Nevertheless, that this situation was in the long term to change suggests that there was no innate reason why these groups should remain forever resigned. Rather, perhaps the most important barrier to their participation was that this substantial component of the working class were disenfranchised non-citizens. Most immigrants (aside from certain defined categories such as 'repatriated' *pied noirs* and those from the few remaining colonies such as in the Caribbean) were foreign nationals, and consequently had no legitimate ideological claim to a say in the French polity. The set of people who lived and worked in France, and the set of people allowed to participate in French democracy were not identical. Only a few years before, considerable effort had been expended to claim that 'Algeria is France', in the words of François Mitterrand as Interior Minister at the start of the Algerian War. But what Todd Shepard has termed the 'post-Algerian Republic' now did its best to forget not only 'French Algeria' but also 'Algerian France'. The number of French deputies and senators of North African origin fell at a stroke in 1962 from fifty-five to zero – and stayed at zero until 2004. After 1962, deeply embedded notions of the inadmissibility of foreigners meddling in the affairs of the Republic now applied not only to 'old' foreigners from other European countries but also from the newly independent ex-colonies who had suddenly become 'foreign'. As foreigners, they were considered bound by a code of strict political neutrality.[140] So when immigrants did participate in strike movements, such as Portuguese in the La Cellophane factory near Lyons in 1967, it was fairly easy for management to victimise and sack the strike leaders, who being foreigners, were not allowed to hold official union positions, so lacked any legal protection.[141]

For even the politically aware immigrant worker, the more attractive ideological claims in this period were those of the newly independent states. Among migrant organisations, the Senegalese UGTSF was unusual in staking out a position independent of its home country government. The UGTSF's oppositional example would be much copied after 1968. But before, there was only the Association des Marocains en France, founded in 1961 by the famous thirdworldist leader Mehdi Ben Barka, and the Mouvement des Travailleurs Ivoiriens en France, founded in 1964. In 1967 a group of Malian workers in Paris issued a tract denouncing the official Association des Travailleurs Maliens, but such murmurings of discontent were still the exception rather than the rule.[142] Much stronger were the Amicales, nationality-specific welfare/friendly societies for migrant workers, with official or semi-official links to consulates and home country governments, of which the paradigmatic example was the Amicale des Algériens en Europe (AAE). Activists from countries with continued close relations to France, such as Morocco, Senegal or Ivory Coast, could portray their home governments as pawns of neo-colonialism – thus Ben Barka's 1965 kidnap in front of the Brasserie Lipp on the Boulevard Saint-Germain and subsequent disappearance is one of the great unresolved mysteries of de Gaulle's presidency. Algeria, by contrast, exuded an air of revolutionary transformation. By extension, Algerians in France who had struggled for independence had a reputation among the French as troublemakers. There is a certain mirror image between the right-wing stereotype of the 'cunning Arab', the 'Arab terrorist' and the more favourable view of one CGT activist that Algerians 'have behind them the revolution and a certain sense of *combat.*'[143]

So what had happened to the previous political energy of Algerian emigrants in France, seen notably on the demonstration of 17 October 1961? The Algerian nationalist movement was, after all, born in France during the 1920s and 1930s. But this did not necessarily equate to continued politicisation in the post-1962 period. Certainly, the FLN's pre-1962 Fédération de France had been of considerable importance to the Algerian struggle for independence, as contributions from migrant workers were the main source of funds for the FLN's armed struggle. Yet this had left little role for open political mobilisation by the mass of emigrants, since the FLN always feared that they might become too independent. The Fédération was more bureaucratic apparatus than open political party. Leaders who had never been migrant workers were parachuted in from outside, marginalising and in some cases physically eliminating existing cadres amongst the migrant community. As a mass action 17 October was exceptional, and even then the FLN sought to control it tightly.[144] Algerian migrants were used to putting up with what most French people would have considered an intolerably hard life. It took something extraordinary to push them over the edge into open protest, as in 1961 when the terrorisation of the Algerian community 'had become so remorseless that the great majority of immigrant workers was ready to seize any opportunity to break the stranglehold of terror and humiliation in which they were locked'.[145] With a return to more 'normal' times after 1962, the daily grind was not – by comparison to such events as men being taken at the point of a machine gun from their homes at night in front of their terrified wives and children – in itself sufficient to produce open revolt. Indeed, the silence about 17 October on the part of survivors throughout the Sixties helps put the weakness of political activity on other lesser issues into context. In some cases, people were too frightened, judging realistically that the French state was simply not willing to listen to them.[146]

The Fédération was itself disbanded in 1962, replaced with a more compliant AAE. This background of coups from above was not conducive to self-organised activity from below. Any attempt to break the hold of the Amicale would present formidable difficulties. The priority was to build socialism at home, and many former Fédération de France cadres returned home to do just this. (So did many militants from sub-Saharan Africa: it was rather symbolic that whereas *Présence Africaine*'s 1956 and 1959 conferences had taken place respectively at the Sorbonne and in Rome, its 1966 one was held in Dakar, and the 1969 Pan-African Festival in Algiers). If the 'best' militants had returned home, then by contrast, to have remained abroad was in some sense a failure – as was leaving Algeria after independence, for it suggested that they had failed to find a place in Algerian society. Those who remained in France after 1962, the historian Mohammed Harbi suggests, felt like victims, abandoned.[147] In that sense, Algerians were victims of what the sociologist Abdelmalek Sayad termed a 'double absence'. They were absent both from mainstream society in France and from Algeria, an absence often experienced by emigrants with feelings of guilt, even of having betrayed their country. One way to mitigate this perceived failure was to justify their exile to those back home by pretending that their life in France was much happier than it really was.[148] Another was to use the time abroad to serve the revolution at home. Film footage of one Amicale meeting in the working-class Paris suburb of Gennevilliers in 1963 shows the Algerian speaker instructing workers to learn a trade so as to build the country and remove the legacy of colonialists and exploiters. He concludes by leading a cry of 'Long live the socialist revolution!'[149] For migrants to question this Algerocentrism by joining French struggles was extremely difficult. Although after Ben Bella was overthrown in a coup in 1965 small groups of exiles did question the legitimacy of Houari Boumedienne's new government,[150] it remained the case that to join a French group was not the most obvious way of doing so. Given the bloody recent history between the two countries, to abandon the Algerian ideological sphere for the French one made little sense. The legacy of the war of independence meant Algerians could be forgiven for not feeling the French Left was their natural home. Why invest your hopes in a hypothetical revolution in France when a real one was in progress in Algeria?

A different set of concerns impeded the political engagement of migrants from Southern Europe. Since it was decades since there had been any opportunity for normal politics, new young migrants had grown up entirely under dictatorship. Conventional wisdom in the French labour movement regarded the Spanish and, especially, the Portuguese as fearful, deferential and hard to organise. This was usually attributed to their Catholicism, their rural origin, and to coming from countries without free trade unions. French employers often preferred Portuguese (or Africans) to Algerians precisely because they considered them docile and uncomplaining.[151] In retrospect, we might challenge this stereotype. Catholicism did not necessarily equate, as French secularists had traditionally assumed, to right wing. Catholic organisations openly hostile to the regime in Portugal, such as the journal *Presença Portuguesa*, founded in Vitry in 1965, were gaining ground among emigrants to France.[152] And rural origins were neither unique to the Portuguese nor necessarily a determinant of right-wing politics, as diverse historians have shown in their debunking of the myth of 'rural idiocy'. The idea that peasant origins equates to right wing rests on the assumption that real proletarians spring fully formed from a sociology textbook ready to purchase their copies of *L'Humanité*, rather than undergoing the complex and contradictory processes of class making that social historians since E.P. Thompson have explored. What, after all, was the revolutionary working class of Petrograd in 1917, if not a rough and ready conglomeration of ex-peasant migrants who retained half a foot in their home villages?[153] Indeed for the period just after 1968, one author goes as far as to suggest that the Portuguese 'effectively assumed political leadership among immigrant groups'.[154] But before 1968, the stereotype appeared to have been widely believed, and to have some basis in reality. One Portuguese worker, while considering that the unions were perhaps right to object to them working extra hours and not taking holidays, stated that he did not trust unions, because in Portugal unions were controlled by the state.[155]

However, rather than essentialising whole nationalities as 'active' or 'passive', we need to acknowledge that in every group there were active and passive individuals, and examine differences *within* national groups. In both the Portuguese and Spanish groups, some use can be made of a distinction between those who came to France as political refugees and those who came for work. However, there was not necessarily a clear-cut boundary between a handful of antifascist militants and a mass of workers seeking economic gain. Just outside the Spanish centre in Saint-Denis, the Spanish Communist Party would try to win over migrant workers by selling its newspaper as they came out from Mass. And perhaps 30,000 of the Portuguese working in France had come in order to avoid conscription to fight in Angola and Mozambique. This had the effect of making Portuguese emigration in France younger and more opposition-minded.[156] But equally others shared the feelings of one Spanish temporary worker, who summed up the reasons why most immigrants were reluctant to become politicised:

> As long as you earn less than them, French workers put up with you. But if one day you earn four centimes more, as a bonus or otherwise, it's as if you were stealing. Some of them also do propaganda on you to get you to join one of their unions; and if you refuse, they call you a scab. But I'm fed up with their unions. First, because they do too much politics, sometimes about Vietnam, or the elections, or the army, or the police. Me, I'm not politicised. I came to France to earn a living for me and my family, to have a bit of comfort and wellbeing, full stop, that's all. What's more, their unions are just another form of exploitation for us. We, emigrants, bring our subs, we bring our number in case of conflict, them they don't bring anything. Our particular problems don't concern them.[157]

Going to the People

Was it true, then, as *Esprit* pertinently but pessimistically suggested that, 'A nation which reserves the hard work for foreigners has definitively renounced all socialist aim'?[158] In fact a few on the New Left felt they could find their way out of this dilemma. A focus on immigrant workers in France was the perfect way of reconciling *tiersmondisme* with a classic Marxist concern with the proletariat. The immigrant worker could become not a passive subject of exploitation to be pitied, but an active agent of revolutionary destiny. Of all the bewildering array of rival factions on the far Left, it was Maoism, a movement whose birth, rise and fall are coterminous with the '68 years', that had the strongest belief in romantic thirdworldism. Informed by the struggle against the French state's recent use of torture and other brutal repression, thirdworldist rhetoric could be very confrontational. The first Maoist magazine in France was launched in 1963 by Jacques

Vergès – France's most controversial lawyer – who had strong links with Third World revolutionaries, and was then married to the former Battle of Algiers bomber Djamila Bouhired. The magazine *Révolution* was only the Paris-based sequel to Vergès' Algiers-based *Révolution Afrique*. Vergès had himself been born in Thailand, the son of a Vietnamese mother and a French father who was a leading figure in the Communist Party of the island colony of Réunion.[159] By 1968 French Maoism had developed two wings, the PCMLF, a party of mainly workers, and the Union des Jeunesses Communistes Marxiste-Léniniste (UJCML), a party of mainly students, many from the prestigious Ecole Normale Supérieure. At the ENS, the Maoists were influenced by their tutor Louis Althusser who, a key influence on Marxist philosophy of the era, was himself an immigrant, representative of that apparent contradiction in terms, the left-wing *pied-noir*.[160]

But the last thing the UJCML wanted was to remain in their elitist milieu. They considered a student movement in isolation to be a petit-bourgeois deviation. Students should instead leave the Latin Quarter for the *banlieue* and, as they put it, 'serve the people'. These young people believed themselves to be a new type of intellectual. Rather than having authority by virtue of being an intellectual, in the traditional manner exercised by intellectuals from Zola to Sartre, the intellectual must instead dissolve their identity by 'going to the people' and develop revolutionary theory by learning from concrete struggles.[161] But their idea of 'the people' was not primarily the Communist Party's electoral base of skilled male white workers; rather it was those living in 'the shanty town concentration camps, surrounded six days a week by the police'.[162] Given the ideological context of militant anti-colonialism, there was a certain exoticism in this: immigrant workers were viewed not only as proletarians, but also as symbols of the various guerrilla movements around the world frequently romanticised by the New Left. As Fausto Giudice has written:

> The Algerian War and the Chinese Revolution, the Spanish Civil War and the Russian Revolution, Palestine and Indochina, the Tupamaros of Uruguay and South American guerrillas, all that, the young revolutionaries were finding, they thought, in Nanterre, Barbès or Billancourt[163]

A few meetings took place, for example, between French leftists and immigrant workers during the Six Day War of 1967.[164] Immigration was thus for the New Left not an isolated issue within French society, but a manifestation of unequal power relations at a global level. Imperialism had not in their view come to an end with formal decolonisation, but continued as neocolonialism: the economic exploitation of the Third World by the First. French capitalism exploited its peripheral regions to bring cheap and apparently pliable labour to the metropolis. Immigration was thus itself caused by imperialism, because it created underdevelopment in the neo-colonies: hence the term *travailleur émigré*, used as often as *travailleur immigré*.[165]

The Maoists were of course not the first and not the last young intellectuals to want to 'go to the people': we may be reminded of the turn-of-the-century Russian Narodniks, Simone Weil in factories in the 1930s, or George Orwell's experiences in *Down and Out in Paris and London*. Nor were they the first in France to try to recruit immigrant workers to their cause. The Communist Party had established language groups for immigrants in the interwar period, and during the Second World War its Main-d'Oeuvre Immigré had played a key (and controversial) role in the Resistance.[166] But the identification with marginalised social groups was a particularly strong element in Sixties international radical culture. In the social context of the time, the new outsiders were migrant groups or ethnic minorities. As students around the world were rapidly to discover, the authorities could easily contain protest confined to campus: no strategy based on isolated 'red bases' was seriously going to threaten the system. But if students protested in public spaces and found another social ally in the same city, urban insurrection might be possible. The problem was finding this fellow agent of revolutionary change. In a context of unprecedented prosperity and economic growth, skilled white workers looked (especially to those that had read Marcuse) a poor prospect, since they appeared to have been bought off with fridges and camping holidays. This was where the most marginal elements, the lumpenproletariat mistrusted by Marx and admired by Fanon, came in.

For some 'going to the people' simply meant going to the suburbs on the metro to hand out leaflets, but even before May 1968, some students or ex-students had begun to disguise themselves and seek work in factories to immerse themselves in 'the people'.[167] From the autumn of 1967, a few dozen Maoists were already following Mao's advice to 'first direct your eyes downward, do not hold your head high and gaze at the sky'.[168] They believed, in the words of the Turin slogan, that 'Vietnam is in our factories'[169] – but in France, with its multinational working class, this was true in a more literal sense. So when the events of 1968 unexpectedly but unmistakeably put class struggle in France back onto the agenda, the time was at last ripe for a more generalised meeting of the two worlds of immigrant and intellectual.

Chapter Two

French and Immigrant Workers, United:
the 'Discovery' of Immigration, May-June 1968

'So, we are no longer nobodies in France?'

These words of Portuguese residents in a hostel for workers making Citroën cars highlight a central aspect of this book. What marked off May '68 from student unrest in Northern Europe was that it sparked a wave of strikes and factory occupations, the largest labour uprising in the history of France. When, during the general strike, the Citroën hostel director attempted to bus workers in to vote for a return to work, many Portuguese workers refused. The director would often tell them, 'You foreigners, you're nobodies in France!' But on seeing he was offering them shiny new coaches to break the strike, the Portuguese retorted: 'So, we are no longer nobodies in France?'[1] By throwing the director's own words back at him, the workers subverted his view of them as economic units. By withdrawing their labour, they had ceased to be nobodies in France. Such events, and the impact they had on the encounter between immigrants and the Left, form the focus of this chapter. Since France's working class included some three million immigrant workers – it was the 'working class of France', rather than the 'French working class'[2] – their response to the strikes is a key question. As we shall see, there were further possible avenues of participation: in discussions and debates, on demonstrations, in leftist groups. But if nowhere else, each immigrant worker must have come face to face with the events at their place of work. How far, then, did they participate in the strikes? The Confédération Française Démocratique du Travail (CFDT) carried out investigations into the extent to which its immigrant members had participated, as did many local branches of the left-Catholic youth movement Jeunesse Ouvrière Chrétienne (JOC), and the French branch of the official Algerian trade union confederation, the Association Générale des Travailleurs Algériens. Such post-mortems both implied that participation was viewed as the default position and, together with other sources, help the historian to assess how far this participation went.[3]

Citroën

The previously unpromising level of organisation amongst immigrant labour in France before 1968 was transformed, at least temporarily, by the strike. This was particularly evident at the factories where Citroën cars were produced, in the western Paris suburbs of Levallois, Choisy and Nanterre, and in the city itself at Rue Balard and the Quai de Javel. Today an elaborate but now neglected-looking park stands on the former site of Citroën-Javel, beneath the corporate headquarters of Canal Plus, leading down to a plaza where tourists can lift off in the world's largest hot air balloon. There is one plaque that in passing hails the efforts of the workers who built the cars but – in contrast to a nearby garden in memory of the Argentinian mothers' protest movement about the disappearance of their post-68 activist offspring – no hint there was ever any conflict here at Citroën. For as we have seen, before May '68, Citroën appeared a classic example of the use of migrant labour to create a docile, repressed workforce.

Yet paradoxically, the strike at Citroën proved as fierce as elsewhere, and rather longer lasting: it went on until 20 June, well after workers elsewhere had gone back to work. The evidence strongly suggests that immigrants played a substantial role in this. For the Maoists Alain Geismar, "Erlyne Morane" (a pseudonym) and Serge July, today editorialist for the centre-left daily *Libération*, immigrant workers were a guarantee of the revolutionary character of the movement. As an example, they claimed in 1969 that immigrants had started the strike at Javel.[4] However the evidence for immigrant workers actually starting this strike is not so clear-cut. Police files do indicate some activity by a group of Spanish activists, whose allegiance is variously given as Trotskyist or Guevarist. Two semi-skilled Citroën workers and one outsider were said to hand out tracts and sell *Lucha Obrera*, a Spanish-language version of the Trotskyist newspaper *Lutte Ouvrière*, at the factories. They were all members of the Grupo de Accion y de Union Proletario, which aimed to liberate Spain by violent means. Portuguese workers at a JOC meeting disagreed, however: 'It is false to say that it was foreigners who started the strike. They put up with the strike to begin with. The leaders were mostly French, but there were some immigrant workers among them.'[5]

An examination of the events of 20 May 1968, the day the factories were occupied, bears this out. Students at the occupied Censier university annexe, active in the Comité d'Action Travailleurs Etudiants (CATE, a mainly anarchist group that hoped to bring immigrant workers into the movement)[6] had already set up a Comité d'Action Citroën to push for an occupation at the factory. At around 5.45 am on 20 May, the students arrived at Balard bearing leaflets, some of them specifically aimed at foreign workers, to convince the arriving workers to occupy. But the CATE activists were surprised to find a group of union delegates affiliated to the Confédération Générale du Travail (CGT) already calling for an occupation. At this stage the mass of foreign workers appear to have remained passive, standing outside while a small group of union activists went inside in an unsuccessful attempt to occupy the factory. Though the CGT men were predictably hostile to the outside *gauchistes*, it appears that an agreement was then reached for the students to do the picketing they had intended to do themselves, either because the students feared no repercussions from the management, or because they could speak the languages of the foreign workers. So the students spoke through loudspeakers in French, Spanish and Arabic.[7] However, the CATE activists Roger Gregoire and Fredy Perlman unduly flattered themselves in stating that 'The result was that, after about two hours of direct communication between the foreign workers and the Action Committee members, most of the foreign workers were inside the factory, participating in its occupation.'[8] In fact other sources indicate that most of the workers were still hesitating after the students had spoken. It was not until a group of young workers from another Citroën factory arrived, shouting 'Bercot assassin' (referring to Citroën's hated boss, Pierre Bercot), at 7.45 or 8 am, that the mass of workers streamed in and the red flag was raised over the main entrance.[9]

However, once the strike was underway, there is ample evidence of participation by Spanish and Portuguese workers:[10] 'Since Monday 20 May, the Citroën factory workers, French and foreign, have been on strike.'[11] By 23 May, a group of workers from Choisy drew attention to the solidarity shown by their immigrant fellow-workers in an article for the Maoist paper *La Cause du Peuple*. Even the Communist *L'Humanité* considered that one the most remarkable features of the Citroën strike was the 'firmness' of immigrant workers.[12] Multilingual leaflets and posters were addressed to the strikers by everyone from unions to Maoists.[13] Indeed, one of the most celebrated posters of May, 'French and Immigrant Workers United', may have been made with the participation of Citroën strikers.[14] At least two Citroën workers, the Algerian Amar Daoud and the Spaniard Nicolas Del Rio, were expelled from France as a result of their role in the strike.[15]

Nevertheless, relatively few workers, French or foreign, actively participated in the occupations, for Citroën was an example of what the historian

Antoine Prost calls 'absenteeism in occupied factories'.[16] Many were stuck in company hostels, unable to get to the factory because they relied on company buses that were not running during the strike. This meant real hardship, even rumours of starvation.[17] It also meant that outsiders like the Action Committee *gauchistes* had to travel to the hostels if they wanted to make contact with them. They were shocked by what they found, as were a group of doctors and nurses who followed to document allegations about conditions. Regulations forbade all visits, even by family. There was no breakfast, only a meagre lunch, and no health care. No newspapers were allowed. Spying and bullying were encouraged 'by hostel superintendants recruited among former foreign legion soldiers'.[18] One consequence of the strike, therefore, was the 'discovery' by French leftists of the conditions in which the hostel residents lived. It was a two-way process: trying to spread their ideology among the immigrants, but also learning from the immigrants about the realities of their own society. Attempts were made by management to use immigrant workers as strikebreakers, but as the hostel example demonstrates, these were remarkably unsuccessful.

Renault: the 'Workers' Fortress'

One sunny evening in May 2004, prompted by a television report that the remains of the Renault factory at Boulogne-Billancourt, which closed in 1992, were about to be demolished, I went to see the factory before it was too late. Making my way from Billancourt metro station (where Maoists had once encouraged workers to leap over the barrier without paying) I passed around the outside of the disused works, past an African hostel and a Turkish restaurant opposite Renault's personnel department – whose deputy director had been kidnapped by Maoists in 1972. I went up to the bridge leading to the factory's main entrance on an island in the Seine, and thought about its significance. What now appeared as a decaying pile of junk, with vegetation growing on top, the area deserted but for a few fishermen, was in fact a key site in the history of twentieth-century France. In contrast to Citroën, Renault was a legendary bastion of the French labour movement. Nationalised in 1945 as punishment for Louis Renault's collaboration with the Germans, the 'workers' fortress'[19] was famous for its CGT and Communist militancy. Indeed, the very word 'Billancourt' was synonymous with the class-conscious worker, as in the famous phrase 'we must not make Billancourt despair'.[20] Billancourt was therefore traditionally a key location where intellectuals went to meet 'the people'. Jean-Paul Sartre himself had spoken where I was standing. And the best known fact about Billancourt in May '68 is that the CGT locked the gates to students as they attempted to fraternise with the workers, undermining, so we have often been told, their idealistic hopes of worker-student harmony.[21]

But if by 1968 Billancourt was not only the largest car factory in Europe, at its very height in the numbers employed, it was also one of Europe's most cosmopolitan workplaces, employing as many as 60 different nationalities. Contemporaries referred to it as the 'Casbah on the Seguin' and 'the united Babel of the exploited'.[22] The story of the workers of Billancourt is not, therefore, that of French Communists alone. It is also the more hidden history of France's immigrant minorities. There is ample evidence of immigrant participation in the '68 strike at Billancourt. Yet, as at Citroën, immigrants did not start the strike alone. On 13 May, the unions called a one day general strike to protest against police brutality on the 'Night of the Barricades'. One observer watching workers arrive was 'struck by the number of Algerian and black workers'[23] among those looking as if they had come for work rather than mass meetings, unaware of what was happening. On 16 May, an all-out strike and occupation began at Renault in departments where French workers were in the majority.

But once underway, immigrant workers joined. As one of them put it: 'Our entry into the fight was massive and total.'[24] Once they saw the strikers were numerous, black workers in one workshop threw off their gloves and joined the strike. The walls of the factory were covered with posters in three or four languages expressing solidarity with immigrants. Among the entertainment provided for the strikers was the Spanish singer Leny Escudero. Speeches were made in Spanish and Portuguese at a meeting attended by as many as six thousand foreign workers.[25] The CGT to some extent acknowledged the specific grievances of immigrants, publishing a 'platform for the defence of immigrant workers' and calling for a new immigrant hostel in Billancourt (though this did not question the idea that they had to be housed separately). When the CGT's leader, Georges Séguy, made his famous speech unsuccessfully attempting to sell the Grenelle agreements with government and employers[26] to the Billancourt workers and thereby end the strike, he was literally standing on a platform above a sign saying 'Immigrants are workers in their own right.'[27] The CGT's newspaper for Algerians even considered that 'In this sector the heros of the strike are called Mohammed, Hocine, Vendidi or Martinez.'[28]

Some foreign workers at Billancourt were, however, critical of the CGT. It appears that on 26 May a separate list of demands was compiled that went beyond the CGT's 'platform', making the absence of these extra demands in the Grenelle negotiations a point of controversy. Whereas the CGT tended to favour separate meetings by nationality, the 1968 Billancourt strike, and that at Renault's other factory at Cléon, was significant for solidarity between workers of different nationalities on the basis of their occupational grievances as unskilled workers. One Billancourt worker, Antonio, a CGT member himself, did not come to the factory on the last night of the occupation, because he was angry with the CGT for wanting to end the strike. One leaflet in Spanish and Portuguese called for the strike to continue. The CGT's great rival, the CFDT, felt its image had improved among Spanish workers because the CGT had forbidden the use of Spanish at meetings.[29] While historians have often shown how the CFDT, traditionally less militant than the CGT, used May '68 to outflank the CGT on its left,[30] this suggests that some migrant workers were among the radicalised constituency the CFDT tried to attract. This perception reflected the reality that many immigrants were members of the strike committee or pickets. While this could lead to 'greater mutual comprehension'[31] between French and immigrants, it could also irk racist elements among the workforce. One electrical engineer later complained that 'there were workshops where the pickets were almost completely composed of foreigners'. One French worker even left the CGT on the grounds that it was more concerned with Algerian than French workers.[32]

Renault's most modern factory lay some way to the west of Paris, at Flins. Flins was to gain a special place in *gauchiste* mythology, chiefly as a result of the events of 7-8 June 1968, when fierce battles followed the ending of the factory occupation by riot police and an ensuing attempt to reoccupy it. It was this battle, joined by mass reinforcements of student flying pickets from Paris, which resulted in the drowning of the seventeen-year-old schoolboy Gilles Tautin, French Maoism's first martyr. A film evocatively titled *Oser lutter, oser vaincre* ['Daring to Struggle, Daring to Win'] made during the events by the young director Jean-Pierre Thorn, portrayed Flins as the new hotbed of proletarian militancy.[33] Given the New Left's penchant for migrant workers, it is tempting to think Flins' reputation may have had something to do with the presence of immigrants. But while immigrant-led strikes were to break out there in 1973, it was only from 1969 onwards that there was a large scale recruitment of foreign workers, especially Moroccans. The newly proletarianised migrants working at Flins in 1968 were more likely to have come from the French countryside than the other side of the Mediterranean, though a significant minority of the unskilled workers were foreign.[34]

Yet in spite of their relatively small number, observers reported 'a high percentage of immigrant workers'[35] on the picket line. As at Citroën and Billancourt, this was an effect of the strike rather than the cause of it: in the early days, Portuguese and Africans were reported to gather outside the factory, watching but not participating. There was as much pressure on them to break the strike as elsewhere: trade unionists suspected that Spanish and Portuguese secret police were operating in the factory. Unlike elsewhere, the pressure had some success. The vote in a secret ballot to end the strike was ascribed by some observers to foreigners who did not understand what they were voting for. Still, young Spanish, Portuguese, African and North African workers were among those joining the students in the fighting of 7-8 June, with eight immigrant workers arrested. When the smoke cleared, the students had left behind a 'French and Immigrant Workers United' poster in a CFDT office in the nearby town of Les Mureaux. At this stage the management formed a group of strikebreakers, including newly arrived Africans, who were involved in scuffles with strikers on 19 June to prevent a reoccupation of the factory.[36]

Class Conscious: The Building Industry and Other Workplaces

If the most visible presence of immigrants was in the large-scale confrontations of the car industry, many worked in smaller workplaces, especially in the building industry. Spanish, Portuguese, Moroccans, Yugoslavs and Italians were reported as participating in strikes on building sites on motorway junctions, new housing, hospital and administrative buildings in the eastern suburbs of Paris, the new wholesale food market being built outside the city to replace the historic one at Les Halles, and in provincial locations like Perpignan and Lyons – where one strike won the right to two months holiday for migrant workers to spend time with their families. This does not mean that they were necessarily at the forefront of starting strikes. As with French workers, some were happy for others to take the lead. But one picket on a site in Perpignan, for example, was composed of eight Spaniards, four Portuguese, two North Africans and four French. One Portuguese building worker in the southern suburbs of Paris was threatened with deportation for 'forcibly opposing a return to work'; he was also accused of secondary picketing at a Carrefour supermarket. Both the CFDT and the Censier students made efforts to build links with foreign building workers. Attention was drawn by building workers to the fact that, while building houses, they had none to live in themselves.[37]

There were also strikes involving immigrant workers in joineries, textile factories, mineral water factories and refuse collection.[38] The informers of the Renseignements Généraux characterised immigrants generally as 'passive strikers',[39] obeying calls to strike without great enthusiasm. But, as Xavier Vigna notes, the timing of this report, at the end of June after order had largely been restored, needs to be taken into account, reflecting a desire on the part of officials to play down the extent of strike activity.[40] In fact immigrant pickets could be found across France, from a Spanish worker at a biscuit factory in the Paris suburb of Ivry to North African miners in the northern town of Lens. In many cases they formed part of strike delegations, as essential channels of communication to the foreign workforce. This indispensable role gave the lie to the notion that immigrants were strikebreakers: 'And people will say afterwards that immigrants are strikebreakers, that they come to eat our bread!'[41] At a mineral water factory in the Paris region, the almost exclusively Portuguese unskilled and semiskilled workers were more combative than the mainly French skilled workers.[42] Strikers at the Jeumont-Schneider electrical factory in Saint-Denis included the Vietnamese ex-Trotskyist-turned-anarchist militant Ngo Van – and were entertained by a radical group of Portuguese *fado* singers, who considered themselves, too, exploited by capitalism.[43]

In 1968 the vast majority of immigrants in paid employment were male. But female workers, including Portuguese telephonists and even Spanish domestic workers, also went on strike. In one shop in Toulouse, the strike was started by a Spanish woman who was sacked for making a speech about exploitation. Nevertheless, the attitudes of migrant women as reported at JOC meetings varied. At a department store in Toulouse, the younger women came into conflict with older cleaners, who felt that the young, single ones, could only go on strike because they had no family to feed. This irritated one of the young women, as she had not eaten that day and sent what little she earned to her family in Spain. Another said that whereas previously when she had been unemployed and needed money she would cry the whole time: 'now that I need money even more because I am a striker, I feel it less, I'm even happy, because we are struggling to have something.'[44]

Both women and men, of varying political attitudes, shared a perception of the utility of uniting for better conditions. One Italian at Citroën's Nanterre factory, for example, was adamant that the strike should continue until all its demands were satisfied, although she was not unionised and preferred Gaullism to Communism. These were rational sentiments, given that the reasons for worker dissatisfaction, especially low pay, affected immigrants hardest. But the strikes were not viewed only in terms of material benefits. Another motivation was class solidarity. There was reported to be general agreement among Spanish workers that if they were to benefit from the strike, it was only fair that they should take part in it.[45] Solidarity could be altruistic, with many participating even though they did not think they would remain in France long enough to see such benefits as higher pensions. As Manuel, a Portuguese worker at Citroën, put it: 'We are workers and we have to act, not in political demonstrations, but for everything affecting the living conditions of the workers, even for pensions which does not concern us.'[46] As many observers noticed, it was highly significant that employers were in the main unable to use their 'traditional arm'[47] of forcing immigrants to be strikebreakers. Indeed, in one case the reverse of the expected situation arose, and management attempted to break a strike by doing a deal with French skilled workers and not foreign unskilled workers. In the event this was unsuccessful and the French workers invited local North African families to eat in the factory.[48]

So while few immigrants conformed to the New Left's exalted expectation of what a revolutionary worker should be, many displayed a high level of class consciousness, identifying with the working class as a whole. Bonds were therefore forged between French and immigrant workers where they had previously been absent. One of the features of the strike was a relative absence of racism by French workers. Despite some criticism of foreign presence on picket lines, when compared to the atmosphere in French factories during the Algerian War, or to the violent autumn of 1973 – or for that matter, the London dockers who went on strike in support of Enoch Powell one month before May 1968 – the situation was very positive. At one factory it was reported that 'all trace of racism practically disappeared'.[49] As one Spanish worker in Nanterre described it, this situation was extraordinary: 'The only time when I was really friends with French workers was in May '68. At that moment, there was a unity between all the workers.' He considered that this unity had been broken by the unions' overemphasis on wage increases, as opposed to the human contact many sought:

> Our demands were of a different nature. What we wanted was to be able to sit down together, to be able to discuss together, was that there no longer be differences between French workers and immigrant workers. That is why, in May, we took part.[50]

Similar sentiments were expressed by one Citroën worker, who considered that the strike was about something more profound than money: 'It is the dignity of man which is in question.'[51]

Non-Participation: Panic or Rational Behaviour?

But while there was a major dynamic towards unity, this process was neither smooth nor invincible. Few immigrants, apart from *pied noirs*, anticommunist refugees from Eastern Europe, and some Italians,[52] actively opposed the revolt. But a more common reaction was to stay at home, keeping one's head down until the crisis was over. This might be seen as passive participation, since many workers staying at home were on strike, whether willingly or not. Bernard Hanrot, a French worker-priest, was living in a shack near Dunkirk with three Turkish factory workers. When he returned to the hut after collecting solidarity money for them and other strikers, he found them in a pitiful state, having not eaten for three days since they had no money.[53]

A number of immigrants, perhaps ten thousand, even left France at the end of May and the beginning of June. This was reported both in Paris (the eastern district of Belleville, and shanty towns in the northern suburbs) and in rural areas (Spanish fruit-pickers in the Pyrenees and Portuguese agricultural labourers near Paris).[54] This is the crucial piece of evidence that leads both Yvan Gastaut and Geneviève Dreyfus-Armand to consider the primary effect of May '68 on immigrants as one of fear. However, their accounts of people leaving are both entirely reliant on one article in *Le Monde*.[55] Arguably this does not give the full picture: the situation was not as dramatic as it sounds. To begin with, those who left were not 'the great mass of immigrants'.[56] Only Portuguese and Spanish left, out of all the different nationalities in France. 10,000 was less than 0.4 per cent of the foreign population in France.[57]

Even the minority that did leave, far from not understanding what was happening, understood very well that going on strike meant an economic sacrifice for the duration. They took a rational decision to avoid this, just as others went on strike in the hope of thereby benefiting their position. Significantly, leaving France did not involve as great a departure from normal behaviour as the 'panic among immigrants' thesis implies. Migrant workers usually went home in the summer anyway for their annual holiday and to see their families. This toing and froing had become a pattern of migration especially characteristic of Iberian migrants, in part because they knew it was relatively easy to avoid French border controls in the Pyrenees. The French authorities, in their desperation for cheap labour, had tended to turn a blind eye to this practice.[58] So those who left in 1968 may simply have decided to go home early that year as there was no work during the strike. Strikers had no income other than ad hoc solidarity payments from unions (which not many immigrants were members of), so some could not afford to stay in France. As a Portuguese JOC activist explained: 'For most Portuguese, France means work and so means money. And if there was no possibility of having either, why stay in France?'[59] Since what little savings they had were usually intended for bringing home, fears that the franc, and therefore their savings, could be devalued, were a further threat. Spanish workers at one mineral water bottling factory returned to Spain, but because they had no money, not because they opposed the strike.[60] So the motivation for return may have been economic, rather than panic at the first sign of a social movement.

Where the motivation was political, it was often due to fear of the authorities rather than of the revolt itself. An International Commission of Jurists investigating deportations of foreigners saw the exodus as due to a climate of fear created by the deportations. Immigrants also had reason to fear the Comités pour la Défense de la République, vigilante groups led by Charles Pasqua. Pasqua was representative of the more hard Right, nationalistic and intolerant strain within Gaullism, going on to be the minister for whom the journalistic cliché 'hard-line Interior Minister' should surely have been invented. It is also worth noting the role of the Portuguese state, whose consulate sent propagandists out to persuade its nationals to leave and laid on coaches to bring them back from Saint-Denis.[61]

Moreover, if the events were really so terrifying for immigrants, why did others continue to arrive throughout? Even as some Portuguese were leaving Saint-Denis, others were taking their place. Algerians and Portuguese were still arriving in Marseilles and along the Spanish border, alongside Spanish agricultural labourers. Even at the height of the events, coaches were being laid on to enable the return to France of Italians who had gone home to vote in elections. The number of immigrant workers entering France fell only modestly, considering that there was little work available, with 27,216 and 13,689 recorded entries in May and June 1968 respectively, compared to 29,712 and 14,912 for the corresponding months of the previous year.[62] Since these are likely to be an underestimate, excluding clandestine entries, it can safely be concluded that more immigrants arrived in France during the events than left.

Even those who left were not so afraid they intended never to return. Rather, they went home temporarily while keeping an eye on how the situation developed in France. Explicitly downplaying the idea of fear, a French diplomat in Madrid predicted the Spaniards would come back after a return to work,[63] while the Renseignements Généraux agreed: 'Most will come back in a month or two.'[64] In mid-June, the flow of leavers was slowed down by a rumour in Portuguese shanty towns that, unusually, the French authorities at the Spanish border were taking down the names of those leaving, in order to forbid them re-entry.[65] The response to this rumour implied that returning to Portugal for good was not an option. Being prevented from returning to France was a more severe danger than any posed by the events. The economic forces driving migration would continue to apply regardless of political circumstances. May '68 did not lead to any sustained decrease in the numbers entering France. In fact, the reverse was true: by July, numbers were already higher than 1967, and annual totals for 1968, 1969 and 1970 all saw year-on-year increases.[66]

Indeed for some young foreigners, May '68 could be a positive reason to come to France. An organiser of au pair placements found that, far from being put off, none with placements that summer had cancelled: 'The English girls, particularly, are very excited at the idea of coming to make the revolution in Paris.'[67] Another au pair who found Paris an agreeable destination was the Norwegian-born future anti-corruption magistrate and Green presidential candidate Eva Joly. Although Joly had already arrived in 1964, after May '68 she set up a CFDT branch at the record company where she worked as a secretary. For 'Moktar', then a young miner in Morocco, hearing radio broadcasts of the events was a major factor in his decision to move to France. Asked why he migrated to France, one Mexican later recalled translating slogans from May '68 as a student rebel in Mexico City that October.[68]

This was not always the case, however, for May '68 could also be reason for a certain sort of foreigner to give the apparent danger of revolution in France a wide berth. Ilich Ramírez Sánchez, the young Venezuelan man who later became the notorious terrorist 'Carlos the Jackal', was at the time studying for his 'A' Levels at a crammer in London. His father, a Communist who named his son after his hero Lenin, actually cancelled plans for his son to study in Paris because of the events. Ironically, Carlos' father's reaction was typical of many wealthy older foreigners. American Express laid on buses to enable tourists to escape, while guests at the Cannes Film Festival were picked up by boat in what the director Roman Polanski remembers as being like 'a second Exodus'.[69] Even French people with large bank accounts were withdrawing their money in cash and taking it in suitcases to Switzerland, Belgium or England.[70] This exodus of the bourgeoisie puts the movement of immigrant workers into context: the rich may have had as much if not more to fear.

Nevertheless, immigrant workers were not the revolutionary vanguard romanticised by Maoists. They did have grounds for concern. Some viewed de Gaulle's as being a good government for foreigners – not unreasonably, since it actively encouraged immigration – albeit a bad one for the French. Some feared the possibility of the Communist Party coming to power: 'Many Algerians think: if it is the Communists who are in power, we can pack our suitcases.'[71] De Gaulle's radio broadcast about the dangers of 'totalitarian communism' was primarily aimed at the French bourgeoisie. But some Spanish and Portuguese workers shared similar sentiments, having grown up under rulers whose mainstay was anti-communism. The flying of red flags over occupied buildings contributed to this: 'Abdelraouf explained to friends the meaning of the red flag which some had planted on the factory gate: some were concerned by the flag, they feared a Communist takeover.'[72] In reply, Abdelraouf, a JOC activist, tried to persuade them that the red flag was associated with the Paris Commune and the strikes of 1936, not just the Soviet Union.

References to 1936, however, were not necessarily encouraging. On the one hand, older French workers remembered the year of the Popular Front with fondness for victories such as the right to paid holidays. Some of this rubbed off on immigrants:

> I work with a French worker who went on strike in 1936. He explained to me what a strike was. He told me that the advantages won't perhaps come immediately, that they perhaps won't come for us! But, what is for sure, is that they will come one day for the working class. I thank the worker who helped me understand.[73]

But for Spaniards, 1936 conjured up a different set of associations, when an uprising had led not to socialist utopia, or even paid holidays, but civil war and dictatorship. 'They have a collective memory of '36 back home. They are afraid of any civil war.'[74]

Rumours circulated that led people to believe the violence was worse than it actually was. In one shanty town, it was falsely rumoured that five Portuguese had been killed by strikers. By the time such stories had found their way back to home countries, where television, radio and newspapers tended to portray the revolt negatively, they were exaggerated still further. It was reported on a farm in Portugal that: '"My son has been killed", a mother told us. "There are train loads of corpses".'[75] But this was not on account of any especially credulous mentality. The French responded to rumours too, many returning to work on rumours of tank movements around Paris. With seven dead and thousands injured, there was real violence.

If French citizens had reason to fear the use of force by the state, this was all the more so for immigrants. It was only six and a half years since 17

October 1961, when immigrant protesters had, far from being listened to, been beaten to death and thrown into the Seine. To a limited extent, and although this time no immigrants were among the dead, May '68 revived memories of those events. As vanloads of police once again filled the streets of Paris and lashed out with their *matraques* – the word itself derived from Algerian Arabic – it was possible to be reminded of the bloody autumn of 1961, even if the comparison looks exaggerated today in the cold light of hindsight. The anti-racist pressure group MRAP juxtaposed photographs of victims of the two events: 'In May 1968, Paris had its new *ratons*, the students.'[76] On the other hand, awareness of the 1961 massacre was at this time limited among the French to such relatively small circles of militants. One historical irony is that after his retirement from the police, Maurice Papon was the director of the aircraft manufacturer Sud-Aviation, whose Nantes factory was, famously, the first workplace to be occupied in May 1968. Yet when the Sud-Aviation workers – by all accounts, among the more politically conscious in France – drew attention to Papon's shady past, they were somewhat confused about even the date of the massacre, giving it variously as 17 October and 12 November.[77]

In the circumstances, therefore, what is surprising is that so many immigrants did participate. Defying the stereotype of the deferential Portuguese, at one mineral water bottling factory Portuguese workers hardened the strike beyond the intentions of French union activists. The Spanish were also supposed to be passive – but at Citroen's Levallois factory they were the most solid.[78] So immigrants were neither straightforwardly revolutionary nor straightforwardly passive. With significant exceptions, a temporary unity between French and immigrant workers arose during the general strike of 1968. Starting from a low base and with some initial hesitancy, immigrant workers joined the strike movement en masse and to an unprecedented extent. Although most visible in the large car factories, this was not confined to any one industry, size of workplace or gender.

'Long Applause and Frantic Cries of Joy': Discussions and Debates

It was, arguably, this collective strength which forced politicians and activists to react to the presence of immigrants that had previously gone unnoticed. The involvement of immigrant workers was an important moment for the Left, as French activists theoretically convinced of the importance of Third World liberation met face-to-face with immigrant workers, often for the first time. The atmosphere of May '68 has often been described as one of interminable talking and debate, an 'endless political talk fest'[79] or 'revolution of words'. Discussions on all manner of topics went on, especially in occupied university buildings, well into the night. What became known in leftist parlance as 'student-worker liaison' was the order of the day. So having joined the movement as strikers, to what extent did immigrants take the next step and participate in the internal debates of the movement? And were their voices heard?

There certainly appeared a multitude of voices seeking to speak to, but sometimes also on behalf of, immigrant workers. The unions were enthusiastic, the CFDT distributing in Paris alone more than 30,000 copies of multilingual leaflets with stirring phrases such as 'Immigrant and French workers, all united in the same fight we shall win'.[80] The most iconoclastic voices, though, were far Left activists. The Maoist newspaper *La Cause du Peuple* broke taboos about the republican model of individual integration by demanding that French nationality be bestowed on all immigrants, 'collectively, immediately and without condition'.[81] Committees proliferated to examine issues such as the existence of shanty towns, discrimination against foreigners, and how to unite French and immigrant workers into the movement.[82] Activists from other countries formed short-lived committees such as the Comité d'Action Maghrébin, which issued a leaflet that, beginning as it did with the words 'We, Maghrebi workers', is an apparent exception to Vladimir Fisera's claim that 'the few texts about immigrant workers and women which do exist are produced by foreign and women students, not by workers'.[83]

Some critics have dismissed the French Left's newfound interest in immigrants as mere revolutionary posturing. Frederick Ivor Case, a black British teacher who spent May '68 in the Lille area, argued that the cries he heard of 'The immigrants are with us!' were 'empty' and 'hypocritical', because nothing was actually done about their suffering – a charge later echoed by Peter Fysh and Jim Wolfreys.[84] But while there was certainly an element of rhetoric, demands made by French activists about immigrants derived not merely from ideological abstraction but also from the concrete experience of meeting immigrants during the events. Such experiences had all the more impact since it was usually the first time for both parties. As one Portuguese worker told a student audience, 'Until now, many among you were unaware of the difficulties of immigrants, perhaps even their existence. We pass alongside you without you seeing us.'[85]

A case of this relationship between experience and ideology were the posters produced at the occupied Ecole des Beaux-Arts, of which several specifically mentioned immigrants. The most eye-catching of them, featuring a behatted capitalist trying without success to keep apart a stylized French and immigrant worker whose arms were linked, bore the legend

'French and Immigrant Workers United'. This poster was apparently 'in great demand by foreign workers in May and June'.[86] Significantly, the poster was made on 22 May with the participation of strikers from Citroën, as probably also was a second poster bearing the slogan 'For Equal Work, Equal Pay'.[87] This prefigured the egalitarian demands that would appear in immigrant-led strikes of the early 1970s.

The events thus sometimes inspired attempts to actively seek out and present in some detail immigrants' own grievances. ATD-Quart Monde, for example, distributed money and food in the shanty towns during the general strike, and in response to demands articulated by the people they met there, drew up what they termed *Cahiers de doléance* ['Books of grievances'], the title recalling a similar exercise in 1789. The *Cahiers* included various material demands, such as calls for affordable housing, better primary education, more libraries, job security and easier access to social security benefits. But just as importantly, shanty town dwellers demanded to have the same rights to be consulted on issues affecting them as everyone else.[88] Arising from contacts between French people and immigrants during the events, ephemeral newspapers began to appear with an emphasis on voicing immigrants' own demands, in an anonymised format to avoid reprisals from the authorities.[89]

It was one thing to participate in meetings laid on specially for immigrant workers, such as those arranged by the JOC; or by the Comité des Trois Continents, a grouping of militants from Asia, Africa and Latin America, at the Sorbonne on 8 June.[90] Activism by foreigners was widespread within occupied university buildings, as the British poet Stephen Spender described:

> One day there was a table for Kurds, Turks, Arabs and Algerians ... The Sorbonne is cosmopolitan French culture. Among the bewildering assortment of advertisements, appeals bulletins posted everywhere or leaflets thrust into your hand, I noticed directives to Greek, Spanish, Portuguese, and German students, some of them written in their own language. And of course there were Americans.[91]

In a typical week at the occupied Sorbonne, there were meetings being held by at least 9 different immigrant committees.[92] But it was quite another to speak on equal terms in general meetings, outnumbered by French activists who knew the rules of the game. Despite this, some immigrants were frequent attenders. There were Vietnamese, for example, who spent almost 24 hours a day listening to debates at the occupied Sorbonne.[93]

Was this merely passive participation? After all, many people, French and foreign, attended the debates out of curiosity – the Sorbonne was the 'shop-window' of the revolution – rather than because they necessarily agreed with what was being done there. One young Romanian scientist went along to 'see what happens first hand', only to dismiss the debates as 'everybody shouting down everybody else', 'bouts of leftist hysteria' and 'Gallic agitation'.[94] But others were enthused by what they heard and saw, finding the debates compelling. As the Algerian writer Assia Djebar put it, 'I was only a witness, but a witness from nine in the morning to midnight'.[95] Moreover, many were speakers not just listeners, although this was more common among foreign students than workers. Foreign speakers at the Sorbonne ranged from 'rooms in which Africans debated Third World problems in impeccable French' through German SDS activists to a Spanish militant who organised meetings on 'the promotion of new structures in the university and capitalist society'.[96] Foreigners loudly advertised their presence, and their participation was greatly welcomed, implying little fear about speaking within such 'liberated zones'. Thus at midnight on 14 May, the Algerian flag was carried into the Sorbonne, followed by a banner proclaiming 'Revolutionary solidarity of the Algerian students of France with UNEF'.[97] The occupation of the prestigious college Sciences Po was largely carried out by international students, its rather conservative, briefcase-carrying home student body of trainee bureaucrats having mysteriously disappeared.[98] Gamé Guilao, a student from Guinea, recalled that at the end of a speech he gave to students in Poitiers 'the room vibrated with long applause and frantic cries of joy.'[99]

Moreover, the content of what foreigners said was often bold, challenging or heckling other speakers. In the Sorbonne, one Asian Maoist shouted down a Communist-supporting Renault worker as a traitor, for suggesting that the students were heading for defeat and needed to be disciplined. At a debate picturesquely entitled 'From Che Guevara to Jesus Christ', one Arab worker was scathing of the debate's Christian organisers: 'I'm fed up with Christian charity! A foreign worker has better things to do than be talked to about religion. He'd prefer that people find him a place to live.'[100] It is true that in both these cases the speakers were expressing views that French *gauchistes* in the audience would probably have agreed with. This was not so with a Spanish worker at the Odéon theatre, whose pro-Communist speech, describing the students as far from the reality on the street,[101] is further evidence of an atmosphere where foreigners could speak their mind.

Racism towards foreign speakers was not entirely absent, but there seems to have been a strong taboo against it. In the Odéon, when an African speaker was interrupted with a shout of 'Get back to your bush, Zulu!', the audience reacted sharply, booing the heckler and asking him to leave. The Odéon crowd again booed a racist, when a Portuguese worker's speech was heckled by a man saying 'You're foreign, you have no right to make revolution in our country!'[102] This did not mean foreigners were put on a pedestal, for like other speakers, they could find agreement as well as disagreement. At the Cannes film festival, the (Swiss) Jean-Luc Godard's call for the festival to be abandoned in solidarity with the students and workers was vigorously contested by the Irish film maker Peter Lennon. Lennon found his film *Rocky Road to Dublin* in great demand by audiences ranging from the Sorbonne to the Renault factory, so much so that fighting broke out amongst the audience when it was screened at Assas law faculty.[103]

'Elements Foreign to France and Outside the University': Demonstrations

Demonstrations, barricades and riots are perhaps the best-known images of May '68. As this was a key arena for political confrontation, here is a further test for the level of immigrant participation. Because of its public nature, demonstrating in the street was a higher risk activity than striking or speaking inside occupied buildings. For foreigners, it entailed breaching the French state's traditional requirement that they obey strict political neutrality. It could and did lead to arrest and deportation. Many, even if on strike, therefore felt they had no right to demonstrate in France.[104] The notoriously brutal behaviour of the police towards demonstrators (and sometimes non-demonstrating bystanders) was exacerbated by xenophobia. From early on during the student unrest, this was encouraged by political pressure on the police to portray a leading role as being played by 'elements foreign to France and outside the university'.[105] One police commissioner was rumoured to instruct his men to get arrest figures of 40 per cent foreigners. As one deportee, the American Paul Werner, recalls, being selected for arrest or deportation was likeliest for those who fitted 'a certain visual profile' of a what a 'foreigner' looked like. Werner suggests that this unwritten rule made Jews, North Africans and South Americans especially vulnerable.[106] (This makes sense in the light of recent history, given that some of the policemen involved could have been veterans of the round-ups of the Algerian War, or even of Vichy). He recalls a policeman reading out his decision: 'Hooked nose, frizzy hair, sinister-looking expression. Immediate expulsion.' Werner was arrested with a Senegalese friend – David Diop, son of the owner of the Présence Africaine bookshop, but Diop was not deported.[107]

Foreigners were arrested from the first and second days of major rioting in the Latin Quarter, Friday 3 and Monday 6 May. Many of these were students, though already by 6 May about half were non-students, including Gregory Brandenburg, a Canadian cook, and Paul Bruppacher, a Swiss woodturner. When they appeared in court, some foreigners accused of assaulting policemen that day denied having participated on the demonstration at all, including James Koss, a medical student from Detroit, and Ekkeard Wohlrapp, a German student. Wohlrapp explained that, far from ripping up paving stones to throw at the police, he was in fact picking up his glasses from the pavement. Some of the foreign students had been picked up after the demonstration finished, on a late night raid on a café full of language students from the Alliance Française. While 6 May saw the first involvement of *blousons noirs*, leather-jacketed youths from the working-class suburbs, the evidence for immigrants amongst them is only patchy. There were some suggestions of North Africans throwing paving stones at the police, though both from hostile sources that may have had an interest in seeing rioting North Africans where none existed.[108]

The following Friday night, the 'Night of the Barricades' followed the creation of a 'liberated', police-free zone in the Latin Quarter. When riot police stormed the barricades in the early hours of the morning the 'worst street fighting of the century'[109] ensued. While some of the 61 foreigners arrested may have been bystanders caught in the wrong place at the wrong time, such as a Swiss cabaret singer leaving his performance that night, there is clear evidence for the participation of foreign intellectuals at least. One German teacher was injured in the foot by a tear gas canister exploding, and his British journalist wife was knocked over and trampled by the crowd. The Scottish journalist Neal Ascherson recalls seeing the injured couple with their small children sometime afterwards, and confirms that the German was a revolutionary, rather than a bystander. The family were subsequently deported from France. One Spanish student, possibly linked to the Maoist newspaper *L'Humanité Nouvelle*, was blinded in one eye. The artist Jean-Jacques Lebel wrote in the British underground newspaper *Black Dwarf* that his group organising the barricade at the corner of rue Gay-Lussac and rue Saint-Jacques included some Italians. According to a recent biography of the Belgian Trotskyist Ernest Mandel, he, his wife Gisela and the Argentinian Trotskyist guerrilla Roberto Santucho also helped construct barricades on the rue Gay Lussac.[110]

The evidence for immigrant workers participating on 10 May is less clear. The wife of a policeman told the Canadian writer Mavis Gallant the next day: 'When my husband came in this morning, he told me the barricades were manned by North Africans, aged forty and fifty. That was why the police had to be so rough.' The historian would be wise to share Gallant's scepticism about this:

> This is believed. Indignant housewifes. "Send them back to North Africa!". I have a queer feeling this is going to be blamed on foreigners – I mean the new proles, the Spanish and Portuguese. And, of course, the North Africans are good for everything[111]

Nevertheless, that it was believed that foreign workers were already taking part – officers in the riot police reported North African, Portuguese and Spanish involvement – is itself of significance. 10 May also brings the first evidence from sources favourable to the demonstrators of immigrant worker participation. The Maoist *L'Humanité Nouvelle* reported Algerian workers offering to give blood to wounded students and agreeing to hand out leaflets. Thus the wider public sympathy for the students – bringing down hot drinks to the barricades and so on – was beginning to affect immigrant workers. For Djemmaa Boulemnadjel, an Algerian cook at the Sainte-Anne hospital, participating in the barricades was her first political experience in France.[112]

The mood of revulsion against police brutality led to a one-day general strike on 13 May, accompanied by a march of hundreds of thousands across Paris. This time, there is overwhelming evidence for immigrant workers having gone on the march. The Trotskyist newspaper *Lutte Ouvrière* reported: 'No demonstration has included such a large number of Caribbean workers. Several hundred marched shouting "Two centuries, that's enough".'[113] This was not simply because those from the French Antilles felt, as French citizens, able to protest. Many Spanish workers, including from Renault, went on the march, as well as some 500 members of the Spanish Communist Party. One Portuguese JOC activist later recalled going with thirty compatriots.[114] Other Portuguese workers shouted: 'Franco, De Gaulle, Salazar, murderers!'[115] One banner read: 'Let's break the isolation of the shanty towns. Long live the united struggle of French and immigrant workers.'[116] This participation reflected the nature of the demonstration. In contrast to the chaotic scenes in the Latin Quarter, there was safety in numbers on a peaceful mass march, organised by the trade unions with many coming into Paris from the 'red suburbs'. Still, not everyone who wanted to participate could do so. Ali, a young Algerian living in the Nanterre shanty town, persuaded several friends to go on the demonstration, but they were unable to get into Paris because the trains were on strike.[117]

Four days later, the students went on their famous 'Long March' to the by now occupied Renault factory at Billancourt, hoping to link up their struggle with that of the workers. En route, they passed through parts of the south-western suburbs with a large immigrant population. Judging from an account by a British activist, their attitude was one of cautious approval:

> In some streets many Algerians line the pavement. Some join in the shouting of "CRS-SS", "Charonne", "A bas l'Etat policier".[118] They have not forgotten. Most look on shyly or smile in an embarrassed way. Very few join the march.[119]

This might lead us to nuance the implications of the march's famous lack of success on arrival. Immigrant workers, though still inhibited from full participation, were showing some sympathy even for the students so disapproved of by the CGT leadership.

Violent demonstrations returned to Paris on 22, 23 and especially 24 May. Earlier that day, Moroccans, Algerians and Africans had joined peaceful CGT demonstrations in the northern suburb of Saint-Ouen. In the evening, some 200,000 demonstrators gathered in the forecourt of the Gare de Lyon. Fighting followed all around Paris, with the stock exchange set on fire and police stations sacked. Although one story goes that a group of Arabs were heard chanting the slogan 'We are all German Jews', there is a surprising absence of any suggestion that immigrant workers had rioted.[120] There was an element of truth to the Renseigements Généraux' assertion that: 'Passive strikers, most foreign workers did not take part in rioting'.[121] Attention on 24 May focused more on the role of the criminal underworld and *blousons noirs*. Lack of immigrant participation on 24 May is understandable, since the readiness of some demonstrators to use violence was a deterrent. Even if otherwise sympathetic to the movement, many migrant workers considered violence a tactical mistake, and found it strange that students overturned cars and set them on fire, objects which they as workers made and perhaps aspired to. This did not prevent police violence against foreigners reached a peak, with reports of North African, black, Chinese and Vietnamese bystanders being badly beaten in police vans and holding centres.[122]

The situation on 24 May was, if anything more desperate in France's second city. When a crowd of demonstrators in Lyons tried to cross the river Rhône to march on the prefecture building, barricades and fighting ensued. One policeman, Jean Lacroix, died that night. At the time it was believed he was crushed to death by a lorry sent careering into police lines. While some blamed 'youth from the underprivileged housing zones in the city outskirts' for the violence and looting, foreigners were not directly implicated in Lacroix's death, for which two young French men were prosecuted, and which has been more recently attributed to a heart attack he suffered in hospital.[123] Nevertheless, reports from both sides of the barricades mention the presence of immigrant workers: 'Given the turn taken by events, the students retreated, replaced by groups of young hoodlums, foreign workers, and even prostitutes.'[124] 'Those who on the night of 24-25 May refused the power [of the bourgeoisie] by putting up barricades, were workers, were students, were unemployed, were immigrant workers.'[125] The nationalities of the foreigners arrested that night were, in contrast to the early student demonstrations in Paris, representative of the immigrant worker population, the largest contingents being Algerian, Portuguese and Spanish. So with the situation now outside the control of the authorities, more felt confident to join non-respectable demonstrations. Saïd Bouziri, later one of the leaders of the immigrant workers' movements of the 1970s, had left Tunis in 1966 to train as a bookkeeper in Lyons. Having already been involved before May in attempts to link students and immigrant workers in the city, and during May in student committees, the 20-year-old Bouziri was in the crowd that night. Although he recalled the number of Arab demonstrators being low, North Africans bore the brunt of the police crackdown that followed. Police combed Algerian districts and selected immigrant workers for arrest and beating. Thus while ten Algerians were arrested on the night itself, by 30 May as many as fifty Algerians were being held.[126] Some indication of the tense situation in the city even a month later was given in a letter from an Algerian CFDT activist:

> I am astonished not to see any news arrive and I think it is serious.
> I ask you once again not to forget me because in Lyons we are going through a period of repression, other arrests have taken place recently of immigrant comrades notably Algerians, Malians, one Chinese detained at Vauban and about to be deported.[127]

Immigrants continued to participate in more orderly marches, such as Spanish, Italian, Portuguese, Algerian and African workers from Citroën and Renault on one organised across Paris by the CGT on 29 May.[128] But following de Gaulle's broadcasts and dramatic return to Paris, a million-strong counter-demonstration on 30 May and the calling of elections for June, the government began to regain control – and inter-ethnic solidarity began to break down. In Belleville, generally known for a history of mutual tolerance between different immigrant groups, North African

Jews and Muslims fought each other from 2 to 4 June.[129] Demonstrations by those wishing to continue the movement became more isolated and confrontational. At Flins on 7-8 June, Paul Werner and David Diop were among the many people intercepted by police as they attempted to reach the Renault factory. This was a predominantly intellectual crowd, including many artists such as Lucien Taieb and Jean-Ange Msika from Tunisia and Julio Le Parc and Hugo Demarco from Argentina. While the artists claimed to police that they were present merely as observers out of artistic duty, this needs to be treated with some scepticism. Subsequent retrospectives have highlighted the role of Le Parc and Demarco at the Atelier Populaire producing the posters of May '68.[130] In the thick of events, there was little distinction between observer and participant. As Werner puts it: 'I don't see a difference. Everybody participated in one way or another. And being an observer was a form of participating. It's called bearing witness.'[131]

On 11 June, renewed fighting ensued both inside and outside the Latin Quarter following the death of Gilles Tautin at Flins. The police station in the mainly North African district of La Goutte d'Or – future scene of many of the immigrant mobilisations of the early 1970s – was damaged. Many of the participants, however, appear to have come from outside the area. More typical of the foreigners arrested elsewhere that night were Patrick Crossan, an Irish café waiter and Alliance Française student, and David Morgan, an American poet who, when arrested with a paving stone in his pocket, claimed it was a souvenir paper weight for his father's secretary.[132] The movement was thus in the process of being re-confined to the student ghetto from which it had escaped during the last three weeks of May. A similar demonstration took place in Toulouse, on which many foreigners were arrested and deported, including Portuguese, Spanish and Africans, but also an Iranian medical student who was arrested leaving a cinema.[133] Foreigners were among those arrested during further disturbances when the Sorbonne, followed by the last strongholds of the student revolt, Censier and the Halles aux Vins, were retaken by riot police on 16 June, and early July respectively, and again in the Latin Quarter on 13 and 14 July. At the Sorbonne, just over half the foreigners arrested were minors, all of whom were male non-students, suggesting that a substantial number of youths, whether young immigrant workers or the sons of immigrant workers, were attached to the hard core of the student movement.[134] On the night of 13 July, an isolated group of young men threw Molotov cocktails at police stations and Gaullist offices in Bordeaux. Though all but one were French, they included a 25-year-old Algerian student, Mohammed Hadj Cheraïa.[135]

Although figures for foreign nationals arrested need to be treated with some caution given the bias in selection, 481 out of 2974 people arrested over the course of the events, nearly one in six, were foreigners.[136] So even if considerably more foreigners than French were wrongly arrested bystanders, the proportion of genuine participants arrested would be at least as high as the proportion of foreigners in the population as a whole (about one in nineteen according to the 1968 census). While many of these participants were students or teachers, the majority of those deported from France in connection with the events were neither. Of those deportees whose profession is given in the Interior Ministry archives, some 64 per cent were either in a manual occupation or unemployed. This picture is supported by records of deportees' nationality, age and gender, which show a preponderance of young male Algerians, Spanish, Portuguese and Italians – who together made up the bulk of foreign workers in France at the time.[137]

Moreover, we need to compare like with like. It would be all too easy to compare, say, a Tunisian building worker to Dany Cohn-Bendit, and show that the latter attended more demonstrations than the former. As the historian Richard Evans once pointed out, labour history has too often involved unfair comparisons between real workers and an ideal-type of a perfectly class-conscious revolutionary, dedicated one hundred percent to the struggle, who has never existed outside the fantasies of the philosopher György Lukács.[138] But a more appropriate comparison would be the participation of French workers. A study by American political scientists found that only 8 per cent of the whole French population attended a demonstration in May '68. While this figure rose to 30 per cent among young males, the participation rate among the working class was lower than that for professional and managerial groups (although the total *number* of working-class demonstrators was still high due to the numerical weight of the group). Considerably more people participated in strikes than demonstrations.[139]

In this context, the real but limited level of participation by foreign workers on demonstrations was not dissimilar to that of the working class as a whole, just as the high level of participation by foreign students and professionals mirrored that of their French counterparts. Many immigrant workers participated without being arrested, particularly on the large, predictable set-piece demonstrations like 13 May. They wanted their voices to be heard, but were reluctant to be involved in high-risk confrontation with the police. Many deported foreigners – Richard Tôle, a Malian Citroën worker in Lyons, for example – admitted to some political or trade union activity (in the CFDT in Tôle's case) whilst denying having rioted or associated with students.[140] It was possible, therefore, for immigrant workers to be *soixante-huitards* in the broadest sense of the term without conforming to the narrow stereotype of international subversion that the authorities tended to equate with any activism by foreigners. So if there was some truth in the portrayal of the Latin Quarter demonstrators as children of the bourgeoisie, these most spectacular of demonstrations were only the tip of an iceberg-sized, mixed-nationality social movement beneath and beyond.

Immigrant Protests

Moving up the ladder of involvement, a minority of politicised immigrants took advantage of the temporary retreat of state power in France to stage their own protests, often related to the situation in their countries of origin. Migrants from the French overseas territories (DOM-TOM) occupied three buildings, each selected for its official or semi-official role in the French state's management of migration from the DOM-TOM: the welfare organisation Jeune Guyane, occupied for two and a half weeks; the Amicale des Travailleurs Antillais, Guyanais et Martiniquais en Métropole; and, more briefly, the Bureau pour le développement des Migrations Intéressant les Départements d'Outre-Mer (BUMIDOM). In each case, responsibility was claimed by the Comité d'Action des Travailleurs Etrangers et des Pays sous Domination Coloniale Française, whose members came from the Caribbean, French Guiana and the Indian Ocean island of Réunion. They combined demands for independence and messages of solidarity to the French movement with a critique of BUMIDOM, which they accused of running a 'new slave trade'. The occupiers may have had links to organised nationalist groups: one of the Jeune Guyane occupiers had been given a suspended prison sentence in the trial of Groupe d'Organisation Nationale de la Guadeloupe militants for their part in the Guadeloupe uprising of May 1967. But they were not without wider support. Hundreds of workers and unemployed came to the occupied buildings for mass meetings.[141] This may be explained by the fact that DOM-TOM migrants, as French citizens, were not liable for deportation like foreign nationals. They were also active in strikes in the public sector, including hospitals, railways and post offices, which only French citizens were eligible to be employed in.[142]

Foreign nationals, by contrast, targeted their own home governments. On the afternoon of 30 May, a group of students occupied the Senegalese embassy in Paris. That evening, having persuaded the ambassador to send a message to the authorities at home, they vacated the premises. The message denounced the government of President Léopold Senghor, and expressed solidarity with the student movement in Dakar – which as in France, had set off wider social unrest and a general strike. The embassy occupation was thus primarily an offshoot of what was happening in Senegal. While some French observers saw the crisis in Senegal as a spin-off from the French events ('In Africa, May explodes in June'), the historian Abdoulaye Bathily has criticised this attitude as francocentric, pointing to the domestic causes of the Senegalese crisis. Yet the occupation also had roots in the prior politicisation of Senegalese students in France. The occupiers were all members of the Fédération des Etudiants d'Afrique Noire en France (FEANF), which, while expressing solidarity with French students, played little role in the French student revolt itself. Two FEANF activists were nevertheless deported from France.[143] On 11 June, Mauritanians in Paris followed suit, a group of between one and three hundred occupying their embassy. Again, the issue was African, not French: the killing of seven striking iron miners by Mauritanian security forces at Zouérate on 27 May. The occupiers also left once the ambassador agreed to transmit their demands back home, though not before damaging a portrait of President Ould Daddah and daubing slogans on the wall.[144] Conversely, some French consulates and embassies abroad were the target of demonstrations, including in Algiers, where a crowd of French *coopérants*, among them the future immigrants' rights campaigner Paul Oriol, forced their way into the building. They managed to hold daily meetings there thanks to negotiations with sympathetic diplomats including, according to Oriol, Stéphane Hessel – who at the age of 92 was to write the bestselling pamphlet *Indignez-vous!* ['Time for Outrage!'] which inspired the 2011 mass movement in Madrid's Puerta del Sol.[145]

Another prominent outburst of foreign activism was the occupation of the Cité Universitaire Internationale. An extensive complex of halls of residence for international students on the southern outskirts of Paris, it was a product of an earlier period of internationalist idealism after the First World War. The casual visitor having lunch in its cafeteria today can still get a flavour of this atmosphere. Nevertheless, the halls are divided by nationality, a fact that sits ill at ease with the French state's republican emphasis on integration. Beginning with the Spanish hall on 18 May, the Argentinian, African, Moroccan, Greek, Portuguese, Brazilian and international halls were all in occupation by the end of the month. Some of the occupations continued for two months or more: while the occupation of the Italian hall began as late as 9 June, the Africans were still holding out on 20 August and the Moroccans until 2 September, well after most French university buildings had been cleared.[146] Denouncing home country authorities, the occupiers also made accusations of corruption in the ways the residences were run. Thus in the

Argentinian case, the director was accused of embezzling residence funds to pay for fitted carpets, a garage, sliding doors, a dishwasher, doorframes, cupboards, a marble nest of tables and twelve crystal whisky glasses for his personal use. While theoretically the residence was designed for students or intellectuals on low incomes, many were in fact wealthy middle-aged lawyers and doctors, well connected to the regime in Argentina, treating the residence as a 'tourist hotel', and who fled during the occupation.[147] There was thus sometimes conflict among residents over the occupations, with the international hall of residence broken into at one point by residents hostile to the occupation committees. Some sources portrayed these as dominated by small groups of militant exiles keen to make links with their compatriots among migrant workers living elsewhere in the Paris region. The Renseignements Généraux, for example, blamed the occupation of the Portuguese and Italian halls on the secretary of a Portuguese Maoist front organisation and that of the Spanish hall on a refugee living in the northern suburbs who was a former leader of the leftist Frente de Liberación Popular (FLP). They even alleged that the occupiers had a machine gun, three rifles and Molotov cocktails, which may not be so outlandish, since the FLP did advocate the liberation of Spain by violent means.[148]

Revolutionaries Without Borders

Paris, then, had become something of a showcase for international insurgency by politicised minorities. Most of this, though, was aimed at change in their countries of origin, since permanent settlement in France was not yet on the agenda. The Situationists were particularly impressed: 'Rarely have so many national flags been burnt by so many foreigners resolved to finish with the symbols of the State, before finishing with the State itself.'[149]

The final logical step after other involvement in protest might then have been for immigrants to actually join a *gauchiste* group. However it would have been unwise for foreigners to publicly identify themselves as members, since this would undoubtedly lay themselves open to deportation. Hence this was the least likely avenue of participation. Some New Left intellectuals of foreign birth, like Cornelius Castoriadis, André Gorz and Nicos Poulantzas, kept a cautiously low profile during the events themselves.[150] Even so, a few individuals can be identified as active *gauchistes*, albeit mostly students and intellectuals, reflecting the social composition of the groups involved. For many this was the highlight of a lifetime odyssey. Dany Cohn-Bendit aside (who, having been born in France, was a foreign national, not an immigrant), perhaps the most prominent was the 22-year-old Benny

Lévy, whose Jewish family had fled Nasser's Egypt in 1956. Adopting the French pseudonym Pierre Victor, Lévy was a member of the Maoist Union des Jeunesses Communistes Marxiste-Léniniste, and after the UJCML was banned in June 1968, the leading ideologue of its successor the Gauche Prolétarienne. Lévy later became Sartre's secretary before spending the latter part of his life as a rabbi in Jerusalem, where he died in 2003. Omar Diop, the first ever Senegalese graduate of the Ecole Normale Supérieure, had already acted in *La Chinoise*, Jean-Luc Godard's 1967 film about Maoist students, and was a prominent member of Nanterre's Mouvement du 22 Mars. Diop later returned to Senegal and was reported to have died in prison in 1973 after being tortured and strangled, following a 1971 demonstration on which Molotov cocktails had been thrown at the cortege of the visiting French President Georges Pompidou. Nidoish Nasseline, from New Caledonia, was also a member of the Mouvement du 22 Mars. On returning to New Caledonia, he became active in Kanak nationalism, which he attributes to the Parisian students' admiration for non-Europeans that had for the first time made him proud to be Kanak. Mustapha Khayati, the Tunisian Situationist who had written the famous pamphlet *Sur la misère en milieu étudiante* ['On Student Poverty'] was deported from France during the events. Provincial examples can also be found, such as Voldodia Shahshahani, born to an Iranian father in the USA, who was a Maoist activist in Grenoble.[151]

But alongside the cosmopolitanism of the French revolutionary Left lay the activity of foreign revolutionary groups. In the latter case, there are more examples of worker activists. In the midst of the *banlieue* in Saint-Denis, Portuguese Maoists were said to have written graffiti denouncing the dictator Salazar and his secret police.[152] The Renseignements Généraux's 'foreign agitator' file for May 1968 gives details of four Latin Americans, two Italians and one Portuguese Maoist activists living in France. Space was also given to 11 Spanish residents in France who were members of various Maoist, Trotskyist, anarchist and Guevarist groups. Untypically for the file as a whole, six of the Spaniards worked in manual occupations: a painter and decorator, a chocolate factory worker, two Citroën workers, a chef and a sheet-metal worker. Some of the Spanish and Portuguese were alleged to have been involved in the Cité Universitaire occupations. Though the Spanish anarcho-syndicalist CNT in exile – heirs of the legendary Civil War protagonists – appears to have played relatively little part in the events, the Renseignements Généraux did note the involvement of three young workers in Paris who were CNT members.[153] The *Economist* reported that Spanish anarcho-syndicalists carrying their red and black flag through Toulouse 'were surprised when middle-class onlookers applauded them',[154] having mistaken the flag for the colours of a local football team.

More numerous still in the Renseignements Généraux file were 35 deserters from the US army in West Germany, who had fled to France to avoid being sent to fight in Vietnam. However only a few were alleged to have participated in May '68; the rest were under suspicion purely because of their desertion, or in some cases for vagrancy. One exception was Schofield Corryel. Raymond Marcellin, the new Interior Minister appointed at the end of May with a brief of crushing the revolt, singled out Corryel in a speech, for leading a group of American deserters in occupied university buildings. While denying this accusation, Corryel admitted having founded the Paris American Committee to Stop War. Another was Thomas Schwaetzer, aka Max Watts, originally a Jewish refugee from Austria, who was heavily involved in supporting fellow American war resisters, to the extent that one obituary claims he was kidnapped by French security forces.[155]

But it was the German SDS that seems to have had the greatest direct impact on events. Both the Nanterre students and Alain Krivine's Jeunesse Communiste Révolutionnaire (JCR) had already developed close links to the West German student movement, which predated its French counterpart as a mass movement. Krivine and others travelled to Berlin in February 1968 for a major international anti-Vietnam War demonstration. At the time, Neal Ascherson was Berlin correspondent for the London *Observer*, and an SDS sympathiser. In early May, Ascherson came to Paris and, with an SDS contact, tried to push the SDS's line at meetings of French students. Having discovered this in the Renseignement Généraux's 'foreign agitator' file in Fontainebleau, in 2001 I interviewed Ascherson at London's Institute of Archaeology. He confirmed the file's report on his activities was broadly correct, and recounted how the already experienced SDS were rather disdainful of what they viewed as the chaotic approach of the French. While minimising his own role, Ascherson considers the SDS enormously influential on the tactics of the French insurgents, by getting them to turn street confrontation with the police into a political learning process. This goes some way to explaining why so many Germans were arrested in Paris during the events. While no doubt some were simply victims of anti-German xenophobia, there was also a small hard core of SDS activists in Paris, speaking, marching, running up and down staircases, passing messages. On 10 June, the police raided the Latin Quarter flat of the German-British couple who had been injured on the Night of the Barricades. At least ten people were deported following the raid on their flat, which the French authorities alleged served as SDS headquarters in Paris – but which

Ascherson recalls as a room with bare boards that did not look like anyone's headquarters.[156]

Ascherson's story points to how, during May, Paris became a magnet for 'revolutionary tourists' from across Europe, as well as those already in France. French officials were ever paranoid about international conspiracies: for Raymond Marcellin, May '68 was a plot orchestrated by foreign powers. There was a large element of fantasy in such notions of 'remote control': the governments of China or Cuba would have required a startling degree of political brilliance to persuade millions of people in a country thousands of miles away to go on strike and take to the streets. In so far as there were people in France on the eve of May '68 seeking to foment revolution, they were surprisingly few in number, mostly French, and as much taken by surprise as everyone else at the largely spontaneous events of early May.[157] But once the events were underway, individual revolutionaries did head for the French capital. The authorities quickly became wise to this, drawing up a banned list of international revolutionaries likely to attempt entry. They included the Italian New Left publisher Giangiacomo Feltrinelli, who in 1972 was to accidentally blow himself up whilst attaching explosives to a Milan electricity pylon, and the German student leader Rudi Dutschke, who had been the target of an assassination attempt in April 1968. Those who made their political affiliations too obvious – such as a German theatre troupe who aroused the suspicion of Strasbourg border police by flying Chinese and Vietnamese flags from their minibus – fell foul of this attempt to seal off international contagion.[158] Two leading SDS activists were arrested and deported at Orly airport on 9 May as they attempted to travel to address a JCR meeting. Activists quickly wised up to getting through clandestinely: one of the pair later managed to enter by land on 12 May. Cohn-Bendit famously did the same, after temporarily fleeing to West Germany in a car borrowed from Bernard Kouchner – the original 'doctor without borders' who later became Nicolas Sarkozy's foreign minister. Belgian and German Trotskyists managed to keep the Fourth International's cars supplied with fuel by arriving every other day with cans of petrol. A number of Italian activists from far Left groups such as Potere Operaio did manage to get to the French capital.[159]

In later years tremendous prestige was to be attached in leftist, intellectual and artistic milieux outside France to having 'been in Paris in '68'. One British postgraduate, for example, claimed to have been 'the navy of the revolution', spraying the Boulevard Saint-Michel with water pumped from his houseboat on the Seine to disperse the tear gas.[160] Having made it there was important even to those later sceptical of the significance of the events, such as Tony Judt, who followed 'so many of my friends and contemporaries' to Paris.[161] Indeed, not having gone there could become something to be apologised for, as did another British historian, Sheila Rowbotham:

> Some friends went over to Paris but it always seemed to me that I should be in Britain, arguing through the political implications of what was taking place in France. This was certainly a less glamorous position to be in.[162]

Even so prominent a figure in the British version of '68 as the Pakistan-born activist Tariq Ali was later to describe his own decision to cancel his travel plans, following a tip-off that the British authorities would not let him back in the country again if he left, as 'unforgiveable'.[163] A failure to have made it to Paris in May would need to be explained away – the American anarchist thinker Murray Bookchin only got to Paris on 13 July, but still made the most of it – or even a cause for fabrication. The Sex Pistols manager Malcolm McLaren later claimed to have been in Paris, although he was in fact staging a sit-in at Croydon Art College.[164]

As the fog of tear gas cleared, it was clear that there had been substantial participation in the events of May by a variety of immigrants in a variety of ways. While only a small minority were active *gauchistes*, and even participating on demonstrations was a risky affair, the larger numbers participating inside occupied buildings were evidence of the movement's genuine internationalism. True, many spectacular actions were the work of middle-class activists far removed from the shanty towns which surrounded Paris. But such revolutionary minorities would not have been able to influence events in the extraordinary way they did in the Paris of 1968 had they not been able to capitalise on wider feelings of discontent. Many more immigrants participated not as agents of international revolution, but as ordinary inhabitants of France. There were large numbers of immigrants who neither instigated revolutionary committees, nor conformed to the stereotype of the fearful and deferential migrant worker, but were somewhere in between. In terms of numbers, by far the most significant avenue of participation was as strikers. Both French and immigrant workers went on strike in a remarkably widespread range of industries and geographical locations.

An impressive dynamic towards unity was thereby forged. Contemporaries such as Sally N'Dongo of the Senegalese UGTSF recognised the importance of this breakthrough: 'We came out of the night.'[165] The Algerian writer Kateb Yacine was also greatly impressed: 'I was very surprised to see

Algerian immigrants participating in the events, in the first ranks of May. I asked myself if there was a force organising them. It became clear that it was spontaneous.'[166] So was Jean Daniel, editor of *Le Nouvel Observateur*:

> The young people are not right because they are young. They are right when, taking a German as leader, and including Tunisians, Portuguese and Spanish in their marches, they invite us to return to the sources of internationalism.[167]

In short, the working class which carried out the largest labour uprising in French history was a multi-national class. By striking it had shown itself to be a force to be reckoned with. Immigrants were indeed, if only for a few weeks, 'no longer nobodies in France'.

Chapter Three

A Time of Spectacular Action, 1968-1971

'In Nanterre, things are stirring.'
Mahiou Roumi, who grew up in the shanty town
adjacent to Nanterre University.[1]

Fear and Repression

Now that the events of May-June 1968 had dramatically highlighted the issue of immigration, over the following years it was to rise further up the political agenda. A wave of anti-racist protest began, that would eventually become a full-scale immigrant workers' movement. But for the three years immediately after the events, the most typical form this took was less by immigrants themselves than on their behalf by New Left intellectuals – who saw in the immigrant worker what they wanted to see, namely a new agent of revolutionary change. The aftermath of 1968 has been characterised as one when revolutionaries set themselves impossibly ambitious goals, in excess of the forces actually available to them.[2] Yet the hopes aroused by May '68 among migrants and their supporters were far from being immediately fulfilled. Indeed, the historian Arthur Marwick was to claim:

> With regard to the French events of 1968 it is possible to say that in practically every area of French life there were, indirectly if not directly, in the longer term if not immediately, benefits of some sort. For North African immigrants, on the contrary, the effects were an almost unmitigated disaster.[3]

How far does the evidence support such a bleak assessment?

First, as we have already seen, a number of foreigners were deported from France for their real or alleged part in the events. It is not possible to give a definitive figure for the number of expulsions – newspapers reported around 154-161 in June, the Interior Ministry counted 215 cases, and contemporary accusations ranged as high as 700 – but the police archives suggest it cannot have been less than 160, in addition to a further 57 struck by separate legal measures.[4] An early sign of the crackdown was the police offensive in Algerian districts of Lyons after the riots of 24 May: 33 expulsions resulted, of which eleven were young Algerians, all either workers or unemployed.[5] The crackdown intensified as the authorities reasserted their control during June, the month that a firmly right-wing National Assembly was elected in reaction against the events of May. At least twelve people were expelled after having been arrested on their way to the Renault factory at Flins on 7-8 June.[6] At least a further ten expulsions followed the 10 June raid on the Latin Quarter flat suspected of being the French headquarters of the German SDS.[7] The following days' rioting in Paris and Toulouse produced a further 41 and 22 expulsions respectively.[8]

There was to be no let up for at least another month: expulsions followed of three Latin Americans for 'intense political activity' in the Alpes-Maritimes and two people arrested in a raid on a meeting of a Comité d'Action Ouvriers-Etudiants in Paris. In normal times, expulsion was a surprisingly leisurely process in which it was usually left up to those issued with expulsion orders to leave the country on their own initiative, leaving most expulsion orders unimplemented.[9] But in the tense atmosphere of June 1968, foreigners were bundled into police vans and taken straight to the border, or put on planes and deported with great haste. Little attention was paid to legal niceties, creating embarrassing problems for the authorities. For example, the French authorities tried to deport Boris Fraenkel – Lionel Jospin's mentor into Trotskyism – along with other individuals found in the raid on the German revolutionary's flat, only to find Fraenkel refused entry to West Germany on the grounds that he was a stateless person. Fraenkel was therefore instead issued with an order forcing him to reside far from Paris, at Sarlat in the Dordogne.[10] Fraenkel and many other expellees were more active than they admitted at the time: in June there was an understandable tendency to play down the foreign participation loudly proclaimed during May – in order to avoid lending credence to conspiracy theories about international subversion. But a number appear, from the legal documents appealing against their expulsions, genuinely to have been innocent bystanders caught in the wrong place at the wrong time, including Pablo Parades, a Peruvian student and journalist, and Wada Hildebrands, a Dutch student and waitress. Francesco Lanzini, an Italian cutter and toolmaker living in Paris, was almost blinded by a tear gas canister as he was trying to park his car during a riot. He then had insult added to injury by being sent back to Italy where he was unable to afford treatment for his eyes, having paid social security contributions only in France.[11]

A second piece of evidence supporting a pessimistic reading is that May '68 led to new restrictions on immigration. In June, a quota was imposed of 1000 per month on the number of Algerians allowed to enter France for work. Given that there was up to this point no limit at all on such entries, this measure can be identified as a turning point from a laissez-faire to a more restrictive policy, a precursor of the complete halt to primary immigration in 1974.[12] Writing in 1979, Gary Freeman argued that the quota was partly a reaction against the involvement of immigrant workers in the events, though he added two other factors: a short-term increase in unemployment due to the crisis, and a reprisal against the Algerian government's recent nationalisation of some French-owned firms.[13]

While Freeman's other two factors also seem valid, there is new evidence to support the notion that immigrant participation in May '68 was responsible for the restrictions on immigration. Even before the quota for Algerians was announced on 18 June, documents in the Interior Ministry archives show that a wider-ranging measure was decided on, although there is no evidence that it was implemented. It was envisaged to stop temporarily from 7 June *all* new entries of immigrants for work, except EEC and Swiss nationals. This was also to apply to existing immigrants returning from holiday, if they could not show how they were to reach their usual place of residence (even if they had the right papers) and to family reunions. The reason given was essentially the practical one of the difficulty of transport and finding work in the midst of a general strike.

But an underlying political motive for the measures is given in a longer, revealing document in the same official file. This explained that:

> Current events lead us to examine problems relating to immigration under two particular aspects:
> -The intrusion of foreigners into French political life and their participation in demonstrations of a violent character.
> -The possibility of inserting immigrants into our economy, and therefore, the conditions of admitting job seekers to live here.

It went on to examine what it saw as the disproportionate participation of foreigners on demonstrations, and drew a connection between the two issues: 'These concerns of the maintenance of public order, of social peace and of harmonious relations between communities must feature among the essential factors of a migration policy.' It recommended that the current situation of 'spontaneous immigration' – immigrants entering as tourists, finding a job and then regularising their situation only later if at all – be stopped completely or at least heavily restricted. The document also argued that Algerians were a particular problem, citing their large number and problems of unemployment, poor housing, health and delinquency, and called for their special legal status to be removed. It seems likely, given its timing, that the arguments presented in this document influenced both the implemented Algerian quota and the unimplemented 7 June suspension.

The document ended on a chilling note: 'It is above all important in this field to try to avoid the racial upsets which periodically trouble the world and which have not spared recently a neighbouring European country.'[14] This was presumably a reference to the storm created in Britain by Enoch Powell's 'rivers of blood' speech in April 1968. The worst nightmare of French policy-makers was that they should face a situation as in Britain where migration had escaped from being a matter for non-controversial management and become a political quarrel. In their eyes, the participation of immigrants in May '68 had threatened to do this.

A third reason for pessimism is that, though the economic situation of immigrants as workers did improve in some cases, their specific problems as immigrants were largely ignored. Some lost their jobs – 925 by the end of June at Citroën – though equally others were taken on, especially at Boulogne-Billancourt. There were a few tangible gains in working conditions: at Renault, temporary three or six month contracts, which contributed to the insecurity faced by foreign workers, were replaced by permanent ones. Moreover, there were substantial improvements in pay as a result of the general strike. Many immigrants were likely to have gained from the increase of some 35 per cent in the minimum wage, and wages as a whole. At Citroën, for example, unskilled workers saw their pay increased by 13 per cent, for a working week reduced by half an hour.[15]

Yet the Grenelle agreements which led to an end to the strikes did not deal with immigrant workers' special concerns. Immigrants do not even appear to have been specifically mentioned in the positions adopted by any of the main union confederations in the negotiations; hence it was not surprising they did not feature in the final agreement. This was despite the fact that the immigrant workers' branch of the second biggest trade union confederation, the CFDT, had set out a number of demands for the negotiations, including an end to work permits and residency permits, and union co-management of immigrant hostels.[16] It looked, therefore, as if immigrants had given more to the French labour movement than they had taken. As delegates to a meeting held in October of Spanish activists in the CFDT put it: 'Immigrants have not solved any of their problems during these events. Grenelle brought them nothing. Enormous disappointment.'[17]

Resisting Deportation

Yet too pessimistic an account of 1968's effects on immigrants leaves out another important consequence: an increase in the collective self-consciousness of immigrants, and in the willingness of others to stick their neck out for them. This had clear origins in the international solidarity of May '68 itself. The expulsions of foreigners were counterproductive in that, in not a few cases, they provoked a protest movement in response. This is best known in the case of Dany Cohn-Bendit, who was able to single-handedly provoke demonstrations in his favour, inspire the creation of new slogans and draw on networks to smuggle him back into the country. In historical perspective, for large crowds of French men and women to shout 'We are all German Jews' was no mean achievement.

Rather less well known is that other expellees who lacked Cohn-Bendit's cult following were also able to inspire protest on their behalf. Even before the expulsions were officially announced, on 10 June posters appeared advertising a demonstration for the evening of 12 June at the Place de la République under the slogan 'Stop the expulsion of our foreign comrades'. Ironically, the posters advised foreigners not to participate,[18] suggesting that the organisers' idealistic internationalism was tempered with a dose of realism. The days of international participation were now ending as the Gaullist state reasserted its control, and foreigners would no doubt be the first to be arrested. Protestors' worst fears were confirmed when on 12 June the government unveiled a package of measures including not only the expulsions but also a ban on all demonstrations. The planned demonstration was therefore rapidly cancelled – though too late to prevent a hundred and fifty demonstrators being arrested as they tried to make it to République – and replaced with a meeting on the lawn of the still occupied Cité Universitaire Internationale that evening. Even at this stage, foreigners were still actively participating: two Africans were among the speakers who addressed the thousand-strong crowd that night.[19]

The student movement continued to make propaganda use of the expulsions in posters and declarations. But they were on the defensive. Further plans for massive street demonstrations every Wednesday did not reach fruition.[20] Another meeting was held at the Cité Universitaire on 28 June, but broke up in acrimony when the mainly African audience refused to hear prepared speeches from French writers like Marguerite Duras and Pierre Vidal-Naquet, preferring to watch an Algerian film instead. There were a few dramatic incidents of direct action against expulsions, including the occupation of court buildings.[21] In the autumn the Marseilles branch of the fledgling Maoist group, the Gauche Prolétarienne, mounted a

Molotov cocktail raid on a police station where deportations were about to be authorised in the mainly North African Porte d'Aix district.[22] But this only served to underline the movement's re-confinement to an ultra-leftist ghetto.

At the same time, the expulsions were drawing protests – though mainly of the verbal variety – from more respectable sources. The MRAP was first off the mark in June, swiftly followed by a joint statement by Catholic, Protestant and Jewish leaders, and the CGT, the largest union confederation in France, followed suit. However, the MRAP's archives reveal that the CGT's Georges Séguy refused an offer for joint protests by Daniel Mayer of the Ligue des Droits des l'Homme. When granted an audience with the prime minister in August, Séguy brought up the issue only after a long shopping list of economic demands,[23] which suggests that expulsions were not a priority for the CGT leadership. A Comité pour la Liberté et contre la Répression, comprising many of the 'usual suspects' of famous intellectuals, denounced the expulsions at two meetings in July and one in October at the Mutualité, though only as part of a wider campaign against 'repression'.[24] An international commission of jurists found the French government to be in breach of both common law and the European Convention on Human Rights, while the West German government made a formal complaint about the treatment of its citizens.[25]

But it was individuals who aroused the most vociferous protest campaigns. An outstanding example was the case of Roland Rutili, an iron miner of Italian origin. Rutili, in his late twenties, lived in Audun-le-Tiche, a small town in Lorraine, where France's iron and steel basin borders Luxembourg. Like Cohn-Bendit, Rutili was born in France. Furthermore, his father had arrived in the 1920s as an anti-fascist refugee. This background made him the ideal focus for protests. Rutili enjoyed the support of a close-knit local working-class community, largely Italian and Polish in origin, in a town anchored a long way to the Left, in a region where people had little difficulty combining Catholicism and Communism, with a still growing PCF vote of not far off 40 per cent. He had the additional good fortune to have a French wife and children – and, as a CGT activist, the resources of the mainstream French labour movement.[26] Above all, Rutili's supporters drew on the fact that his father had died as a deportee to Mauthausen concentration camp in 1943: 'The name Rutili figures on the Audun-le-Tiche monument to 'Those Who Died for France'.[27]

Rutili therefore inspired large general assemblies of the town's population, strikes in local mines, an impressively broad regional defence committee, a generous collection at the CGT's national conference and representations by the national leaderships of the CGT and its Italian counterpart the CGIL. As a result, Rutili's expulsion was cancelled, but it was replaced with orders banning him from living in Lorraine and forcing him to reside elsewhere in France. Some years later, all measures against him were overturned by the European Court of Justice in what became an important test case for the principle of freedom of movement within the EEC.[28]

Rutili's case suggests the importance of workplace solidarities in determining the extent of defence campaigns, in a society where people were still very much defined by their work. Other CGT activists could occasionally succeed in similar campaigns, even if like Jorge Ferre-Artal, a Spanish iron craftsman, they had flirted with leftist ideas like worker-student dialogue.[29] Since an innovation of 1968 was the spread of strike activity to intellectual occupations, it was not surprising that quasi-strike activity was in some cases deployed as anti-expulsion protest. The expulsions of Julio Le Parc, Hugo Demarco, Lucien Taieb, and Jean-Ange Msika led to fellow artists withdrawing their works from official exhibitions in protest. Indeed, the newspaper *France-Soir* considered it had made Le Parc and Demarco the biggest names in contemporary art. After his expulsion, Msika went on to play a prominent role in the Poster Workshop set up by London radicals that summer in imitation of the Atelier Populaire. Meanwhile French psychologists threatened to cancel international conferences until the security of foreign participants could be guaranteed. The expulsion of a French-Canadian physicist, Pierre Roberge, led to motions being passed by his university colleagues and open letters written to de Gaulle drawing attention to the irony of the expulsion given de Gaulle's past support for the Québécois cause.[30] The government also scored an own goal by attempting to deport political refugees back to Franco's Spain. The cases of Angel Campillo Fernandez from Bordeaux and of Georges Fernandez, a doctor from the south-western town of Alès, sparked an outcry. It was alleged that the Spanish tortured Angel Fernandez for 17 days following his deportation, while his namesake was also directly handed over, a telephone call from the authorities in Perpignan to their counterparts in Barcelona having warned of the arrival of a 'dangerous subversive individual'.[31]

A few expulsees had the confidence to openly mount their own protest campaigns, including American anti-Vietnam War activists, like Warren Hamerman and Alfred Schmidt, or Thomas Schwaetzer, who became something of a cause célèbre among students at the Paris science faculty, as well as the leading international Trotskyist Ernest Mandel. More than once in the following years, Mandel managed to sneak into France, on one occasion holding a press conference in the middle of Paris with the equally banned Tariq Ali.[32] Letters in the Interior Ministry's archives show that 24 of the foreigners expelled succeeded in getting their expulsion orders overturned, often by using behind-the-scenes contacts. A Yugoslav man arrested for stealing a bicycle to escape from a demonstration was let off when his employer sent a glowing character reference to the Ministry. The reference, drawing attention to the facts that the company's director was a member of the Legion of Honour, and that the Yugoslav's father had been shot by the SS, struck the right chords with Gaullist officials. A Swiss cabaret singer arrested on the Night of the Barricades had his order revoked in 1969, apparently due to his family's friendship with a prominent French politician. A Greek student succeeded in having his case reopened after interventions from an official whose nephew was a student at the same faculty, despite the fact that there was other evidence contradicting his denial of political activity.[33] Daniel Guérin, the anarchist writer who had spectacularly broken with his bourgeois past in the 1920s, made use of his remaining links by sending telegrams to the Elysée Palace on behalf of an expelled British anarchist, Martin Kay. By 1969, Kay's expulsion was overturned.[34] As for Neal Ascherson, he was not even aware, until I told him in 2001, that he had been branded a 'foreign agitator' by the Renseignements Généraux, since he was never subsequently prevented from entering France.[35]

Manual workers of non-European origin, though, were rarely as fortunate. Only in exceptional circumstances were protests aroused, for example in the case of Ahmed Merahoui, an Algerian factory worker in Vitry-sur-Seine. The 'strong emotion'[36] aroused among Merahoui's workmates by his expulsion can partly be explained by the fact that the chemical factory concerned, Rhône-Poulenc, had had an unusually radical strike whose aim was explicitly to 'contest the organisation of society' rather than purely bread-and-butter economic demands.[37] Merahoui was also a CGT activist, leading to interventions on his behalf by a local Communist deputy. Those lacking such exceptional circumstances went without protest, meeting only silence. Dozens of cases survive to history only as names in the archives, with no-one in France to protest on their behalf.

From the Factories to the Streets

June 1968 did not, however, mark the complete 'return to normal' the government had hoped for. Though it had seen off the immediate challenge from the movement, veterans of '68, emboldened by the experience, continued a multi-faceted low-level insurgency for years afterwards. This was not least the case on the issue of immigration, which became an increasing preoccupation of the *gauchistes* in general and of the Maoists in particular. In the highly optimistic aftermath of 1968, many leftists across Europe saw foreign workers as a potential new revolutionary vanguard. (Trotskyists, by contrast, rejected the idea that the rest of the working class had become bourgeoisified, so while they did carry out some activity in support of immigrant struggles, these remained less central to their overall political strategy than was the case for Maoists.[38]) Given the role played in May-June by factories with many immigrant workers, one of the first actions of the reformed Maoist *groupuscules* in the autumn of 1968 was to seek 'proletarianisation and militarisation'.[39] In other words, to seek recruits in these factories by stirring up immediate confrontation on the factory floor. At Renault, it appears to have been a young Italian worker known as 'Bouboule' who set up the first Maoist 'struggle committee'.[40] In other cases, committees were initially set up by the *établis*, intellectuals who had become workers to infiltrate the factories. But the classic account of this experiment, Robert Linhart's *L'établi* [translated as *The Assembly Line*] underlines the initial disillusionment as this graduate of the Ecole Normale Supérieure encountered the monotonous drudgery of work at Citroën's Choisy factory and the sense of powerlessness on the part of its diverse immigrant workforce that belied Linhart's romantic ideas about the working class.[41] An immigrant-led worker revolt inside the factories was still a little way off: immigrant participation in the general strike of 1968 appeared something of a false start.

Yet the dogged resistance that Linhart detected 'disguised beneath a simulated resignation'[42] finally burst into an open revolt in early 1969. The issue was an attempt by Citroën to make workers put in extra time at the end of each day to make up for the hours lost during the previous year's strike. Following a month of secret planning, when the extra time began on 17 February around 400 strikers downed tools. It is a moot point whether or not the strike would have begun without Linhart's intervention, but an equally prominent role was played by 'Primo', a Sicilian immigrant who was already an active trade unionist before Linhart's arrival. Other participants in their 'struggle committee' included Yugoslavs, Algerians and a Malian. Few of Linhart's fellow workers were shocked to discover that an intellectual was working in a factory, since they all had their own individual itineraries and dreams before working at Citroën. For example, one of the most militant workers, 'Mohammed', had been a shepherd in the Algerian region of Kabylia, before coming to Paris in the forlorn hope of studying literature.[43] New Left intellectuals like Linhart thus hoped that they could somehow transcend the social hierarchies of French society by linking up with immigrants, and young French workers less schooled in these rigid boundaries than were the traditional French working class. Linhart's dreams of 'the shanty towns marching towards Neuilly' were not easy to fulfil – the strike collapsed within two weeks in the face of threats from management and consular interpreters, and the ringleaders sacked – but the memory of the strike remained alive at Citroën for years afterwards.[44]

Nevertheless, solidarity between French and immigrant workers was not the norm, outside such exceptional circumstances as May '68. For the most part, pro-immigrant campaigning was at this embryonic stage an affair of intellectuals. This included both a new generation of revolutionaries forged on the barricades and their patrons among older elite but dissident intellectuals, whose radicalism had been given a second wind by 1968. The first group, sometimes with the assistance of the second, began to carry out propaganda activity in the form of spectacular, exemplary actions in an attempt to break the wall of public indifference. The immigrant issue was being pushed on the streets, though largely by proxies. Linhart was a member of the Gauche Prolétarienne, who emerging from the ruins of the banned UJCML together with their newspaper, a re-launched *La Cause du Peuple*, came to incarnate the spirit of the post-68 New Left. Their penchant for marginalised groups made them ideal proponents of the immigrant cause, and their leadership included a Moroccan, Anis Balafrej. 1969 was a time of ultra-leftist enthusiasm, when the GP was making the extravagantly melodramatic claim that France was heading 'Towards Civil War',[45] and when the Trotskyist presidential candidate, Alain Krivine, was calling for the formation of armed workers' militias. That year *gauchistes* concentrated their efforts in favour of immigrants on harassing Communist-controlled municipalities in the red belt around Paris. They accused the mayor of Argenteuil, for example, of evicting local shanty town dwellers without providing alternative housing, and of making racist comments about the percentage of local school pupils who were Algerian. The *gauchistes'* leafleting and postering campaign in Argenteuil culminated in a demonstration at the town hall. It drew a furious response from *L'Humanité* as the work of 'fascists' from the prosperous parts of Paris in league with the billionaire proprietor of *Combat*. Returning the compliment, accusations flew that Communist Party members had attacked leafleters with stones.[46]

By 1 May 1969, the *gauchistes* were sufficiently confident to eschew the traditional Communist-led May Day march and mount their own. It is no coincidence that they chose to do this in the largely immigrant-populated area of Belleville, the scene of the Arab versus Jewish riots of June 1968. Yet May Day '69 in Belleville proved a fiasco, resulting only in unwanted police harassment for the local North African population. One Maoist postmortem on this failure blamed the arrogance of *gauchistes* in arranging the march without consulting the local population. They had done this largely because they had misinterpreted the previous year's Belleville riots as a proletarian uprising.[47]

The author of this characteristic piece of 'self-criticism' was a little-known group called Vive le Communisme, which had been founded in late 1968 by Maoist ex-students like Tiennot Grumbach and Roland Castro. Castro was himself the son of Greek immigrants and a veteran of the campaign against the Algerian War, later a leading adviser on town planning to President Mitterrand: he would himself attempt to stand for President in 2007. He had edited the first series of *La Cause du Peuple* which highlighted the immigrant issue during the events of May.[48] Renamed Vive la Révolution in 1969, VLC/VLR generally merits only a footnote in the history of the French New Left – not surprisingly for a group with only a few hundred members, and which lacked the high media profile of the GP. VLR is usually noted for its unusually anti-authoritarian, quasi-anarchist bent and emphasis on sexual liberation that seems to have more in common with Anglo-American counterculture of the period than the rather austere Marxism-Leninism of rival French groups.[49]

Yet the group's history also provides a fascinating case study of the New Left's relationship with immigration on the ground, in no less emblematic an area than Nanterre. It was there that questions about the relationship between immigrants and the New Left were posed most acutely, since both were in plentiful supply at close quarters. Castro chose to set up as a full-time activist in Nanterre, because of its unique triple reputation as hotbed of student revolution, working-class suburb and site of Algerian shanty towns. As he described looking back in poetic form in his memoirs:

> I settled in Nanterre,
> Where it had begun.
> The sons of bourgeois
> In the middle of the shanty towns
> Behind the railway,
> In the zone,
> Deep in the suburbs.
> Nanterre-la-Folie.

Castro like other 'sons of bourgeois' (in the derogatory Communist description of the time) found the revolt and authenticity they were searching for at the place where the railway line, the university and the shanty town met, Nanterre-la-Folie:

> You go elsewhere, where things are real,
> In the noise, the revolt. '
> And in Nanterre you don't lack
> Subjects for revolt. [50]

For VLR immigrants were, along with women, regional minorities, students and workers, one of several potential bases for social movements. Together they represented a potential for 'fusion' along the lines suggested by Jean-Paul Sartre in his *Critique of Dialectical Reason* – a group of people coming together collectively to free themselves. Immigrants were also one of the 'enemy's weak points', because they were not integrated into electoral politics. The subject also tied in with VLR's international agenda, which displayed particular penchants for the American Black Power movement and the Palestinian cause, which attracted some North African recruits. Indeed, one young Algerian supporter from Nanterre would end up being killed as a volunteer guerrilla fighter, a *fedaï*, in Jordan in 1970.[51]

But *gauchistes* were interested in the here and now of immigrants' situation as much as far-away struggles, especially in a context where immigrant-based struggles were gathering pace. An early sign of this was in the south-eastern suburb of Ivry-sur-Seine. If you head out on foot from the furthest reaches of Left Bank Paris, past the Vietnamese restaurants of the Avenue de Choisy, you have already passed the line between a place where most people on the street appear to be white to a place where they do not. The Périphérique approaches, that brutal final frontier between Paris and *banlieue*. Motorists speed underneath towards Nantes or Bordeaux, as you cross to Ivry, a place where Parisians generally go only to be buried in its cemetery. The contrast is rude: the visitor is greeted by factory chimneys, enormous tower blocks, the ruins of long-forgotten import-export businesses, and pavements with holes in reminiscent of the developing world. Taking a left turn past the bus depot and an eponymously-named bar, you reach the Avenue Maurice Thorez, named after the historic leader of the French Communist Party, that winds down towards the town centre. Unexpectedly, above anarchist posters denouncing deportations, there are stairs to cobbled streets and a church, whose noticeboard demands beatification for two pre-war evangelists who came here with the intention of serving the proletariat – like the *gauchistes*, and like one disillusioned middle-class Communist apparatchik who described Ivry in his autobiography as 'the promised land'.[52] Ivry is where the Malian residents of a disused chocolate factory used as makeshift accommodation went on rent strike in May 1969, and persisted for many months despite their landlord's attempts to end the strike by cutting off water and electricity. What became known as the 'Battle of Ivry' set a pattern for activism where there would be a delicate balance between the desire for immigrants to themselves lead the struggle and a continued role for French supporters.[53] Though they received the support of a number of French lawyers and other individuals who had been providing literacy classes for them since May '68, this 'Comité Alpha' insisted that: 'No action will be undertaken, no leaflet produced without prior discussion with the workers in the hostel and their agreement.'[54] The implication, clearly, was that this prior discussion had not always been the case in the past.

Commandos and Intellectuals

In the very first days of 1970, the housing issue came suddenly to the attention of a wider public. Five African workers were killed by a fire in the northern suburb of Aubervilliers because, having been housed in a run-down hostel with no heating, they had no alternative but to make a wood fire to keep warm. The incident led to a good deal of media attention to the previously 'undiscovered' issue of immigrants living in modern day Paris in nineteenth-century conditions worthy of an Emile Zola novel. The New Left led the cries of outrage, turning the victims' funeral into a political denunciation of the iniquities of capitalism, as a large crowd singing the *Internationale* followed the five coffins on their journey from the morgue. A motley crew of young Maoist militants and famous intellectuals, including the novelists Marguerite Duras and Jean Genet, and the historian of ancient Greece Pierre Vidal-Naquet, occupied the headquarters of the employers' pressure group, the CNPF, in protest. Maurice Clavel, writer and philosopher, TV critic of *Le Nouvel Observateur*, former wartime associate of General de Gaulle turned Maoist sympathiser and an outspoken critic of the mistreatment of foreigners in France, was reported to have been pushed down the stairs by CRS riot police. For his part, Genet came away with a broken wrist; Vidal-Naquet with blood on his face. Roland Castro was arrested, but made a spectacular attempt to escape from the police van en route to the commissariat before being recaptured and beaten. The slogan the occupiers daubed on the walls – 'Imperialism kills in Aubervilliers like in Chad' – summed up how the New Left viewed anti-racism and anti-colonialism as one and the same, by referring to the French-assisted counter-insurgency operation then underway in Chad. Some 150,000 leaflets in French, Spanish and Arabic were distributed to justify the occupation, though accusations were made in the press that the *gauchistes* were making political capital out of other people's suffering. Meanwhile the Malians of Ivry also seized the opportunity to publicise their cause, deciding to occupy their landlord's office in the company of French supporters like Michel Leiris of *Le Monde*. At the end of February, the CNPF occupiers were put on trial, accompanied by speeches from Clavel, Genet and Jean-Paul Sartre about the exploitation of immigrants. Such prestigious support led the occupiers to get away with what their lawyer Henri Leclerc considered surprisingly light sentences.[55]

The CNPF occupation, in the tradition of small-group actions of the type that some foreign activists had carried out in May 1968 itself, set a pattern for this early phase of pro-immigrant protest. It typically took the form of small groups of individuals mounting exemplary actions, most symbolically on 8 May 1970 when Maoists stole foie gras, champagne and cakes from the Fauchon luxury food store and handed them out in a shanty town.[56] Though immigrant workers themselves were usually absent from such 'commando' actions, this was not only the consequence of a certain revolutionary arrogance on the part of the 'commandos', but also the fruit of bitter experience. The Malians of Ivry brought in French supporters because they feared a repetition of a similar dispute at a hostel in Saint-Denis in 1969, which had led to the deportation of two Malians and the imprisonment of a third, a naturalised French citizen. Sometimes participants were responding to the concrete grievances of immigrants they personally knew. In March 1970, for example, Maoists mounted a raid on the town hall of Meulan to publicise the fact that workers they had been in contact with had to pay large sums of money to be hired at Renault-Flins: the Maoists went to prison as a result. Such actions – a particular speciality of the GP – could also take a lower level form such as helping immigrant workers at Renault-Billancourt pass through metro ticket barriers without paying.[57] Yet 'commando'-type actions sometimes proved controversial within the movement. As Sally N'Dongo argued:

> Maoist groups have often taken their desires for reality, they believed that immigrant workers were an outright vanguard class. So they led some immigrants into suicidal struggles leading too often to deportations from France.[58]

Nanterre I: The Shanty Town Seen From the University

During the spring of 1970, the immigration issue was to intermesh with a major re-emergence of student protest at Nanterre University, where pitched battles between right-wing and left-wing students led to a heavy police intervention on campus.[59] This was where the VLR *groupuscule* came into play, for the unrest was marked by the appearance on campus of people from the neighbouring Algerian shanty-town, actively encouraged by the *gauchistes* and VLR in particular. Perhaps the most interesting aspect of this was VLR supporters setting up what they called a '*crèche sauvage*' to provide childcare for children from the shanty-town. The creche, which lasted from February to June 1970, illustrates the lengths to which the New Left were prepared to go to present themselves as immigrants' number one champions.

VLR's justification for the *crèche sauvage* rested on three principal ideological grounds: economic, pedagogical and anti-racist. First, it was an economic issue: existing authorised crèches were not open to all, but only to parents in paid work, and only if they could afford to pay for a whole week rather than as and when needed. Algerian and Moroccan mothers were thus in practice excluded. In any case, VLR argued that there were not anything like enough places to go round. The *crèche sauvage* was, by contrast, held to turn life in bourgeois society upside down by being free, making use of unoccupied space, and by not being officially recognised. This economic justification had a feminist dimension to it, mixed with VLR's anti-capitalist libertarianism: it was argued that official crèches only freed women to go to work for capitalists, whereas the *crèche sauvage* freed women to do what they wanted during the day.[60] Secondly, VLR justified the creche by presenting it as an experiment in progressive education. Whereas traditional education merely prepared children for work, the *crèche sauvage* allowed them to play freely, whereby, it was hoped, they would learn to live together in a living model of how to 'change life': 'A place where social relations are no longer those of the hierarchy of money.'[61] This drew on previous experiments at the Sorbonne, Censier and Vincennes during and after 1968, which had challenged the methods used in official crèches.[62]

What was distinctive about the Nanterre case, however, was the juxtaposition of university and shanty town, which made anti-racism a key issue behind the *crèche sauvage*: 'It is *sauvage* because the bourgeois cannot bear to see students in the shanty towns and shanty town dwellers in the universities.'[63] This third justification was encapsulated in the choice of slogan, for the crèche was advertised to workers at the Citroen factory in Nanterre with the words: 'French and immigrant babies...same bottle!'[64] accompanied by a drawing of a hammer and sickle in which the hammer had been replaced by a baby's feeding bottle. This slogan was clearly a twist on the 1968 slogan 'French and immigrant workers, same struggle'. The hammer and sickle emblem further underlined this Leninist emphasis on unity. However, the baby's feeding bottle demonstrated a move away from orthodox ideas of where the class struggle should be waged – in the workplace, at the point of production – towards a typically New Leftist concern with the politics of everyday life.[65] Even such a relatively minor deviation from Marxist orthodoxy was controversial, for one Trotskyist militant had told those protesting the Aubervilliers fire: 'But in truth, comrades, the main thing is not in the hostels, but in the factories. It is in the factory that workers produce, it is in the factory that the bosses exploit them.'[66]

There were also tactical and strategic reasons behind the creche. It is significant that the creche was located on campus – a stronghold of the far Left not just by comparison with the rest of France but also with the rest of Nanterre. The town of Nanterre, centred further along the railway line out of Paris, away from both university and shanty town, was dominated by a quite different, defensive French Communist working-class culture. Dominated by older men like Raymond Barbet, who had been member of parliament for and mayor of the town since 1935, Nanterre's municipal Communism was the legacy of a different world, chronologically and socially, from that of the radical young students. Local Communists were consistently hostile to the university-based *gauchistes*, presented as irresponsible vandals objectively in league with Gaullism. Nor was there much sign of the Nanterre Communists being outflanked on the Left by their own constituency. The strike of May-June 1968 was well followed in the town, with 50 workplaces on strike including factories and the local branch of Monoprix, but it was an orderly and respectable affair with little radical experimentation or much in the way of contacts between workers and students.[67] When during the 1970 troubles, Nanterre students went to the Gare Saint-Lazare to explain their position to commuters returning to the western suburbs, they were faced with hostile comments from members of the public along the lines of 'Why do you want to smash everything?', 'Work instead of smashing everything up' and 'We're fed up with students'.[68] VLR's attempts to recruit in Nanterre town, by issuing factory bulletins, met with little success. In short, it was becoming abundantly clear that France was not heading 'towards civil war'.

In the absence of a wider support base, then, a rather more promising prospect for local allies was the Algerian shanty towns. In the league table for numbers of people living in shanty towns in 1968, Nanterre came second in the whole country with estimates ranging upwards from 9700, twice as many as in the whole of Marseilles. It was outdone in numbers only by the eastern suburb of Champigny, which had no comparable focus of student leftism. The possibility of connection between the university and shanty town was therefore real in Nanterre, feared by the authorities and desired by the New Left. A list drawn up by the government in 1970 of immigrant housing locations that had been visited by *gauchistes* found five in Nanterre – two shanty towns, two hostels and one transit camp – more than in any other suburb or district of Paris, except for Saint-Denis.[69]

Anti-racism was thus central to VLR's ideology: when the police entered the campus, VLR attributed the intervention to racist hostility to the *crèche sauvage*. It was further alleged that university security guards had called Algerian women bringing their children to the creche 'dirty silly bitches'.[70] Though in public the university authorities avoided making reference to the ethnic origin of the non-students coming on to campus, it appears that in a committee meeting complaints were made about 'young Arabs' and 'North African teenagers'.[71] Moreover, their justification for calling in the police specifically mentioned the youths from the shanty town. The Dean, the leftwing philosopher Paul Ricoeur, saw himself as facing a particularly grave situation with two interconnected problems of armed political bands of students and juvenile delinquents on university property, blaming these twin threats on the juxtaposition of university and shanty town.[72] Ricoeur's response was nevertheless considered too soft by the local Gaullist member of parliament, the no-nonsense future Interior Minister Charles Pasqua. Pasqua was moved to write to the prime minister to complain about the 'indulgence' given to 'so-called students who are driven by the mania of destruction and reinforced by hoodlums.'[73]

It was perhaps inevitable that the more the shanty town youths were condemned by the authorities, the more they were welcomed by the *gauchistes*. Attempts were made, for example, to allow people from the shanty town to eat in the university restaurant, including the children from the crèche. During the troubles of early 1970, identity checks at the restaurant – abandoned as unworkable after 1968 – were reintroduced. VLR dismissed the financial reasons given for this measure as a mere pretext to conceal the alleged real reason of racist hostility to North Africans. It was also argued that by demanding the restaurant be open to all, students were 'rejecting their privileges', and enabling workers to eat more cheaply than in workplace canteens.[74]

But ironically the students' altercation at the university restaurant brought them into conflict with some of the workers. There had been an ongoing campaign denouncing the restaurant manager for the alleged racist dismissal of Tunisian workers at the restaurant. Though the campaign resulted in one such sacked Tunisian being reinstated in early 1969, a similar mobilisation some time later resulted in the restaurant being closed with the support of some of the staff. Both the students and the CGT accused each other of trying to divide French workers from immigrant workers. Then, when a new manager was brought in, the students accused him of taking photographs of children from the shanty town. Meanwhile, the restaurant staff, who felt intimidated by the students' campaign of non co-operation with the identity checks, actually threatened to go on strike in protest. Along with a defamatory poster, the threatened strike action led to the authorities closing the restaurant for two days in June 1970.[75] So protesting too vociferously in support of immigrants could mean alienating other parts of the local population.

The national political context also goes some way in explaining the *crèche sauvage*, since in a climate of concern about political violence, the government was enacting the so-called *loi anti-casseur*, which made the organisers of any demonstration legally responsible for any damage caused during it. To gain public acquiescence in this measure, the government was trying to portray the Maoists as dangerous *casseurs* ['vandals'] bent on the destruction of society. In this context, the *crèche sauvage* was a way of showing, especially to immigrants, that they were not simply vandals. The provision of welfare services was a tried-and-tested method of gaining the political confidence of immigrant shanty town dwellers. The authorities had tried it during the colonial period and beyond; during the Algerian War, the FLN had tried it with a considerable degree of success; now it was the turn of the *gauchistes*. The Nanterre creche was only one example of this, and it was not the only one to involve children. In the northern suburb of Villeneuve-la-Garenne at the same time, *gauchistes* built a new neighbourhood centre for Portuguese immigrants living in a shanty-town there, complete with childcare facilities, meeting rooms and bathrooms. A central aim was to turn the charge of vandalism on its head: 'Here, the *casseurs* are building.'[76]

Similarly in 1970, activists of the GP and the Secours Rouge – an organisation that can be described as the humanitarian, cross-party arm of *gauchisme*, along the lines of the Communist Party's Secours Populaire Français – persuaded Algerian children in the Goutte d'Or district of Paris to do drawings on the theme of 'Why do the rich go on holiday, why not the poor',[77] and took the children to the seaside. Perhaps inspired by this example, the following year VLR took 30 children from Nanterre shanty towns and estates for a seaside holiday on the Channel coast. VLR's internal report on this '*weekend sauvage*' is quite revealing of its attitude. Even when performing such an ostensibly non-political activity, the emphasis remained firmly on politics. The aim of the exercise had been twofold: to give the children a holiday, and to distribute VLR propaganda to other holidaymakers on the beach. Yet the first aim was also subordinated to the propagandistic aim: taking the children on holiday would make the VLR appear in the estates and shanty towns 'as a real force capable of initiatives in the face of the revisionists'. This internal report criticised the outing for its failure to 'educate politically' the children. Nevertheless, it concluded that there had been fruitful discussions with the parents of the children. Some who were initially hostile changed their mind after the children were returned safely: 'This type of action really gains people's confidence while destroying the stereotype of the Maoist gangster.' The whole report judged the weekend on what it had done for the party, not what it had done for the children.[78] Thus for all VLR's apparent libertarianism, its relationship with immigrants was in danger of becoming one where what the immigrants could do for it was more important than what it could do for them.

The organisation was, however, well aware of such problems. An internal document on racism and anti-racism was sharply critical of VLR members for being 'anti-racists in words but racists in the gaze'. We accept immigrants as comrades, the report argued, provided they abandon their identity for ours – what it labelled a 'Robinson Crusoe' attitude.[79] Since this document went on to call for the recognition of difference and diversity, this can be identified as one of the first signs that the New Left perceived a problem with the emphasis on unity so prominent in 1968.[80] VLR had explicitly defended, with some qualifications, the concept of integration, in accordance with conventional wisdom on the Left: 'The term "integrate" is a bad one but there is no other one. If immigrants are kept in isolation, how can their unity with all of the people be reinforced?'[81] By November 1970, however, they were candidly admitting that 'To be the trophy immigrant of a French group is not an enviable destiny for a revolutionary immigrant worker.'[82] In a polemic with a rival group, VLR even whipped themselves with the admission that 'We have by forgetting the role of French imperialism in the world developed theses of an integrationist and chauvinist character on the working class in France.'[83]

But diversity raised as many questions as it answered. The New Left was meant to be sensitive not only to racism but also to other forms of oppression, notably that of women by men. In practice, however, there were times when it failed to do this. The former GP militant Claire Brière-Blanchet, for example, accuses her organisation of being so misogynistic that it turned a blind eye to domestic violence committed by one Algerian activist in Grenoble, which later culminated in murder.[84] The two issues could come into conflict, as in the arguments that raged in the pages of VLR's newspaper *Tout!* in 1971 following the suggestion by one Arab militant that French women were racist for refusing to have sex with him.[85] Likewise, having thought they had left France for good because of their feelings about what it had done in the Algerian War, Anne Couteau and Paul Oriol returned from Algeria in 1972 because of the situation of women there, Couteau finding it impossible to leave the house alone.[86] In France, the New Left wanted to bring immigrants out of their ghetto into a wider struggle, but could this be done without imposing French values onto them? This was a dilemma that was to resurface again and again in the following years.

The Birth of the Palestine Committees

The dilemma was particularly acute since political actions among foreigners and their New Left allies in France were still as much orientated towards international issues as towards French ones, if not more so. This was not altogether surprising, for why should immigrants or political exiles waste the opportunities afforded by a stay in a relatively free country by becoming foot-soldiers in some parochial battle on the fringes of French politics? For politicised immigrants, planning the freedom of their own country had a more immediate appeal, especially since so many envisaged their stay in France as a temporary sojourn. Bulletins flourished detailing the latest allegations of torture and repression in home countries. For example, in 1969 the suppression of the Marxist student movement in Tunisia provoked some attention in leftist circles in France. On the other hand, there was usually no clear separation between international and domestic issues. One avenue of meeting between the New Left and North African immigrants was pro-Palestinian activism. Young Maghrebi intellectuals in France were marked as much by the Arab defeat of 1967, and the subsequent emergence of radical Palestinian nationalism, as by May 1968. Periodicals devoted to the Middle East proliferated, bearing titles like *Fedaï* ['Guerrilla'].[87] Some French intellectuals had similar preoccupations: the Comité de Soutien aux Luttes de Libération Nationale des Peuples Arabes, which had formed during May 1968, first suggested the idea of local campaigns in solidarity with the Palestinians. Their journal *Résistance Populaire* argued that, since there was little love lost between French and Arab workers ever since the Algerian War, the two could only be united by a locally-based international solidarity campaign.[88] Indicative of the gap to be overcome was a series of machine-gun and Molotov cocktail attacks on Algerian targets in the Paris region in 1969, which were virtually ignored by French public opinion.[89]

Local Comités Palestine first started appearing in late 1969. For future leaders of the immigration struggles of the 1970s like Driss El Yazami and

Saïd Bouziri, this was their most sustained period yet of political activity in France. Important meetings, in which activists from different factions mixed, took place in the Moroccan hall at the Cité Universitaire Internationale, as well as the North African student club on the Boulevard Saint-Michel.[90] The period was strongly marked by the civil war of September 1970 in Jordan between the Palestinian *fedayeen* and King Hussein's forces, viewed as stooges of Western imperialism. First hand accounts indicate that Black September led to many heated discussions in Arab cafés in Paris, and major mobilisations in symbolic areas like the Goutte d'Or. Most significantly for the future, committees soon attracted significant support among North African workers, of whom some 1500 attended a meeting at the Mutualité on 14 February 1971: 'For the first time since the Algerian War, hundreds of workers came down into the street, alongside French people, in Barbès, in Clignancourt, for Palestine, against racism.'[91]

Not surprisingly, a Comité Palestine was started in Nanterre: a leading role in the Comité Palestine Ouvrière de Nanterre was played by Gilbert Mury, the sociologist and Maoist ideologue. Mury was a master of rhetorical flourishes linking local and international issues, declaring in 1970 in relation to a dispute over conditions at a hostel for immigrant workers in Nanterre that: 'In its shacks and in its cellars, in its furnished rooms and in its hostels, facing the exploiter like the *fedayeen* face the Zionists, Shanty town will win!'[92] Such extravagant language, crudely amalgamating the Palestinian struggle and that of Arab workers in France, lay Mury open to ridicule. The director of SONACOTRA, the organisation which ran the hostel, ridiculed the notion of a 'Nanterre Workers' Palestine Committee' on the grounds that there were no Palestinians in his hostels in Nanterre. To follow through his principles, Henri Laborie suggested, Mury should go to Damascus and become a real *fedaï*.[93] The rage behind Mury's declarations landed him in serious trouble in 1971, when he was prosecuted for incitement to murder for writing of the foreman responsible for the death of a Portuguese building worker: 'But there is no longer any justice if someone does not get him.'[94]

Nevertheless, it was a real sense of personal responsibility – Mury was a Resistance veteran – that drove intellectuals to respond to the poverty they saw around them in Nanterre:

> I am a civil servant, I could go home, put on my slippers, and watch television. Is this the life that I must lead? I fought yesterday so that Jews could be Jews and not *youpins*, I fight today so that Arabs can be Arabs and not *bicots*.[95]

Mury's references to racist terms for Jews and Arabs respectively are reminiscent of the declaration in Jacques Panijel's film about the 17 October 1961 massacre: 'That everybody is a *youpin*! That everybody is a *bicot*!'[96] There was a continuity: in the early Seventies as in the early Sixties, the New Left sought to mark itself out by identifying with marginalised groups against racism. This was given an added twist by the fact that many of the New Left intellectuals identifying with Arab and Palestinian nationalism were of Jewish background. Benny Lévy, one of the leaders of the GP, recalls being shocked by hearing antisemitic remarks from Arab workers they had recruited, but saying nothing, out of deference towards the 'popular masses'.[97]

The whole movement received added impetus from the behaviour of successive governments. While young people of unconventional appearance and leftist opinions were in general treated roughly, being foreign was an aggravating factor. It was also not unknown for French activists to face prosecution for crimes as apparently minor as handing out leaflets to Portuguese building workers at their university. After Georges Pompidou replaced de Gaulle as President in June 1969, foreigners continued to be expelled on the slightest suspicion of political activity: an Algerian worker in Roubaix for being an opponent of the Algerian government; two Mexican students for organising a talk on 'Imperialism and Africa' at the Cité Universitaire; Syrian and Palestinian students for pro-Palestinian activity; a official in FEANF, the African students' union, for attacking French neo-colonialism at a meeting at Clermont-Ferrand town hall; an Algerian student for going on anti-racist demonstrations in Marseille; a female Italian worker for striking: these were just some of the cases documented across France between 1969 and 1971.[98] Much publicity was aroused by the case of Laureta Fonseca, a Portuguese mother in the southern suburb of Massy, whose husband was avoiding conscription into the Portuguese army. Fonseca was issued with an expulsion order for occupying the Socialist-run town hall to demand local replacement housing for the inhabitants of the shanty towns. In the course of helping Portuguese residents with their immigration paperwork, Fonseca had uncovered a corrupt official in the local bureaucracy. In September 1971, more than a thousand people, including the future prime minister Michel Rocard, demonstrated in her support, and Fonseca's case received much press coverage and even support on an international level, forcing a government U-turn.[99]

So far from silencing the governments' critics, 'repression' only served to encourage those who liked rhetorically to portray France as a police state little different from Spain or Greece, even if in practice they were aware that it was more open to public pressure. Particularly since the New Left were mobilising at the same time against Franco or the Greek Colonels, comparisons which may appear exaggerated in retrospect came readily to hand: 'Paris had taken on the face of Madrid.'[100]

Demonstrations in support of immigrants or in which they participated lent themselves particularly well to the creation of 'martyrs', like the journalist Alain Jaubert, who was badly beaten during a demonstration in support of independence for the Antilles on 29 May 1971 – despite the fact that he was a white Frenchman and had not even participated in the demonstration. An unintended consequence of the Jaubert affair was the entry into the mainly North African Goutte d'Or district of northern Paris for the first time of Michel Foucault and Claude Mauriac, to meet with an Algerian witness to the beating. We will see in the next chapter that this meeting was to have far-reaching effects.[101] It was symptomatic of the way that immigration issue received the attention of some of France's most highly respected intellectuals, partly from ideology and partly from such chance encounters – which underline the huge social gulf that needed to be breached. A relatively small number of big names such as Simone de Beauvoir, Maurice Clavel, Marguerite Duras, Daniel Guérin,[102] Jean-Paul Sartre, Pierre Vidal-Naquet and, following his return from Tunisia, Michel Foucault, crop up time and again in petitions and demonstrations from 1968 onwards, over expulsions, over the CNPF occupation, over the GP's 'commando' actions, over the Fonseca case. It was at around this time, for example, that Sartre appears to have noticed that, in the title of a speech he gave in 1970, 'The Third World begins in the *banlieue*'.[103] Such support, a product of the renewed radicalisation of France's intelligentsia in the wake of 1968, lent added credibility and publicity to what were still quite small movements.

Nanterre II: The University Seen From the Shanty Town

So while it is important not to ignore the role of immigrant workers themselves, there is no doubt that prior to this stage it was French activists, plus dissident intellectuals from exile communities, who had made much of the running in the growing contestation over immigration. This leads to all sorts of questions that can be asked in retrospect – and were sometimes asked at the time – about who had the authority to speak for whom. While ideological debates about immigrants were filling the pages of leftist publications, what did the immigrants of Nanterre and elsewhere themselves make of the *gauchistes*?[104]

One means of assessing this, at least for the younger generation who had come to France as very young children, is depictions of *gauchisme* in retrospective autobiographical narratives. The Beur autobiographical novel is a genre more readily associated with the 1980s and 1990s than the 1960s. Nor do such works typically contain much about explicitly political activity.[105] Yet the age profile of the group of writers published from the mid-1980s onwards was such that many were teenagers, a time of life often depicted in the genre, around 1968. And at least four such books, by authors born in Algeria in 1952 or 1953, do contain material on 1968-era *gauchisme*: *La menthe sauvage* ['Wild Mint'] by Mohammed Kenzi, *Le sourire de Brahim* ['Brahim's Smile'] by Nacer Kettane, *Confessions d'un immigré* ['Confessions of An Immigrant'] by Kassa Houari and the ironically titled *Vivre au paradis* ['Living In Paradise'] by Brahim Benaïcha. Benaïcha, Kenzi and Kettane grew up in the shanty towns (Benaïcha and Kenzi in Nanterre), while Houari arrived in Paris from Algeria as a young adult. In addition to the novels, there is also the life story, recorded in a magazine by Mogniss Abdallah, of 'Mohammed', who having come to France with his parents aged eight in 1959, lived in a 'temporary' transit camp in Nanterre for twenty years after 1962. A further two books mentioning *gauchisme* were written down by French authors from the oral autobiographical narratives of Algerian youths, also both from Nanterre: *Un nom de papier*, written by Celine Ackaouy from the story of Mahiou Roumi, and *Du bidonville à l'expulsion*, amalgamated by François Lefort from the stories of a number of young people. Finally, there are later interviews, such as by the Moroccan-born writer Tahar Ben Jelloun, with Houria, the daughter of Algerian immigrants to Lyons, who was 14 in 1968; by the journalist Phillippe Bernard with Saïd Bouamama, once a teenage militant in the Maoist Parti Communiste Révolutionnaire Marxiste-Léniniste; and an enquiry into racism in Marseilles by the British travel writer Bruce Chatwin.[106]

The positive and negative images of *gauchisme* in these sources can be balanced against each other. On the positive side, the young Algerians generally approved of the students' revolt against authority. This was in part because they were also revolting against their parents' generation. As we have already seen, immigrants were not a homogenous group: a further internal division to take account of is generation. 1968 has often been considered as, amongst other things, a generational conflict, since many of its prime movers were young people. One of the key ways to tell the difference between a New Left and an Old Left activist was simply that one was usually younger than the other.[107] But generational differences over political attitudes arguably existed as much within immigrant communities as in the rest of French society. Saïd Bouziri, for example, emphasised that those who formed the Comités Palestine were generally under 25.[108]

This theme clearly emerges from the autobiographical sources, which indicate a differentiated reaction to the student revolt along lines of generation. Kenzi's account describes how his parents' generation in Nanterre reacted in a hostile manner to the troubles at the university:

> People considered this revolt as a contradictory act, a youthful madness. They did not understand how this group, supposedly the elite of society, could contest the system from which it had emerged. My father formally prohibited me from associating with these individuals.[109]

This response was remarkably similar to those of both older French Communist trade unionists and conventional French *bourgeois*: the students were spoilt kids who had everything, so why should they revolt in such a destructive manner? But, in behaviour typical of the Sixties generation, his father's admonishment only encouraged Kenzi to do the opposite, making friends with students distributing leaflets at the entrance to the shanty town: 'Here the student revolt had ripened a certain hope for change in the minds of young people.'[110] The similarities with French contemporaries are again striking. Arguably the young people of the Nanterre shanty town shared, if perhaps little else, with 'philosophy students building barricades on the Boulevard St Germain' and 'sullen youths playing pinball in provincial towns',[111] this 'certain hope for change'. Generational conflict could cut across lines of class and national origin.

Nevertheless, immigrant parents had an additional argument at their disposal – that the unrest was nothing to do with them because they were not French. This was shown in the experience of Houria: 'In 68, I wanted to go and demonstrate with my friends. My father said, "Do you really think you're at home in France? What has what's been going on here got to do with you?" And he gave me a slap.'[112] There was a clear difference in perspective between adults who had spent most of their lives in Algeria and adolescents who had come to France as very small children. For the parents, taboos about participation by non-citizens in politics were strong. The teenagers, by contrast, saw no reason not to have a say in the only society they knew. This was especially so if a political movement came along that was explicitly committed to the ending of such distinctions between citizens and non-citizens – distinctions which made little sense to those who had grown up in France. Nevertheless, parental influence on this issue was not easy to shake off: 'I soon faced the facts: no, I wasn't French.'[113]

In Nanterre, there was also approval for the students on the grounds that they had seen through the hypocrisy of French society. Benaïcha, for example, became friends with a group of students, whom he admired for their selfless devotion to him and his friends – they were taken on outings to the swimming pool and the cinema.[114] He felt they were motivated by their realisation of the flaws in French society. Their experience of the reality of Nanterre contrasted to what they had been taught about 'la Grande Nation': how could such a 'clean' society have such 'dirty feet' at the gates of its capital?[115] This group of students were, according to Benaïcha, popular in the shanty town, even among adults: 'Jean was welcomed as a liberator, like a highly popular head of state. If elections had been held here, he would have been elected with 100% of the vote.'[116] 'Mohammed' similarly had a political awakening as a result of contacts with the students in 1968, both in the 'transit camp' where he lived and in the university. For the first time he questioned why his family had to live in such poor conditions, and this made him consider that they should have equal rights to French people: 'What led me to this conclusion was in part having hung out at the university, with students and intellectuals.'[117]

The university campus also had its attractions from an apolitical point of view. It was a great playground, being the nearest large open space to the shanty town. The modern facilities in particular were a source of diversion, given the contrast with the desperate material conditions of the shanty town. Benaïcha, for example, stresses his amazement at seeing automatic drinks dispensers for the first time. This playground atmosphere was all the more so during the unrest of 1970. The narrator of *Du bidonville à l'expulsion*, who encountered VLR when they were called VLC, particularly enjoyed the provision by the *crèche sauvage* of free-for-all painting sessions for older children.[118]

The Algerian youths' awe at the wondrous facilities of the university is ironic in view of the fact that students and academics at Nanterre often complained that their concrete brutalist campus lacked the facilities open to their counterparts in the Latin Quarter: parks, shops, cafés, and so on.[119] The fact that the Nanterre students were in revolt despite the fact that they had a whole new campus provided for them prompted accusations of hypocrisy. This charge that the revolting students were just spoilt middle-class children of the welfare state was perhaps more prevalent among the older generation in the shanty town. According to *Un nom de papier*, Maoist students at Nanterre came to hand out potatoes in the shanty town, even though the residents had told them not to. The book describes the reaction:

Some, seeing the lorry came to buy, but when the 'Maos' said it was for free, they left again, furious. They knew that the students were running riot everywhere, that it was because of them that police controls were starting again like during the Algerian War.[120]

The diary of Monique Hervo, a Frenchwoman who had lived in the shanty town since 1959, confirms this incident, and dates it to 16 March 1968.[121] The Algerians did not want to be treated as charity cases. Nor did they welcome the increased police harassment that was a consequence of the student upheavals.

Yet some of the young Algerians, though far readier to flirt with *gauchisme* than their parents, also came to the conclusion that the students were hypocritical. For example, the narrator of *Du bidonville à l'expulsion*, together with a student, decided to let down the tyres of cars parked at the university, on the grounds that 'those who had a car were fascists'. In this account, the two of them were arrested together, but treated in a discriminatory manner: the narrator and not the student were beaten up by the police, and two of them were let out thanks only to a telephone call by the student to his father. The next day the narrator was shocked to see the student arrive at university in a car himself. Disillusioned by this experience, he vandalised the student's car and never came back to the university again.[122] For Benaïcha, his honeymoon period with the students had been ended by May '68. One day it was suddenly announced that the campus was burning and he and his friends could not understand:

> They've got everything and they aren't happy. They've got a swimming pool, a gym, a library (under construction) and even the freedom to live with their girlfriend. If with all that they're in revolt, it's because they've gone mad.[123]

For Bouamama, it was the telling details which convinced him to abandon Maoism:

> It was the university comrade who made the people at a meeting called at his home wait because he had not finished his dinner; it was the pre-prepared speech that a mumbling African friend was made to read, in the name of the expression of the oppressed; it was finally the appearance before a people's tribunal for having burnt the potatoes on a summer camp.[124]

Many of the youths were also bewildered by the students' penchant for the wooden language of ideological abstraction. The students would constantly use terms such as 'mao', 'facho' and 'réviso'[125] which meant little to anyone uninitiated to the different factions of student politics: 'The distinctions between Left, Right, far Left, far Right, Fascist, Revisionist, Marxist, Trotskyist, etc., totally escaped me. I was like a spectator who did not know the rules of the game.'[126] The ideological foibles of the students could even be a source of amusement:

> In the lecture theatre sometimes I yelled to amuse myself: for Mao, Lenin, Stalin and Trotsky, the students had unbelievable susceptabilities! We couldn't care less about these big famous guys. Our problem was more those cops that went past like mushrooms with their big round helmets.[127]

The narrator of this extract, who was excited enough by May '68 to help in the ripping up of paving stones to build barricades in Paris, was nevertheless unmotivated by the grand abstractions of the students. He even admits to having taken advantage of the confusion caused by demonstrations to steal things from shops – though he only did this after seeing some well-dressed men do the same.[128]

In *Le sourire de Brahim*, the eponymous hero takes part in one of the more orderly marches of May '68. Though impressed by the size of the social movement he sees around him, which is described as 'joyful masses', Brahim is slightly put off by the sameness of the slogans chanted and worried about his parents' reaction to his being out late. Also it is someone external to the immigrant community – his French friend Roland – who tries to give the march an air of grand historical significance, to which Brahim is comparatively indifferent:

> He had just lived without knowing it through a grandiose moment of history. Hadn't Roland said to him before leaving him: 'What do you want my brother, that's life. You'll see later, like others say I did 1914-1918, you'll be able to say, "Me, sir, I did '68".'[129]

Kenzi became similarly sceptical as a result of his activity in the Comité Palestine in Nanterre. Although he felt this issue brought him back to his roots, Kenzi was critical of Gilbert Mury, who he met through the committee. Though committed to the cause, Mury was, Kenzi suspected, after power for himself. Moreover, Kenzi suggested, Mury was too obsessed with Palestine, to the detriment of campaigns for better conditions for immigrants in France.[130] Chatwin encountered a similar view in Marseilles:

> Another source of trouble comes from the Maoist or Trotskyite
> Left: students and staff from the universities, who use Algerian
> immigrants as shock-troops in their confrontations with the
> Right. From time to time they pour into the Algerian quarters
> and smear them with revolutionary graffiti. The sex-starved boys
> get all worked up over the girls, and follow them to political
> meetings they know nothing about. But the Leftists are a broken
> reed when things go wrong – and it is the Algerians who get hurt.
> The vehemence of one Algerian social worker amazed me: '*Cette
> cochonerie de la Gauche*!' he sneered. 'Chile! Chile! ... Always
> Chile! And when our people get killed they run like mice for their
> holes.'[131]

On the other hand, the intellectualism of the New Left could attract as
well as repel. For Houari, who as his autobiography makes clear, had great
respect for Western high culture, one point of entry into this world was
the New Left. For example, he often went with his student friends to plays
by Bertold Brecht. That he received his education from this source had
interesting consequences. When working as a porter delivering laundry to
the Jussieu science faculty in Paris, he asked a young woman looking in a
microscope what there was of interest in it; she replied that she was looking
at a cell. Houari did not understand this, for he had only previously heard
the word 'cell' used by his comrades in its political sense as a tightly-knit
local branch of a revolutionary party.[132]

Nevertheless, Houari did not passively accept what his *gauchiste* friends
told him. For example, they did not discuss religion, as they took it for
granted that atheism was so obviously correct it did not need to be stated.
By contrast, for Houari, atheism was a new idea, and he only became a
convert to it after discussing science, and in the light of the culture of his
own background: he opposed the Kabyle proverb 'tomorrow is death'
to the Islamic notion that the only true happiness is in paradise. He was
also critical of the *gauchistes*' belief in the superiority of manual work to
intellectual work. As a manual worker himself, who would have liked to
have been an intellectual, he felt quite the opposite – that the amount of
manual work should be radically reduced.[133]

These various ways in which second generation youths felt misunderstood
by the New Left were, however, arguably as much a matter of class as of
national or cultural difference. After all, they perceived the Algerian

community's own equivalent of *gauchistes* in much the same light. The Parti de la Révolution Socialiste (PRS), an opposition movement led by the future President Mohammed Boudiaf, was at this time based among a group of political exiles in France. Houari joined the PRS after he drifted away from the French *gauchistes*. His view of the former was similar to his view of the latter: he admired the PRS intellectuals for their modest, generous, self-sacrificing nature and their vision of a just society, but felt them to be somewhat out of touch with reality: they were not interested in the situation in France, and being exiles were cut off from life in Algeria.[134] Or, more succinctly, the ambivalence towards student leftists could be compared with the young Southern Italian migrant to Turin, who, on receiving an invitation to meet with students, declared: 'What the fuck, I've got nothing to lose, I'll go and see what these turds have to say.'[135]

Despite the initial disappointments and dashed hopes, then, 1968 was a pivotal moment in the history of anti-racism in France. The years immediately after saw repeated attempts to run with the issue of immigration. In this respect May-June 1968 was not an isolated outbreak but, as the slogan put it, 'only a beginning'. From well-known intellectuals in the Latin Quarter to VLR in Nanterre, there were *gauchistes* committed to improving the lives of immigrants at a time when few other forces in French society were aware of them. They were willing to do this in deed (witness the *crèche sauvage*) as well as word, and in their own locality, even when – perhaps especially when – the authorities tried to obstruct these initiatives and other sections of the public were hostile. There was also a continuity between 1968 and 1971 in terms of prevailing ideological attitudes. This was still a world in which class, imperialism and the politicisation of everyday life mattered more than latter-day obsessions such as 'integration' or the 'right to be different'.

The clear generational divide that emerges from the autobiographical narratives shows that there is some truth to the idea that the generation who came to France in the 1960s were less willing to act politically than their children. But contrary to the conventional notion that the 'second generation' became politicised only with the Beur movements of the early 1980s, here I have suggested a different chronology. The 'second generation' had in many cases already been exposed as adolescents to leftist political movements, of both French and Maghrebi origin, a decade or more earlier. 1968-era *gauchisme* was Janus-faced: though in many respects ideologically backward-looking, we can also identify within its penchant for immigrants the pre-history of the anti-racist movements of the 1980s and beyond. Already by the early 1970s the failure of a wider revolution to materialise was giving rise to a recognition – in practice at least, more grudgingly in theory – that there was not the 'only one working class' that had been proclaimed in 1968.

Yet the association between immigrants and the New Left was ambiguous. The relationship between middle class *gauchistes* and working-class immigrants was often deeply paternalistic and patronising in practice. The New Left's intellectualism could repel the very people it aimed to attract. The young people of the shanty towns, who were with the New Left in their spirit of revolt, were easily disillusioned, because of the contrast between the social worlds of shanty town and university. The New Left certainly had internationalist ideals. But the rhetoric of solidarity did not always translate into a lived experience of solidarity on the ground. We will now see how frustration with these methods gave rise to initiatives for autonomy within immigrant communities, after hunger strikes broke out in 1972.

Chapter Four

The Birth of an Autonomous Movement, 1971-1973

'We came to France as free men to enjoy our rights
and not to suffer racist injustice, scorn and discrimination.'
Hunger strikers in La Ciotat, 1973[1]

Outside an otherwise unremarkable block of flats, but in a remarkable area of Paris, there stands today at number 53, rue de la Goutte d'Or, a plaque marking an emblematic moment in the history of antiracism in France:

INNOCENT, THEY DIED VICTIMS
OF RACISM AND INTOLERANCE

The plaque is in memory of a 15 year old Algerian boy, Djellali Ben Ali, who on 27 October 1971 was shot dead by Daniel Pigot, the husband of the concierge of the block. The crime was to rapidly become a *cause célèbre*, which would split the local community, mobilise some of France's best-known intellectuals, and open up a whole cycle of immigrant activism over the ensuing years. We have seen how immigration had already been established as a major theme of contestation by a confident, if fringe, element of the French Left. But their efforts were sometimes perceived as external meddling even by the younger generation within immigrant communities sympathetic to ideas of revolt. The significant change was that after Djellali Ben Ali's murder, this fertile but problematic alliance developed and matured, from actions on behalf of immigrants to actions by immigrants themselves, and from spectacular individual raids to popular mobilisations. Rather than a simple two-sided interaction between 'immigrants' and 'intellectuals', the group dynamics involved a more complex relationship between four groups, at least one of which overlapped this boundary. Moving from those with most to least power (or 'cultural capital'[2]) the movement by the mid-1970s included Intellectuals with a capital 'I' like Michel Foucault and Jean-Paul Sartre; the younger generation of French Maoists who had some access to the Intellectuals; a group of marginal students and ex-students from North Africa who would form the principal cadres of the Mouvement des Travailleurs Arabes, the most important immigrant political group of the period; and immigrant workers themselves. In the course of this chapter, we will survey this movement at its height, and examine the difficulty of creating solidarities between it and French workers.

To understand the movement, we must not only consider those who were both immigrants and intellectuals, but also look both outside and inside the borders of France. We have already seen how political actions by foreigners were often orientated towards international issues. The next major development, though, would be for this to feed into the politics of immigration within France, as encounters via the world of pro-Palestinian activism led to interest among both French and Maghrebi intellectuals in the situation of immigrant workers.[3] The Palestine issue was particularly worrying for the authorities because, since Black September, it had mobilised Arab workers as well as intellectuals, notably in the classic and emblematic area of La Goutte d'Or in northern Paris. In contrast to today's identification of immigrant issues with the high-rise *banlieue*, the main geographical focus then was the inner city areas typified by La Goutte d'Or. This area of the 18th arrondissement, also sometimes known as Barbès after the main avenue adjoining it, had played a key role in the Algerian independence struggle of a decade earlier.[4] La Goutte d'Or had a significance well beyond its own 6,000-strong North African community, as a focal point for weekend socialisation and shopping for as many as 15,000 people from across the Paris region: it was probably the most important meeting point for Algerians in France. As the unofficial capital of North African France, agitators of all sorts saw the streets of La Goutte d'Or as fertile terrain for political militancy.[5] Through recruitment there, the Arab Left in France took on a more proletarian ambience than had hitherto been the case: 'Simply, the workers had got into the habit of coming to see us, to talk, to participate in our activities, and even to become an integral part of the life of the movement.'[6]

Above all, it was this worker involvement that was to lead the Comité Palestine activists away from exclusive concentration on Palestine and towards mobilisation on the condition of Arab workers in France. For as the activists soon came to recognise, the workers had more immediately pressing problems in their lives: 'One cannot ask a worker who is afraid of getting killed just going home in the evening to fight for the Palestinian Resistance.'[7] Thus – in contrast to other groups of North African exiles who remained more concerned with the situation in the Arab world – the group of activists who would form the Mouvement des Travailleurs Arabes (MTA) made a conscious decision to reorientate themselves towards the problems of immigrant workers in France. Saïd Bouziri, for example, had already made this decision by the end of 1968, asking 'Are we here to change things over there ... Or are we here to change things where we are?'[8] The activists realised that unless they dealt with issues within the immediate experience of immigrants, like racism and discrimination, they would soon become irrelevant. Palestine still remained important to these activists – the struggles of North African workers continued to be rhetorically identified with those of the Palestinians[9] – but more as a symbolic reference point: the day-to-day focus of activity was now on immigration.[10]

First Encounters: The Ben Ali Affair

By 1971, then, there was already a significant politicisation of North African workers, but the wider public were not necessarily aware of it. What publicised this movement for French eyes were two major *affaires*, the Ben Ali affair of autumn 1971 and the Bouziri affair of autumn 1972. The murder of Djellali Ben Ali, midway between the massacre of 17 October 1961 and the Left's victory of 1981, was a revealing moment in the social history of Paris. Its protagonists were a microcosm in one appartment block of many of the social issues of modern France, from poverty and overcrowded housing to divisions within the working class. The ill-fated Djellali's father worked nights as a labourer building the RER rapid transit system that now carries travellers across Paris. Djellali, who suffered from epilepsy and had previously been in trouble for minor delinquency, lived with his uncle and aunt at 53, rue de la Goutte d'Or because there was no space with his family, who were living nine to a room in a nearby street. Djellali's killer, Daniel Pigot, was known for making racist remarks about Arabs. He had often argued with, and threatened with a gun, Djellali's aunt and uncle, who ran an oriental silk shop in the neighbourhood.[11]

As Djellali was leaving the flat that October morning, Pigot shot him in the back. Militants from the Comités Palestine and the Secours Rouge, suspecting intuitively, but unlike other observers, that this was racially motivated, not simply a dispute between neighbours, immediately mobilised in protest. On 30 October, a demonstration was forcibly dispersed by police. The next week, on 7 November, there was a rally of at least 2000 – some claimed as many as 4000 – local inhabitants and French and North African militants. The police also mobilised *en masse*, with *Le Nouvel Observateur* describing scenes of 'a frightening police cordon, which had never been seen here since the Algerian war'. Some media attention was attracted by the court appearance of the singer Dominique Grange for allegedly throwing a bucket of wallpaper paste at the police on the demonstration. Grange, known for her recording of the Maoist anthem *Les Nouveaux Partisans*, shocked the court – including North African defendants – by making a political speech about racism. Grange spoke of the insults that immigrants suffered, about reports of bodies of North Africans being found in Parisian canals, about a workplace death at Renault, and related that at the police station she was asked, 'So, you are being the whore for the *bougnoules*' (racist slang for North Africans). By 27 November, a Comité Djellali had been formed. This was the first sustained encounter between the four groups identified above: the big Intellectuals, the young French Maoists, the North African / Middle Eastern students, and the workers themselves. All the 'usual suspects' were out in force: a star-studded list of writers joined the committee, including Jean-Paul Sartre, Michel Foucault, Jean Genet and Gilles Deleuze. In fact, that first meeting of the Comité Djellali was the very first time that Sartre and Foucault had spoken to each other. Both of these intellectual celebrities were themselves to speak through megaphones in the street during the course of the affair. But equally, the Djellali campaign relied on the efforts of French Maoist activists and marginal intellectuals from the Maghreb like Saïd Bouziri, as well as the North African population of the Goutte d'Or itself, especially teenagers. Further meetings brought the different sides together, and the committee ran campaigns on issues like local housing conditions.[12]

Nevertheless, the intellectuals were outsiders in the Goutte d'Or, an area of extreme poverty – as late as 1990 40 per cent of households did not even have a toilet – where the middle classes did not live.[13] As the journalist Fausto Giudice notes, it is rather ironic that the two main published first-hand accounts of the Ben Ali affair are by Claude Mauriac, the Gaullist and deeply bourgeois son of the writer François Mauriac, and Catherine von Bülow, the daughter of an aristocratic Prussian army officer and former dancer at the New York Metropolitan Opera, who took Djellali Ben Ali's sister Fazia under her wing. Mauriac, rapidly shifting leftwards, was director of the new *Libération* press agency, ancestor of the daily newspaper of the same name. His diaries for the period, published as *Et comme l'espérance est violente* ['And How Hope Is Violent'] makes for rather contrasting reading. For the first half of the book, Mauriac hobnobs with de Gaulle and his Minister of Culture André Malraux, then almost overnight he is plunged from the top to the bottom of society in the Goutte d'Or. *Et comme l'espérance est violente* shows how the leading intellectuals associated with the affair seem to have wandered into it almost by accident. The first time that they set foot in the Goutte d'Or was in June 1971 as a by-product of the Alain Jaubert affair.[14] An Algerian living in the Goutte d'Or, whose name is not recorded, was the main witness to the police beating of Jaubert. Foucault and Mauriac were therefore dispatched to the Goutte d'Or by the Comité Jaubert to interview the witness. Mauriac's description of this underlined the huge social gulf: even to mix with assorted young French leftists on the committee was a big step down socially for him: 'I suddenly had the impression ... that I had passed onto the other side of the curtain which in our society separates those for whom the State acts – and the others.'[15] There is then a rather Orientalist moment when Mauriac and Foucault, expecting a place of mystery and danger, are surprised to find that the streets of Barbès are similar to any French boulevard: 'Not the Medina that Foucault was waiting for, he said ... but calm, spaced out, provincial streets.'[16] Anticlimactically, the Algerian failed to turn up due to a train strike. But the meeting having been rearranged for the following day, Mauriac could not quite believe his informant, when he said that three corpses had been found in the Canal Saint-Martin, and two or three Algerians deliberately run over on pavements. There was a gulf in comprehension to overcome between North Africans' lived experience of violent racism, where rumours like that would be believed, and the little idea that those living in bourgeois areas of Paris had about such matters. Nevertheless, in November during the Ben Ali affair, Mauriac went round from café to café with an Arabic-speaking comrade to announce the opening of a drop-in centre to 'listen, intervene and prevent if necessary'. Mauriac's feelings are expressed thus: 'Sudden plunge into another world. Brutal and total transformation into a militant among militants – with this impression of fraternity.'[17] Unlike Jean Genet, who had been a homeless petty criminal before becoming a writer, Mauriac shows signs of being somewhat out of his depth in a rough proletarian environment, nervously noting 'a (European) garage mechanic observing me with defiance' as he visited the victim's apartment block. Mauriac also found himself in a difficult position being surrounded by pro-Palestinian activists, as his own sympathies were pro-Israeli (again unlike Genet, who had recently returned from a Palestinian refugee camp).[18]

One Saturday Sartre himself stepped out of a Citroën 2CV into an Algerian café, accompanied by one Algerian and six or seven Secours Rouge militants, to announce the opening of the drop-in centre. However, the centre, offering legal assistance and help filling in forms, was not, it would appear, a success with the local population. Though for a while the intellectuals continued to come to the area to socialise with local activists, the committee itself was short-lived, with tensions emerging between different agendas. Foucault, for example worried that Sartre was taking it over. Networks associated with the Algerian state, like the Amicale des Algériens en Europe, resisted the committees' challenge to their authority – strong given the Goutte d'Or's past as a centre of FLN networks – by reasserting control. Three 13-year-old Algerians denounced the committee and the Maoists at a meeting on 26 December, for producing leaflets instead of the promised revenge for Djellali. In January 1972, embarrassment was caused to the campaign when youths associated with it smashed the windows of a hotel. By February 1972, intellectuals had moved on to the next big 'cause', namely prisons, and it could be argued that the most lasting relationship formed was between themselves – Mauriac went on to smoke a joint with Foucault – rather than with the inhabitants of the Goutte d'Or. By the time Djellali's murderer was finally brought to justice in 1977, Giudice suggests, immigrants were no longer the latest fashionable cause. Foucault was too busy arranging a reception for Soviet dissidents to even turn up to court.[19]

Giudice's charge is not one hundred per cent correct. Several of the Comité Djellali intellectuals were arrested on a demonstration about another racist murder in November 1972; Foucault and Mauriac were at the front of a march against immigration controls in March 1973; and as late as 1984, the two intervened on the issue of housing evictions in the Goutte d'Or.[20] But it has an element of truth to it. The commitment of the French leftists to the Goutte d'Or was also questioned by Ben Ali's sister, Fazia Ben Ali, who wondered:

> It was all very well to denounce racist crimes, but when you started to denounce the housing and the filth in the neighbourhood, I asked myself "Why have they only noticed this now" ... I felt that you had only come when there was something important and spectacular, like my brother's death.[21]

Such a judgement reflected the sense of unfamiliarity felt on both sides in this encounter between different worlds – summed up by one incident in which Mauriac and his fellow activists were mistaken for policemen by a young North African they had come to visit.[22] The French militants Fazia encountered dressed differently, travelled differently (by car), and had different expectations of what constituted normality: 'I remember that as soon as one of them came to our home, he immediately said '"Good God, it's not possible to live like that, ten to a room!" OK, for *you*, it wasn't possible, but we had always lived like that.' Until the affair, Fazia stated that she had no idea what a 'militant' was, associating those who came to intervene about her brothers' death with the hippies she sometimes heard strumming guitars outside the Sacré Coeur.[23]

Fazia was not alone in her suspicions. The charge that *gauchistes* used immigrants to score cheap political points was also made by older established anti-racist organisations like the MRAP.[24] As was suggested by the autobiographies we saw in Chapter Three, class was the major barrier to uniting immigrants and intellectuals. Another group of Arab intellectuals, grouped around the newspaper *Al Kadihoun* ['The Worker'] had the same problem. *Al Kadihoun* appears to have foundered on a communication failure between the haute-Marxist theorising of its originators, who had a propensity for wordy articles replete with footnotes and political jargon, and its intended worker audience. As they admitted in one editorial: 'Arab workers (like most other workers) don't like reading and aren't used to pouring over texts.'[25] Similarly, the British anthropologist Ralph Grillo found that North African students giving literacy lessons in Lyons were 'viewed with suspicion bordering on resentment by the mass of ordinary immigrants'.[26] Attempts by North African activists to start Arabic literacy classes for the children of the Goutte d'Or during the Ben Ali affair appear to have been similarly unsuccessful.[27]

Conversely, North African intellectuals involved in Seventies politics were often clearly on the same wavelength as the French intellectuals, in a way that working class immigrants often were not. Saïd Bouziri had nothing but praise for Sartre, Foucault and Mauriac, who he described as 'a very great friend'. Indeed, for Bouziri, the Intellectuals represented a vital link between the immigration movements and French public opinion. Without them, mobilisations might have gone unnoticed; with them doors were opened to mainstream opinion. Bouziri considered this link important, because he did not want immigrants either to remain in their own ghetto, or to have their links to French society confined only to the far Left fringe of that society. Nevertheless, the French far Left themselves were important intermediaries between immigrants and the big-name Intellectuals: without this link, Bouziri questioned whether the likes of Sartre would have become involved.[28]

Inventing the *Sans-Papiers* Tradition:
The Bouziri Affair and the Hunger Strikes of 1972-1973

Which brings us to the second major turning point of immigrant mobilisation: the adoption of a new tactic, the hunger strike. Saïd Bouziri's was not strictly speaking the first immigrant's hunger strike – there are others recorded in Lille and Marseilles in 1971, as well as that of the Tunisian

Sadok Djeridi in Amiens in April 1972.[29] But it was probably the single most influential one. Faouzia and Saïd Bouziri were important figures in campaigns with both French and Arab militants, having been involved in all the key events from the Comités Palestine through to the Djellali affair. So when, on 26 October 1972, the couple went to renew their residency permits as usual, only to be told that they should have done so sooner and were therefore being expelled from France, the authorities got more than they bargained for. The couple suspected, plausibly enough given Raymond Marcellin's track record on deporting political activists,[30] that the real reason for their expulsions was political. On 6 November Saïd Bouziri began a hunger strike. Faouzia Bouziri, however, did not join him in this, since she was six months pregnant. The Bouziris' decision needs to be viewed in the context of the legal situation of foreigners at the time: essentially any 'normal' political activity such as going on demonstrations was illegal, and also of the new forms of direct action adopted more generally since 1968. Saïd Bouziri chose to go on hunger strike because he considered it unlikely that he would otherwise be able to mobilise enough people in time to stop his expulsion – on 3 November, he had been given ten days to leave the country – and because of his personal belief in non-violent action. He went underground to avoid arrest, a more public hunger strike was carried out by a small group of Tunisian and French supporters, and a support committee was rapidly set in motion, attracting prominent figures on the Left like the writers Daniel Guérin and Gilles Deleuze. Sartre, Foucault and Mauriac all came to visit Saïd Bouziri. Nearly a thousand people signed a petition, in which seven public figures, Sartre and Foucault amongst them, declared themselves publicly responsible for the maintenance in France of the Bouziris, while a demonstration was held on 19 November. Meanwhile, the Interior Ministry appeared to change its story, by confirming in a press release that the Bouziris' expulsion was indeed for failing to obey the rule of political neutrality. It listed a number of demonstrations and meetings between 1970 and 1972 at which one or the other had been questioned by police, and alleged that Faouzia Bouziri had previously been issued with an expulsion order for her part in an occupation of the Tunisian hall at the Cité Universitaire in February 1972. Yet ultimately the strike was a success. The same day that two thousand people turned out for a demonstration in support of the Bouziris, the police offered them a 15 day authorisation to stay in France. Despite what might appear the miserly nature of the offer – astonishingly, they were made to renew their papers every 15 (or later 30) days for a whole decade until the return of the Left to power in 1981 – they decided to accept, and called off the hunger strike.[31]

Why, then, was this strike remembered when others were not? First, because it was successful. Expulsions were two a penny: they were running at over 3000 a year at this time, and the majority did not arouse any serious protest. For the Bouziris to fight and win was a remarkable breakthrough for the emerging politics of direct action. It was not the only successful example: Sadok Djeridi also won his campaign, after mobilising a thousand demonstrators in his support,[32] but it was a relatively rare one. Secondly, because Saïd Bouziri's hunger strike took place in the Goutte d'Or. This neighbourhood was a 'place of resistance', as he put it when, 32 years later, I interviewed him there at his home on Boulevard Barbès. Mobilisations of immigrant workers had historic local precedents, and a heavily populated area could be quickly covered with leaflets and posters.[33] Bouziri was part of a group of militants who had formed the MTA – probably at a conference held on 17 and 18 June 1972[34] – whose activities were centred on the Goutte d'Or. Thirdly and consequently, it involved the right people in the right place at the right time to attract the attention and support of big-name Intellectuals, whom the Bouziris already knew from the Ben Ali affair. Most immigrants facing expulsion were not political militants and could not draw upon such prominent French supporters. Indeed, as unlikely a figure as a Gaullist member of parliament, Louis Terrenoire, spoke up on their behalf, on the grounds that they were only being expelled for their pro-Palestinian sympathies.[35] (It could not necessarily have been predicted in 1972 that in November 2004, my interview with Saïd Bouziri would take place while Faouzia Bouziri attended a vigil outside a military hospital on the other side of Paris, where the Palestinian President Yasser Arafat lay dying as an honoured guest of the French state).

But above all, the importance of this moment also lay in the way that hunger strikes suddenly caught on to become a national phenomenon. This was because it happened to coincide with new government attempts to restrict immigrants' rights. The Bouziris' support committee, which soon changed its name to the Comité de Défense de la Vie et des Droits des Travailleurs Immigrés (CDVDTI), was to support some 29 further hunger strikes in protest against the so-called Marcellin-Fontanet decrees. The decrees made the situation of existing immigrants much less secure, by merging the procedures for obtaining residency and work permits, thus making the residency permit dependent on having a job contract and housing certificate approved by an employer. The *carte de séjour* has totemic status among foreigners in France – one 1980s rock group named themselves after it – since without it, nothing is possible. Significantly, the decrees made it impossible for immigrants to retrospectively regularise their situation, the normal procedure prior to this point, thus severely disrupting habitual patterns of migration and inventing a hitherto unknown bureaucratic category of *clandestin* ('illegal immigrant'). They also meant that if an employer did not renew a worker's contract, their residency permit became invalid and they could not claim unemployment benefit. Leftists suspected that, by making the right to stay in France effectively dependent on the goodwill of a single employer, and by conveniently bringing together all the paperwork on an individual into a single file in their local police station, the decrees were deliberately designed as 'a drastic attempt to nip in the bud the rudimentary immigrant workers movement'[36] – to be replaced with fresh and not yet politicised recruits directly from abroad. During the summer of 1972, there had been some activity in far Left circles around the decrees. It was, however, only when they entered into force in the autumn, provoking pressing fear on the part of many concerning their future in France – and when Saïd Bouziri had demonstrated the possibilities of a hunger strike tactic – that mass action erupted. Activists working against the circulars went to visit Bouziri during his strike, and after it ended, presented his as a great victory to their contacts elsewhere.

Rabah Saïdani, a Tunisian worker who had joined Bouziri in his hunger strike in Paris, returned to the Provencal town of Valence where he lived, and began with seventeen other Tunisians the first hunger strike against the Marcellin-Fontanet decrees. The Valence strike was very successful in attracting publicity to the issue, becoming one of the first occasions on which immigration was front page news. By March 1973, hunger strikes were taking place in most major cities, mostly by Tunisians, but sometimes also by Moroccans, Portuguese or French supporters. While Bouziri was keen to caution would-be hunger strikers that it was not easy, earlier hunger strikers like him were able to give tactical advice to those who had decided to take this 'politically courageous' step. The numbers involved in each individual strike grew – 68 in Toulouse, for example. Many more became actively involved in support. In Marseille, 24 North African hunger strikers were supported by some hundreds mobilising on a regular basis and up to two thousand on one demonstration through the city centre. By April, the different hunger strikers from across the country had met in a Lyons suburb to form a national coordinating body. The strikes were increasingly proactive rather than reactive, public rather than private, the tactics ever more bold and contestatory. A group of 56 hunger strikers in Ménilmontant in eastern Paris staged an occupation of government employment offices.[37]

One declaration by hunger strikers in the Mediterranean town of La Ciotat is worth extensive quotation, since it illustrates in dramatic fashion the issues at stake:

> We are workers in La Ciotat. We have been on hunger strike. So why?
>
> You know, brother worker, that our life was not secure; we have no rights. If something happened to us, an accident at work for example, the boss sacks us and doesn't want to know. He says 'Get lost or I'm calling the police'. Naturally, the worker is scared, he leaves and abandons his rights. Why? Because he hasn't got his papers in order.
>
> Why, brother Arabs? Until when will we remain silent? You came to France to work. You earn a crust thanks to your arms, to your sweat. You came to France as a worker and not as a tourist. Don't believe you are a tourist, this is propaganda. Tourists don't live in dirt like us: they don't live in cardboard shacks; they stay in hotels.
>
> Brother Arab worker, think carefully! You work without papers, your life is in danger, you do the most dangerous and difficult work for the lowest wages. Don't forget that. Wake up and claim your rights. Arab unity is with you and at your service. Speak and demand what is owed to you, all Arabs will be with you. We came to France as free men to enjoy our rights and not to suffer racist injustice, scorn and discrimination.[38]

The hunger strikers thus claimed their rights as workers, not as 'guests'. They were eventually successful in achieving their own regularisation, and that of 35,000 others, and a watering down – though not complete withdrawal – of the governments' proposals. This was therefore a crucial point in the development of an autonomous immigrant workers' movement. It was in fact the first movement of *sans-papiers* ['without papers']. The phrase came into existence during the strike, to designate a movement which, adopted by successive waves of new arrivals, was to sustain itself into the twenty-first century. The form of action that Bouziri and others initiated has been copied ever since by immigrants confronting expulsion with their own self-organised activity, often supported in the background by early pioneers like Bouziri. Throughout the 1970s, immigrants in industrial disputes ranging from seasonal agricultural workers in the Midi to workers in sweet factories adopted the hunger strike tactic.[39]

It was no coincidence that both Bouziri and the Valence strikers were Tunisian. First, because of French prejudices, North Africans were the prime targets for arrest and deportation, while Tunisians (and Moroccans) lacked the special status of Algerians under bilateral agreements that protected them from the worst impact of the Marcellin-Fontanet decrees. Secondly, Tunisian migration to France was a recent phenomenon of the post-colonial period that included many educated urban young people from Tunis. In a country sometimes referred to as the 'Latin Quarter of the Maghreb',[40] these were precisely the people most obviously receptive to the ideas of May '68, especially since Tunis itself had a major student movement (which Foucault had supported as a visiting professor). Indeed, during the summer of 1973 the Tunisian government went as far as to organise a major publicity campaign, warning emigrants who had returned for the summer against 'the ravages of contestation' in France.[41]

Setting a pattern for the future, many of the hunger strikes took place in churches with the support of Christians, who alongside the far Left represented the second principal ally of immigrants. Although the church was initially reluctant to let their premises be used, Saïd Bouziri carried out the latter part of his hunger strike in an annexe of the Saint-Bernard church – the same church famously raided by riot police during a later *sans-papiers* movement in 1996. Bouziri later described the Abbé Gallimardet, one of the Saint-Bernard priests, as 'the soul' of the *sans-papiers* movement. Gallimardet, a founder member of the Comité Djellali, had played an important part in the Djellali affair, by allowing the church annexe to be used for the drop-in centre. As the treasurer of the CDVDTI and a fellow-traveller of the MTA, 'Galli' was by all accounts a popular figure in Barbès, overcoming the traditional suspicion of French priests amongst Muslim immigrants. Meanwhile the pregnant Faouzia Bouziri was looked after by a group of nuns, who had originally come to the Goutte d'Or for missionary work with prostitutes and who had started a newsletter detailing local people's experience of poverty. The Valence hunger strikers, also in a church, were supported by four priests who refused to celebrate Midnight Mass in protest, attracting considerable publicity over Christmas. By the spring, even most bishops and archbishops came out in support of the movement, a measure of how far the post-Vatican II Church had travelled from its traditional association with the most reactionary elements in French society. Although churches had been occupied before (the Sacré Coeur by Maoists in February 1971 for example) the *sans-papiers* movement was the first time this had happened with the approval of the ecclesiastical authorities, rather than to denounce their complicity with capitalism. Although priests occasionally worried that they and the immigrants had become pawns in a game of chess played by the *gauchistes*, the church link was an important means of broadening support for the immigrant movement beyond the far Left alone, and invaluable practically in providing physical spaces to hide from the authorities.[42]

Nevertheless, the predominant organising force of the movement was immigrant-led. Certainly it was organisationally sheltered by French activists and intellectuals in the CDVDTI, including Maoists, Christians, and supporters of the Parti Socialiste Unifié (PSU). At the height of the movement, on 31 March 1973, the CDVDTI organised a march in Belleville of some three thousand people from across France. But behind the CDVDTI usually lay the now expanding MTA. As the movement developed, MTA activists who had been on hunger strike themselves were able to pass on their experience and advice. Saïd Bouziri was present, for example, in May 1973 with Tunisians on hunger strikes in the crypt of a church in Ménilmontant; one witness considers, not surprisingly, that he was already a leader of the movement. Ménilmontant was the occasion for innovative tactics, the strikers drawing attention to their hunger strike by the ironic gesture of leafleting cinema-goers who had just seen the film *La Grande Bouffe* ['Blow-Out'] in which people die from over-eating. As the Valence strike indicated, the MTA was not confined to Paris, but was putting down roots in the South of France. Though there was some traffic between them, two distinct centres of MTA activism emerged: one in Paris and another in Aix-en-Provence and nearby Marseilles. The hunger strike in Aix was led by the MTA activist Driss El Yazami, following a movement there in spring 1972 among Arab workers against overcrowded hostel conditions. The MTA was by now producing a regular newspaper, *Al Assifa* ['The Storm'], which Foucault agreed to act as nominal director of publication for – although at first he considered Sartre would be more suitable for this role.[43]

French and Immigrant Workers, United? Problems of the Movement

Yet too triumphalist a view of the immigrant movement of the 1970s would be misleading. Above all, questions might be asked about representation. As Alana Lentin puts it in relation to more recent antiracism, 'Who Says What, for Whom and From Where?'.[44] The general tendency of French organisations to paternalism was labelled as 'the 1973 version of the Colonial Exhibition' (of 1931).[45] The Fédération des Associations de Solidarité avec les Travailleurs Immigrés (FASTI), for example, revealingly defined its role as being 'to be the spokesperson for immigrants where they cannot yet express themselves'.[46] One Portuguese researcher studying Portuguese migrant workers in the southern Paris suburb of Orsay, found that the local ASTI branch could be somewhat patronising, and interpret the economic behaviour of the Portuguese incorrectly. Their extremely frugal living conditions, which ASTI members attributed to poverty and ignorance, were actually caused by saving to build houses in Portugal.[47]

Such continued paternalism reflected a certain continued dependence of the movement on French allies, given the high vulnerability of foreign activists to repression and deportation. In July 1973, Mohammed Selim Najeh, a former Paris street-sweeper, general secretary of the CDVDTI, and one of Bouziri's main supporters in his hunger strike, was himself expelled. During the Bouziri affair, Najeh claimed he had been paraded by police around the Goutte d'Or, handcuffed and at gunpoint. Other political expulsions of that year included a Syrian CNRS researcher involved in pro-Palestinian activism and resistance to the demolition of shanty towns in Marseilles, an Algerian worker found in possession of Maoist newspapers, and a Tunisian student accused of supporting Arab workers' struggles in Toulouse. Even Europeans were not exempt from this risk: in September 1973, Andrew Parker, a British priest, was expelled for his work with immigrants, as also was Berthier Perregaux, a Swiss Protestant pastor who had played an important role in hunger strikes and literacy campaigns in Marseilles.[48]

There were also splits over tactics. The CDVDTI faced criticisms from a rival group, the Comité Unitaire Français Immigrés (CUFI), based in the 13th arrondissement of Paris. The CDVDTI-led movement was portrayed as too groupuscular, taking too many risks and, because based around human rights rather than class struggle, over-reliant on the support of French intellectuals, 'progressives' and students as opposed to workers. As one leaflet put it: 'This type of small-group, spectacular action, without mass support behind it, not only exposes immigrant workers to repression but cuts them off even more from French workers.'[49] Critics also raised the problem that the collective purpose of the hunger strikes – to change government policy – could be lost in the individual hunger striker's personal aim – to stay in France. The day after the Belleville demonstration of 31 March 1973, fighting broke out between two rival factions of Tunisians at a CDVDTI-organised conference at the Mutualité, one supporting the 'humanitarian' line and one the 'class struggle' line. The undoubted growth of pro-immigrant activism among French militants concealed a more fundamental problem. While effective on one level, the sans-papiers hunger strikes did not, the sociologist Manuel Castells suggested, create either a mass movement or real unity with the labour movement beyond slogans. He was not the only contemporary sympathetic to the movement who asked whether the hunger strike tactic was a sign of weakness rather than success. Was the movement overly dependent on alliances with the French middle classes, cut off from the organised working class, too individualistic in its immediate goals, even irresponsible in dangers it exposed immigrants to? Certainly French supporters were often middle class: in Grenoble, a Comité de Vigilance Anti-Raciste was formed, but it was entirely composed of lecturers, an administrator and a chaplain at the local university.[50] This implied that outcomes would be highly variable, depending on the distribution of the 'right sort' of left-wing intellectual. The historian Ed Naylor suggests that anti-racist protests in Marseilles had considerably less impact on public opinion than high-profile Parisian events like the Ben Ali affair.[51]

Looking back on this period, it is worth asking whether it marked the beginning of a trend that has continued ever since, in which the middle-class antiracist Left forged links with ethnic minorities, but thereby undermined its relationship with French workers. Was this a turning point in a long term shift among leftist intellectuals from seeing their role as to serve the French proletariat – the classic position of 'we must not make Billancourt despair' – to seeing their role as to serve immigrants? Did the CDVDTI anticipate the politics of human rights that later became highly fashionable in France as a replacement for Marxism?[52] For Saïd Bouziri, the intellectuals were a key link making the immigrant movement more visible, by allowing it access via the media to French public opinion. But how far did ordinary French people really listen to Sartre and Foucault? As Bouziri, himself a committed far Left militant at the time, acknowledged in retrospect: 'It wasn't possible, whether we like it or not, to see French society through the prism of the far Left.'[53]

After all, the 68-era far Left, though it did temporarily make some inroads into immigrant communities, never managed to appeal to more than a smallish fringe of, mainly young, French workers. The fact that parts of the far Left sometimes had a tendency to glorify young delinquents as a revolutionary force may not be unrelated to the hostility of many older French workers. As Giudice suggests, the problem with the GP's aspirations to unite in the factories 'the generation of the Resistance', 'the generation of May [1968]', and the 'in-between generation' with immigrant workers was that the 'in-between generation', having fought as conscripts in colonial wars, was, though often trade unionists, not always known for its anti-racist internationalism.[54] Thus if we take the emblematic example of Billancourt, it is true that Algerian former Renault workers interviewed by Jacqueline Costa-Lascoux and Emile Temime are often nostalgic for the strong feeling of fraternity and solidarity that they associate with Billancourt, portrayed as safe by comparison with the racism experienced in the world outside. Yet the authors also acknowledge a certain feeling of superiority felt by the predominantly European skilled workers over the predominantly non-European unskilled workers. Costa-Lascoux and Temime also downplay the use in factory floor banter of shockingly racist terms like *bicot* as merely a colonial vestige,[55] which surely points to the salience of the colonial heritage as a barrier to unity between workers.

Moreover, solidarity on the factory floor did not often translate into solidarity in residential areas. As one CGT activist in Lyons put it, 'At the factory gate everyone puts on their bourgeois mask'.[56] For example, any analysis of the Ben Ali affair must take into account the fact that though local businesses were mainly North African, a significant minority of local residents were not. The *petit blanc* racism of Ben Ali's assassin, Daniel Pigot, was shared by many French local residents, of whom 285 signed a petition arguing that it was 'legitimate self-defence'. An association, the Comité pour l'Amélioration et le Renouveau de la Chapelle-Goutte-d'Or, was formed to denounce what they described as the 'Harlemisation' of the area. Even some anti-racist activists admitted that the fact that Ben Ali was known as a troublesome individual, while not justifying his murder, posed problems for the campaign. The Comité Djellali ran campaigns that brought them into direct conflict with part of the local population, about for example the scornful behaviour of shopkeepers to Algerian customers. Posters and graffiti appeared denouncing a local baker and a local pharmacist as racists; their addresses were given in far Left newspapers, and graffiti daubed on the shops; the baker in question was at one point looted by children taking sweets and adults taking bread. Such tactics were controversial even within the far Left. On all sides, the atmosphere was incendiary: on the one hand, children daubed graffiti such as 'We will avenge Djellali' and 'Death to the racists', while on the other a certain 'Groupe de Vigilance 18' openly celebrated the 'execution' of Djellali.[57]

Indeed, the Djellali murder could be viewed as an early ancestor of the phenomenon which would see, a decade and a half later, large swathes of the working and lower middle classes voting for Jean-Marie Le Pen. The perception of an equation between immigration, juvenile delinquency and insecurity, an amalgam that would become such a powerful populist theme at an electoral level, was already established at an informal level, as the following testimony from a teacher of Arabic at Pigot's trial in 1977 indicates: 'In the name of security and property, a climate of denigration reigned in 1971 in the Goutte d'Or. Young people were assimilated to the criminal underworld.'[58] The national press for the last month of 1971, during the Djellali affair, already has an alarmingly certain familiarity when viewed with hindsight. An Algerian claimed to have been beaten in a police station; the quota for the number of Algerians allowed to enter France was lowered; a Communist mayor asked for a cap on the number of foreigners in his area; and the far Right *groupuscule* Ordre Nouveau announced its intention to form a 'Front National' to unite the 'anticommunist, anti-system, national and popular' opposition for future elections. Indeed by 1986 the 18th arrondissement was to give the FN its highest vote in Paris.[59]

But there was resistance to racism too. The MTA denounced the systemic nature of racist violence in French society and the official impunity that seemed to reign. In November 1972, Mohammed Diab, an Algerian lorry driver, died in custody after being seized by police in hospital and taken to Versailles police station. The same people who had mobilised over Djellali Ben Ali, both the MTA and the French intellectuals, once more took to the streets. A demonstration about Diab on the *grands boulevards* of central Paris[60] on 16 December attracted considerable media attention. Contrary to de Gaulle's dictum that 'one does not arrest Voltaire', Claude Mauriac, Michel Foucault and Jean Genet were all arrested and Mauriac struck in the kidneys by a police truncheon. In this affair as in other racist killings, a key issue was that of truth: contesting the official version of events, and demanding that the truth be told. Typically, home-made posters would appear of the victim, accompanied by appeals to demonstrate for justice. An unofficial enquiry was carried out into Diab's death by academics and students at Paris 7-Jussieu, demonstrating that police claims that Diab was the aggressor or had died in an accident were not true.

State racism, not just the racism of individuals, was in question. The authorities persistently refused to accept that there was a racial motivation in the Ben Ali case, or to listen to Diab's family's account of what happened. Initial newspaper coverage had presented uncritically the police version of events.[61] When a Moroccan worker, Mohammed Bekri, was killed in Marseilles in August 1972, his friends and family claimed that the police were treating them as suspects, instead of finding the killers. To modern British eyes, such cases might bring to mind the words 'Stephen Lawrence' and 'institutionalised racism'. But mobilisations around racist killings were becoming more frequent and more autonomously immigrant-led. Of the estimated two thousand people who demonstrated in the centre of Marseilles despite an intimidating police presence to protest against Bekri's murder, just fifty were French.[62] The situation had thus moved on since the days of small-group, French-dominated 'commando' actions in 1968-1970. In contrast to such artificial actions, by 1972-1973 mobilisations were springing up in a variety of locations and with real mass support.

The Radical Immigrant Milieu

The MTA was only the most prominent of a whole galaxy of autonomous organisations that thrived in the immigrant worker/far Left cross-over milieu of this period. While the growth of immigrant associations is conventionally associated with the period following the removal of legal restrictions in 1981, many existed on the fringes of the law a decade earlier. There was a growing demand for radical and critical alternatives to home government-controlled Amicales. Sally N'Dongo's Union Générale des Travailleurs Sénégalais en France already existed as a template for such an alternative. N'Dongo himself became a prominent, if controversial, figure on the Left during this period. Some French Maoists claimed N'Dongo was essentially a clientelist, in the pay of the Senegalese government, accusations which French Trotskyists defended N'Dongo against. N'Dongo's critics included the *groupuscule* Révolution Afrique!, which had arisen from encounters between two young ex-JCR members, Madeleine Beauséjour, a black Nanterre graduate from Réunion, and the white cartoonist Gilles de Staal (aka 'Harpo'), and a group of young West African workers involved in hostel rent strikes in the Paris *banlieue* – notably Mamadou Konté, later a well-known organiser of world music festivals. The group's lively style was typified by carrying off lightning-speed leaflet distributions in Barbès cinemas showing Indian or Egyptian films to packed houses, in the short interval between the film ending and the lights coming back on.[63]

Other home country or countries-specific oppositional groups like the Union des Travailleurs Mauritaniens en France, the Association des Travailleurs Maliens en France, the Fédération des Travailleurs d'Afrique Noire Immigrés, the Union Générale des Travailleurs Réunionnais en France, the Movimento dos Trabalhadores Portugueses Emigrados, the Comité des Travailleurs Algériens and the Union des Travailleurs Immigrés Tunisiens attempted during the 1970s to emulate the UGTSF's early success. The Association des Marocains en France (AMF) especially became more influential at a time of growing Moroccan immigration, denouncing the monarchical regime in Morocco from underneath an umbrella of protection provided by the French CFDT union confederation. Its base in the Parisian suburb of Gennevilliers 'became the laboratory of an original working-class and political culture',[64] followed by thousands of people as student leftists united with migrant workers. Meanwhile the Portuguese alone had at least eight associations and three political parties active in France on the oppositional Left during this period, producing as many as 50 ephemeral publications.[65] There was an increasing feeling, however, that separate organisation by nationality was insufficient, especially since all groups had a common interest in defending themselves against French government policies. The different groups therefore came together to coordinate their action in the Maison des Travailleurs Immigrés in eastern Paris, which organised France-wide festivals to celebrate immigration. Many of the groups worked together in the mobilisation against the Marcellin-Fontanet decrees. Local networks like the Comités Français-Immigrés brought together immigrants and leftist militants for political and social activities.[66]

The autonomy of the movement from its allies on the far Left was in part an ideological fetish of the time. The idea of autonomy had such disparate intellectual origins as Selma James, C.L.R. James and the 'Johnson-Forest tendency' of American Trotskyism, the French-based *Socialisme ou Barbarie* and dissident Italian Marxist thinkers like Raniero Panzeri. At just this point in the early Seventies, it was starting to be widely advocated internationally by women's and gay liberation movements.[67] But it was important too for the MTA because they wanted their message about racism to reach ordinary French opinion without the baggage that came from being pigeonholed as a partisan extreme Left protest. As Saïd Bouziri emphasised, 'What we wanted, was to talk to the French, ... was to be heard by the French, was to not only go through the prism strictly of the far Left.'[68]

This was a significant development, for as one contemporary pointed out, French activists were ready to accept the autonomy of small groups of foreign activists, especially if they belonged to the same ideological family, but rather less so the autonomy of mass organisations[69] – which by their nature were harder to control. Even in its 1968 guise, the French Left was reluctant to shed the idea that everyone should be struggling together in one fight, with anything smacking of separatism liable to be denounced as petit-bourgeois nationalism. Whereas MTA activists were insistent that 'for us to simply be in a battle where we were the menials of the far Left, was impossible'. They asked themselves 'was a certain autonomy, a strong autonomy, of immigrant workers needed or were we completely dissolved in an undifferentiated movement'.[70] At the beginning of 1973, one group of immigrant activists explicitly called for the movement to be autonomous on the grounds that 'Experience shows us that French comrades, being organisationally the strongest, objectively tend to impose their points of view on us (see the Comités Palestine experience), and that 'in production, in society, we belong to another universe from French workers'. They criticised not only the mainstream parties but also the Trotskyists and Maoists, for either subsuming immigrants' specific interests in the general struggle, or using them for individual spectacular actions designed for the needs of the *groupuscules* rather than immigrants themselves.[71] It was not hard to find examples of far Left initatives that had backfired: following the racist killing of Arezki Rezki in Lyons in June 1972, for example, a Gauche Prolétarienne-led demonstration swiftly ended in the police badly beating Algerians with their batons.[72] This extension to a mass immigrant movement was a consequence of the Ben Ali affair, which MTA literature used as a precedent. When in June 1975, militants in Toulouse responded to a racist killing by holding meetings in front of a café whose owner they held responsible, the MTA commented: 'It takes up the tradition of immediate mass riposte by Arab workers, which is present since the Djellali affair ... in the whole history of the MTA.'[73]

Autonomy, though, was a delicate balancing act. By 1974, hunger strikes involved Mauritians and Pakistanis who were actively supported by the MTA. But the very prominence of the MTA meant that there was a danger of the movement being dominated by North Africans at the expense of other groups. Some African workers complained that the MTA's emphasis on mobilising 'Arab workers' excluded them. The idea of autonomy was becoming sufficiently developed that at one point French supporters even demanded autonomy *from* immigrants. Activists in the 20th arrondissement of Paris set up a 'Comité Français Immigrés' with only French members, because they had the impression of being 'used' by immigrant fellow activists, who would suddenly tell them to change the wording of a leaflet after large numbers of copies had been laboriously reproduced. And the militants of Révolution Afrique! found themselves simultaneously accused by black nationalists of manipulating Africans and by Révolution!, the French group from which they had originated, of neglecting French *gauchisme*. At the same time, they were undergoing internal battles over how to manage the sensitive issue of Franco-African relations within the group itself.[74]

The movement was thus never completely self-sufficient. Whatever the rhetoric, most immigrant activists, with the exception of an African group known as FETRANI, who refused to have anything to do with French activists because of the danger of 'recuperation', sought French allies of some sort. This was as necessary in practice – French activists often had resources that the nascent immigrant workers' movement lacked – as it was in theory, for the MTA's ideological approach was open, universalist, and far from anti-French. It has to be stressed therefore that isolation was not the intended outcome. As Yvan Gastaut has suggested, the MTA was perhaps less autonomous than it presented itself to be: its strategy was one of high visibility and an appeal to the media.[75] A movement of people vulnerable by their legal status to state repression and aiming to act within the French public arena was to some extent dependent on its fellow travellers among a certain layer of French leftists and intellectuals.

But the autonomous approach brought with it the risk that immigrant struggles would, though widely supported within immigrant communities, not be supported by ordinary French people. The messy reality on the ground was not always as idealistic as the theory would have it: active solidarity with immigrants was only a minority, if confident and growing, interest among the French. This was not always apparent, since activists suffered from the perpetual tendency of the far Left to exaggerate minor victories: 'At the first meeting, we were 28; the following ones have been even more massive (up to 35 militants).'[76] But occasionally, activists would frankly acknowledge the problem. As *Vie et luttes des travailleurs immigrés*, a brochure brought out by activists in Marseilles and Aix put it, 'Why are these struggles not popular?'.[77] Or, in the words of one Algerian striker in Lorraine in 1973, 'There should above all have been a support committee of French people who are workers themselves, who work in factories ... But I noticed that among the supporters there were too many intellectuals, people who live outside factories.'[78] When militants in Belleville held multicultural festivals in December 1973 and March 1974, they attracted a good mix of North Africans, Spanish, Portuguese, Pakistanis and Mauritians, but a 'low number of French workers from the neighbourhood'.[79]

Challenging Exploitation: Strikes for Equality

Although less publicised than the hunger strikes, probably a greater number of immigrant workers were involved in what has been termed a 'veritable wave of foreign worker strikes'[80] beginning in 1971. The exploitative and discriminatory situation experienced by migrant workers, working longer hours for less pay, facing more precarious employment status, and risking more danger in the workplace than French workers, produced industrial unrest now that the initial period of fear had been broken by events since 1968.[81] To go on strike with a whole workplace presented less immediate risks than to attend a street demonstration, 'I personally support the trade unions, but I never go on demonstrations'.[82] Laure Pitti attributes this strike wave to a combination of the political impact of 1968 with the economic context, namely attempts by metallurgical employers to concentrate, reorganise and speed up production by breaking it down into very fragmented operations that alienated the workforce.[83]

The long and hard strikes by Moroccan and Algerian workers at the Penarroya factories in Saint-Denis in January-February 1971 and in Lyons in February-March 1972 were a much cited formative experience, and the subject of two films widely viewed in leftist circles. The strikers' grievances, publicised by the Cahiers de Mai leftist group, concerned both lead poisoning and poor and discriminatory sanitary conditions: many more showers were provided for 'European' than 'immigrant' workers. In the second of the films, *Dossier Penarroya: les deux visages du trust* ['The Penarroya File: The Two Faces Of The Cartel'] the slick boardroom image of a modern, successful company – the world's biggest producer of lead – was contrasted to the burns on the bodies of its workers who, not allowed to eat in the canteen during working hours, were forced to eat with lead on their hands. The strike ultimately led to a change in the law recognising lead poisoning as an illness caused by the workplace.[84] In November 1972 at the Câbles de Lyon factory in the north-western Paris suburb of Clichy, Algerian, Moroccan and Portuguese workers went on strike after a *gauchiste* was sacked.[85] Attempts were made to bring together strikers from different disputes: the same month, six hundred workers were bussed in from across France for a Maoist-run congress in Paris on these new workplace struggles. Portuguese, Moroccan and Algerian workers spoke at the conference, described by *Le Monde*'s correspondent:

> The orator speeds up his delivery, gets agitated and expressive, and, suddenly, he mumbles and stops. Nobody breaks the silence: "I don't know how to say that?" Again, silence. The immigrant hesitates, finds his words again, stumbles again, and to applause, continues his speech in Arabic.[86]

This context helps explain further why the Bouziri hunger strike, mentioned at the Maoist conference, had such an impact. Workplace strikes and protests against immigration controls fed into each other during 1972-73.[87] For the MTA, immigrants' struggles were a battle for workers' rights. As their magazine *Al Assifa* put it in response to claims that foreigners should just work and shut up: 'We are not goods that one country sells to another, we do not live off charity, we are workers, we are taking up the right to struggle and claim our dignity.'[88] Workers at the Margoline recycling factory in Nanterre – who were housed in sheds on the second floor of a hangar with no toilets and accessible only by ladder – linked up with the *sans-papiers* movement and went on strike to demand regularisation. By the spring of 1973, the strike wave had reached the French labour movement bastion of Renault-Billancourt. A three week long unofficial dispute took place, over the key issue of equal pay for equal work also highlighted in some of the other strikes of the period.[89]

Nevertheless, industrial disputes were characterised by 'a large number of half-victories and half-defeats'.[90] The strikes often posed a challenge to trade unions, especially the Communist-run CGT, viewed as old-fashioned and insufficiently attuned to the current grievances of workers, especially broader issues of human rights and dignity rather than simply bread-and-butter claims. Workers contested not only the fact that they had to work, and live, in worse conditions for less pay than French workers, but also the way that they were excluded from having a voice.[91] Pitti suggests that the Penarroya dispute was really about what would today be called a 'glass ceiling', whereby workers initially classified as unskilled were permanently excluded from promotion. Similarly her study of the Billancourt strikes argues that their real significance was not so much the 'immigrant' aspect, as the divergence between workers and unions that emerged.[92] Conversations outside the factory gates taperecorded and published – admittedly by *gauchiste* sympathisers – in a journalistic enquiry into the Communist Party confirm this view of a disconnection between the two. Immigrant workers described the CGT as 'bogus' for its propensity to hold only inadequate one hour-long strikes, and for presuming to speak on immigrant workers' behalf in radio interviews.[93]

The Fixations of the Far Left: from Pierre Overney to Alain Krivine

Even leaving aside specifically immigrant-focused movements, two of the most legendary incidents of the final apogee of post-1968 *gauchisme* were originally about immigrants, though this was obscured by grandiose political posturing. The first was the Pierre Overney affair, when a young Maoist militant was shot dead by a security guard outside the gates of the Renault factory at Boulogne-Billancourt on 25 February 1972. Overney's funeral was attended by an astonishing 200,000 people, including anyone who was anyone on the Left, from Jane Fonda[94] to the future Interior Minister Jean-Pierre Chévènement. The funeral and its aftershocks are generally seen as the emblematic endpoint to *gauchisme*, because this was the crucial stage at which the movement in France teetered on the brink of plunging into Red Brigades / Baader-Meinhof -type terrorism, but held back.[95] The Nouvelle Résistance Populaire, an offshoot of the Gauche Prolétarienne, staged its first and only, half-hearted, act of terrorism, by in revenge kidnapping Renault's deputy head of Human Resources, and then changed their minds, releasing him unharmed. Traumatised by the experience, and by the failure of the 'popular masses' to join them, both the NRP and its parent organisation disbanded themselves (although some years later others did assassinate the security guard who had killed Overney). Many ex-GPers radically changed direction in the mid-70s to become anti-totalitarian 'New Philosophers', rejecting the whole leftist inheritance. This is what the Overney affair is remembered for, as part of the narrative of the intellectuals' journey from revolution to reform.[96]

But what was Overney actually doing when he was shot? He was not an intellectual, he was a worker handing out leaflets protesting against the sacking of three of his Renault colleagues. Overney, the son of French agricultural labourers, was also a convinced anti-racist, who appears to have been assigned by the GP to mobilise immigrant workers. The *gauchistes'* fascination with Billancourt was in part to conquer the legendary 'workers' fortress', but this was tangled up with a specific fascination with the potential of the migrant workers who made up a good proportion of the non-unionised workers they targeted. The so-called Milice Multinationale Ouvrière, in which some of those involved in the Overney affair had been active, had organised many physical confrontations with racist supervisors in this and other factories. Of the three sacked Renault workers, only one was French: Christian Riss, who had been sacked for taking part in an attack on the Jordanian embassy in July 1971, in which he had himself been shot by embassy security. Saddok Ben Mabrouk, from Tunisia, had been sacked in January 1972 for his combative role in industrial relations inside the factory, as had José Duarte, from Portugal, for allegedly smashing up a supervisors' office in revenge for Ben Mabrouk's sacking. All three went on hunger strike in a nearby presbytery which, until Overney was shot, attracted relatively little publicity – despite visits from, amongst others, Sartre, Régis Debray, the famous actress Simone Signoret and the film directors Costa-Gavras and Chris Marker. Overney's leaflet informed workers that Ben Mabrouk had just been hospitalised, and that there would be an anti-racist demonstration that evening at Charonne metro station, to commemorate the tenth anniversary of the 1962 police massacre there. The more immediate cause of this demonstration was the latest spate of racist crimes, since it was reported that the bodies of several North Africans had been found floating in the Seine. This prompted the leading GP figure Alain Geismar to evoke 17 October 1961, alongside Charonne, in a speech to a preparatory meeting in the Ecole Normale Supérieure some days earlier.[97]

Yet back in the presbytery, only the night before Overney's death, an immigrant worker accused the intellectual-dominated GP leadership of once again using immigrants, by planning to provoke a fight with security guards so as to mobilise support for the anti-racist demonstration. Although the GP leadership attempted to cancel their Charonne plans following Overney's death, at least 3000 people still turned up. They carried pictures of both the 1962 Charonne victims and recently killed North Africans including Djellali Ben Ali – as well as French Resistance martyrs Jean Moulin and Missak Manouchian,[98] reflecting the Maoists' curious populist recycling of Gaullist and Communist, French and immigrant iconography alike. A few days later, among those who actually carried Overney's coffin was Ali Majri, an MTA militant, who insisted that the cortege go past Barbès metro station as a mark of respect to Overney's support for the immigrant cause.[99] But who now remembers this context, or the names of Ben Mabrouk or Duarte?

A second example of a hidden anti-racist motive behind a major leftist moblisation was the events of 21 June 1973. On that day, the *service d'ordre* of the Trotskyist Ligue Communiste led a premeditated Molotov cocktail charge by thousands of crash-helmeted *gauchistes* into the police lines guarding a meeting at the Mutualité by the far right group Ordre Nouveau. In a reversal of the habitual superiority of the police in matters of violence, they fled in panic, with many officers badly burned. This incident is generally remembered for the excessive violence that led to the LC being banned, its leader Alain Krivine briefly imprisoned, and the party questioning the ultra-leftist excesses (its 'period of militarist deviation' as it is put in the film *Mourir à trente ans*) that led to the debacle.[100] The riot was thus in part due to the macho cult of the leather-jacketed revolutionary tough guy then ascendant within the LC's *service d'ordre*, and the territorial issue that Ordre Nouveau were daring to trespass on the Left's turf by holding a meeting at the Mutualité.

But the ferocity of the LC's response can also be explained by the issue which sparked it off. The Ordre Nouveau meeting had been called to denounce what they termed '*l'immigration sauvage*', and marked the culmination of an early attempt by the far right to stir up anti-immigrant racism. Ordre Nouveau had just managed to unite the warring tribes of the French far Right in the Front National founded in late 1972 precisely by a new emphasis on immigration and 'anti-French racism', the main theme of the FN's first election campaign in 1973. On 9 June, Ordre Nouveau had begun a campaign on the issue. This marked a turning point, since immigration had previously been of relatively minor significance in the programme of the far Right. In the intervening 12 days tension had mounted, with the murder of a Portuguese worker fishing on the banks of the Seine, apparently by Ordre Nouveau militants out fly-posting who had mistaken him for a North African. Meanwhile on 12 June, in the perfume town of Grasse on the Côte d'Azur, a *sans-papiers* demonstration outside the town hall had been violently repressed by police and hose-wielding firemen ordered in by the mayor, soon spontaneously joined by local shopkeepers, leaving several migrants seriously injured. On the day before the Ordre Nouveau confrontation, Krivine had flown from Paris to Nice to speak at a meeting to denounce these attacks – which had the added advantage of getting him well out the way for the police crackdown on the LC's Paris leadership that they anticipated would follow the next day's events.[101]

Both Ordre Nouveau and the LC thus recognised the potential of immigration to hurt in the coming economic downturn, and acted accordingly. It was rather prescient for a future in which the Left would be reacting against the far Right's agenda on immigration rather than setting the agenda themselves, as they had done since 1968. Indeed, one of the leaders of Ordre Nouveau was a young man called Gérard Longuet, who after a long time recycling himself into the mainstream Right would in 2011 be appointed France's Defence Minister.[102] Yet the specifically anti-racist logic of the 21 June riot became, not for the first time in the history of the French Left, lost in a display of anti-fascist unity, as the rest of the Left – rather surprisingly in some ways – rallied around Krivine as a martyr: 'The reason for the clashes and the Ordre Nouveau meeting – the incitement to murder immigrants, especially Arabs – became of secondary importance, eclipsed by the "anti-fascist" struggle.'[103]

Death in Marseilles: The Hot Autumn of 1973 and the MTA Riposte

But two months later there would be a major outbreak of violence, to make the Grasse incidents pale into insignificance. On 25 August 1973 a French bus driver, Emile Gerlache, was stabbed to death in his bus in the centre of Marseilles by a mentally ill Algerian man, Salah Bougrine. Bougrine's severe brain damage had stemmed from having his head split open in an axe attack by two Frenchmen and a *harki* in Nice in 1969 where Bougrine worked in the sewerage system, in addition to trauma suffered during the Algerian War. The affair thus revealed the seedy underside of the beautiful Mediterranean coastal region of Provence and the Côte d'Azur. Different groups, many of whose presence originated in France's colonial adventure across the Mediterranean, coexisted superficially but uneasily: *harkis, pied noirs* nostalgic for the French Algeria they had lost, even trying to recreate it under the hot southern sun, North African labour migrants doing much of the work, Italians, Corsicans, French workers in port cities with leftist traditions but now entering economic decline, corrupt police, criminal mafias and wealthy retirees prone to extreme right-wing views. Incited by a vitriolic editorial in the Marseilles local newspaper *Le Méridional* after the killing of Gerlache, at least ten people were killed in petrol bomb and machine gun revenge attacks on North African cafés and hostels in the first week alone – including Ladj Lounès, aged 17, shot dead as he left a bar. Many observers detected the hand of far right groups like Ordre Nouveau behind these events.

Algerian workers responded to the violence with street mobilisations and wildcat strikes in protest. On 1 September, some two thousand people joined, in silence, the funeral procession of Ladj Lounès down through the immigrant districts of Marseilles to the port to return his body for burial in Algeria. Calls were made that day for a general strike.[104] The Amicale des Algériens en Europe, however, urged restraint, fearing that the strikes were organised by far Left groups hostile to the Algerian government. Which indeed they were: probably the high point of the MTA's influence was carrying out a series of successfully followed one-day general strikes in the Marseilles area on 3 September, in Toulon on 4 September and along the Côte d'Azur on 11 September. The 3 September strike was followed, according to official figures, by 60 per cent of North African workers (especially in construction) in the Bouches-du-Rhône department that includes Marseilles, and 100 per cent in the historic university town Aix-en-Provence, where the MTA was particularly strong.[105] However the fact that the strike was also followed virtually 100 per cent in the industrial port of Fos-sur-Mer, with which MTA militants had had relatively little contact, suggests that the strike responded to a more generally held resentment against racism: 'In vain does one ... look for someone in charge, for a representative. It's a useless reflex, a habit of a European used to the structures of trade unionism. "No, no-one gave out a strike call. We were all agreed that something needed to be done."'[106] Indeed, a strike had already broken out in the shipbuilding yard in La Ciotat on 31 August, one day before the MTA gave its strike call. The movement did not remain confined to the Midi. The Paris MTA group, encouraged by success in the South, announced to a meeting on 8 September that a one-day strike would be held on 14 September.[107]

The September strikes were highly distinctive: an autonomously organised, North African-only affair, bypassing French trade unions, involving shopkeepers as well as workers, and stationing pickets in unusual venues like bus stops, hostels and cafés. The Paris strike, if not perhaps living up to the billing of 'general strike', given that the MTA did not have activists everywhere, was nevertheless followed by a majority of workers in key factories like Renault and Citroën, and was marked by the widespread closure of shops in areas like Barbès and Belleville, despite shopkeepers' initial reluctance. The day culminated with an open-air meeting of more than a thousand people outside the main Paris mosque, including a minute's silence for the victims of racism.[108] However the mosque's director was keen to distance himself from the strike: hence Abdellalli Hajjat goes as far as to identify an 'objective alliance' between the religious authorities, the Amicales, the Interior Ministry and the French trade unions against the threat posed to them by the MTA, citing meetings by French government agents with the Amicales and other Arab notables.[109] For the sin of challenging the French labour movement's rather one-dimensional notion of what constituted a strike (in a factory, organised by a union, with pickets at the gate), the strikers in the Midi were at first condemned by the CGT for 'dividing the working class'. By the time of the Paris strike the CGT's emphasis had shifted to welcoming the movement, whilst advising it to operate through the usual union channels.[110]

Yet on its part, the MTA sought to rebut accusations of separatism, citing one Arab worker's account: 'The day after the strike, whereas he didn't normally speak a word to me, a French worker bought me a drink.'[111] In fact the MTA went out of its way to appeal to a French audience in French ideological terms. Footage of the 1973 *sans-papiers* struggle shows activists including Saïd Bouziri leafleting in a metro station and a market to passersby, French and immigrant alike. On 2 September, the MTA and the CDVDTI held a ceremony at the Paris memorial to the French men and women who had been deported to Nazi concentration camps, to declare that their struggle was for all the victims of racism. After reminding an audience that 'Fascism and racism made 6 million victims', the names of seven recent victims of racist murders were read out, as a mix of invited guests listened in silence. These included Michel Foucault, the human rights lawyer Jean-Jacques de Felice, Marie-Claude Hamchari, widow of the PLO's assassinated representative in Paris, and two concentration camp survivors, together with representatives from the PSU, the CFDT, the Ligue des Droits de l'Homme and the CIMADE.[112] French intellectual sympathisers like Daniel Guérin intervened angrily in the crisis, accusing the government of, rather than dealing with the racist attacks, choosing this of all moments to expel Berthier Perregaux for taking too active a role in support of immigrant workers. Perregaux himself made a tape-recorded message, played at a meeting attended by 700 people in Marseilles on 7 September: 'Faced with attacks by racists, we keep our *sang-froid* and affirm with force our determination to defeat all tyrants and exploiters, let's continue the struggle wherever we are.'[113]

A satirical fake edition of Le Méridional was distributed by the GISTI as a riposte to the newspaper's role in stirring up racism. It imagined life in

France if the immigrants were to leave: a cartoon depicted rubbish piling up in the streets, roads left half-finished, 'sleep merchants' out of business, prices rising, and the Mediterranean coast filled with French people carrying placards begging them to come back.[114] But the French government's perceived inability or unwillingness to ensure the physical safety of immigrant workers, in spite of President Pompidou's pronouncements that 'France is profoundly anti-racist', led President Boumedienne of Algeria to take the drastic step of suspending further emigration to France.[115]

Though a period of apparent calm followed, it was put under strain by the Middle East oil crisis, when Arab countries turned off their supply of oil to the West in protest at American support for Israel during the October War of 1973. Some French cafés refused to serve North African customers: 'No petrol, no coffee!'. The calm was definitively shattered on 14 December when a bomb exploded in the waiting room of the Algerian consulate in Marseilles, killing four and seriously injuring twelve. The consulate bombing provoked a still greater mobilisation than in August/September. On 17 December, a predominantly Algerian crowd of up to twenty thousand people, described by Le Monde as being of 'unequalled power and intensity', staged another one-day strike and filled the streets of Marseilles to accompany the funeral cortege. It was the single biggest demonstration of North Africans in France since 17 October 1961. The demonstration was accompanied by another one-day strike in southern towns and cities, while significant demonstrations took place elsewhere, including of several thousand people in Paris.[116]

So if the summer and autumn of 1973 had witnessed the worst racist violence since the end of the Algerian War, they had also seen probably the biggest, and most autonomously-led, anti-racist mobilisation since. Indeed, autonomy took on a new meaning in one factory on the morning of 17 December, when workers told MTA leafleters to stop, because they had already decided to strike anyway and were capable of doing this without outside assistance.[117] This vigorous reaction may be compared to the relatively limited response to another outbreak of deadly violence in May-June 1971, and especially to the near silence at a series of machine-gunnings of North African cafés in summer 1969.[118] It was not only that the violence was on a larger scale in 1973: something seemed to be shifting in the political consciousness of immigrant workers.

But solidarity from ordinary French people beyond leftist circles was often difficult to come by. On the one hand, the workmates of Emile Gerlache, the bus driver whose murder had sparked the crisis, had boldly declared that they 'would not tolerate any racist demonstration to mark the funeral of our comrade'.[119] Yet beyond the solidarities of organised labour in the workplace, where a certain internationalism was still expected, in residential areas the situation was more divisive. On 27 September, the Comité de Solidarité avec les Travailleurs Immigrés held a debate in a youth club on the Marseilles estate where Gerlache had lived. The response, according to the organisations' own newsletter, was not great. Members of the committee felt incapable of providing an adequate constructive response to questions from French workers such as: 'A saturation point has been reached in the number of Arabs, I can see it because many people are very worked up against the Arabs and it will end up badly.' At one point a *gauchiste*, having trotted out his theoretical stance, called the people who he was talking to racists, with disastrous results.[120]

So during the right-wing presidency of Georges Pompidou, a new and dynamic anti-racist movement had formed from an alliance of different social groups. Immigrants changed from a passive recipient of French political debate to a force to be reckoned with. From the Ben Ali affair to the 'general strike' of 1973, and from Barbès to Aix-en-Provence, migrants were speaking out, expressing a demand for rights as workers and a refusal to put up with racist discrimination. Though the upsurge in antiracism had been sparked and initially structured by the far Left, an autonomous immigrant workers' movement was now born. Yet problems and controversies remained for this new social movement. Relations between big-name Intellectuals, young French and immigrant activists, and migrant workers themselves were not always ones of equality. And a wider solidarity between French and immigrant workers was even harder to achieve. Many of the more tricky issues around popular xenophobia that subsequently became a more overt part of French politics were already present below the surface. In the next chapter we will see how the anti-racist movement started to effect real change by entering the mainstream of French political life.

Chapter Five

Into The Mainstream, 1973-1976

'Our struggle is that of all of the workers of this country, French or immigrant.'
Mouvement des Travailleurs Arabes, 1973[1]

The immigrant workers' movements of the 1970s did not exist in a vacuum. They were to have far-reaching effects on politics and society more broadly. This chapter will ask how far the politicisation of migrants in France affected the dramatic events that were to follow in Southern Europe, before moving back to assess its effect on French political life. We shall see that the immigrant movement was a campaign that crossed class boundaries, and had a major impact on progressive opinion as a whole – shocked by the sordid realities that the movement exposed, from degrading conditions at work to a secret prison for immigrants. In particular, by standing an immigrant 'candidate' at the 1974 presidential election, immigrant campaigners dramatically raised the civil rights issue that they were excluded from supposedly universal suffrage. In the course of the decade political parties, from the 'New Left' PSU to the 'Old Left' PCF, and trade unions, from the 'New Left' CFDT to the 'Old Left' CGT, engaged positively with immigration in a serious way. This chapter will question just how wide was the supposedly unbreachable chasm between 'Old' and 'New' Left. Finally, we must dare to ask the underlying question: just how far did internationalism on paper translate, at both leadership and rank-and-file level, into a lived experience of solidarity?

Spain, Portugal and Greece in Upheaval – the French Connection

The exile politics of the '1968 years' was not only a history of marginalisation and failure. If, in the short term, the experience of many home countries in the 1970s, notably in the Maghreb, were characterised by the defeat of movements for political change, future developments were in motion. The new radical university at Paris 8-Vincennes provided an early institutional home, in the shape of the Groupe d'Etudes Berbère (1972-77), for the Berber movement that would burst onto the Algerian political scene after the 'Berber Spring' of 1980.[2] Similarly, the Islamist movement, though tiny at the time, found some early expressions among exiles in France. They derived their critique of the West paradoxically from interaction with it, strengthening its future appeal to those who 'wished to understand, in order to refute, the ideologies of Western aggressors'.[3] The Ayatollah Khomenei, future leader of the Iranian Revolution – and future crusher of the Iranian Left – was during the final part of his exile in the late 1970s a resident of Neuphle-le-Château, a quiet village to the west of Versailles. Ali Shariati, the more progressive early ideologist of the revolution and an advocate of 'red Shiism', had studied at the Sorbonne between 1960 and 1964, and was familiar with the writings of Sartre and Fanon, Marxism, existentialism and other Western ideologies.[4]

More immediately, there was the outbreak of the Portuguese 'Carnation Revolution' of 25 April 1974, and the death of Franco in 1975, to which can be added, though their numbers in France were much smaller, the overthrow of the Greek Colonels in 1974. May '68, and the political space opened up by it in France and Europe more generally, was a contributory – though probably not decisive – factor in the revolutions that swept Southern Europe a few years later. It may not be too far-fetched to see a certain correspondence between the far Left's relationship to events in France and to those elsewhere in Southern Europe. An authoritarian *ancien régime* (Gaullism, the Colonels, Salazarism, Francoism) is challenged at first by marginal groups of dissidents writing much but doing relatively little (the pre-1968 'dream years' in France, the small and isolated groups of Maoists and Trotskyists in Greece, Portugal and Spain or in exile in Western Europe). Discontent mounts in the universities. Suddenly there is an explosion (May '68, the 17 November 1973 uprising centred on the Athens Polytechnic, the 'Carnation Revolution', the mass unrest in Spain during the five years before Franco's death) in which the *groupuscules* suddenly find themselves with more influence than they could previously have dreamt of. An important aspect is some joint action between students and workers.[5] Significant formal change occurs to the political system as a result (de Gaulle's replacement by more reform-minded successors, the transition from dictatorship to democracy in Greece, Spain and Portugal) but it is limited enough for the Left to still have much to complain about. Euphoric utopian expectations on the far Left rocket through the roof and they perform dramatic acts of street theatre, imagining *la lutte finale* is at hand (the 1973 Ordre Nouveau riot, similar pyrotechnics by Maoists and Trotskyists elsewhere).[6] But meanwhile, it becomes apparent that the wider public does not share a desire for total socialist revolution and the far Left hits either disillusion, retreat, or for a certain fringe, ultra-radicalisation into a long-term campaign of terrorism (the French Action Directe, the Basque ETA, the Greek November 17).

The difference, of course – glossed over by the rhetoric of the time – was that the French Fifth Republic, for all its faults, was not a dictatorship. By providing a space for comparatively free political activity in exile, it served as a significant rear base for the far Left of Southern Europe. This was also true of West Germany and Great Britain, but the more similar social, ideological and cultural structures shared between France and Southern Europe, and the scale of the May '68 social explosion in comparison to the more student-confined unrest of the German and British cases, made for a closer, more intense relationship. Even at a linguistic level, Tony Judt recalled 'both the necessity and the sufficiency of French as a medium of communication among students from Barcelona to Istanbul as recently as 1970'.[7]

So what, then, was the role of returning migrants from France in the revolutions of 1974-1975? As we have already seen, Spanish, Portugal and Greek militants in exile had all participated in May 1968. To a significant extent, it was students and other intellectuals and activists, together with the books and ideas they brought back with them, who played an important role in radicalisation. In a period still marked by the after-effects of '68, ideas had, to the authorities, the unfortunate habit of crossing national borders. As one history of the Portuguese Revolution notes: 'Possibly as an outcome of the student unrest that was occurring in Europe and America, many Portuguese young people became interested in the ideologies of the ultra-left.'[8] In both Greece and Spain (though not much in Portugal) the last years of dictatorship saw a relative liberalisation in the limits imposed on freedom of expression.[9] In Spain this allowed a flood of Marxist literature, generally originating from either Italy or especially France, into the country: 'the authorities will tolerate a learned study on Debray or Fanon where they will cut comment on popular issues like divorce or the role of the clergy.'[10] Even the French Communist Party's publishing house found itself much in demand for translations of its books.[11] Such were the unintended consequences of attempts by all three regimes to move away from autarchy towards the Western capitalist mainstream by opening up to foreign investors and tourists. Authorities could not always distinguish those foreigners who were, as the historian Gerd-Rainer Horn puts it, 'suspected to be more interested in the vagaries of far left politics than the beaches of the Algarve',[12] since the young militant often had the same dress sense as the young tourist. Indeed there was often an overlap between the two, as is clear from the wall slogans in Paris in 1968 urging students, 'Don't go to Greece this summer, stay in the Sorbonne'. In the Greek case, Marxist journals smuggled in from Greeks abroad in western Europe played a significant role, and May '68 itself was regarded with some reverence as a point of inspiration. Immediately after the downfall of the junta, foreign books were positively devoured by the intelligentsia. So high were the expectations surrounding a visit to Greece by Alain Krivine that he arrived to find no less than four rival fractions of the Trotskyist Fourth International competing with each other to pick him up at the airport.[13] Indeed, the rather less francophile approach of the Greek 'enraged citizens' of 2011 makes the post-68 period look by comparison like a golden age of France's international reputation: 'Flags jibe at the *rive gauche*: "The French are sleeping – they're dreaming of '68".'[14]

Similarly in Spain, although the student movement inside the country dated back to as early as 1956, more widespread travel abroad during the Sixties, and a certain francophilia among parts of the intelligentsia, especially in Catalonia, meant French authors were widely read and discussed. Even in the Fifties, when many French pop songs, let alone Sartre and Camus, were banned in Spain, reading such authors clandestinely was a mark of internal defiance. In a country where 'the mere fact that a book was written by a foreigner was enough to convince middle-class readers that it was profound', the limited relaxation of censorship in the Sixties only exacerbated the demand for the latest trends from 'Europe' to the young Spanish mind. And at that time, for 'Europe', we can often read 'France'. Even young Spanish priests copied the more socially aware attitudes of their French counterparts.[15] José Maravall's study of student radicals in Spain found that three-quarters of those who had travelled abroad – which in view of its geographical proximity and cultural pull often meant France – said they had been radicalised by the experience. As one interviewee put it, 'It is amazing to remember what the journey to Paris means to a lot of people.' The visit to François Maspero's bookshop in the Latin Quarter became something of a pilgrimage for the young Spanish leftists.[16] Conversely, the French Ligue Communiste had, by spring 1972 when its leading intellectual Daniel Bensaïd went on a political mission to Barcelona, an offshoot in Spain, as did the Confédération Française Démocratique du Travail (CFDT) union. At various points, French *gauchistes* staged a raid on a Spanish bank in Paris and even an occupation of Notre Dame Cathedral in protest at late-Francoist repression. France was still home to the historic

Spanish Left exiled since 1939. The leader of the Catalan government in exile lived in the Loire valley, while the leader of the Spanish Communist Party, Santiago Carillo, resided in the Paris suburb of Champigny – until Raymond Marcellin, in a sop to the Spanish, deported him to Switzerland in 1971. Though many Spanish exiles remained politically quiescent for fear of suppression by the French authorities, and ultimately were edged aside by a younger generation of political leadership in Spain, broader cross-Pyrenean influences were at work none the less. Some younger anarchists brought up in France to Spanish parents mounted cross-border raids, and associated with their counterparts from inside Spain, like Salvador Puig Antich – who in 1974 became the last political prisoner in Spain to be executed by garotte.[17]

Nowhere was the French connection more controversial than in the Basque country. Longstanding nationalist grievances and the struggle against dictatorship had cross-fertilised with the Marxism-Leninism of the period to produce ETA. Although ETA emerged from the internal situation inside Spanish-controlled territory, the French Basque country served as a *de facto* rear sanctuary for ETA refugees granted asylum in France, that helped enable ETA to carry out attacks inside Spain. The cross-frontier nature of ETA has been vividly portrayed in the film *Lobo* ['Wolf'], where social events and crucial planning meetings take place in the French Basque country, before the participants stock up near the frontierspost on the left-wing newspapers – and pornography – freely on sale in France but not Spain.[18] Indeed, the relative leniency of French governments towards ETA was a familiar complaint of Spanish governments before and after the restoration of democracy. From 1975 onwards they spawned a clandestine 'dirty war' by the Spanish authorities against ETA in France, that was among the most violent series of incidents in mainland France since the Second World War and only concluded with the reversal of French policy in 1986. Any suggestion of a crackdown on the ETA refugees had at first been bitterly resisted in France. Much of the French Left had little sympathy for Basque separatism in France, traditionally viewed as conservative and clerical. But refugees from Franco's dictatorship were a different matter. In the Spanish town of Burgos in 1970, six Basque militants nearly faced the death penalty. The Burgos trial provoked not only the worst rioting in Spain since the Civil War and the smuggling into France of a kidnapped West German diplomat, but also a very considerable outcry among the French Left.[19] Hunger strikes in 1970, 1971 and 1972 provoked by attempts to remove the Basque refugees from the border area to northern France attracted widespread support, including visits from big-name intellectuals like Simone de Beauvoir, because they seemed to be a direct response to demands from the Francoist regime that France do just that. These were separate from the Tunisian-led hunger strikes over the Marcellin-Fontanet decrees. But both suggested that a repressive immigration policy, conditioned by the need of Gaullist *Realpolitik* – more interested in arms sales and other considerations of self-interest than human rights[20] – for good relations with repressive regimes elsewhere in the Mediterranean, was being more directly contested than in the past.

But if Southern European political militants made much use of their sojourns in France, how radicalised were the much larger group of migrant workers, of whom there were some half a million Spanish and three quarters of a million Portuguese by the mid 1970s? Emigration was supposed to be a safety valve for social discontent at home. Yet could it, as leftists like Tariq Ali suggested, become 'an important transmission belt for new and, in certain cases, radical ideas'? It needs to be pointed out here that such radical ideas were not confined to the university. As Maravall and Horn have both argued, that student and worker movements were interconnected only looks peculiar from an insular Anglo-Saxon viewpoint. Recent Spanish historians have questioned the idea that Francoism was accepted by the general population, pointing to a rising arc of unrest among workers and priests as well as students and intellectuals. It was not only the university campuses but also the trade unions that were, by the 1970s, filled with 'long-haired beardies'.[21]

Large proportions of the Spanish and Portuguese workforce had some exposure to life in more 'normal' European environments, especially as politically vigorous an environment as France in the aftermath of 1968. This meant that horizons other than those of anachronistic pre-war moral orders could now be imagined. Many had witnessed or taken part in the events of '68 and it is likely that the stories they brought home had some impact. Although radicals complained of the lack of a mass organisation of Spanish labour migrants in France, during 1969 and 1970, radical 'Workers' Commissions' on the model of those challenging the regime inside Spain appeared in France. The campaign against the Marcellin-Fontanet decrees was a further source of radicalisation, spawning a Coordination des Travailleurs Espagnols de la Région Parisienne. That the Spanish Communist Party (PCE), with its long established structures in France, acrimoniously fell out with Moscow in 1970, and therefore by extension with its erstwhile hosts in the notoriously pro-Moscow leadership of the French Communist Party, made the PCE look more radical than it actually was, an impression which Carillo's expulsion would only have reinforced.[22] May '68 had already contributed to the breach between the two parties, since the Spanish Communists took a much more favourable view of the student movement than the French. There was real hostility between the two over the status of Spanish immigrants in France: at one meeting in 1974, Georges Marchais, *de facto* leader of the Parti Communiste Français (PCF), vituperatively attacked Carillo for suggesting that the Spanish should be granted national minority status. Marchais considered this a 'false and dangerous thesis, one without objective foundation and sure to contribute to xenophobia and racism in France'.[23] Later they were at loggerheads over the prospects of Spanish entry into the EEC, the PCF championing the interests of French farmers against Spanish competition. Indeed neither man ever once visited the other at home, despite living just 300 metres apart. French *gauchistes* reasoned, therefore, that any enemy of the PCF must be a friend of theirs. The PCE participated, for example, in the demonstrations accompanying Pierre Overney's funeral.[24] Given this radicalisation, it is not surprising that recent Spanish labour migrants in France were active inside Spain. Many of the most active participants in popular struggle in regions such as Cádiz had been migrant workers abroad, especially in France; indeed they had often been the seasonal agricultural workers written off as mere strikebreakers by the French labour movement.[25]

But the Portuguese case is more ambiguous. On the one hand, the potential impact of returning migrants was considerable, given that a higher proportion of the population of Portugal were in France than of any other sending country. Through its attempts to make it a crime to emigrate without permission,[26] the Salazarist dictatorship had not exactly endeared itself to Portuguese living abroad. There was no firm dividing line between refugees and apolitical economic migrants, as the former sought to conceal themselves among the latter, both to avoid being detected by the Portuguese secret police or their contacts within the French police, and to propagandise amongst their compatriots. Some eighty-six Portuguese opposition newspapers were published in Paris between 1960 and 1974.[27] The fact that student and worker unrest, and attempts at armed struggle, had been fairly quiescent inside the country since 1962 gives the prominent efforts of Maoist exile groups such as the Comité Marxista-Leninista Português in Paris – 'romantic, dogmatic and sectarian' though they were – all the more significance as a possible trigger mechanism. Student unrest then did begin inside Portugal in November 1968, followed by a marked upturn in student and worker strikes and armed attacks in 1969-73, during which the exile-based ultra-left began to have some limited influence at home. This was both to some extent a consequence of the French May and a necessary background to the 1974 revolution. Indeed, the wildly leftist course of events in Portugal in 1974-75, like that in Russia in 1917, could be said to be conditioned in part by extremist ideologies nurtured in exile.[28] For a certain and now largely forgotten time, Portugal enjoyed an international aura not dissimilar to that of France in May '68, that attracted foreign leftists like bees to a honeypot – a veritable 'Kathmandu of leftism at the end of the motorway'.[29] Another prominent figure in the Portuguese transition, the future Socialist President Mario Soares, was at the time in exile teaching at Vincennes, and in 1973 co-organised with Mitterrand a seminar on Marxism. However Soares' underlying sympathies were with moderate social democracy, precisely because of his familiarity with the mainstream western European model.[30] Certainly the key triggers of the coup of 25 April – like the Nanterre students in spring '68, they moved swiftly from corporatist demands to insurrection – were discontented army officers who had served in the colonies. But the role of those who spent the colonial war years in the shanty towns of Saint-Denis or Champigny rather than the jungles of Angola or Mozambique should not be entirely neglected.

Yet there was a sociological and geographical problem. The large-scale social unrest of 1974-75 largely happened in Lisbon and southern Portugal. In those parts, a real social revolution seemed to be in progress, with massive land seizures by landless farm labourers, workers taking control of factories, much sloganising about popular power, and both Communists and the far Left highly influential. Yet most Portuguese workers in France came from the rural north of the country, where smallholding and a deeply entrenched Catholic traditionalism (though as we saw in an earlier chapter, ambiguous in its relationship to the old Salazarist regime) held sway. The Canadian anthropologist Caroline Brettell found that they were attached to ideas of individual self-improvement via emigration, rather than political action.[31] The ultra-leftist ideas of political exiles were thus at best of limited interest to most Portuguese migrant workers. The unfolding of events in Lisbon, such as an assault by leftists on a Catholic radio station, indicated a less than wholehearted commitment to democratic means by the Portuguese Communist Party. They provoked embarrassment as far away as Paris, where the French Communist Party defended the PCP's actions. So a violent anticommunist reaction set in among the northern peasants. A situation where relatives back home were burning down Communist offices, while vacant properties, sometimes built with migrant labourers' life savings, were being threatened with seizure, was not one in which migrant workers could be expected to display leftist fervour. Indeed, it was necessary for Portuguese army captains from the revolutionary Armed Forces Movement to go on speaking tours of France before fears were assuaged and emigrants reassured that in fact their property was safe, since redistribution measures were aimed at the large landowners in the South rather than the small landholdings of the North.[32]

Both the revolution *and* the counter-revolution in Portugal, in other words, had echoes and links in France, in a complex and contradictory process. Even the fears over property seizures should not be taken as confirmation of the stereotype of the conservative Portuguese migrant. It was not only apolitical migrants who had concerns over the course of events during a worrying and uncertain time. Ambiguity remained, for example, over the legal status of army deserters in exile, who had to stage an occupation of the Portuguese consulate in Paris before they were assured of obtaining passports allowing them to return. Additionally, it could be argued that the conservative reaction in the rural areas was partly a product of all the young people having left abroad, leaving only the traditionalist elderly behind. Thus it does not necessarily imply unadulterated conservatism on the part of the migrants themselves. Though some were worried by the nationalisation of the banks and stopped sending money home, most welcomed the advent of freedom through a relatively bloodless transformation. The 1974 revolution had consequences in France, notably a proliferation of associational activity among Portuguese emigrants given the new atmosphere of freedom. The French government was sufficiently concerned about a possible newfound spread of subversion among what they had previously considered a docile population, that it attempted to prevent the Portuguese captains entering France, and refused permission for French government buildings to be used as polling stations for migrants during the first free elections in Portugal.[33]

Crossing Boundaries

But a shift was already underway from the politics of exile to a politics emphasising immigrants' struggle to live freely in France. The classic dilemma for migrant activists was that of 'here' or 'over there': should they be asserting their place in French society, or should they, on the contrary, consider themselves as anti-imperialist, anti-government cadres preparing to take the struggle home? Despite their turn towards a France-orientated direction of struggle, the militants of the Mouvement des Travailleurs Arabes still existed partly within a North African leftist milieu in which the central point was to make the revolution back home.[34] The 'myth of return' still had a powerful pull, especially among those recently arrived, for both political refugees and migrant workers. Musical evocations of the immigrant experience tended to emphasise the sorrows of exile, and look forward to a future return home. 'Moktar', a twenty-four year old Moroccan worker interviewed for a book about Maoists, argued there was no difference between the struggle in France and the struggle at home: 'The struggle that I lead here and the struggle that I will lead over there, is the same.'[35] But this revealing word 'will' still shows that he was intending to return. Others were already making the mental leap that happened at different times for different people, which saw their future as lying primarily in France. Workers sometimes reacted to propaganda about oppression in their countries of origin not by becoming revolutionaries, but by remaining in France and aspiring to the lifestyle of a French worker. Those Algerians who were in France had, after all, chosen after independence to remain in France rather than help build socialism in Algeria. By the 1970s many were finding that, despite everything, they rather liked living in France. And besides, could they afford to return if the post-independence dream of economic development in their village had failed to materialise? So the hitherto unquestioned expectation that their stay in France would be temporary was slowly but surely being undermined. The tightening of restrictions on immigration by Marcellin-Fontanet inadvertently accelerated the transition: male migrants, given that it was now increasingly difficult to travel back and forth, instead brought over their wives and children to stay in France for good. By 1973-74, some militants in hitherto home-country-orientated groups like the AMF were thinking in terms of staying in France for the long term, with significant consequences for the future direction of the organisation.[36]

The fluidity of the migratory situation was matched by a fluid political situation. Anti-racism was one of many post-68 new social movements, whose very unpredictability was precisely what attracted young people to this type of politics. Saïd Bouziri emphasised to me that the MTA was not a political party, it was 'a movement for freeing people's minds' and raising their consciousness, an anti-authoritarian movement, where there was 'a liberation of speech'.[37] (In that sense it was very much a prolongation of the spirit of '68: though the period saw more than its fair share of dogmatic micro-parties, it was also characterised by a suspicion of the notion of the party as such. Even the Gauche Prolétarienne had no membership cards or clear boundary between those inside and outside the group.)[38] Bouziri considered that a key aim of the MTA was to allow Arab workers a space where they could express themselves. This was in most cases new to them, coming from countries which were not free, and because until then they did not feel they could say anything about their situation because they simply did not belong in France:

> That period was a period where ... people began to consider
> themselves – today you would say as citizens, in any case at the
> time, to consider themselves as being from here, then, as being
> from here, and that they shouldn't put up with things ... whereas
> before there was a total inhibition

At the height of the movement, he recalled, it only took 40 or so activists
to turn up with a hundred leaflets, and hundreds of workers would follow
them off to demonstrate.[39] The movement was in this sense a breath of
fresh air contrasting to the 'functional and dehumanised'[40] role assigned to
immigrant workers at the time.

Socially, the movement was fluid too. The MTA leadership, composed
for the most part of educated activists like Bouziri, served as an important
intermediary between the French far Left (who in turn had access to the
big Intellectuals) and migrant workers. By the mid-70s the MTA militants
were thoroughly immersed in the life of Goutte d'Or, to some extent
overcoming the class barrier that separated them from immigrant workers.
Not least, because since they could read and write in French, they were
much in demand to help with official paperwork.[41] One could thus concur
with Catherine Polac's suggestion that although the MTA leadership were
not originally 'immigrants' in the widely understood sense of immigrant
workers, the Goutte d'Or had made them into 'immigrants'.[42] As the
sociologist Johanna Siméant has argued, there was a blurring of the line
between the 'intellectual' and the 'immigrant'. The key activists of the period,
though they had usually been through some higher education in France,
had typically been in the less prestigious vocational end of the system (Driss
El Yazami went to a business college in Marseilles, and Saïd Bouziri to an
accountancy school in Lyons). Their families had looked forward to upward
mobility: El Yazami's mother paid for his plane ticket to France by selling
her six olive trees.[43] But they often became *déclassé* in the sense of not finding
employment commensurate to their level of education – an all too frequent
occurrence for educated Maghrebis in France owing to discrimination. As
Bouziri told me, few of the MTA militants were at the time intellectuals in
the professional sense of being teachers, etc, though many of them did find
modest upward mobility later on.[44] A crucial role in the movement was thus
played by this intermediary layer of people who, as Jim House puts it, 'are
difficult to fit into some typologies which reduce intellectual intervention
to petition-signing on the Left Bank'.[45] The Algerian sociologist Abdelmalek
Sayad, who had already worked with as prominent a French intellectual as
Pierre Bourdieu, and was himself a later influential theorist of the immigrant

experience, spent many years doing odd jobs to get by, such as a salesman in open-air markets, between moving to France in 1963 and being recruited to the state-funded CNRS research body in 1976.[46] Tahar Ben Jelloun, the later famous novelist, had been a student activist in Morocco during the 1960s, and discovered the immigrant worker community after arriving in Paris as a postgraduate in 1971, through reportages he wrote for Le Monde, devoting many of his early works to the plight of immigrants, whilst painting houses to supplement his grant.[47]

This kind of cutting across conventional categories should not surprise us. As Kristin Ross emphasises, the '68 era was all about crossing boundaries.[48] It was precisely at locations on the margins of formal institutions that the fluid boundary crossing so crucial to the activism of the Seventies could take place. Cafés were central to this, as meeting places for the circulation of information and ideas. Of course, these included North African cafés,[49] but university cafeterias, frequented by students, ex-students and non-students alike, also served a crucial role. As we have already seen, taking North African residents from the adjoining shanty town to eat in the campus cafeteria was an important aspect of student activism at Nanterre University. Driss El Yazami ran a branch of the Comité Palestine which revolved around the university cafeteria at the arts faculty in Aix-en-Provence.[50] Discovering this fact from Siméant's book rang all kinds of bells for me, since I personally experienced in Nice in 2001-02 the central role of university cafeterias – where informal mixed groups of people, whether French or North African, and whether formally registered as students or not, can spend all afternoon talking undisturbed over one cheap state-subsidised cup of coffee – as a site for free-flowing political and social dialogue.

There was also, though, an ideological motive for the blurring of class boundaries. Anti-intellectual populism – 'a culture of guilt'[51] – led many middle-class French activists to become établis and choose to work in factories. Some North African intellectuals joined them in this. One typically helter-skelter career path led from Tunisia to being a penniless law student in Aix doing the washing up in a restaurant, then via MTA militancy to a three and a half year stretch as an établi at Peugeot, through agit-prop theatre and writing for the magazine Sans Frontière at the end of the 70s: the individual concerned is now a successful restaurant owner in Paris.[52] Today this might not appear so unusual: anyone who has been through the contemporary graduate job search will be familiar with an oscillation between what are referred to in France as petits boulots ['little jobs'] and higher status work. Indeed graduate underemployment is now a major issue in the Maghreb itself, dramatically exposed by the Tunisian Revolution of

2011.[53] Yet in 1970s France it was an ideological statement, radically cutting against the rigid and socially segregated career paths typical of France up to that time. Though even these had never applied as strictly to foreigners as to the French. As Siméant suggests, *déclassement* is a constant in the sociology of migration. The stereotypical Parisian taxi driver of the interwar years was a Russian aristocrat in exile; in *Down and Out in Paris and London*, George Orwell's best friend was a former captain in the Tsarist army working as a waiter in Paris.[54] Indeed in the post-68 period, *déclassement* was an issue even among immigrants whose only experience of France was as manual workers. The historian Nicolas Hatzfeld has identified many Algerian, Moroccan and Tunisian car workers with high levels of secondary education, but who were denied the white-collar opportunities they had expected: not surprisingly, such individuals were often motivated into activism.[55]

Sociologists and Militants: Immigration and French Progressive Opinion

Good evidence of such boundary crossing was the way the emergence of an autonomous immigrant workers' movement had really put immigration on the map amongst progressive opinion. Disturbing stories of exploitation emerged from beneath the surface of consumer-based, 'advanced liberal society' that the new, modern, official France presented. Workplace exploitation was bound up with housing issues, since employers often provided workers with substandard accommodation. In Savoy, for example, activists attacked 'one of these bosses "of divine right" who still live in our region'. He made Turkish workers in his factory work a sixty-hour week for the minimum wage, pay high rents to live in huts with no running water or sanitary facilities, and pay for a shower at work. Newspaper reports suggested that Moroccan workers building a path up Mont Blanc were being made to sleep outdoors at an altitude of 2800 metres in temperatures of minus 10 degrees.[56] While the most notorious *bidonvilles* were gradually demolished in accordance with government pledges, there was frequently little housing to replace them with. In Montbéliard, near the Swiss border, Algerian building workers being threatened with eviction displayed on placards the poignant slogan, 'We build houses, but we have no bed!'[57] Where there was alternative accommodation available, this often consisted of depressing hostels, where migrant workers would be under surveillance and, unlike in shanty towns, have to pay rent. In some cases, as in the southern Paris suburb of Châtenay-Malabry, workers refused the hostel alternative, leading riot police to come and demolish the shanty town while its residents were out at work.[58]

The concentration of many lone male workers in the hostels presented an obvious target for *gauchiste* agitation.[59] They attracted attention not only for the poor living conditions emphasised when they had first become a site of contestation after 1968, but also as part of a broader critique of authoritarianism. In 1974, a report highlighted some of the more absurd regulations that prevailed. Residents were treated as hotel guests, thus, contrary to French law, denying them their rights as tenants. In some hostels, visits were permitted only at certain times, and female visitors, even family, forbidden altogether 'for reasons of morality'. Hostel authorities were increasingly paranoid about political activism amongst the residents, the report found:

> The recording and surveillance of immigrants are pushed to such a caricatural extent [in one hostel] that a monthly confidential report is asked of the manager – he must note down 'everything which could be recorded, especially the distribution of leaflets', describe the 'state of feeling of the users' and a note is added to the managers' instructions: 'Information must be asked for directly but gathered incidentally, in the course of the month, through day-to-day contacts, general conversations, and perhaps from certain reliable subjects who can be considered as responsible informers.'

In short, residents were treated 'either as dangerous elements .... or as big children'.[60] Abdelmalek Sayad similarly found that, in contrast to shanty towns or shared hotel rooms, the hostels constituted an 'impossible community', a 'totalitarian universe' where managers sought to avoid collective action at all costs. This was in the best colonial tradition of 'protecting' residents from subversive influences (the SONACOTRA hostels had been founded during the Algerian War). 'Anti-French' or obscene books, images, leaflets and posters were forbidden.[61]

Such critiques mirrored those offered by libertarian leftists of the authoritarianism of pre-1968 French universities: paranoid and repressive, refusing to treat people as adults, anachronistically maintaining outdated standards of bourgeois morality. Little wonder, then, that Foucault with his interest in power and surveillance, should become involved in immigrant solidarity. It was, after all, precisely the issue of excluding visitors of the opposite sex to halls of residence which, when combined with a wider political attack on authoritarianism and imperialism, had proved so explosive at Nanterre in 1968. And yet, while social hierarchies were to some extent becoming less authoritarian for students and other French people, Valéry Giscard d'Estaing's 'advanced liberal society' had little place for immigrant workers. Especially if still in the hostels, they were still being kept in a pre-1968 timewarp that was ripe for satire. Tahar Ben Jelloun carried the logic of the hostel regulations to absurdist conclusions:

> - It is forbidden to: repaint the walls; touch the furniture; break windows; change the lamps; be ill; get diarrhoea; engage in politics; forget to go to work; think about bringing the family; have children with French women; flirt in church; wear pyjamas in the street; complain about the objective and subjective conditions of life; sympathise with leftists; read or write curses on the walls; fight amongst yourselves; strike blows; play with a knife; or seek vengeance.
> - It is forbidden to die in this room, or in the area of this building (Go die elsewhere, in your own country, for example – it is more convenient).[62]

At least 13 books about immigration were published in France between 1971 and 1974, five of them by the New Left publisher Maspero.[63] Amongst the new titles we might single out Juliette Minces's *Les travailleurs étrangers en France* ['Foreign Workers in France'] (1973), both because its publication by Seuil was evidence of mainstream publishing interest, and because of its emphasis on extensively quoting what immigrants had to say for themselves in a long series of interviews. This style of direct *prise de parole* ['speaking out'], showing immigration as a fundamentally human issue, was typical of a post-1968 emphasis on self-expression,[64] in contrast to the dry demographic and statistical fare that made up much of the relatively little written about immigration before 1968. However, the interview content was not especially comforting to the *gauchiste* worldview: indeed Minces specifically rejected *gauchistes'* offers of their immigrant contacts as interviewees on the grounds that they would be atypical. Minces found her interviewees complained less about their working and living conditions than she would have expected. Many were either unaware that they were being paid less than their French counterparts, or justified it on the grounds that they had not been in France long enough, or were less well qualified: only a minority attributed this to discrimination or injustice. She found that Portuguese, Yugoslav and Turkish workers in particular tended to lack, especially if they came from rural areas as yet unpenetrated by modern ideology, a sense of common interest with other workers, at least on first arrival. Their preference for individualistic solutions – working harder and better to increase their individual salary – mitigated against attempts at collective struggle. Indeed they often considered French workers lazy, regarding as bizarre their propensity to consider it a great victory to be able to work fewer hours. As one Turkish worker told the sociologist Maryse Tripier: 'They are kind but they don't have the same conception as us: they want to work little and earn a lot. As we work a lot more, we make them uncomfortable.'[65] Nevertheless, *gauchistes* could take some consolation from Minces' observation that the older established communities of Italians, Spanish and especially Algerians were more willing to stand up for their rights collectively, having more experience of the working-class movement, and in the case of the Algerians, of anti-colonial struggle. Minces' picture, of patchy rather than across-the-board solidarity, sometimes reliant more on consciousness of being exploited as a foreigner than of being exploited as a worker,[66] was a more sober and realistic picture than revolutionary propaganda claimed, but it suggested a potential for further struggles ahead.

The sociology of this period when, as Adrian Favell puts it, 'Marxists roamed the earth',[67] had a marked militant dimension, with many postgraduate students and young researchers working on migration themselves involved in political struggles on the issue. Stephen Castles, for example, recalls spending his days writing his thesis and his evenings attending teach-ins 'surrounded by helmeted pickets to keep out right-wing intruders'.[68] The Spanish sociologist Manuel Castells had been deported from France for his part in May '68, but was allowed to return in 1970 thanks to the intervention of his former PhD supervisor, Alain Touraine. Castells chose to study events on the ground in Belleville, for as he later recalled:

> Belleville was, as for so many immigrants throughout history, my entry point to Paris in 1962. As a 20 year old political exile, without much to lose except my revolutionary ideals, I was given shelter by a Spanish construction worker, an anarchist union leader, who introduced me to the traditions of the place. Nine years later, this time as a sociologist, I was still walking Belleville, working with immigrant workers' committees, and studying social movements against urban renewal.[69]

It was in a similar ideological context that the British writer John Berger and the Swiss photographer Jean Mohr produced their 1975 book *A Seventh Man*. The text interspersed Marxist underdevelopment theory with the powerful words and images of an individual migrant worker's-

eye view 'dream / nightmare' sequence of the whole migrant experience
– collated from examples across Europe, including France, and drawing
on the findings of Minces.[70] Indeed the volume of studies in France was
such that union officials became exasperated with the number of students
approaching them for information about immigrants.[71]

Sociologists debated with each other about the effects of immigration on
advanced industrial societies. Were they a factor for stability, providing a
docile workforce more willing than French workers to be exploited, as André
Gorz, Roger Girod and Bernard Granotier tended to argue? An observer of
France prior to the radicalisation of the early 1970s, particularly if influenced
by the structuralism then dominant in the social sciences, might well have
come to this conclusion. Yet there was also a hint of optimism in Gorz's
analysis, as he suggested that since May 1968 'Immigrants are sometimes
at the origin of actions and play an important role in their outbreak, which
was simply unimaginable in the sixties'.[72] Some asked whether more recent
events had actually made immigrant workers, in the words of the American
political scientist Mark Miller, *An Emerging Political Force.*[73] Miller, who
observed the situation by spending his summer vacations working alongside
foreign workers on a building site near Nice, attempted to refute the 'thesis
of foreign worker political quiescence'. He argued that, by passing the official
channels denied to them and finding new means of political expression,
workers were less voiceless and powerless in practice than in theory.[74]
Castells, on the other hand, took the more pessimistic view that 'the utility
of immigrant labour to capital derives primarily from the fact that it can act
towards it as if the labour movement did not exist, thereby moving the class
struggle back several decades'. He suggested that – 'impressed as we are by
the violence and audacity of certain immigrant struggles' – such necessarily
risky and minority ventures left untouched the fragmentation within the
working class caused by the presence of immigrants. These divisions could,
Castells argued, only be overcome by a (very difficult) generalised battle
against capital for equal rights.[75]

Radical film-makers also increasingly turned their attention to
immigration as part of their critique of French society. Fitting in with
the general tendency to view immigration in terms of exploitation, the
predominant style of these films has been described as 'miserabilist' and
as the ' "battered suitcase" genre'. For example in 1970, Robert Bozzi, a
Communist activist, made *Les immigrés en France*, which depicted the
Portuguese inhabitants of a shanty town in Saint-Denis as a social group
oppressed by capitalism. But as Bozzi later confessed, the film was made
without finding out much about them as people, even their names.

Commissioned by a cultural centre in the Communist-controlled Seine-Saint-Denis, in 1976 Claude Dityvon made *Est-ce qu'ainsi que les hommes vivent?* ['Is This How Men Live?']. The film juxtaposed stark images of shanty town poverty to a Malian hostel resident, Diara Bassirou, expressing his disappointment at the reality of life in France compared to the paradise he had expected. Bassirou went on to discuss, though, the developing consciousness of the residents of the Allende hostel, then at the beginning of a long rent strike. So as the decade moved on, films were reflecting the rise in active political struggle. Other films reflected classic *gauchiste* themes like the necessity of acting independently of the trade unions, portrayed as useless and ineffectual.[76]

By 1974, contemporaries noted: 'Immigrant workers are today in fashion',[77] something that could not have been said a decade earlier. The newspaper *Libération* – a good measure of what was trendy in the post-*soixante-huitard* milieu – was highlighting immigration even before it was launched. Its press agency had produced a special feature on the Djellali Ben Ali affair, while a dummy issue of 22 February 1973 carried a discussion between Foucault and an immigrant worker at Renault sacked for his political activities. *Libération*'s founder Jean-Pierre Vernier had himself participated in one of the *sans-papiers* hunger strikes.[78] The very words 'immigrant worker' had become *the* symbolic figure of the oppressed, even to describe quite different contexts. In March 1974 the 'New Philosopher' André Glucksmann described the Russian dissident Alexander Solzhenitsyn's character Ivan Denisovitch as the 'epitome of the immigrant worker, the absolute *ouvrier spécialisé*' ['unskilled worker'].[79] Many leftists spent their spare time teaching immigrants French. The Fédération des Associations de Solidarité avec les Travailleurs Immigrés (FASTI) had by 1974 some 4500 members and 153 branches, mixing the functions of literacy provider and pressure group. The Groupe d'Information et de Soutien aux Travailleurs Immigrés (GISTI) was founded in November 1972 by lawyers such as Jean-Jacques de Felice, intellectuals like Jean-Marie Domenach (editor of *Esprit*) and social workers and activists in contact with immigrant workers. The GISTI vigorously defended immigrants' rights in the French public arena via the provision of free legal support, which it explicitly defined as part of the class struggle. It mounted a legal challenge to the Marcellin-Fontanet circulars, which eventually resulted in their partial annulment.[80]

This interest was linked to a growing subculture of French people concerned with Third World issues, indicated by the foundation in 1975 of the publishing house L'Harmattan. The difference with the *tiersmondisme* of the anti-colonial and immediately post-colonial period, though, was that immigrant struggles were now bringing the issue closer to home. Immigration was challenging a Europe that, following decolonisation and with the onset of economic crisis, was beginning to turn in on itself. Whereas in the 1950s and 1960s the exciting struggles had appeared to be in Africa itself, now that independence had been achieved, as the then Trotskyist militant Benjamin Stora recalls, 'to my mind not much was happening in Black Africa or the Maghreb'.[81] When one activist, Paul Oriol, who had spent nine years as a *coopérant* in Algeria, returned to France in 1972, his party wanted him to become a specialist speaking about issues of underdevelopment in the Third World. But – having found on arrival to his new home in the 20th arrondissement of Paris a leaflet about the impending eviction of African workers from a nearby hostel – Oriol replied that there was underdevelopment in France, and chose to prioritise immigration in his political work.[82]

Elections, No Longer a 'Trap For Fools': Djellali Kamal and the 1974 Presidential Election

By spring 1974, the MTA was sufficiently confident to put up an immigrant 'candidate' in the French presidential election that followed the death of Georges Pompidou. This was in spite of the fact that as foreign nationals they did not actually have the right to stand or vote in the election. 'Djellali Kamal', a young Tunisian MTA activist who adopted this pseudonym with reference to Djellali Ben Ali and a militant named Kamal who was being deported,[83] explained his reasons for standing: there are millions of immigrant workers in Europe contributing to the wealth of the 'Common Market of slavery', but recognised only as a labour force and expected to keep their mouths shut. In summary, 'My candidacy is not a joke, it is not a publicity stunt, it is the cry of millions of men reduced to serfdom in the middle of the twentieth century'.[84]

Bending over backwards not to be accused of separatism, Kamal explained that they simply wanted to enjoy the same rights as French workers. Indeed, he criticised French parties like François Mitterrand's Parti Socialiste (PS) which demanded a new and improved special status for immigrants.[85] As Rabah Aissaoui suggests, Kamal's message was grounded in universalism, emphasising the similarities between the struggles of Arab and French workers. While the MTA sought the recognition of cultural difference, it did so within 'a universalist and open political discourse of inclusion and solidarity'.[86] If one compares the discourse of the 1970s with that of earlier movements (or later ones for that matter), the striking thing is the emphasis on class as opposed to particularist identities such as religion. The 'Arab' element of the MTA's title, although it drew on identification with the struggles of the Palestinians, was not an exclusively nationalist appeal. It was also a recognition of the numerical preponderance of North Africans among those most subject to racism and oppressive living conditions; a way of uniting them by breaking the hold of the three separate North African government-controlled Amicales; and a certain internalisation of the popular French tendency to conflate the terms 'immigrant' and 'Arab'. Despite its title, in practice the MTA campaigned with and alongside Spanish, Portuguese, Mauritians, Pakistanis and others.[87] Contemporary documents from the time of the election confirm this emphasis on communicating their positions to the French, at public meetings, in cafés, at film evenings, in the pages of *Libération* and in street theatre.[88]

The need for Kamal's 'candidature' can also be understood in the context of an absence of immigration as a major theme amongst the main candidates. Neither Mitterrand nor the eventual winner Giscard d'Estaing mentioned the subject much in either a negative or positive sense, except for some warm words about the need to favour the integration of foreigners – though this was a slight advance on the total absence of the subject in the previous election of 1969.[89] Even, ironically, Jean-Marie Le Pen, the entirely unsuccessful candidate of the newly founded Front National, did not mention the subject once in the four pages and ten points of his manifesto.[90] It was, by contrast, the post-1968 alternative Left that considered the issue of greatest importance. Although Lutte Ouvrière's Arlette Laguiller did not refer to the subject, the Ligue Communiste Révolutionnaire (LCR)'s Alain Krivine not only pledged in his manifesto full equality of union and political rights for immigrant workers, but gave up his allotted television airtime to Djellali Kamal. So too did the ecologist Réné Dumont, who as an agronomist was well versed in the economic problems that drove migration in the first place. This suggests a certain deference on the part of Krivine and Dumont towards the autonomy of the immigrant workers' movement. Kamal's 'candidature' was accompanied in the run-up to the election by what was described as the 'first foreign worker congress held in France', in Marseilles in April 1974. A Front of Foreign Worker Movements was proposed, to unite the MTA with like-minded organisations of other nationalities, in a more co-ordinated fashion than had been the case during the largely nationality-specific hunger strikes of 1972-1973. At the Marseilles congress and at a second in Montpellier, delegates strongly emphasised the need for an autonomous space for foreign workers within the movement.[91]

Although Kamal's 'candidature' had relatively little impact at the time – he probably had more influence on French opinion in his later role as manager of the raï music star Khaled[92] – taking the long view it was an event of great significance. As an early attempt to raise the issue of foreigners' voting rights, this was the start of a passionate debate that remains unresolved nearly four decades later.[93] Fundamentally, it can be seen as an issue of civil rights, or to put it in more French terms, it is about making universal suffrage truly universal. Although the historiography sometimes tends to see this debate as starting under the impact of European integration,[94] a case can be made for the role of the 1974 'candidature', given how radical a step forward it presented. It directly challenged, in *soixante-huitard* fashion, entrenched republican notions of the 'strict political neutrality' required of non-nationals. Yet it was a bold and challenging move to make even within the movement, given the context of a 68-era far Left that was sometimes contemptuously dismissive of elections as a 'trap for fools', and more importantly the national pride of immigrant communities themselves. To participate even symbolically in a French election was still controversial, little more than a decade after the successful conclusion of nationalist struggles for independence from France. Not until the 1980s was the demand for the right to vote in France to achieve near-universal acceptance among immigrant activists.[95] During the hunger strikes of 1972-73, Paul Oriol was startled to find strikers coming to see him exclaiming, 'Come, because the Communists want to make us French!' They had been perturbed to find Communist posters pasted on the wall of one hunger strike venue, demanding, amongst other things, that naturalisation be made easier. Oriol's own party, the Parti Socialiste Unifié (PSU), was also in favour of this, and the right to vote for foreign residents, but discovered that some immigrant organisations were against, on the grounds that they wanted to return home to continue the struggle in their own countries. Oriol thus considers that Kamal's 'candidature' went against the grain of the time. Oriol's fellow PSU activist Guy Phillippon agrees, recalling one meeting in 1973 at which Tunisians found the idea of the right to vote insulting.[96] Yet by intervening precisely at a time when the lived reality of immigrant life in France was becoming a permanent one, undermining the myth of return, the Kamal candidature marked the beginning of a decisive shift in such attitudes.

The Movement Continues

Although it has sometimes been suggested that France entered a 'period of relative calm' after 1974,[97] this was not entirely the case regarding immigration, at least to begin with. Giscard's incoming government, headed by a young prime minister named Jacques Chirac, may have brought an end to the six year reign of Interior Minister Marcellin, but a new Interior Minister simply meant a new bogeyman for the immigrant movement. Michel Poniatowski, himself of Polish origin, was so keen to fit into the job description of 'hardline Interior Minister' that he became known for personally leading police charges into metro stations for random identity checks in search of drug dealers and illegal immigrants. But if Poniatowski was the 'hard cop', the role of 'soft cop' was played by immigration minister Paul Dijoud. During the first three years of the Giscard presidency, there was a lot of talk from Dijoud about 'insertion', 'dialogue' and even respect for cultural difference: television programmes and other cultural activities were now to be produced in association with the sending countries. This could be seen as marking a break with old-school republican assimilationism (though more cynically, it could be viewed as keeping the option of repatriation open, by subjecting migrant culture in France to the approval of home governments). There was a crackdown on 'sleep merchants', and from 1975 immigrants were allowed to be union delegates. Giscard himself went to visit a shanty town in Marseilles. This self-consciously more enlightened approach needs to be seen in the context of pressure from below during the mobilisations of the preceding years. The government was now being forced to treat immigration as a social issue of major public policy concern, rather than simply relying on a pool of cheap labour with little concern for the broader consequences. The authorities had belatedly come to realise that immigration was not just a question for the workplace, but one for society. Dijoud's was the first government department for immigration since the 1930s, indicating how far the issue had moved up the agenda.[98]

Such pressure from below showed no immediate signs of letting up. 1974-75 saw the *sans-papiers* hunger strike movement spread to seasonal agricultural workers in Provence and Languedoc, following a meeting with urban-based activists including Driss El Yazami of the Aix MTA group. In contrast to the French-speaking, literate activists, and to the mainly urban, educated Tunisian hunger strikers of 1973, these *sans-papiers* were Berber-speaking peasants straight from the Moroccan countryside, who El Yazami had first come across when a group chanced upon his leftist café salon in Aix, wanting to know where the trade union was. It turned out they were living in a greenhouse in a village outside Aix, and that practices such as having to pay a middleman for the privilege of a work contract of only 40 days were widespread. Hunger strikes ensued in Avignon and Montpellier, where on 11 January 1975 the Protestant church in which 180 Moroccans were taking shelter was stormed by three hundred riot police, leaving some hunger strikers sufficiently badly injured to be hospitalised. Three days later, however, activists claimed victory with the declaration by France's highest constitutional authority, the Conseil d'Etat, that the Fontanet circular was actually illegal. The movement culminated with a large nation-wide rally in Montpellier.[99]

Yet some *gauchistes* were already detecting the beginnings of disillusion. By 1975 the AMF was beginning to tear itself apart in bitter internecine disputes over the Moroccan occupation of Western Sahara. And writing in a March-April 1975 special issue of the journal *Politique aujourd'hui*, Fouad Lamine and Bernard Navacelles contrasted the confident and mature state of the movement during 1973-74 to a situation which had now been stabilised on terms unfavourable to immigrants. The government was now able to implement its policies: the ability of the last group of immigrants able to enter France relatively freely, from sub-Saharan Africa, was now being curtailed. Unemployment was beginning to sap the movement's strength. Activists were disheartened by recent arrests of leftist militants in Tunisia and Morocco – which had both seen major student-based far Left movements in the early Seventies, but which were now being smashed with an iron fist. To this can be added the way the Montpellier incident, and a similar one in Avignon, demonstrated the French government was no longer respecting the right of sanctuary in churches. Indeed because of his role in the Montpellier movement, Poniatowski ordered that El Yazami be deported back to Morocco, where he was imprisoned, tied up and kept blindfolded in a detention centre in Rabat.[100]

But Morocco was not the only country to operate a clandestine prison. In April 1975, it was sensationally revealed that for more than ten years the police had been operating a secret prison for foreigners intended for deportation, in a hangar at the Arenc port in Marseilles. The journalist Alex Panzani made the discovery after concerns were raised by friends of a Moroccan worker, Mohammed Chérif. Chérif was legally resident, but because of his friendship with opposition activists back home, had been beaten up by officials at the Moroccan consulate when he went to sort out some paperwork. Upon obeying instructions from the French authorities telling him to attend a police station, Chérif simply disappeared, and officials refused to explain to his lawyer what had happened. Investigating the story following its being taken up by a lawyers' union, Panzani stumbled across the mysterious hangar, broke the story in the local paper *La Marseillaise*, and it was taken up in the national press. Officials, while confirming that Chérif was being deported, actually denied the existence of Arenc, until photographs of it were published in *La Marseillaise*. The Interior Ministry then changed its line, now explaining that it was perfectly normal that such a centre should exist. Further journalistic enquiries showed that some three thousand prisoners had been held at Arenc during 1974, and that since April 1975 alone at least three prisoners had attempted to commit suicide with sardine tins. In February of that year, African detainees had revolted, setting their mattresses on fire in protest at the poor quality and quantity of food.[101]

All this was grist to the mill of the Left's critique of the repressive treatment of immigrants in France. Communist deputies tried in vain to shut the prison, and Panzani published a book about it. He raised not only issues of institutionalised arbitrariness – the existence of this extrajudicial prison contravened the Declaration of the Rights of Man – but also of public collaboration with its existence. As Panzani noted, the truth had only emerged because Chérif's lawyer had refused to play the same game of pretending not to know about Arenc that other lawyers and officials had. One court had refused to do anything about the attempted suicides on the grounds that it was not aware of the prison's existence. As the prison was in the centre of Marseilles' port area, many people must have seen comings and goings from it, but said nothing. Panzani compared this to the inhabitants of Munich not wanting to know that Dachau concentration camp existed on their doorstep. In future, he suggested, such secret prisons could be used Pinochet-style for domestic political opponents.[102]

Such exaggerated comparisons were in keeping with the rhetorical heritage of the New Left, dating back to the clandestine resistance to the Algerian War, when only a small minority had actively opposed the war and so were often frustrated by what they saw as the acquiescence of the wider public in colonialism.[103] Yet such rhetoric risked casting the anti-racist movement as an elite of lone warriors, fighting the indifference of the public. The relative secrecy in which Arenc was maintained until 1975 – and the scandal that accompanied its exposure – suggests, by contrast, that the authorities were somewhat more shamefaced about possible public reactions than their predecessors building internment camps in the 1930s and 1940s.[104] Recent research by Ed Naylor questions the notion of a sudden 'discovery' of Arenc in 1975, since its existence was referred to in both Algerian and French newspapers in 1967, yet 'scarcely raised an eyebrow'. This actually underlines the importance of the post-68 political context, which was more favourable than previously for highlighting abuse of immigrants.[105] In the problem of starting as an avant-garde, though, the 1970s anti-racists were not unique. A perennial issue facing political movements is being in a minority to begin with: even the French Resistance were in this position once. The question is how to make the transition from minority to wider movement.

Political Parties: The Left Jumps on the Bandwagon

By the mid-1970s, there were signs that such a transition might be beginning to occur. Immigration became a salient issue more widely on the Left beyond those directly linked to *gauchisme*, for the growth of anti-racism as a social movement had political implications. First, while much of the growing contestation over immigration was taking place outside the orbit of the established Left, the mainstream parties were beginning to sit up and take notice. Though somewhat caught napping by the Marcellin-Fontanet decrees, they were changing as a result of pressure from the autonomous movement below. Superficially it might appear that there were few votes to be gained in sticking up for literally and metaphorically disenfranchised immigrants. But both PS and PCF had to make some positive noises, if only to fend off embarrassing accusations from the far Left that they were hypocritically betraying the tradition of proletarian internationalism. Hubert Dubedout, the mayor of Grenoble, actually centred his campaign for re-election to the National Assembly in 1973 around the record of his Left coalition council in improving conditions for immigrant workers.[106] Secondly, a multiethnic society was becoming an undeniable reality, precisely in those parts of France controlled by local authorities of the Left. By the late 1970s, even voting rights for immigrants was no longer an outlandish suggestion from the extreme Left and had entered the mainstream agenda. Some local authorities carried out consultation exercises to respond to the views of foreign residents denied the formal right to vote.[107] Thirdly, trade unions, especially the CFDT, but in some cases the Communist-dominated Confédération Générale du Travail (CGT) as well, provided cover for the activities of leftist foreign opposition groups to an extent that would have been unusual elsewhere in Western Europe. The CFDT allowed the MTA, for example, to use its premises in Aix. In the Lyon suburb of Villeurbane, an immigrant defence committee was run by Georges Valero, a postman and trade unionist of anarcho-syndicalist leanings and Spanish descent who was successively a member of the CGT and then CFDT.[108] Finally, the *gauchiste*-linked anti-racist movement of the 1970s did not begin with a *tabula rasa*, but rather had to coexist with longer established anti-racist movements. While the efferverscence of the period did create tensions within such associations, portrayed by the far Left as ineffective and paternalist, they did not reach the polemical heights of the struggle within the Institute of Race Relations in Britain.[109] Organisations like the MRAP had a leftist background and campaigned on many of the same issues, such as housing and the Marcellin-Fontanet circulars. Having in 1972 succeeded in its long-held demand of a law against racial discrimination, the MRAP persisted in campaigning to ensure that the law was implemented.[110]

This wider support has to be seen in the context of a Left completely excluded from national power since 1958, and therefore tempted by a stance of leftist oppositionism. The emergence of the PS under Mitterrand's leadership from the ashes of the old Section Française de l'Internationale Ouvrière was in no small part built on the recuperation of the themes of 1968. The dividing line between Left and far Left was not as sharp in France as in most Western European countries. Indeed, there is some evidence (as photos of Mitterrand alongside Alain Krivine in the aftermath of the 1973 banning of Krivine's Ligue Communiste illustrate) to suggest that the PS viewed the *gauchistes* as exuberant younger siblings, and sometimes a source of ideas to borrow, rather than as dangerous wreckers. The party's initial programme, *Changer la vie* (1972) was written by the left-wing CERES faction that, despite its traditionalist Jacobin leanings, included many young people politicised by May.[111] Its title was a direct lift of a *gauchiste* slogan about the need to change everyday life, itself taken from the nineteenth century poet Arthur Rimbaud, that had been particularly associated with Vive La Révolution. During what the political scientists Rémi Lefebvre and Frédéric Sawicki call the PS's 'militant parenthesis', many activists in the new party were themselves involved in the new social movements of the period.[112] That the party was almost, yet not quite, on the verge of coming to power at the parliamentary election of 1973 and the presidential one of 1974, heightened expectations. As Régis Debray, by then returned from his Latin American adventures and rallied to Mitterrand, put it: 'The 1970s, that time of electoral defeats, was our *Temps des cerises* (love of failure being a left-wing virtue). How beautiful 1981 looked from the courtyards and plane trees of 1973!'[113] Debray's reference was to a nineteenth century love song often sung by French leftists to express nostalgia for the revolutionary hopes of yesteryear, particularly the Paris Commune. In the spring of 2010, for example, I heard *Le Temps des Cerises* sung by a choir of former Parti Socialiste Unifié activists, presided over by a bearded hippy on an organ, gathered at a Paris town hall for a reception to mark the fiftieth anniversary of the founding of the party. Yet in the 1970s there were distinct echoes of such a tradition even within the more mainstream PS, far from the party's social-democratic managerialist image of today. Rhetorically at least, the PS's pitch had strong anti-capitalist and anti-establishment aspects. The then highly fashionable cause of *autogestion* (workers' self-management) was the classic case in point.

But a reasonably internationalist stance, or at least a judicious amount of bandwagon-leaping, can also be detected on immigration. Early policy documents like *Changer la vie* promised a suspension of expulsion and a greater judicial control over them; equal pay and workplace rights for immigrant workers, plus an improvement in the housing, training and education offered to them; and even the holy grail of the right to vote in local elections and to be elected onto bodies dealing with immigration. Immigrant workers would also, along with aged French workers, get priority in being given municipal housing. By 1976, the party was in favour of full freedom of association for foreigners, implying the repeal of the 1939 law which heavily restricted this.[114] While the PS was not itself a major player in street-level contestation over immigration, it was quick to reach for accusations of human rights abuse whenever governments sought to crack down on foreign activists. Stressing civil liberties enabled the PS to demarcate itself both from the SFIO's own past record in Algeria and from the PCF with its links to the Brezhnev-era Soviet Union (at one point during the Arenc controversy officials stated that 'there is no Gulag in France', perhaps a dig at the fact complaints were coming from the PCF). Mitterrand himself was especially adept at claiming the moral high ground on such 'rights of man'-type issues.[115]

The Role of the PSU

The PSU, originally formed as a left-wing breakaway from the SFIO to oppose the Algerian War, was an important transmission belt, as the party most capable of bridging the gap between the young *enragés*[116] and mainstream politics. No one straddled this divide better than the PSU. Adopting a position mid-way between reform and revolution, the PSU represented the themes of 1968 both in *gauchiste* street politics and, comparatively successfully, in electoral politics. The party's name belied its bewildering array of different factions, from respectable former Radicals like former prime minister Pierre Mendès-France right through to the wilder shores of Maoism. Though the PSU had peaked by the mid-1970s, it was to continue in existence until as late as 1990, and the desertion of Michel Rocard's followers from PSU to PS in 1974 helped inject more of the *soixante-huitard* milieu into the mainstream.[117] The PSU, considered as the 'conscience' of the Left,[118] with its origins in anti-colonialism, provided a natural home for those concerned with migration, with many members involved in literacy and political campaigns with immigrant workers. For example, one public meeting in support of hunger strikers in Paris in February 1973 was addressed by leading PSU figure and nationally respected Resistance veteran Claude Bourdet.[119]

This concern, emerging in large part at a local level from activists, was, however, only one of a series of competing priorities for the party nationally. Its national structures for immigration postdated developments on the ground, especially in the French capital. Despite the PSU's championing of the theme of decentralisation, a disproportionate number of its members were in the Paris region, which would play a major part in the sliding of the party to the far Left after 1968, and where the caricature of the PSU as a party of middle-class intellectuals had more basis than elsewhere.[120] Nevertheless, the party's first Commission Immigrés was set up after the hunger strikes in the 20th arrondissement, one of the most deprived areas of the city. Sociologically, this can be linked to the combination of one of the biggest concentrations of immigrant workers in Paris with what might be termed a progressive, intellectual, *petite bourgeoisie*. Such inhabitants of the 20th arrondissement would later come to be caricatured as 'bourgeois bohemians'. This term is probably too anachronistic, though, for the activists of the 1970s led a lifestyle that was considerably more modest and less defined by consumption than the latter-day stereotype. The founders of the Commission Immigrés were French activists with both experience of Third World issues and a developing sense of how these had become directly relevant to the local environment of eastern Paris, something that became clear to me when in 2006 I interviewed Anne Couteau and Paul Oriol in an Alsatian restaurant on the Place de la République. Former *coopérants* in post-independence Algeria, Couteau and Oriol were marked by their experiences of a local hostel dispute in a disused cardboard factory in the rue Bisson in 1971. Members of the PSU's local branch were then active during the movement against the Marcellin-Fontanet circulars in other organisations such as the CDVTI. About ten of the hundred-odd members of the local party branch participated in the Commission Immigrés. They also created a Groupe Action Français Immigrés including not only PSU members but also those of other parties, associations and unions. Meetings took place, often weekly, at Couteau and Oriol's flat and that of the party branch secretary, Guy Phillippon. Such groups continued to be active on living conditions in the rue Bisson hostel, and went on to develop other initiatives such as the production of a film about the children of migrants in nearby Belleville. Memorably, they produced a giant four metre-high poster of an immigrant gagged by a boss and a policeman, with the slogan 'Freedom of speech for immigrant workers'.[121]

Though Oriol went on to be involved in the PSU's Commission Nationale Immigrés, he considers that the party's leadership did not give sufficient priority to the issue. When I asked him from when immigration was important to the PSU, his immediate response was 'never', relating that at one press conference, the PSU's national secretary failed to mention the subject at all, despite repeated hand signals from Oriol. This marginalisation was a more general problem on the Left, as a cartoon in a party journal suggested. At an open-air rally where the massed ranks of followers dutifully listen to the orator's speech, at the back an immigrant worker points outs to a French activist, 'He hasn't spoken about immigrant workers', to which the activist replies: 'But oh yes he has, he said "etc" '.[122] Compared to the rest of the parties, the PSU became fairly outspoken on immigration. While in 1969 Rocard had not mentioned immigration at all in his *Le PSU et l'avenir socialiste de la France* ['The PSU and the Socialist Future of France'] he spoke out as a member of the National Assembly against expulsions. PSU documents from the Seventies, from the first major feature on immigration in the party journal, placed some emphasis on this theme. The party went well beyond the PS' demands, arguing for a general right to vote and the abolition of residency and work permits. The PSU also favoured autonomy for immigrant workers' movements, as a logical corollary of the party's beliefs in internationalism and *autogestion*. Immigrants should be entitled, for example to teaching in their own languages and support for cultural and religious events – a major deviation from republican orthodoxy. The PSU was severe in its criticism of those who merely proclaimed the unity of French and immigrant workers, and of other forms of 'paternalism' and 'manipulation'. For Oriol, the challenge to what he considered as the 'myth' of assimilation was one of the most important achievements of 1968.[123]

On the other hand, the PSU might itself be accused of paternalism, since in practice it had few immigrant members. The party's Commission Nationale Immigrés had only one foreigner on it, and he was an old Swiss Trotskyist. One 'Groupe Information Immigrés' in which party members in the 20th arrondissement participated did not actually include any immigrant workers. But this was arguably less a French/immigrant problem than one of class: in Paris, the PSU did not have many working-class members of any nationality, tending to attract only foreign students to its meetings. Critics' characterisation of the PSU as a *petit-bourgeois* party of teachers and intellectuals was (with certain exceptions such as Charles Piaget, leader of the 1974 Lip watch-makers strike and a longstanding wing of Christian workers) not far off the mark. Nevertheless, Couteau, a teacher, and Oriol, a doctor from a working-class background – his father was a builder in a village near Carcassonne – were sociologically typical of a certain type of PSU activist, who sought to use their professional skills to make a long term commitment to helping immigrants: giving out information to prevent people catching tuberculosis in hostels, teaching the children of migrants, and so on. There was thus a clear element of altruism motivating the PSU activists' concern with immigration, that found a home within the party's 'ethical conception of politics'.[124] In fact the party took account of its sociological makeup by evolving an innovative approach that has been described as the opposite of Leninism: instead of trying to use the movements to build the party, the party followed, and built an intellectual strategy around, the movements themselves. A rather telling anecdote holds that a PSU member, one of four activists regularly handing out together leaflets about immigration, discovered one day that, unbeknown to him, all the others were also PSU members. PSU views on autonomy thus tended towards a hands-off approach of supporting immigrant workers struggles, and publicising them to a French audience, rather than attempting to lead them. Party activists' relationship with immigrant workers tended to be second-hand, via associations and groups like the MTA.[125]

The PSU's intellectual leanings were not without their achievements, such as the CEDETIM.[126] After 1968 governments in both France and Africa cracked down on leftist infiltration of overseas development institutions – with some home governments, including Algeria, now playing the postcolonial card of depicting troublesome *coopérants* as colonialists. So the *coopérants rouges* associated with CEDETIM returned to France and became more concerned with the situation of Third World immigrants in the metropole itself.[127] The organisation took an increasingly militant but eclectic turn in the 1970s, at one point being taken over by the PSU's extreme left wing, the Gauche Ouvriers et Paysans,[128] but providing a space for *gauchistes* generally from different currents to campaign together on international issues. It also provided a home for immigration campaigns via yet another initiative, the Collectifs Unitaires Français Immigrés, and by providing facilities and political training for autonomous groups of North African, African and Spanish militants. From 1973 onwards, CEDETIM had its own building in south-western Paris, known as the Centre International de Culture Populaire.[129] In 1975, it published a book providing many recent examples of immigration struggles in France, which is still a useful source for historians. It was a sign of the times that the authors felt defensive about justifying 'yet another' book on immigration, on the grounds that they were presenting a detailed account of *political* actions.[130]

The Communist Party and Immigration: Failure or Success?

Even the apparently stale and monolithic Communist Party, long considered to be decidedly lukewarm on non-European immigration, was not entirely immune from fresh thinking. Our general image today of the post-war

PCF is as Stalinist dinosaurs living off their Resistance past, droning on about the absolute pauperisation of the working class, little changed in the aftermath of 1968 by a half-hearted flirtation with Eurocommunism, interested only in the sectional demands of French workers and oblivious to the Third World. We are more than familiar with the idea of the PCF as a caricature of *ouvrierisme* and Jacobin nationalism, upholding the red flag and the tricolour, as it were fiddling in Billancourt while Algiers burned. Authors such as Etienne Balibar have tended, not without good reason, to be highly critical of Communist duplicity on this subject. Indeed, so much of the 1968 generation of intellectuals' *tiersmondiste* critique of the PCF has seeped into the consciousness of post-colonialist historians that it is hard to study the subject without preconceptions.[131] But was the PCF always as hostile or indifferent to North Africans as it has been made out to be? Arguably its record on Algeria and Algerian immigration, though clearly far from unproblematic, had more positive features than we are sometimes led to believe. Historians are usually quick to seize on the party's undoubtedly spectacular failures – to cite two frequently given examples, its vote for 'special powers' in Algeria in 1956 and the 'bulldozer affair' of 1980-81, when a Communist local authority was accused of racism when it demolished housing for Malian workers.[132] But they consequently tend to overlook attempts to reach out to immigrant workers at repeated intervals, that were less headline-grabbing but perhaps just as revealing of the underlying values of party militants.

At least at the level of grand rhetoric, the PCF rarely differentiated between French workers, European immigrant workers and non-European immigrant workers. A worker was a worker. It was precisely the party's crude *ouvrierisme* that led it to argue that the only true division in society was between classes, and that immigrant workers were therefore 'our class brothers'. Indeed, Yvan Gastaut suggests that the PS lagged behind the PCF in its positions on immigration.[133] For all the *gauchistes*' spirited critique of PCF 'revisionism' – and whatever might rightly be said of the party's history of deep complicity in human rights abuses in Eastern Europe – it was still the first electoral choice for workers. It was still recruiting trade unionists amidst increased workplace struggles in the aftermath of 1968. Despite the PCF's by then deeply unfashionable image amongst the intelligentsia, for working-class people seeking to get politically involved, it was still the obvious choice, the 'number one reality' by virtue of its sheer size on the ground, for which more than five million people still voted. Immigrant workers were also faced with this reality: estimates for the readership of the party's foreign-language press range from 40,000 to 80,000. The party actively recruited foreign members: it was claimed as late as the beginning of the Eighties that some 25,000 immigrant workers belonged to the PCF, more than any other party in Western Europe. This is all the more remarkable given that they did not have the opportunity to vote for it. In spite of their often acute criticisms of the Communist record on immigration, no far Left party could remotely claim such a figure even for their total membership, let alone for the number of immigrants within it. Even the PCF's assimilationist-chauvinist tendencies, though real enough, should not be exaggerated: it supported, for example, language classes for children in their parents' mother tongue. Arguably the principal targets of PCF chauvinism in the 1970s, apart obviously from the USA, were capitalist West Germany, or even their fellow communists in Italy, rather than the Third World.[134]

Meanwhile the CGT had an active organisation for immigrant workers, presided by Marius Apostolo, a former Renault worker and union official previously responsible for the education of metal workers and himself the son of Greek immigrants to Marseilles. As a result of a conversation in a bar with the CGT leader Benoît Frachon at a union conference in 1966, Apostolo was put in charge of the immigrant organisation, a position which he occupied until 1980. In an autobiography published after his death in 2007, Apostolo admitted that 'racist and xenophobic reactions were a reality in the working class, including among CGT militants', but also highlighted the CGT's achievements. The organisation won the right for foreign nationals to be elected as union delegates, succeeded in the practical application of the free circulation of workers within the EEC, and campaigned – rather less successfully – for all immigrants working in the EEC to have the same rights as those from member states. In its attempts to maintain an audience among migrant workers, the CGT could also draw upon the considerable leadership skills of both Mohamed Djeghri, an Algerian Communist who moved from labour correspondent for the *Alger Républicain* newspaper to active organiser for the French union confederation, and Jean Saliba, a Communist *pied-noir* and militant former building worker who had been to prison for his refusal to serve in the French army.[135]

What did greatly irritate Communists, though, was any suggestion of control over immigrant workers' struggles slipping out of the hands of the CGT into those of 'irresponsible' *gauchistes*, whether French or immigrant. According to Driss El Yazami, the first time he was picked up by the French authorities was when a Marseilles docker, active in the CGT, grabbed him by his long hair and took him to the police station opposite the port.[136] The CGT in Marseilles condemned the MTA-led general strike of 3 September

1973 with reference to an alleged conspiracy by government and employers to manipulate violent racist groups and far Left groups responding to them. The day after the strike, the front cover of the Communist daily *La Marseillaise* tersely stated:

> A certain number of workers of North African origin went on strike, yesterday, in the Bouches-du-Rhône. The Union of CGT branches denounces this manoeuvre which isolates immigrant workers and divides the working class.[137]

For the CGT, a good immigrant was one who followed the proper union channels, not the *gauchistes*. Thus often in industrial disputes involving immigrants, there would be three-way faction fights, pitting PCF and CGT activists against PSU and CFDT on the one hand and Maoists on the other. In the Penarroya dispute of 1972, the CGT and PCF in Lyons had made a number of allegations regarding the role of the *gauchiste* group Cahiers des Mai ('outside non-working class elements') in the strike, including the disappearance of strike funds – allegations strongly denied by the CFDT. During the Renault strike of 1973, CGT delegates came into conflict with José Alvez, a sacked Portuguese worker of Maoist leanings, and were reduced to hurling insults at him, including the allegation that he had served as an officer in the Portuguese army.[138] There was certainly some ideological division, the PCF not sharing the *soixante-huitard* view that nationality was of itself wrong:

> When the pseudo-revolutionaries proclaim that the workers have no homeland, they are going back to slogans which, for more than a century, Marxists have rejected and they place themselves, objectively, on the side of the workers' class enemy.[139]

Yet the distinction stereotypically made between the supposedly immigrant-suspicious CGT and immigrant-friendly, New Left-friendly CFDT was not total in practice. Though the CFDT tended to be more supportive of relatively isolated groups of immigrant workers in struggle, presented by the CGT as risky minority actions, the MTA was sometimes critical of both CGT *and* CFDT for an overly bureaucratic style. While tolerating the hunger strikes of 1972-73, the CFDT continued to view them as an inferior form of struggle. Indeed, one internal CFDT document was highly critical of the *sans-papiers* movement, its recuperation by *gauchistes*, and the support given by local CFDT branches to it. The document argued that hunger strikes were individual actions which undermined trade union norms by taking the struggle outside the workplace. It described demands made by the *sans-papiers* movement for across-the-board regularisation as 'demagogic', because it would leave immigrants at the mercy of unscrupulous employers. There were frequently internal disagreements within the CFDT: in 1973, while local activists in the 20th arrondissement were issuing leaflets supporting the hunger strikes against what they termed the 're-establishment of slavery', a split nevertheless opened up in the confederation over whether to allow a hunger strike to take place in their premises.[140] Thus the CGT was not alone in its suspicions of *gauchiste* infiltration, for the difference was not so much doctrinal as between two contrasting styles of politics: a trade union style inherited from before 1968 and the more impatient, spontaneist approach of post-68 militants.

But to adopt too Manichean a view of the New Left / Communist divide – which is a danger if the '68 years are equated exclusively with the family saga of a certain Parisian in-crowd – would be to ignore some of the ambiguities and complexities that the loud rhetoric of mutual hostility concealed. On 29 April 1970, the hard Right deputy Charles Pasqua caused uproar in the National Assembly by telling a Communist opponent of the government's legislative crackdown on the Maoists:

> It's logical for you to defend the *gauchistes* because, in fact, they were brought up in your innermost circle, and most of the *gauchiste* leaders … came out of the Communist Party's cadre schools.
>
> I've already told you, you lit the fire. Today, it's burning your fingers! Too bad for you![141]

Though characteristically crude, Pasqua's tirade touched a raw nerve because there was some truth to it. Many far Left parties, from the LCR to the Maoists, *had* been derived from splits from the official Communist movement, and carried over elements of its political heritage. Both PCF and far Left, for example, celebrated the 'Manouchian group' of Polish, Jewish and Armenian Resistance fighters shot by the Nazis in 1944 (and more recently dramatised in Robert Guédiguian's 2009 film *L'armée de crime*). While the far Left posited themselves rather than the official PCF as Manouchian's true heirs, emphasising the foreignness and the Jewishness of the Manouchian group which the PCF played down,[142] they thereby tacitly acknowledged their debt to older Communist traditions of solidarity with immigrants. The *gauchistes* wanted to be seen as quarrelsome schismatics from France's official labour movement, rather than something completely alien to it. Similarly, until he was shot dead in the lift of his Paris apartment block in 1978, the Egyptian-Jewish stateless refugee Henri Curiel ran a network entitled Solidarité that furnished false papers and other material support to various Third World liberation movements, just as he had done to the Algerian FLN. A wartime Gaullist, former leader of the Egyptian Communist movement, organiser of early Israeli-Palestinian peace talks, and something of an international man of mystery, Curiel's internationalism was in many ways that of a Moscow-loyalist Communist intellectual of the old school, sceptical of some of the more extravagant claims of revolutionary *tiersmondistes*. Yet it is telling that Curiel's network was ideologically broad enough to avail itself of the services both of Jean Tabet, who until he resigned over the 'bulldozer affair', was a member of the PCF Central Committee's commission on international politics, and such *soixante-huitard* militants as Thomas Schwaetzer, expelled from France in May 1968.[143]

Conversely, there was no absolute barrier shielding the PCF itself from contamination by post-68 ideas. Even among older CGT union militants, there were those like Apostolo who did not conform to the Communist ghetto stereotype. Apostolo had been active in left-Catholic organisations after the war, and was critical of the PCF's assumption that the CGT should act as a transmission belt into the party. This heterogeneity was, however, most apparent among younger members of the PCF. It is easily forgotten today that the party accelerated extremely impressively its recruitment of new members during the Seventies, of whom a disproportionate number were young, of working-class origin, and often female. Some studies estimate as many as 358,000 new recruits passed through the party between 1972 and 1976. Although many left before long – which was true of the *gauchiste* groups too – the lasting legacy is that babyboomers are still consistently more likely to vote Communist than their elders *or* their youngers.[144] So though the historiography depicts 'a tale of clashing countercultures',[145] paradoxically a subset of the babyboomers are actually the last generation of Communists in France. The age and size of the entrants belies any argument simplistically counterposing the party to the '68ers. Even apparently orthodox young apparatchiks were in a real sense members of the '68 generation. Future General Secretary and presidential candidate Marie-George Buffet joined up in 1969 at the age of 19, having been on strike as a lycée student in May '68.[146] Or to name another future political leader, the young François Hollande, before he went to the Ecole Normale d'Administration, met his long-term partner the future presidential candidate Ségolène Royal and rose himself to become the PS's First Secretary and a presidential contender, was in the 1970s a PCF sympathiser. Although involved in the school students' movement of the early Seventies, Hollande gave the *gauchistes* a wide berth, did not go to Pierre Overney's funeral, and enjoyed his military service: but he read *L'Humanité*, had many friends who were Party members, and as late as 1980 was justifying the PCF line in support of the Soviet invasion of Afghanistan.[147] Hollande's case shows how the PCF was in a sense the more 'square' option, for those who found the *gauchistes* just too disorganised.

But in an important sense this was no longer the party of Maurice Thorez.[148] To become a Communist in 1969 or 1979 was not the same as becoming a Communist in 1939 or 1949. Moreover, many joined with the intention of changing it from within, for a certain degree of susceptibility to *gauchiste* themes was not in practice incompatible with membership of the PCF or CGT. Mimouna Hadjam, the daughter of Algerian immigrants working in a biscuit factory near Lille, chose to join first the PCF's youth wing, and then the party itself, as the obvious choice for those fighting redundancies in the economically declining North of France. Yet at the same time she became a sympathiser of the clandestine Algerian Parti de l'Avant-Garde Socialiste, then being suppressed by the Algerian government with the complicity of the PCF. Considering herself one of the 'inheritors of '68', Hadjam also adopted outspoken positions on feminism, homosexuality and family planning that led more socially conservative elements in the party to consider her a *gauchiste*. Equally, Gérard Noiriel, now France's leading historian of immigration, joined the PCF as a student in Nancy, despite being a member of the '68 generation – one of his proudest boasts is to have seen Jimi Hendrix and Jim Morrison perform at the 1970 Isle of Wight Festival – because the party's ample educational opportunities for those from working-class backgrounds appealed to him more than the know-it-all attitude of the *gauchistes*. Yet, under Althusserian influence, Noiriel was far from uncritical of Communist orthodoxy. Ali El Baz, a future leader of the radical Association des Marocains en France's successor organisation, maintains that he came across the AMF via the CGT and not vice versa – but also hung out with the hippies and anarchists who gathered outside the Pompidou Centre. The Arenc detention centre scandal first broke in the Communist newspapers *L'Humanité* and *La Marseillaise*, yet was published in book form by Maspero.[149]

The PCF's attitude to immigration, then, needs to be considered as the responses of actors in an evolving historical situation, rather than the cartoon villains of the piece. Having gradually arrived at this conclusion myself over a number of years, I was intrigued to discover that the film historian Tangui Perron, who works as a cultural organiser in the Seine-Saint-Denis, similarly critiques the tendency in academic literature to see the CGT only as one-dimensional bad guys. Perron argues that the CGT was harsher at a national than a local level, where many branches had a more libertarian culture. His documentary film centre Périphérie has re-released the 1970 documentary *Etranges étrangers* ['Strange Foreigners'] made by the former television journalist and PCF member Marcel Trillat about shanty towns in Aubervilliers and Saint-Denis – only one of many immigration-themed films made by Communist directors. A recent interview of Trillat by Perron reveals on the one hand Trillat's deep attachment to the CGT and a similar distaste to Noiriel's for the *gauchistes'* tendency to be givers of lessons. Yet on the other hand Trillat comes across as a rebel who was often deeply uncomfortable with the party line, describes himself as basically an 'anar', against authority, and had *gauchiste* friends, including the film's co-director Frédéric Variot, a Maoist sympathiser.[150]

It is not self-evident, though, that the PCF's half-heartedness on immigration can entirely be attributed to its leadership. The xenophobia of at least part of the popular electorate of the Left – something of a taboo subject even to the party's leftist critics, who preferred to speak of bosses or revisionists dividing French from foreign workers, rather than openly criticise French workers – was a reality that historians have to acknowledge. The events of 1973 in Marseilles were a case in point, witnessing popular mobilisations that were essentially communitarian in nature. On 28 August, 5000 French people, including trade union representatives, turned out for the funeral cortege of the murdered bus driver Emile Gerlache, while North Africans stayed at home.[151] A good illustration of the problem can be found in *Vivre à gauche* ['Living on the Left'], a 1974 journalistic survey of ordinary voters who had voted for the Left in that year's presidential election. It contrasted the rousing ovation received by Mitterrand when, at a rally in Marseilles, he called for solidarity with immigrant workers, to the rather less noble sentiments expressed in private by left-wing voters, including committed activists:

> All through this investigation, often, too often, racism was present: aggressive or shamefaced, conscious or unconscious. There is an enormous gap between what the Left says in a loud voice and the whispers that can be observed within its ranks.[152]

For example, one painter at the naval shipyard in Nantes, a long-time CGT member who wrote to Mitterrand after the election to commiserate with him on his defeat, and had even participated during the Algerian War in demonstrations blocking conscript trains, openly said that he would not allow his daughter to marry an Algerian: 'It's not really their race which bothers me, but their way of seeing life. Perhaps in a few years they will be better. For the moment, no. I know this because I've worked with them.'[153] Television documentaries of the period often discovered alarming levels of openly expressed popular racism (though it is a moot point how far they also helped to create it).[154] On the rare occasions when leftist discourse did confront this issue, it could often come across as patronising, especially when coming from middle-class intellectuals, outside the Communist Party. In 1971, for example, the PSU's weekly *La Tribune Socialiste* had carried a feature on immigration which argued that the priority should be to struggle against chauvinism within the French working class, as the biggest obstacle to proletarian unity:

> For 70 years, [the French working class] has adopted a chauvinist and colonialist attitude very similar to that which Marx and Engels reproached the English proletariat for. The indifference of French workers during the Algerian War is still in everyone's memory.[155]

Indeed looking back as a historian in 2007, Noiriel attributed a significant amount of the blame for a dangerous re-ethnicisation of social relations to the largely middle-class far Left of the Seventies. By reducing immigration to its post-colonial component only, he suggests, they succeeded merely in inverting previous negative stereotypes, and also in reintroducing prejudices about the 'ordinary racism' of the French.[156] Noiriel's book is in many ways a timely reminder of the importance of class inequality, that not everything about the history of immigration can be reduced to ethnicity or the colonial heritage. But the evidence base on which he makes these particular claims about the far Left is quite limited, and contradicted by the significant interest it showed in Spanish and Portuguese migrants. And while the view of the French as racist was clearly a gross stereotype, it hardly, as we have seen, lacked possible foundations in reality.

But nor was it a simple case of the Left having xenophobic grassroots. One study of blue-collar workers in Lorraine in 1974 found that, although Algerians were the second most disliked national group after Germans, when asked if any group had too much power in France, no-one responded 'immigrants' – in fact the most popular answer was 'the bosses'.[157] Similarly, workers interviewed by sociologists Guy Michelat and Michel Simon in 1978 generally refused to express any dislike of immigrants, preferring a discourse of class defence, where anti-immigrant sentiment was seen as a trap set by the government and bosses and therefore to be avoided.[158] The Peugeot factory at Sochaux in eastern France, where two workers had been killed in the brutal storming of the factory by riot police in June 1968, was an example of the forging of class solidarity between French and immigrant workers in the years that followed. Peugeot workers later interviewed by Stéphane Beaud and Michel Pialoux recalled the 1970s primarily as a time of conviviality between themselves and 'my immigrant mates'. Indeed, Beaud and Pialoux see a kind of class contempt in the obsession of latter-day elites with working-class racism.[159]

We need to recognise that the same people could hold contradictory attitudes. One interviewee for *Vivre à gauche*, a 24-year-old aviation worker, CGT activist and recent recruit to the PCF, who did have black and North African friends, admitted to having once stopped dancing with a black woman out of what he attributed to unconscious racism, and to differentiating between friends of different 'races':

> At the start it is certain that you are more tempted to make friends with a bloke who is like you than a bloke who is not. Perhaps this is racism, but it can't be denied. You can't say that you spontaneously accept a North African as you accept a Frenchman. But even so there's a difference between this sort of racism and the violent racism of those guys who refuse to have anything to do with Arabs. Now that is disgusting racism![160]

This honest response reveals the complexity of attitudes to difference. Rather than racism being a simple issue that could be resolved by sloganising about unity, it was deeply entrenched in the structures of a society only just emerging from its colonial past. Here a worker was making an effort to overcome his own prejudices – indeed argued back with workmates who expressed the more virulent form of racism he referred to, by telling them that North Africans were workers too – yet had clearly not fully succeeded in this. Abraham Behar, writing in *La Tribune Socialiste* in 1971, had similarly detected the beginnings of a change in attitudes amongst younger French workers, but remained rather pessimistic about its extent:

> Eight years of the Algerian War are there to prove to us that imperialist chauvinism is not a vain word. Luckily, recent class conflicts reveal the growing power of a new generation of French workers less affected than preceding ones by reformist and

chauvinist ideology. But this process of renewal is only at the beginning of its evolution. How many more racist roundups will we witness before it reaches maturity?[161]

Yet while real enough, colonialist ideology was not necessarily all-pervasive, or stronger in the working class than elsewhere. If the memory of French Algeria was later transferred into anti-Arab racism in France, as Benjamin Stora argues, this does not mean that the ordinary worker on the production line in metropolitan France can simply be amalgamated to the *pied-noirs* and the OAS. During the Algerian War itself, workers had actually been more likely to agree with Algerian independence than other classes.[162]

Though the PCF did sometimes attempt to propagandise its own members against racism,[163] this was not always welcomed. In February 1974, Communist militants told two journalists allowed to sit in on a party branch meeting that other party members were resisting their attempts to produce foreign-language party material: 'The blokes refuse to pay for "propaganda in Arabic" as they put it. This is normal.'[164] A more subtle issue – of the party failing fully to confront racism by others, as opposed to direct racism – was thus posed. But it cannot be denied that PCF-controlled municipal councils contributed to the problem, by espousing the pseudo-scientific concept of a 'threshold of tolerance', in common with councils of all political shades of opinion. Communists gave the concept a Marxist twist by arguing that Right-wing councils were deliberately not building public housing, so as to pass on to Communist-run working-class areas the social costs of reproducing a labour force that the capitalists could continue to exploit for free. Immigration was thus portrayed as a conspiracy by sending countries, the bosses and the government to dump their problems onto Communist municipalities. Consequent demands for a more even dispersal of immigrant workers contributed to a public perception of immigrants as a problem.[165] Many of the more tricky issues around popular xenophobia that subsequently became a more overt part of French politics were thus already present below the surface. Outright xenophobia was still, however, impeded, or at least concealed, by the persistence of a strong working-class Left in the shape of the Communists, which could articulate an earthy anti-establishment populism in the language of Marxism, and because the antiracist Left also spoke the language of class struggle, of uniting French and immigrant workers. Once the PCF and the activist Left as a whole went into decline in the Eighties, populism was to find a new home on the far Right.

Yet the responses of French workers to the growing militancy of immigrant workers threw up quandaries for the PCF. In May 1976, for example, during a strike by dustmen in Lyons against proposed redundancies, the Algerians who collected the rubbish suddenly found that the French drivers of their carts, some of whom were *pied-noirs*, ceased after only two days to support the strike. Ralph Grillo, who observed the strike as part of anthropological fieldwork, identified this as part of a pattern whereby French workers were increasingly reluctant to go on strike out of solidarity with 'Arabs', thereby posing real dilemmas for the CGT. But as Grillo noted, ethnicity was only one of three connected lines of dispute between the two groups of workers: there was also an occupational cleavage, and an inter-union rivalry of CGT versus CFDT. Indeed, at the time he was hesitant to see this dispute as an issue of 'race'; only when writing it up for publication a decade and a half later did it seem to retrospectively make sense in the light of the rise of the Front National.[166] It is possible, therefore, that he exaggerated this element of the dispute. Since the principal organisations of the Left retained a strongly class-based paradigm at the time, far from the identity preoccupations of the present day, ethnic conflict is sometimes only visible by reading between the lines.

So by the mid-1970s immigration was becoming politicised, but mostly in a positive way, rather than the negative way more readily associated today with France by Anglophone observers. The exploitation of immigrants had become accepted as a problem: immigrants themselves were, for the greater part of the political spectrum, not. Immigration was an issue of the Left, in contrast to the way the terms of debate from the 1980s onwards were often set by the extreme Right. The fate of anti-racism was increasingly determined by the complex dynamics on the Left more widely, not just the far Left. Influenced by the post-1968 new social movement of anti-racism, the Left tried often ambitiously to grapple with the changing nature of French society. But the relationships between immigrants and the Left, and between workers and intellectuals, were far from unproblematic. The relationship between 'Old' and 'New' Lefts was complex. All parties of the Left were ideologically committed to internationalism, but this did not always translate into practice. In the next chapter we shall see how the movement both came to an end and passed on to the next generation in the very different climate of the late 1970s and early 1980s. With the long-term economic downturn, a new dynamic was set in motion. From a situation where since 1968 it had been the Left making the running in the debate over immigration, now the Right was to have its revenge.

Chapter Six

Decline and Renewal:
Passing On to the Next Generation, 1976-1983

'We don't need leaders outside ourselves.'
'Mohammed' from Nanterre, 1982[1]

On 16 March 1976, the bulldozers came to demolish what was then the last major shanty town in France. On the outskirts of Nice, adjacent to the main airport serving the Côte d'Azur, the inhabitants of La Digue des Français sat on their suitcases drinking one final mint tea, before leaving on foot, by bus or by lorry for new hostel accommodation elsewhere. Around them were slogans scrawled on the walls by French *gauchistes*: 'Hostel = prison', 'Residency papers for all'.[2] Politicians had been talking about an end to the shanty towns since as long ago as 1949. Now it had finally become a reality. A particular social universe that had dominated political debate about immigration during the years defined by May 1968 was no more, and new formations were taking its place. This chapter is about how that transition took place, both in the lived experience of immigrants and their families, and in the politics surrounding the issue, as the dreams of '68 gave way to the very different landscape of the 1980s.

Revolutionaries in Decline and the Politics of Immigration

There is no agreement among historians as to the date at which the '68 years' came to an end. Looking for a symbolic burial of grand ideals, some would, following Louis Althusser, place the end point as early as the funeral of Pierre Overney in 1972;[3] others would favour that of Jean-Paul Sartre in 1980.[4] For others, the end of the Left's long years in opposition in May 1981 marks a convenient caesura, making the preceding 13 years the 'between two Mays'.[5] As far as the politics of immigration are concerned, the end to primary immigration in 1974 had already changed a lot. But we shall see that there are compelling reasons to favour 1983 as the key turning point, as the moment when the dynamic on the immigration issue shifted from Left to Right. Yet at any rate by the 1980s, a new set of references were shaping political and intellectual life, erasing Marxism from view so effectively that its dominance only a few years earlier became a sheer embarrassment, fit only to be written out of history. As Robert Lumley has written in relation to Italy:

> Until 1980-81 (though it is difficult to pinpoint a date), there was a certain continuity in people's conceptions of themselves with the ideas identified with '68, especially among those who had been participants. Then, from the early 1980s onwards, that past came to resemble a foreign country. It is as if a frontier had been crossed and the language and points of reference had changed.[6]

This anti-Marxist turn coincided with a shift in preoccupations towards those of culture and identity. Right-wingers no longer defined themselves against a now diminished Communist threat so much as against supposed threats to French and European identity from Islam. Though immigration was to become a bigger mainstream political issue, shorn as the debate was of the umbilical cord that had tied it to 68-era Marxism, the terms of argument had fundamentally shifted. The far Left had declined, words like 'worker' were no longer fashionable, and the Left instead adopted the language of cultural difference, decoupled from a critique of capitalism.

Nor is there agreement as to the causes of this shift, for many competing explanations have been advanced for the decline of the 1968-era Left. Indeed, it can be viewed as a kind of murder mystery – who killed *gauchisme*? – for which different theoretical approaches apportion blame differently. The political scientists' explanation would have it that the culprit was François Mitterrand in the bathroom with a copy of the Common Programme, by co-opting the *gauchistes'* rhetoric about *autogestion*, 'changing life' and so on.[7] The intellectual historians' explanation would be that the villains were actually the much-touted 'New Philosophers' Bernard-Henri Lévy and André Glucksmann, in the drawing room with a copy of Alexander Solzhenitsyn's *The Gulag Archipelago*. The 1974 French publication of the Russian dissident's masterwork has often been taken to symbolise a definitive break in the global intellectual context away from the idea of revolution.[8] The sociologists', or social historians', explanation might be that the victim was pre-destined to turn back into a pumpkin at midnight. Many of the *gauchistes* had all along been what Pierre Bourdieu called *The Inheritors*, or in the words of E.P. Thompson, 'the revolting young bourgeoisie ... doing their own thing'.[9] New Left activists tended to be motivated less by material incentives than ideological ones,[10] so it was not surprising they reverted to type in the time-accustomed manner once the going got tough. Finally, a more prosaic explanation would be that the poor unhappy victim simply buckled under the weight of having to sell so many newspapers. The leftists were exhausted after being constantly on the go since 1968 – what some observers termed the 'crisis of militancy'.[11]

Whatever the causes, the failure of the *gauchistes*' immediate political project was becoming evident, even as their wider cultural influence was beginning to bear fruit with a certain diversification of French society. In the 1974 presidential election, Alain Krivine had won a derisory 0.3 per cent of the popular vote: the only even moderate success for the far Left was the 2.3 per cent of Arlette Laguiller, whose austere and old-fashioned approach to Trotskyism, and electoral support from such quarters as elderly peasants in the Auvergne, was never particularly close to the 'spirit of 68'. Most of the Maoist groups folded during the Seventies, leaving only the rump Parti Socialiste Unifié and the Trotskyists as the main, not very successful leftovers of the 68-era Left to carry on into the Eighties. Although the PSU continued to be very active on immigrant solidarity until the end of its days,[12] such as in the prominence given the issue by its 1981 presidential candidate Huguette Bourchardeau, the party was increasingly marginal, attracting only 1.1 per cent of the vote. It was Mitterrand's Parti Socialiste, often radical and *marxisant* in rhetoric but reformist in practice, who were the truly dynamic force on the Left, reaping the benefits of '68 by winning real votes from real people. Only narrowly defeated in the 1974 election, having come first with some 43 per cent of the vote at the first ballot, Mitterrand spent the next seven years as the president in waiting.[13]

So whereas in the Sixties ambitious young political organisers like Alain Krivine had broken with the mainstream Left to join the far Left, by the beginning of the Eighties, the traffic was firmly in the other direction. In 1981, the future founders of SOS Racisme, Harlem Désir, Julien Dray and Didier François, knowing which way the wind was blowing, left Krivine's Ligue Communiste Révolutionnaire, in which they had lost their political virginity as rebellious *lycéens* earlier in the Seventies, and joined the PS. Another Trotskyist mutating into a PS apparatchik, Jean-Christophe Cambadélis of the Organisation Communiste Internationaliste (OCI), played a major role in organising the massive victory celebrations on the night of 10 May, and has even boasted how (in a manner reminiscent of Stalin giving Trotsky the wrong date for Lenin's funeral) he deliberately misled his rival Dray as to the venue. The predominant tendency was thus the difficult journey from revolution to reform, well described in the autobiography of Benjamin Stora, historian of Algeria and 1970s OCI activist, who also gave up Trotskyism in the following decade – partly because of his party's lack of interest in the emerging movements of second-generation French-Maghrebi youth.[14] The relevance of this for the politics of immigration was that the immigrant workers' movements of the 1970s had surfed on the crest of the *soixante-huitard* wave which was now breaking on the rocky shores of the 1980s. Between 1968 and about 1976, immigrants' movements could count on the sympathy of a confident and flamboyant French far Left for the image of the oppressed immigrant worker, a single man living alone in a hostel and working in a factory, exploited by capitalism and imperialism and increasingly prone to fight back. This in turn had been dependent on a number of factors: government-encouraged migration; an economic boom; relative public indifference rather than hostility to immigrants; the absence of a large immigrant-baiting far Right; the continued predominance of class politics – all of which were to disappear in a remarkably short space of time.

SONACOTRA: the Last First Generation Mobilisation

But to some extent the old situation appeared to continue throughout the remainder of the 1970s, notably with a prolonged rent strike by residents of the SONACOTRA immigrant workers' hostels. The strike began in hostels in Saint-Denis in early 1975 in response to attempts by SONACOTRA to put up rents, for rooms that were smaller than industry norms.[15] An equally significant motivation of the strikers, though, was anger at the paternalism and unfreedom inherent in the running of the hostels. As one member of the strike Coordinating Committee put it, the problem with living in a hostel was not that the manager was racist – though they usually were – but that there was a manager, who saw it as his role to open residents' doors to ask what they were up to, had they illegally drunk coffee in their rooms, and so on. The strikers therefore demanded tenant status, in order to abolish this unhappy situation. By the late summer of 1975, the strike had spread right around the Paris region. In 1976, faced with a hardening strike, the authorities responded partly by concessions – training schemes for managers were promised to bury the old colonialist image – and partly by repression, with Interior Minister Poniatowski ordering the deportation of 16 'ringleaders'. This was for a time successful in defusing the strike, frightening other activists into going underground during the summer of 1976.

Such problems turned out to be temporary, though, as in March 1977 the Conseil d'Etat decreed that the government had acted illegally in deporting the SONACOTRA strikers. This was a decision with significance beyond this particular dispute, as it marked a clear shift in the authorities' conception of what constituted a 'threat to public order' sufficient to allow deportation. Throughout the '68 years, and indeed throughout modern French history, foreigners had been deported for going on strike, for handing out leaflets, and for attending demonstrations, but henceforth they could, more often than not, get away with non-violent political activism.[16] The newly emboldened strikers succeeded not only in keeping the strike going, but in spreading it to non-SONACOTRA hostels in January 1978. By the end of 1978, the authorities estimated that nearly 28,000 residents were on strike, in 44 per cent of all hostels.[17] This was despite an increasingly terse polemic between two rival committees, both viewing themselves as the leadership of the strike. On the one hand the Departmental Committee, comprised of an alliance between the CFDT, the CGT, its Communist Party patrons and the Amicale des Algériens en Europe, were trying to conclude a negotiated settlement to the dispute. On the other, a more militantly minded Coordinating Committee, seeking to bypass such institutionalised channels, was resisting attempts to end the strike, arguing that 'For us it is not for organisations, but for those who struggle, to lead the movement'.[18]

Such sentiments typified the growing concern for immigrant autonomy within political struggles during this period, to which French organisations were increasingly sensitive. Established anti-racist organisations like the MRAP were finding themselves in the unusual situation of immigrants not wanting assistance from them.[19] From about 1977 onwards, there was a growing emphasis on immigrant self-expression and autonomy, even within existing organisations: 'The time when French people talked in the name of immigrant workers is gone. From now on it is us who are speaking up to affirm our demands and even our struggles.'[20] French organisations were increasingly aware that this was an issue. They were influenced by a growing trend more widely on the European Left away from old-style Leninism towards a 'movement of movements' approach in which the autonomy of different oppressed groups – youth, women, minorities – to make their own decisions would be respected.[21] The Catholic activist Gilles Verbunt suggested that there were three insidious ways that French militants talked in place of immigrants: first, by pretending that their needs were no different from those of French workers, secondly, by having a token immigrant member who speaks without deviation the line of the French organisation they belong to, given their dependence on that organisation, or thirdly for immigrant leaders to project their own aspirations onto their compatriots, forgetting that a political militant is by definition in certain important respects atypical of other people. Nevertheless, Verbunt argued, 'autonomous' did not mean 'autonomist': immigrant organisations were not systematically opposed to all French organisations, since after all most of their militants had passed through the 'French school of militancy'.[22]

Thus allegations were made by the CGT and the Amicale des Algériens en Europe that the SONACOTRA strikers' Co-ordinating Committee was being manipulated by French Maoist groups. In reality, while it is true that some of the early Algerian strikers had been previously politicised, the role of French *gauchistes* was largely confined to supporting the strikes, attempting to extend them and engaging in polemics about them, rather than playing a major role in instigating them. Indeed one Maoist *groupuscule*, the Union des Communistes de France Marxiste-Léniniste, wrote to a hostel residents committee criticising its emphasis on autonomy, described in the letter as 'false' and 'bourgeois'. On the other hand, the fact that arguments about autonomy went to and fro reflected the growing desire on the part of even the most mainstream parts of the French Left to be associated with the strike. In 1979, when SONACOTRA tried a new tactic by evicting strikers from the hostels, Communist and Socialist local authorities showed solidarity by rehousing the evicted residents. An open-air campsite set up by 240 evicted residents of a SONACOTRA hostel in Garge-les-Gonesses received much publicity. Communist propaganda drew attention to the irony that SONACOTRA residents were being mistreated at a time when politicians were falling over each other to welcome 'good', anti-communist immigrants in the shape of the Vietnamese 'boat people'. Students at Vincennes University produced photo displays in support of the strike, while their counterparts at Nanterre University offered to house the evicted residents in their rooms.[23] Given the relationship during and after 1968 between university and shanty town in Nanterre, this represented history coming full circle. The SONACOTRA rent strike, lasting as it did for some five years, was in many ways the culminating point of 'first generation', immigrant worker militancy: 'Our strike has been, without doubt, the longest, hardest, most combative, most followed and, it goes without saying, the most repressed of all strikes by the immigrant part of the working class.'[24] Demonstrations during the strike were bigger than any over immigration in the immediate aftermath of 1968. In April 1976 for example, 30,000 people hit the streets of Paris to protest the deportation of the strike leaders, whereas turnouts of only a few thousand immigrants had been considered as great victories in 1971-72, as they would again in the late 1990s. The strike brought together people from many different countries and backgrounds, ranging from students radicalised by movements in

Senegal to the illiterate.[25]

The SONACOTRA strike was only the most prominent aspect of a culture of militancy, owing much to the struggles of a few years before, that continued to flourish in some places. The historian Vincent Viet sees it as the culmination of a crisis in the management of immigration, driven by contestation from below, that forced the authorities to liberalise regulations in the hostels.[26] The strikers succeeded in making hostel management more democratic, and in getting their outstanding debts written off, but not in their demand for full tenant status.[27] Although workplace strikes were less frequent than earlier in the decade, some immigrant workers were still flexing their industrial muscle. The mainly African cleaners on the Paris metro went on strike for six months in 1977, and struck again in 1980.[28] In 1979-80, a major battle ensued over redundancies in the steel industry at Longwy in Lorraine, which employed many immigrant workers. The Longwy strike in fact had a lasting impact on the development of a historiography of immigration in France. The later prominent historian Gérard Noiriel, then a young schoolteacher, wrote his first book about this dispute – in conjunction with a Longwy steel worker, Bennaceur Azzaoui – for Maspero, before delving further back into the region's long history of migrant labour for his thesis.[29] But the Longwy strike was symptomatic of a newly defensive tone to industrial struggles given rising unemployment. As a result of discriminatory practices, foreign workers tended to be the first to be laid off. In any case they had the misfortune to be concentrated in precisely those economic sectors which were entering crisis, such as the car, building and chemicals industries.[30]

Meanwhile the cultural scene of the Seventies continued to flourish in festivals and elsewhere. As a legacy of initiatives begun by groups associated with the MTA, such as El Assifa, leftist political theatre about the situation of immigrant workers was highly developed during this period. In Marseilles in 1976, for example, North African female domestic workers put on a play to illustrate their situation. The programmes of El Assifa's pirate radio station – the first immigrant radio station in France – circulated widely on cassette. Significantly, El Assifa spoke in *soixante-huitard* terms of *prendre la parole* ['speaking out'].[31] Newer groups of migrants who had managed to slip through the net of post-1974 immigration controls also became involved in struggle, notably in a new *sans-papiers* hunger strike in 1980 by Turkish workers working illegally in the Parisian confection industry. The strike, led by members of a Turkish far Left group, Dev Yol, and supported by CFDT activists, took place partly in the same Saint-Bruno church annexe as had Said Bouziri's, whose successful hunger strike against his attempted deportation in 1972 had kick-started the militancy of the mid-70s. The 1980 movement spread and was a success, achieving no fewer than 3000 regularisations.[32]

Passing On to the Next Generation: the Role of *Sans Frontière*

But even as first generation immigrant worker militancy reached its climax, its political leadership – often, like the French *gauchistes*, composed of former students – was experiencing its own 'crisis of militancy'. In 1976 the Mouvement des Travailleurs Arabes disbanded. Its former cadres gravitated into less overtly 'revolutionary', more gradual and consensual forms of activism, including journalism and culture. In 1979 they founded an annual street carnival in the Goutte d'Or that still continues today.[33] The decision to wind up the political organisation was partly because it had been weakened by state repression and the deportation of some of its activists, but also partly because El Assifa wanted to become independent of the MTA's propaganda.[34] Two years after the end of the MTA, many of its former leaders, including Saïd Bouziri and Driss El Yazami – who in 1977 had managed to escape from prison in Morocco to France on a sailing boat – decided to launch France's first widely circulated 'newspaper by immigrants for immigrants', *Sans Frontière*. For this venture, the North African ex-MTAers were now also joined by members of other immigrant groups. As El Yazami notes, such diversity, unusual amongst the minority press of the time, was a great strength, but would also prove a source of tension.[35]

The central significance of *Sans Frontière* was that it perfectly illustrated the situation of transition between the post-68 period and the Eighties. Though superficially *Sans Frontière* had some resemblances to a counter-culture paper of the early Seventies like *Tout!*, the style and content had clearly moved on from the *gauchiste* agitational newsletters of that era. Unencumbered by tortuous political jargon, and complete with gig listings and lonely hearts column, it had a modern feel with a trendy logo and lots of photographs. In short, it was the immigrant equivalent of *Libération*, the daily newspaper that had emerged from the post-68 Left in 1973. Indeed, after reading its first issue, one CGT trade unionist wrote in to complain that '*Sans Frontière* is too like *Libé*'. During the 'bulldozer affair' of 1980-81, when Communist local authorities in the suburbs of Paris were accused of playing the race card to pander to anti-immigrant prejudice, *Sans Frontière*'s unsurprisingly robust response was characterised by some critics as 'Anti-communism in the style of *Libé*'.[36] *Sans Frontière* was correspondingly perhaps less critical of the PS than the PCF. In 1981 the magazine welcomed on a visit to its office the future prime minister Lionel Jospin. The new PS First Secretary was standing for election in the 18th arrondissement of Paris, where *Sans Frontière* was based, against a particularly anti-immigrant right-wing incumbent.[37] Fundamentally, though, the magazine's approach was non-sectarian, opening its columns to a variety of political viewpoints. This led it to be denounced by some dogmatic ultra-leftists and accused on different occasions of working for, variously, the KGB, the CIA, the Gulf emirates, Israel and the PLO.[38]

Certainly, *Sans Frontière* remained strongly marked by its founders' political backgrounds in post-68 *gauchisme*. For example in 1979, a debate took place about whether to allow advertising in the paper,[39] a classic sign of a magazine run by recovering 68-ers, in the process of becoming professional journalists.[40] When in 1979 the offbeat activist Pierre Goldman, who had become something of an icon for the *soixante-huitard* generation after being wrongly convicted of armed robbery, was assassinated,[41] he received fulsome tributes in *Sans Frontière* as a man of integrity who was on the side of immigrants against people with power. The fact that Goldman, the son of Holocaust survivors, and whose skin was sufficiently dark for a shot policeman to have confused him in an identity parade with a man from Guadeloupe,[42] had emphasised in his political postures a feeling of not belonging, of anger against the French state, no doubt contributed to this sympathy: 'It is perhaps that he was one of us because [he was] *sans frontière*.' [43] This was not an uncontroversial position to take: one Aziz of Nanterre wrote in to complain that *Sans Frontière*'s silence on the 'anti-fascist consensus between Zionists and yesterday's anti-Zionists' around Goldman's death gave the impression of 'a continued ideological dependence of certain Arab militants on French intellectuals of the Maoist era'.[44]

But *Sans Frontière's* task was complicated by the fact that it had to serve two audiences with conflicting demands. On the one hand, it reported on the last gasps of the struggle of the first generation in the SONACOTRA strike,[45] and served as a kind of 'site of memory'[46] for the struggles of a few years before. So its issue for 1 January 1980 was a retrospective on '1970 – 1980: The Immigrant Years', rather wistfully recalling the glory days when big-name intellectuals had marched alongside immigrants. The implication was that things now were not what they had been then: 'At the dawn of the 1980s, immigrants appear a little as "losers" who will no longer be supported like before. We will no longer see as before, in '71, Sartre, Foucault and Mauriac in Barbès.' [47] The memory theme continued throughout 1980, presenting individuals' life stories under the rubric 'The People's

Memory'.[48] When at the end of the year, the Abbé Gallimardet, the priest of the Saint-Bernard church who had played a key role in the Djellali Ben Ali, Saïd Bouziri and Mohammed Diab affairs died, tributes and reminiscences of those days poured in from readers: 'Galli was a "French immigrant" in a way that the French far Left never were.'[49] Also appealing to an older audience, *Sans Frontière* – from October 1981 subtitled *Immigration and Third World Weekly* – carried much information about events back home. It carried interviews with prominent cultural and political figures from the global South, and served as a forum for debates on such sensitive issues as Islam and sexuality,[50] the place of Jews in Arab societies,[51] the end of the 'myth of return' for immigrant workers[52] and the hostility of Algerian society to returned migrants,[53] the situation of women in North Africa,[54] the first signs of an Islamist movement in Algeria[55] and Mohammed Harbi's revisionist history of the FLN.[56] The magazine could boast among its writers intellectuals like the sociologist Abdelmalek Sayad, collaborator of Pierre Bourdieu.[57]

But on the other hand, *Sans Frontière* sought to address a French-born second generation audience who differed in crucial respects from the first generation militants who founded the magazine. First, they were untied spatially to the locations where previous immigrant militancy had taken place. Rather than in the classic inner Paris immigrant areas like Barbès and Belleville, they lived in the high-rise *banlieue* – where groups like the MTA had always been weaker.[58] Secondly, because they had been born or at least grown up in France, educated in the French school system, they unproblematically saw their future as being there. In important respects they were becoming less ghettoised than their parents had been in the shanty towns and hostels. By 1982 *carte de séjour* did not just mean residency permit, but a band whose name satirised the requirement for people who had grown up in France to get official permission to remain in France.[59] Thirdly, they differed markedly in cultural outlook. The MTA founders had been influenced by a mixture of their cultures of origin and European high culture. But the new generation's cultural landscape was shaped less by the traditional Arabic music of first-generation immigrants than by the Anglo-American rock and pop music shared with their peers. One of the racist killings of the late Seventies took place at a Peter Gabriel concert; groups like Carte de Séjour were heavily influenced by The Clash; and one very popular theatre piece of the period was entitled 'Mohammed Travolta', about an Algerian youth obsessed with being John Travolta in *Saturday Night Fever*.[60] Finally, they were either not tied at all by a political umbilical cord to post-68 Marxism, or this link was tenous and fraying. This gap might be illustrated by the fact that even in 1971, Julien Dray had only managed to persuade his fellow lycée students to attend the LCR's centenary commemorations of the Paris Commune with a (false) rumour that John Lennon and Pink Floyd were going to be there.[61]

Nevertheless, *Sans Frontière* sought to bridge this divide by engaging with the struggles of the new generation. It reported extensively, for example, on the case of Samid and Mogniss Abdallah, two brothers who had got into trouble for politically organising mixed groups of young people, French and non-French, unemployed and students. In 1979, the government attempted to deport the Abdallahs, before being forced to back down after a large mobilisation in their favour.[62] The magazine often carried interviews with second generation youths, talking frankly about their lives in a way that went beyond the simplistic 'miserabilist' dialectic of oppressive France and oppressed immigrants that earlier *gauchiste* papers had been wont to portray.[63] The *Sans Frontière* experience in fact had a lasting impact on at least the oldest generation of Eighties Beur activists, born in the 1950s, many of whom wrote for the magazine. Farid Aïchoune, for example, had been present as a child on the fateful demonstration of 17 October 1961, participated himself in May 1968, had been threatened with expulsion for Maoist activism, and been a founder member of the MTA. As Aïchoune put it, *Sans Frontière* was a 'political training school' and a 'bridge laid down between past struggles and the new generation'.[64]

The Brave New World of the *Banlieues*: Moving Away From '68 Culture

This intergenerational link is important because, though France generally remembers the 1983 'Marche des Beurs' as the beginning of the political expression of the 'second generation', this is somewhat misleading. The prehistory of the Beurs in fact goes back some years before the term was coined to denote the sons and daughters of North African immigrants. As early as 1977, sociologists were identifying the existence of a distinct 'second generation' with its own problems quite distinct from those of immigrants proper.[65] Rapid socio-economic change was altering reality far from the classic situation of the *travailleur immigré* which had held sway only a few years earlier and underpinned the classic leftist view of immigration. Since economic crisis and the ensuing redundancies in heavy industry hit immigrants harder than anyone else, the *travailleur immigré* was tragically often no longer a *travailleur*. He was no longer necessarily an *immigré* either. By 1982 40 per cent of foreign nationals were under 25 years old, and had usually either been born in or grown up in France. And he was now often she, as the previously predominantly lone male migrant population was now accompanied by wives and daughters. The combined effects of unemployment and family reunification meant that by 1982 only 42 per cent of foreigners were economically active. The workplace was simply no longer the defining feature of immigrant life, as unemployment for foreign nationals under the age of 20 rose to the astonishing levels of 35 per cent for males, and 51 per cent for females. It cannot be emphasised too strongly that the new socio-economic landscape of the *banlieue*, defined by unemployment, represented a major challenge to the traditional strategies of trade unions and parties of the Left and far Left. Cheerleading strikes – an activity which took up much of the Left's time in the glory years after 1968 – no longer represented a viable strategy, since the unemployed by definition do not go on strike.[66]

So what political culture was emerging from this new generation? In spite of the media-sociological cliché of the Beur living 'between two cultures', the harsher truth, as the Beur leader Farida Belghoul put it, was that they had proper access to neither: 'We live with the only culture which is really ours: that of the *quartiers*. We call ourselves "Farid from Les Minguettes", "Omar from Châtenay".'[67] It was very much in the *quartiers* that new political movements were emerging, no longer so dependent on French leftist allies, but also feeling unrepresented by the organisations created by first generation immigrants. Autonomy was a multi-faceted concept, for young people wanted to be autonomous not only from French parties but also from nationality or community-specific groups related to country of origin. Instead they tended to favour a social autonomy based on the common experience of living in the suburbs.[68]

This common experience was becoming an increasingly grim one. From 1977 onwards, Giscard's government, having replaced Paul Dijoud as immigration minister with Lionel Stoléru – a technocrat with an economics PhD – dropped the apparently liberal approach of its first few years, and got tough on immigration, to the extent of trying to bribe immigrant workers with 10,000 francs to return home. Voluntary repatriation, the panacea beloved of the Monday Club wing of the Tory Right in Britain, was thus actually tried out in France. It suggested the cynical reading of Dijoud's apparently liberal emphasis on keeping immigrants in touch with their home cultures – that it was intended to pave the way for an eventual return home – was true. But the scheme turned out to be a complete failure. Few workers took up the offer. Of those that did, most were Spanish and Portuguese, happy to return home after the re-establishment of democracy in their countries, whereas of course the measure had been aimed at North Africans and especially Algerians, of whom only 3000 participated in the scheme. Tellingly, the scheme did not include any provision for removal expenses, anachronistically assuming that the immigrant worker was a single man whose worldly goods could be fitted in one suitcase.[69] After the failure of voluntary repatriation, the government fell back on the use of force. Attempts were made to ban radical immigrant groups including the historic FEANF. Moreover, several thousand youths who had grown up in, or even been born in France, were deported for non-political offences of minor delinquency. This practice, today known as *la double peine* ['double punishment'] because it punishes foreigners twice for an offence for which a French person would only be published once, was a major focus of campaigns in the late Seventies.[70] By 1977, therefore, commentators were already speaking of a 'racism of crisis', as the government attempted to solve the problem of unemployment by sending the unemployed 'home'. Worse still, racist killings of second generation youths, sometimes by trigger-happy police, sometimes by estate residents taking pot-shots from their windows, became an alarmingly frequent occurrence at the beginning of the 1980s, on at least fifteen different occasions. The combined effect of racist killings, deportations, and economic crisis produced a serious situation which some observers characterised as one of paranoia and psychosis.[71]

Some young people even chose to take their own lives – one set himself on fire in the Gare Saint-Lazare with a copy of his deportation order in his pocket – and their suicide notes were reproduced in *Sans Frontière* and elsewhere. These depicted the progressively deteriorating conditions in the estates, enlivened only by the chance to live dangerously via rock concerts and less than fulfilling experiences on the margins of *gauchisme*. As the author of one suicide note, who described himself as 'Djamel, 21, Nationality: Immigrant', summarised his experience of the year 1978: 'My school's LCR branch tries to recruit me. "School student comrade, immigrant comrade". I've had enough!'[72] Suicide was not a phenomenon confined to the suburbs, though, for the disillusion and depression experienced by French *gauchistes* as the dreams of '68 died could lead to a similar end. A transition, personally and professionally, into 'normal' life after the extraordinary ferment of the '68 period was far from unproblematic, even for those who had had access to educational opportunities and contacts denied to the youths from the *banlieue*. In 1979, for example, the political theorist Nicos Poulantzas leapt to his death from the Montparnasse Tower. And one of the most celebrated cinematic depictions of the 1968 generation is *Mourir à trente ans* ['To Die At Thirty']. The film depicts the life of Michel Récanti, a prominent activist in the LCR, in charge of security on demonstrations, who threw himself under a train in 1978.[73] Unlike Récanti, though, the likes of Djamel of Nanterre did not generally get films made about their lives which won prizes at the Cannes Film Festival.

The generation of 68er North African intellectuals represented on the editorial team of *Sans Frontière*, however, were often quite ambivalent about the new generation, whose propensity to commit acts of violence against schools and public transport facilities they found rather worrying. The magazine talked of 'a wild and confused revolt against their social imprisonment'.[74] The *Sans Frontière* team were often uneasy with the *banlieue* movements, seeing them as lacking a historical awareness of previous struggles.[75] Some critics, though, detected a tendency on the part of *Sans Frontière* to sweep under the carpet some of the more negative aspects of the behaviour of young people out of embarrassment. In 1981, a right-wing journalist accused the magazine's editors of being 'old lefties, professional anti-racists', only interested in a portrayal of poor oppressed Arabs,[76] while the writer Leïla Sabbar, herself a contributor to the magazine, felt that *Sans Frontière* had changed from its earlier mission to present marginal cultures as they are, both good and bad, and was now disguising the truth 'so as "not to disappoint Billancourt" '.[77]

Beur Activism *Avant la Lettre*: Rock Against Police

Conversely, if young activists like the Abdallah brothers still had some respect for post-68 *gauchisme* – Mogniss for example wrote a tribute to Pierre Goldman[78] – the umbilical cord tying them to it was considerably more fragile than it was for, say, Saïd Bouziri. The MTAers could now be dismissed as 'politicised ex-students who came from the *bled*'.[79] Younger activists accused older ones of *immigrisme*: forging militant careers by purveying a one-dimensional portrait of oppressed immigrants.[80] This can be seen if we consider the background to the Abdallah case, namely the theatre troupe Weekend à Nanterre, who caused a sensation with the eponymous play they put on in 1977 that can be seen as marking the beginning of an autonomous expression by immigrant-origin youth. The link with 68 was clearly there: the play's author Aïssa Djabri had grown up in the shanty town next to Nanterre University and had attended as a child the crèche put on there by Maoist students, which was important for him as the first time he had experienced being welcomed by French people. But Djabri, as he explained when later interviewed for a book by two *Libération* journalists, wished to distance himself from the humanist discourse of the *gauchistes*, preferring a realist portrayal of young people's lives, in which a typical weekend often revolved around bars and pursuing the opposite sex. Hence the outrage from Communists and SONACOTRA workers when the play was put on at the left-wing municipal theatre Les Amandiers. Though the play was instead shown in alternative venues in the estates and autonomist squats, this renewed flirtation with the far Left did not last: 'The leftists have abandoned their leftism. They had disillusionments which were unique to them, and totally retrained themselves.'[81] The troupe's approach in fact, according to Djabri, tried to portray the reality of life for young proletarians whilst getting away from the old militant clichés: 'We didn't want to do the typical Manichean political play with the management on one side and exploited immigrants on the other. These were things that we knew but weren't really meaningful to us and seemed to bore audiences.'[82]

Nevertheless, the political approach of Weekend à Nanterre might be seen as in continuity with the *soixante-huitard* tradition of provocation to deliberately annoy the bourgeoisie. Thus in 1979, they went to disrupt a careers fair at the prestigious Lycée Saint-Cloud – the incident that provoked the attempted deportation of the Abdallah brothers – on the grounds that, as Mogniss Abdallah put it: 'We went to say "Shit" to the bourgeois who were publicly organising the social advancement of their offspring.'[83] But the difference, perhaps, was that in 1968 the leftist agitators were in many cases themselves pupils at prestigious lycées objecting to their own privileges: now the bourgeoisie was being challenged from outside. Relatively few of the early Beur activists, with some exceptions such as the sociologist Saïd Bouamama, had been to university or gained more than a fleeting political education from the far Left.[84] Nevertheless, the higher education system was not entirely divorced from the renewed youth activism of this period. Government attempts to reduce the number of foreign students in French universities were a major source of campus mobilisations between 1978 and 1980. Exams were boycotted, hunger strikes were undertaken, in some cases university officials were held hostage and one student was killed in a riot at the Jussieu campus in Paris.[85]

The dramatically anti-immigrant turn taken by the Communist Party, though, with the so-called 'bulldozer affair' of 1980-81 in Vitry-sur-Seine, led some suburban youth to tar the entire French Left with the same brush.[86] As Neil MacMaster comments, the bulldozer affair 'has generated much heat and little light'.[87] The shameful spectacle of a Communist suburban municipality demolishing the homes of Malian workers was undoubtedly shocking. It has therefore loomed large in critiques of PCF attitudes towards immigration and colonialism, notably Etienne Balibar's 'From Charonne to Vitry'.[88] But it needs to be placed in the changing context of the time, rather than completely overshadowing the history of the previous twenty years. Until his expulsion from the PCF for writing the article, Balibar had himself been a party member, and as we have seen he was far from alone in attempting to reconcile a sensibility to questions of immigration with membership of the largest party of the working class or its trade union. Marius Apostolo, for example, head of the CGT's immigrant organisation, notes that a CGT member actually refused to drive the bulldozer in Vitry. Apostolo himself proposed to an extraordinary meeting of the CGT's Confederal Bureau a motion in protest against the bulldozing – only to find it blocked after the union received a slap on the wrist from the PCF. Not coincidentally, Apostolo's wife Chantal Rogerat, the editor of the PCF's womens' magazine *Antoinette*, was herself simultaneously being accused of deviance from the party line.[89] Vitry came in the aftermath of the collapse of the Union of the Left in 1978, as Georges Marchais attempted to demarcate the PCF from Mitterrand by reverting to a populist pastiche of its Stalinist past, accompanied by a restalinisation of the CGT spearheaded by Henri Krasucki (who, ironically, was a Polish-born comrade of the 'Manouchian group' of immigrant Resisters).[90] This may obscure the more favourable attitudes to diversity that had, cautiously, existed previously even within the ranks of the CGT. Having changed its previous policy, the confederation now tied itself in ideological knots attempting to reconcile its newfound support for immigration controls with the principle of proletarian internationalism.[91]

But for many *banlieue* youths, the effect of Vitry was to turn more strongly towards autonomous mobilisation without adult French allies. Autonomy was thus in part a deliberate political choice, but in part driven by changing necessities. Political activity for foreign nationals was, in the wake of the 1977 decision of the Conseil d'Etat, gradually getting less risky than before. So why rely on the umbrella of established French organisations that previous militants had sheltered under, when the umbrella had developed leaks, and anyway, the rain was stopping? As Catherine Polac has shown, the openness of the MTA/*Sans Frontière* militants to support from French allies, including priests, was not necessarily shared by the new generation, many of whom found this patronising and undermining of their self-expression. The Beur activist Nacer Kettane, for example, accused the 68ers of selling out their erstwhile beliefs, and the political parties of the Left of cynically using post-1968 immigrant movements to gain power for themselves.[92] The analysis of 'Mohammed' from Nanterre was similar, suggesting that the problem was when French people – he cited Catholics and Maoists as examples – stepped over the line from supporting immigrants to substituting themselves for immigrants. Experience of such behaviour had led him to stress the importance of autonomy: 'We don't need leaders outside ourselves. We can deal very well with our problems ourselves. There, I don't accept at all that people speak in our place.'[93]

Also in Vitry, the racist killing of a youth named Kader in February 1980 had led to a thousand people demonstrating and talk of a national school students' strike. In April 1980, the Abdallah brothers formed Rock Against Police to hold a free concert in memory of the dead boy. Similar concerts were organised in suburban estates over the next two years, initially in Paris but also in Lyons, Marseilles and Geneva. The concerts, though reflecting the difficulty that dark-skinned youth had in gaining entry to mainstream nightclubs, were about more than music. They aimed to 'allow the social dynamic of the estates to emerge in a visible manner', and thereby break with the 'tear-jerk antiracism' dominant until then.[94] Borrowing its English name, with an added and extra-militant twist, from the British phenomenon Rock Against Racism, Rock Against Police was an early, if unusually combative, example of the kind of youth-run association that would flourish in the suburbs throughout the 1980s. Unlike say the MTA, the new associations did not always emphasise the representation of one particular ethnic group, often including young people from a variety of backgrounds. Autonomy did not have to mean ethnic communitarianism. RAP's role in the Paris suburbs also had a rough equivalent in Lyons, in the shape of Zaâma d'Banlieue. This group of young women in conflict with both government and parental authority had links to the local alternative-libertarian Left: one of their founders, Djida Tazdaït, later a Green MEP, was influenced by her disillusion at being manipulated by Trotskyists. Zaâma was only one of a number of autonomous womens' groups to emerge from within immigrant communities in the late 1970s, making use of both feminist and anti-racist ideological frameworks. A number of nationality-specific womens' associations were also founded around then, by first-generation refugees from Algeria, Morocco and Latin America.[95]

However, run as they were on an informal network approach, associations of this period failed to put down much in the way of permanent organisation, and were therefore vulnerable to passing events. One exception was in Nanterre, where Algerians rehoused from the La Folie shanty town next to the university were still living, and would stay until 1985, in a 'temporary' transit camp set up in 1971, an especially vigorous and militant local association developed. Following the murder of Abdenbi Guemiah in October 1982, the Comité Gutenberg 'took control' of the Cité Gutenberg. The committee persuaded their parents to go on rent strike until they were rehoused, and expressed deep suspicion of the mainstream French anti-racist movement and associated Christian groups like the CIMADE.[96]

The Politics of Autonomism and its Limits

Such a locally-based autonomous approach had weaknesses as well as strengths, notably the danger of further isolating people on different estates from each other and from wider potential allies in other parts of society.[97] The widespread opposition to the Stoléru measures suggested that the mainstream Left was by no means completely indifferent to the plight of young people in the *banlieue*,[98] but its approaches were now treated with caution. Certainly the associations like RAP did find 'allies of circumstance' in the shape of the 'autonomist' sub-culture that flourished among significant younger elements of what remained of the far Left in the late Seventies, but this alliance was no more durable than previous ones. Apeing similar movements in Germany, the Netherlands and Italy – this was the era when the Italian political theorist Toni Negri was writing of the joys of wearing a balaclava[99] – the autonomists not only sought to appropriate new spaces outside the control of the state or the traditional Left through such means as squatting and free rock concerts, but also glorified violence by young proletarians as a legitimate form of resistance to capitalism by those marginal to the traditional world of work. But the young proletarians themselves were quickly alienated from their flirtation with the ultra-left, feeling, as the Moroccan sociologist Adil Jazouli put it, their rage confiscated by middle-class ideologues looking for an 'exotic annexe'. The more *banlieue* youth got involved with such urban-based groups, the further removed they got from their suburban homes; and for some, turning a necessary struggle against repression into a whole aesthetics of fighting was a step too far.[100]

At the most extreme fringes, some more structured and more marginal groups even advocated organised violence against the state, and one, Action Directe, France's answer to the Red Brigades, put these ideas into action by beginning armed operations in 1979. Such fringe disintegrated elements of *gauchisme* taking a disastrous terrorist turn was perhaps indicative of a wider sense of futility on the far Left, whereas until then France had managed to avoid the violence seen in Italy and West Germany precisely because French revolutionaries enjoyed more prestige within their national political mainstream.[101] There was a limited crossover here with the politics of immigration in that Action Directe used certain ideological tropes characteristic of the thirdworldist *gauchisme* of the post-68 period, connecting France's internal repression of immigrants with its external neo-colonialist policies. Michael Dartnell suggests that this was because, looking for a social base, Action Directe thought they had found it in the autonomist movement, and focusing on the daily oppression of working-class and immigrant youth was a way of doing this.[102] Thus when they bombed the offices of the DST secret services in 1980, they issued a message proclaiming, with reference to a list of recent French military interventions in Africa: 'After Kolwezi, Gafsa, Djibouti, etc, Barbès sends you greetings,' and 'In Gafsa as in Barbès, the same exploitation, the same poverty.'[103] Compare this to the message the occupiers of the CNPF offices in 1970 had daubed on the walls following the fatal fire in Aubervilliers and again referring to a recent French intervention in Africa: 'Imperialism kills, in Aubervilliers as in Chad.'[104] The DST bombing was not the only Action Directe attack purporting to have an anti-racist rationale: in September 1979 for example, they bombed the offices of SONACOTRA. Indeed, some of Action Directe lived in squats in Barbès, and one member of the group, Mohand Hammami, accused of carrying out bank robberies, was of Algerian origin and had written for *Sans Frontière* – although equally other members of the group were of solid French bourgeois background from Neuilly. Nevertheless, the fringe nature of the group in relation to the wider anti-racist scene is suggested by the fact that they wrote vituperative letters from their prison cells to denounce *Sans Frontière* for being soft on bourgeois anti-communism and on Zionism.[105]

The limits of autonomism were suggested by the fact that the most successful and well-publicised protest over the condition of immigrant-origin youths during this period was not by themselves, but by a French Catholic priest. Christian Delorme was the local *curé* of Les Minguettes, a notoriously troubled estate in the Lyons suburb of Vénissieux. Though not a *gauchiste* himself – indeed in some respects an old-fashioned figure who was a scout leader – Delorme, a baby-boomer born in 1950, had rubbed shoulders with the *soixante-huitard* milieu in Lyons ever since 1970, when he had participated in the defence of Michel Raton, one of the Frenchmen prosecuted for the death of a policeman on 24 May 1968. After involvement with prisoners and prostitutes' rights campaigns, he got involved in immigrant solidarity work, including campaigning against the deportation from France of a Mauritian priest. The defining issue of Delorme's campaigning from the late 1970s onwards, though, was *la double peine*. Delorme, influenced more by Gandhian ideas of passive resistance than Rock Against Police's more confrontational approach, went on a hunger strike to protest the injustice of so many young people being deported to their parents' countries of origin. Delorme's hunger strike gained wide support: telegrams of support came in from everyone from Michel Foucault to André Glucksmann to the film-maker Marcel Ophuls, up to and including presidential candidate François Mitterrand. Some 10,000 people demonstrated in Lyons in support of the hunger strike, and Delorme even travelled to Geneva to make an appeal to the United Nations. Nevertheless, the fact that it was a French priest, rather than the young people themselves, who became the focus of attention gave rise to accusations from critics such as Jean-Louis Hurst, a veteran of the clandestine resistance to the Algerian war, that Delorme was guilty of neo-colonialism and speaking in the place of others.[106]

Despite these polemics, Delorme's hunger strike was a success in that the government eventually caved in and, in the midst of the 1981 presidential election campaign, announced a suspension of deportations.[107] Although there was some argument among activists as to how great a victory this really constituted,[108] as a result the 1981 election campaign marked a clear advance from that of 1974, when immigration had been a major theme only for fringe candidates like the MTA's Djellali Kamal. Mitterrand's PS made encouragingly positive statements, especially promising the right to vote for foreign residents in local elections. This built upon a series of experiments at local level with migrant involvement in municipal politics in the late 1970s, and a number of apparently generous declarations on the subject. Even Jacques Chirac, the Gaullist candidate for 1981, had come out in 1979 in favour of the right to vote in local elections for anyone with five years residence in France. Nevertheless, the PSU's Huguette Bouchardeau was alone among the candidates in mentioning immigration in her main four-page election address.[109]

1981: the Left in Power – '68 Continues?

So despite the dire situation in the suburbs, there were some grounds for optimism among campaigners for immigrants' rights, many of whom welcomed Mitterrand's victory as likely to herald important reforms. To some extent, and taking into account the inevitable moderation that comes with office, the early immigration policies of the first two years of the Mitterrand government can be seen in continuity with the demands of the post-1968 Left. More generally, 1981 was at the time seen by critical intellectuals from the '68 era social movements, like Foucault, as a continuation of those movements.[110] Just as radical reforms were carried out in other areas, so the Giscard government's punitive approach to immigration was partly dismantled. There was an amnesty taken up by 131,000 irregular migrants; family reunions and naturalisation were both made easier; and in the wake of the Delorme hunger strike, it was made impossible to deport foreigners born in France. Finally, for the first time foreigners could form associations without having to get authorisation from the Interior Minister, and some now received public subsidies. This measure had perhaps the most far-reaching consequences, giving rise to a flourishing 'golden age' of associational activity at the level of civil society. There were promising signs, too, that the government was more open to cultural diversity, arousing hopes of a 'right to be different'. The incoming government also promised foreign residents the right to vote in local elections. The wind was thus cut out of the sails both of the far Left, many of whose demands appeared to have been met, and of autonomist groups like Rock Against Police, because associations could now be freely formed without the need for such an underground approach.[111]

During the summer of 1981, though, the Mitterrand honeymoon was rudely interrupted by an explosion of violent unrest in the suburbs of Lyons. Rioters stole expensive cars from the city centre, rode them around and then burnt them in Les Minguettes and other areas. The location of the riots was of great future significance, for it was to be from Les Minguettes that a group of youths, in association with Christian Delorme, would decide to launch the 1983 Marche pour l'Egalité et Contre le Racisme.[112] But in 1981, the shock of the violence was such that Adil Jazouli compared public incomprehension of these spectacular events with that experienced in May 1968. Yet, unlike in May '68, Jazouli argued, the violence was an expression of pure rage, uncontrolled even partially by any political or social force capable of acting as an intermediary. Although the mayor of Vénissieux attempted to blame the riots on far Left infiltration – a sign that memories of '68 were still relatively fresh – the more substantial cause was the sheer ghettoisation of an estate deserted by French families, leaving an almost exclusively Maghrebi population experiencing a feeling of oppression by intrusive policing. Far Left groups did attempt to politicise the riots by campaigning over the arrests and heavy prison sentences that followed, but without success: the youths involved rejected their influence and even had little time for autonomous groups like Zaâma d'Banlieue.[113] One youth described the reaction to the *gauchistes* in blunt terms:

> It was only afterwards that the lefties and the intellectuals descended on us to try and explain to the guys the true meaning, as they said, of the joyriding. For us, it was bullshit, and, in any case, we didn't understand much of what they said. It wasn't them who were in the shit, it wasn't their mates who were in the slammer. They quickly understood, and some of them even got a slapping, maybe it was stupid, but you need to understand that we were fed up with everything.[114]

This suggested that a seemingly unbridgeable gulf had opened up between the now declining *gauchiste* movement and their erstwhile allies. By 1982, although the surviving remnants of the *gauchistes* were organising anti-racist demonstrations in an attempt to counter the first signs of resurgence by the far Right, they found that suburban youth were simply not turning up to their demonstrations.[115]

In response to the urban crisis, the Mitterrand government was keen to be seen to be doing something about the *banlieue*. Mitterrand visited many estates, flanked by none other than Roland Castro, the man responsible for Vive la Révolution's forays into the Nanterre shanty towns over a decade before. In a move characteristic of the transition from protest to power by an elite minority of the '68 generation, Castro, now an architect, was put in charge of the Banlieues 89 redevelopment programme which he proposed to Mitterrand. Of course, arriving in suburban estates by presidential helicopter was jarringly different from entering as a revolutionary agitator – but both Mitterrand and Castro were in some senses symbolically still stuck in the '68 years'. On their first meeting, Mitterrand remarked that though the renovation programme interested him, there was still a problem between them, namely May '68; while their next meeting was held on the 30th anniversary of Castro's namesake's first attempt to seize power in Cuba.[116]

1983: The Death of the Sixties

But if '68 survived as symbol, it did not do so as reality. A decisive shift in the politics of immigration was occurring, definitively cutting the links to the post-68 era. Of course, history does not always begin and end with clear cut-off dates. Many first generation immigrant workers were still working, and sometimes, especially in the car industry, still striking. During the Seventies, facing bankruptcy, Citroën had been taken over by Peugeot and shifted production from Paris to the outer suburb of Aulnay-sous-Bois. As late as 1982 a dispute there – inspired by the belief that with the Left in power, improvements could be gained by striking – ended in apparent victory, culminating in a mass open air meeting where the strikers of different nationalities together danced and sang 'We've won!'.[117] So when it came to the suburban riots of the second generation, a few observers still raised the old slogans about proletarian unity. But in a situation where some French workers were carrying out attacks on immigrant workers and starting to vote for anti-immigrant populists, of what relevance was this analysis?

Others still, who had been fed proletarian internationalism with their mothers' milk, proclaimed – without irony – that the solution lay in working class unity. French and immigrants, united together! They quite simply forgot that the killers of Arabs rarely live in Neuilly.[118]

Hostility, not between workers and bosses but *within* the working class between French and immigrants – or between immigrants, such as Africans versus Arabs[119] – was the bald fact that dared not speak its name, the unfortunate reality that the Seventies *gauchistes* had been unwilling to confront. In January 1984, fighting broke out between Maghrebi and African strikers and white non-strikers in the Talbot factory at Poissy, to the west of Paris.[120] This was an exact reversal, in fact, of the historical position of violence between French workers and immigrants accused of strikebreaking (as in the case of the Italians killed in the Provençal town of Aigues-Mortes in 1893). Shockingly, as an injured North African striker was carried out of the occupied Talbot factory, non-strikers yelled 'In the oven, in the Seine!'.[121] This was a far cry from 1968.

Such intra-class hostility was not only an issue of ethnicity, and of divisions engendered during industrial disputes, but also linked to an emerging politics around the dangerously potent concept of 'insecurity'. To some extent this had already been apparent in popular attitudes during the Ben Ali affair of 1971, but by the 1980s, it was becoming more explicit and articulate. Already in February 1980, bus drivers belonging to the CGT were going on strike over the issue of young people dodging fares on the buses,[122] setting a pattern for the future. In Lorraine, Gérard Noiriel found the working class increasingly segmented between 'old' and 'new' immigrants, but also between different occupations and workplaces, and between generations. For young workers, the factory was not a place of solidarity or pride in work, but a punishment for failing their exams, and the Communist Party was not the voice of the workers, but the people who had front-row seats reserved for them at cultural events.[123] Simplistic slogans about unity, however deeply felt because grounded in the utopian experience of 1968 and beyond, were inadequate to address these difficult realities. The Italian theorist Alberto Asor Rosa had already written in 1977 of the existence of 'two societies' and a 'deep divide' between 'the organised working class and marginalised, unemployed youth'.[124] The autonomists openly celebrated not having a job as making youth 'autonomous' from the capitalist system, and were sometimes hostile to the traditional working class as a whole.[125]

A marker of how far the politics of *gauchisme* seemed to have been laid to rest was that the far Left were no longer even used as scapegoats.

In March 1983, strikes broke out in the car industry. In an intemperate remark, Interior Minister Gaston Defferre blamed the strikes on 'Shiite fundamentalists' – in spite of the fact that virtually all Muslims working at Renault were not Shiites but Sunnis, and that first-hand accounts reported virtually no Islamist activity in French car factories, except for a handful of leaflets distributed at Citroën which denounced the strikes as the work of godless communists.[126] The choice of Shiite Islamists as the new whipping boy reflected the beginnings of a shift in global geo-political perceptions, following the Iranian Revolution in 1979, away from one framed by the Cold War and towards a perceived conflict between the West and Islam. Whereas at any time prior to then since 1968, politicians would have blamed similar strikes on Maoist and Trotskyist agitators (in spite of the more prosaic economic causes common to both cases) the leftists had now faded from public consciousness. Indeed, the very word 'worker' was going out of fashion: after the end of the 1970s, in press usage 'immigrant workers' became 'immigrants', even when reporting such workplace strikes, while reference was increasingly made to the problems that immigrants posed to the French, as opposed to the problems they had to face themselves.[127] From 1979 onwards, hostility to the construction of mosques multiplied in many parts of France as a consequence of developments in Iran. Islam, until then conspicuous by its absence as a major theme of public debate in France, had arrived as the new scapegoat – not helped by a series of terrorist attacks against Jewish targets in Paris and at the main railway station in Marseilles.[128]

A series of events in 1983 definitively buried the '68 years' as far as the politics of immigration was concerned, opening up a new era that stretched into the 1990s and beyond, one dominated by the anti-immigration politics of the Right and far Right. In March, the Front National, after a decade of almost total failure since its foundation in 1972, finally achieved its first electoral breakthrough in the local elections – on the theme of immigration. In the 20th arrondissement of Paris, one of the most ethnically diverse areas in France, Jean-Marie Le Pen got over 11 per cent of the vote and was elected a ward councillor. This success was multiplied in Dreux, some way outside Paris and typical of the kind of depressed and isolated town, on the periphery of a major conurbation, which the FN would specialise in targeting. The FN's General Secretary, Jean-Pierre Stirbois, succeeded via an arrangement with mainstream Right candidates, and after a September re-run caused by voting irregularities, in getting himself and three colleagues elected onto the ruling group on Dreux town council with some 16.7 per cent of the vote. As the devil's pact in Dreux suggested, the FN was not alone in playing the race card. The 1983 local elections were the first at which hostility to migration was a major theme for mainstream candidates: the Giscardian mayor of Toulon spoke of France becoming 'the dustbin of Europe', and in one month *Le Figaro* carried some 18 different articles on the theme of crime and immigration.[129] In July, Jacques Chirac, mayor of Paris, responded to growing racist violence – several noted racist killings, including at least three of children under 12, took place that summer[130] – by blaming the victims, explaining that 'France no longer had the means to support a crowd of foreigners who abused her hospitality'.[131]

And, crucially, all this led the Socialist government to a significant change of direction. Just as in economic policy, where the bold experiment with 'Keynesianism in one country' was abandoned in favour of an economic orthodoxy previously unimaginable for a government of the Left, so the field of immigration also saw reality bite, dreams shattered and promises broken. Under pressure from noisy criticism in the right-wing press, the bold pro-human rights approach of Robert Badinter at the Ministry of Justice lost ground to Defferre's Interior Ministry, as the government started to appease opponents of its previously relatively pro-immigrant line. Familiar Giscard-era policies returned, like encouraging voluntary repatriation, punitive clampdowns on those whose papers were not in order, and *la double peine*. New restrictions were imposed on North African visitors to France. Most notoriously, in such an unfavourable climate, the promised right to vote in local elections fell by the wayside, remaining unimplemented even in the twenty-first century save for EU nationals – a betrayal felt keenly by campaigners to this day.[132] And hopes of the 'right to be different' were increasingly shattered, as the mid-Eighties saw a strong revival across the political spectrum of republican thinking that stressed the importance of demanding 'integration' from immigrants, a reaction against the relativism some associated with 1968 – in spite of criticism that integration really meant assimilation, and placed heavier demands on minorities than were expected of anyone else.[133] So in retrospect, it is not unreasonable to view 1983 as the real end to the '68 years'. As Hervé Hamon and Patrick Rotman observed not long afterwards:

> In some way, the millenarian prophesy given a new lease of life by the spirit of May vanished for good in 1983, when the Socialists, like the *gauchistes* had done some years before, stopped dreaming with eyes wide open.[134]

In the year that immigration became a political football for the Right, the FN achieved its first breakthrough, and the Mitterrand government adopted a more punitive approach to immigration, the '68 years' were now ending.

There was, to be sure, a more positive side to the new Eighties politics of immigration. Anti-racists were getting their act together and riposting to racist killings more successfully than in the past. One night in February 1983, 17 year old Nacer M'Raïdi was chased and shot by a drunk policeman on the Avenue de la Division Leclerc in the southern Paris suburb of Châtenay-Malabry – a street on which I often stayed whilst writing this book – as he rode home on a moped from his girlfriend's house. M'Raïdi was shot simply because he was riding without a helmet and had gone through a red light, even though he presented no threat. The mobilisations around racist killings during the MTA years had clearly left their legacy, for in contrast to the delay experienced after the murder of Djellali Ben Ali in 1971 in convincing people that the crime was racially motivated, the very day after M'Raïdi's killing, posters of him went up seemingly everywhere and a rapid response information campaign began. The following Saturday, over three thousand people demonstrated about the killing.[135] Mobilisations on this scale, in unexceptional suburbs, were nothing out of the ordinary in the early Eighties, showing that in a sense things had progressed since the days of Djellali, when getting four thousand demonstrators in the very heart of Arab Paris had been seen as a quite extraordinary achievement.

Above all, the autumn of 1983 saw the Marche pour l'Egalité et Contre le Racisme, when the emergent *banlieue* movements finally gained the media spotlight with a two-month long march all the way from Marseilles to Paris to present the Beurs' grievances. But it too demonstrated that the post-68 era was now giving way to something rather different. The overwhelming feeling around what became dubbed the 'Marche des Beurs', on the part of both participants and the youth-obsessed media, was of a new, exciting and spontaneous breakthrough: 'Happy Beur day', exclaimed *Libération* writer Serge July. Little reference was made to the complex prehistory of the Beur movements over the preceding few years, let alone their relationship to 1968 and the immigrant workers' struggles of the 1970s.[136] Although what remained of the French *gauchiste* movement did support the march, suspicion of them attempting to take it over for partisan objectives was such that heated debates took place between them and youth organisers. As a result, the leftist militants were permitted to go on the demonstration only on condition that they did so without banners raised and not in the traditional manner of separate cortèges for each party, in order to emphasise the non-party political character of the march.[137] This was despite the fact that some of the demands of the march, such as an automatically renewable ten year residency permit, had been included in part because of campaigns by established anti-racist organisations like the CIMADE, GISTI and FASTI, in response to an initiative from members of the PSU. Indeed, activists from the PSU's 20th arrondissement branch busied themselves in preparation for the march by painting a fresco to greet the marchers outside the Gare Montparnasse.[138] After going on the march together, as well as mixing with the *Sans Frontière* crowd, two activists politically formed in the Trotskyism of the 1970s, Benjamin Stora and the Algerian militant Khaled Melhaa, attempted to create a Comité de Défense des Travailleurs Immigrés, but even the title already sounded out of date.[139] The more successful SOS Racisme was also founded by former Trotskyists, but it had the public relations sense and media savvy to conceal the fact, presenting itself as a spontaneous new youth movement unencumbered with the ideological baggage of yesteryear. Visibly, then, the 68-era Left was now in the humiliating position of being airbrushed out of an anti-racist movement that it had, for better or worse, helped to create over the preceding decade and a half.

On 3 December 1983, some 100,000 demonstrators marched from the Bastille to Montparnasse to welcome the marchers. That evening President Mitterrand welcomed the marchers to a reception in the Elysée Palace itself, and conceded one of the main demands of the protesters: a combined ten-year residency and work permit, instead of having to renew them separately and each year.[140] In contrast to other developments of the time, this was the last concrete gain for immigrant communities from the '68 years'. Effectively, it was the opposite of the Marcellin-Fontanet decrees, providing some much-needed stability, for no longer would staying in France be dependent on keeping a particular job. Most of the ingredients of the contemporary scene familiar to us today had already fallen in place: reacting against scapegoating from the Right, the marchers were affirming their rights as members of French society. But how different from 17 October 1961, when North African marchers on central Paris had been treated as enemies of the state. Different too, from May 1968, when immigrants had had to demonstrate cautiously and gingerly. And also from mobilisations like the 1971 Djellali Ben Ali affair, risky ventures by foreign nationals insecure of their status. If the Marxist rhetoric of that era had now been eclipsed, the hundred thousand marchers were greater in number than on any of the immigration struggles of the post-68 period. Many parents of marchers were bluntly hostile to what they viewed as a futile attempt for recognition by a France that would never accept them as equals.[141] This was understandable, for it was a bitter irony that the welcome loudly accorded to the marchers contrasted to the harsh rejection that first generation immigrant workers were experiencing at the very same time, as they were made redundant from the car factories like Talbot to which they had given the best years of their lives.[142] But the young marchers felt differently. For better or worse, they were now part of France, and France would have to learn to accept that. The Beurs would rarely be out of the headlines over the next quarter of a century. But if a new era in the history of French anti-racism was opening that December day, a previous one was being forgotten.

Epilogue

'Today, we finished the job for them.'
Karim Medhat Ennarah, son of a 1968 activist,
Midan Tahrir, Cairo, 11 February 2011[1]

Everyone Back in Their Place?

It was rather ironic, yet accurate, that in 1984 *Sans Frontière* should announce, in its fifth anniversary issue, 'Ciao immigration'. Ironic, because this was just the moment that the French media and political class was becoming obsessed with 'immigration'. But accurate, because by then immigrants themselves had passed from the forefront of political debates in favour of their sons and daughters. As Alec Hargreaves argues, the term 'immigration' has been used in France since the 1980s to denote a wider set of social issues that do not necessarily have anything to do with first generation immigrants, and would in the English-speaking world be referred to as 'race relations'. It was to emphasise this point, that the 'immigrants' were now in fact irreversibly part of French society, that Françoise Gaspard, until the Front National breakthrough of 1983 the Socialist mayor of Dreux, co-authored a 1986 book entitled *La fin des immigrés* ['The End of Immigrants']. By this stage, *Sans Frontière* had become a glossy monthly primarily concerned with Third World issues, and less on the pulse with respect to the second generation. In 1986, little noticed by the outside world, the magazine folded; a successor title, *Baraka*, was more short-lived, in turn closing amid acrimony between different factions on the editorial committee.[2] The complexity of the struggles and controversies of the years that followed, which have been well documented elsewhere, fall outside the subject of this book.

But what, broadly, is the legacy of the preceding period documented in this book for the politics of anti-racism today? We have seen how the idea that 1968 in France was simply French phenomenon is clearly unsustainable. The demonstrations, public meetings and strikes were internationalist in rhetoric, but also in composition. Immigrant workers were not a peripheral diversion or an irritant, but at the heart of the working class that carried out the largest labour uprising in history. 1968 set the tone for the period that followed. The politicisation of the generation of immigrant workers that arrived in the 1960s, and their children, did not begin in the 1980s but in the era defined by the aftermath of 1968. While 1968 clearly did not cure racism from France's body politic, its effect was significant over the intense period of politicisation of immigration issues that followed. People from different social and ethnic backgrounds, French and foreigners, workers and intellectuals, had come together for a common cause. With the prominent role of Spanish and Portuguese alongside Algerians, Moroccans and Tunisians, this was a time when 'immigrant' was not just a cheap euphemism for 'non-white'. Certainly we have seen that not everyone within these movements had an equal amount of power, and that not everyone was convinced by its arguments. If anti-racism has a long back history in France, so does elite and popular racism. We have seen the arrogance and the presumptuousness of the Left, but we have also seen the power of its commitment, solidarity, imagination and idealism.

It was in short, the last time that optimistic visions of a better socialist future still prevailed – in the words of the old slogan 'the tomorrows that sing'. But they would not sing for much longer. Just weeks before the 1981 election, Jean-Pierre Thorn and Eric Pittard released the film *Le Dos Au Mur* ['Back To The Wall'] about a recent strike in the Alsthom electrical factory in Saint-Ouen, a 'red suburb' at the gates of the French capital. Viewing the film today is a highly poignant experience, because it depicts a working class still combative, yet just at the very point of disillusion, like the ex-Maoists Thorn and Pittard themselves, with the revolutionary myths of yesteryear. As Gérard Craplet, an Alsthom draughtsman who articulates in the film a critique of the petty politicking of both Communist and far Left groups, later put it: 'The radical movement was finishing, so we went back to the "traditional" one. It was a bit like the abandonment of the dream of the *grand soir*.'[3] Craplet went on to work in computers, only to be disappointed by his younger colleagues: 'I had the impression that these young people who surrounded me did not live like us. We had ideals, we wanted to change society, we were more collective. They want personal success.'[4]

These social changes were to have catastrophic results. While the share of French national wealth earned as wages, compared to the share being taken by capital, had greatly and steadily increased between 1968 and 1982, it was to decline rapidly in the years that followed.[5] In the economic crisis of the twenty-first century, it is now apparent just how high a price western societies have paid for the destructive inegalitarian turn first taken during the

1980s – what the anthropologist Douglas Holmes terms 'fast-capitalism'.[6] But at the time, this was obscured because the intellectual climate in the 1980s moved so sharply away from Marxism. While it was not surprising that old dogmas were questioned once *le grand soir* failed to arrive, the baby was thrown out with the bathwater, as politics moved onto a terrain overly obsessed with the superficial attributes of cultural difference.

In this context, within anti-racism the 68ers' dream of universal emancipation and liberation gave way to less ambitious, more modest and more fragmented campaigns. The younger generation were less than satisfied with the post-1968 Left's continued emphasis on united struggle, that it had inherited from its Jacobin predecessors. While one year on from the Marche pour l'Egalité, the Convergences 84 initiative saw groups of youths on mopeds from Strasbourg, Toulouse and Marseilles converge on Paris, it was rather symbolic that the next big initiative was called Divergences. The Eighties slogan 'the right to be different', in a defensive context dominated by the rise of the FN and the scapegoating of immigrants, might be seen as a move away from '68's universalism. An emerging commonsense view, perpetuated by the mass media to an increasingly atomised society, portrayed ethnicity as the basic division in society – for as Gérard Noiriel argues, a simplistic ethnicised view of social relations makes for good television.[7] Particularly since the beginning of the second Palestinian *Intifada* in 2000, there have been suggestions of a multiple fracturing in French society and the anti-racist movement along ethnic and other lines. The boundary-crossing of the post-68 era seemed to have evaporated from the air of the time. As Ali Majri, one of the founders of the Mouvement des Travailleurs Arabes, put it before he died in 2011: 'Today everyone has returned back to their place, in their class; both the French and the Arabs; both the bourgeois and the workers; the Christians, the Muslims, the Jews.'[8]

Fundamentally, the decline of the wider Left project since the Eighties has led to the memory of a whole generation of mobilisations being reduced to the saga of an in-crowd of white bourgeois Parisians. The mainstream electoral Left is much less close to social movements than was the case in the 1970s, and has increasingly been portrayed as divorced from both ethnic majority and minority residents in the suburbs. This phenomenon, symbolised by the 'earthquake' of 21 April 2002, when working class voters deserted the main candidate of the Left, beating a humiliated Lionel Jospin into third place by Jean-Marie Le Pen, has been described in one polemic as *The Left Without the People*.[9] The far Left, while apparently resurgent since about 1995, is also not without difficulties in finding an audience in the *banlieue*, remaining as it so often does in its giver of lessons stance.

Amnesia and Remembrance

The heritage from the '68 years, has, therefore, not been fully transmitted, and certainly not its immigrant aspect. The dominance in the media of a selective memory of those years, based purely around elite students, means that '68 appears to lack relevance to the *banlieue*. Many of those involved in the Eighties youth antiracist movement, influenced by the ageism of contemporary society, tended therefore to a misleading self-image of being the first generation to have spoken out against racism. Activists often portrayed their parents' generation, the so-called *zoufris*, as having suffered in silence, resigned to their tragic fate in exile.[10] Yet young activists had their own silences, sometimes dealing with negative feelings about their own earlier involvement in leftism through denial.[11] The post-1968, MTA years, were quietly forgotten. Even when their existence was acknowledged, splits opened up between older militants and the Beurs. The MTA generation of activists were disturbed by this development, fearing that this simplistic generational dichotomy meant that, in the words of Driss El Yazami, 'Rejecting this past, the Beur movement has deprived itself of a part of its future'.[12] As Farid Aïchoune put it, the isolation of the estates was producing 'an amnesiac generation': 'We are seeing the emergence of a generation without memory, which is trying to take its revenge against everyone.'[13]

As the years went by, this effect was magnified. For teenagers of the 1990s and 2000s, even the 'Beur years' of the 1980s were ancient history, let alone the struggles of first generation immigrant workers: 'Sélim doesn't know much about the history of his parents, all that's so distant.'[14] Outside observers also share this amnesia. During the *sans-papiers* movement of 1996, for example, it was thought that this was 'perhaps for the first time' that French people 'had the opportunity to hear the voice of the demonized *clandestins*',[15] erasing the memory of the earlier movement of 1972-73, with historical references being made instead to the more obviously emotive Vichy years. Yet in fact veterans of the first wave of *sans-papiers*, such as Saïd Bouziri, were on hand behind the scenes in 1996 and many subsequent mobilisations.

During the 1980s and 1990s, some of those Beur activists who had been in contact with the French Left during the period before the 1983 March, started to reverse this memory deficit. This was especially evident with respect to the events of 17 October 1961, for it was this early Beur generation, born in the 1950s or early 1960s, that persistently maintained, as 'memory militants', the need to remember the day that others preferred to forget. Associations like Au Nom de la Mémore, Mémoire Fertile and Association 17 Octobre 1961 Contre l'Oubli eventually succeeded, despite dogged resistance from some quarters, in placing the massacre on official institutional agendas. Since 2001, there has been a plaque commemorating the massacre on the Pont Saint-Michel.[16] On the evening of that same fortieth anniversary, I went to an open air screening of a British TV documentary about 17 October in a squatted arts centre in a former army barracks in eastern Nice. By contrast, the immigrant mobilisations of 1968 and after have, arguably, not yet received this level of memorialisation. For a long time they were commemorated only in private by a few former participants: thus in 1993, Saïd Bouziri invited old comrades to mark the twentieth anniversary of the general strike of September 1973.[17] A decade or so later, younger academic specialists and activists started to show an interest.[18] In 2003, activists from the period were joined by researchers at the Centre de Documentation sur l'Immigration et le Maghreb in Marseilles for a one-day conference.[19] But this interest remains limited by comparison to other areas and has not yet filtered through to a wider public consciousness. Djellali Ben Ali, for example, is commemorated only by an obscure plaque outside the block of flats where he lived – on a run-down street visited by few from outside the neighbourhood – dating from the 1980s and referring to him only as part of a longer list of other victims of racist crimes. At best, the Ben Ali, Bouziri and similar affairs are remembered as minor footnotes to the lives of the great and the good of the French intellectual Left, with brief mentions for example, in the more scrupulous biographies of Foucault. I came across no reference to them in the commemorations, including a major exhibition at the Bibliothèque Nationale, which marked the 100th anniversary of Sartre's birth in 2005. Although the MTA is sometimes a point of reference for radical present day campaigners like the Mouvement de l'Immigration et des Banlieues (MIB), such interest, motivated by a search for immigrant-led mobilisations in the past, is rather divorced from the MTA's wider background in 1968-era leftism. Such absence of interest may well be related to the search for autonomy from the French Left prevalent among many second generation activists, that led them to distance themselves from the leftist heritage. It is revealing that, although since 2005 the Périphérie cultural project has been showing 1970s militant films about strikes, in municipal cinemas in Paris' northern *banlieue*, the organisers found they had to produce accompanying books to explain a context that would otherwise be incomprehensible to a contemporary young audience.[20]

The Legacy Today

It is of course easy to be cynical about the legacy of '68, when so much has gone wrong since. The *soixante-huitard* who has 'sold out', now happily settled into the corridors of power in politics or business, retaining nothing of their former beliefs save a narcissistic view of themselves at the centre of the world, is one of the caricatural figures of our age. In 2004, for example, the successful German film *The Edukators* depicted anti-capitalists kidnapping an excessively wealthy businessman who turned out to have been, of all things, a former leader of the student movement SDS. This stereotype is not entirely without foundation, as individual babyboomers reached the heights of power in the Western world, and implemented policies in some respects considerably further to the Right than those of the welfare-state consensus they revolted against. The former spontaneist street-fighter Joschka Fischer, in 1973 photographed beating up a policeman on a demonstration, by 1999 as German Foreign Minister supporting a NATO war led by the dope non-inhaler Bill Clinton and the lead singer of the Ugly Rumours Tony Blair. The media intellectuals and former *soixante-huitards* Alain Finkielkraut and André Glucksmann, virtually alone in France in supporting the Anglo-American invasion of Iraq. The one-time Maoist José Manuel Barroso, spearheading Europe's neo-liberal drive as President of the European Commission with some assistance from Peter Mandelson, the former seller of communist newspapers outside London underground stations. The former contester of all authority, Dany Cohn-Bendit, by the time of the 2005 referendum on the EU Constitution reduced to berating left-wing voters for failing to come to terms with the realities of a market economy. All these are easy targets for ridicule, especially on the part of those 68ers who have made a virtue out of refusing to change their political beliefs.[21] Meanwhile many politicians on the Right have made populist 1968-bashing their stock-in trade, which is itself not without paradoxes. Nicolas Sarkozy was elected President of France by promising to 'liquidate' the legacy of '68 – yet appointed as his foreign minister Bernard Kouchner, who occupied the Paris medicine faculty in May '68.[22]

But these debates are much too polemical and caricatured to permit a full understanding of the impact of 1968. Fortunately, the fortieth anniversary in 2008 suggested a more nuanced understanding of its legacy was emerging.[23] For every obvious tale of someone who has 'sold out', there are dozens of more subtle stories of people still influenced by the ideals of '68. Some have one foot in and one outside the system, suggesting that what the German student leader Rudi Dutschke famously called the 'long march through the institutions' may not have been entirely in vain. The phenomenon that Edwy Plenel, once a journalist on the LCR's *Rouge*, before becoming editor of *Le Monde*, has called 'Cultural Trotskyism', for example, sees many ex-members of the LCR in influential positions in the media, retaining from their previous allegiance at least some of its more libertarian and culturally open aspects.[24] The long *soixante-huitard* wave has even reached the unlikeliest of places, the French Communist Party. In the 1988 presidential election it was a dissident ex-Communist, Pierre Juquin who, backed by the remnants of the PSU and LCR, raised the banner of votes for immigrants. Juquin's campaign director Kaïssa Titous, the anti-racist activist and daughter of an Algerian worker at Renault, was not even a French citizen. Was it more than coincidence that in 1968 Juquin had represented the comparatively conciliatory face of the PCF, dialoguing with the students at Nanterre against party advice?[25] Yet by the 2007 presidential election, the official Communist candidate Marie-George Buffet chose to link herself, in sharp contrast to Communist rhetoric at the time, to images of 1968, when she had first become politicised as a school student. Buffet's campaign broadcasts prioritised the defence of immigrants rights – 'Mummy, what does deportation mean?' said a child's voice – in a way that would have been most unlikely for the party of her predecessor Georges Marchais. With historical irony, though, in the event the PCF was trounced at the ballot box for the second presidential election in a row by the LCR, a creation of '68 if ever there was one.

The links forged between the 1968-era Left and immigrants have in fact left traces in more recent times. Some of the prominent 'memory militants' of subsequent years, such as the sociologist Saïd Bouamama, Mogniss Abdallah, who founded the Im'média press agency, and Farid Aïchoune, once an activist in the Gauche Prolétarienne and now a journalist on *Le Nouvel Observateur*, had been through either the post-68 far Left itself, in Bouamama's and Aïchoune's cases, or at least its tail end during the *Sans Frontière* period, in Abdallah's case.[26] Madjiguène Cissé, who came to prominence in 1996 as a spokesperson for the Saint-Bernard *sans-papiers* hunger strikers, was in her youth an activist in the post-68 upheavals in Senegal.[27] Nordine Iznasni, who was born in the shanty town next to Nanterre University and as a teenager in the Seventies brushed shoulders with leftists as he campaigned against 'rubbish training schemes', today campaigns in the MIB against *la double peine* – a campaign which found unlikely support in the shape of Sarkozy's reform of the policy.[28] One of the first parliamentarians of North African origin, the Green senator and former MEP Alima Boumediene-Thiery, went from anarchism as a teenager to enter immigrant-association activism as a student at the end of the Seventies; she first came to the Greens via friends in the post-PSU alternative Left.[29]

A few of the groups formed in the '68 years' still flourish in the twenty-first century. The Association des Marocains en France, for example, later renamed itself the Association des Travailleurs Maghrébins de France. Another immigrant association active today, the Fédération des Tunisiens pour une Citoyenneté des deux Rives, originally evolved from a group founded by Tunisian leftists in 1974 as a result of the first *sans-papiers* movements. And the CEDETIM, now the Centre d'Etudes et d'Initiative de Solidarité Internationale, provides a base for some 70 different organisations from its current offices in eastern Paris. Ideas first raised in 1968, such as giving foreign residents the right to vote, have steadily grown in public support over the years – partly thanks to persistent campaigning by those who have advocated this right since Djellali Kamal's 1974 candidature, and still seek to extend the boundaries of citizenship, and make universal suffrage truly universal.[30] More generally, the period since the 1980s has seen a large expansion in the number of associations involved with immigration issues. Arguably the associations face many of the same issues as the *gauchistes* of 1968 and after (for example, should social problems in immigrant areas be exposed, or minimised so as not to lend succour to the idea of immigrants as a problem?): it is just that they express it in less ideological terms.[31] Yesterday they might have called themselves revolutionaries; today they are called non-governmental organisations, or civil society.

Many of the most prominent radical intellectuals of today are still the 68ers. For the philosopher Alain Badiou, a long-time Maoist who still seeks to revive the small-c communist project today, the figure of the *sans-papiers* is a central starting point for that resurrection. He envisages this arising from an encounter, as in May '68, between those who do not normally get to meet each other: youth, intellectuals and lower wage-earners on the one hand, and immigrants and the unemployed on the other. Jean-Pierre Thorn, who started making films with *Daring to Struggle, Daring to Win* about the Flins strike of 1968, before spending several years working in a factory as an *établi*, today makes cinematic portraits of ordinary and creative life in the *banlieue* that challenge the sensationalist media images. Etienne Balibar, whose original polemic is where we began, is still very much preoccupied with anti-racism and the ongoing struggle of the *sans-papiers*.[32] The controversial 2005 Appel des Indigènes de la République, denouncing the continuity of colonialist practices in contemporary France, was partly the work of younger activists. Yet their social status as 'challengers',[33] as a frustrated 'micro-elite'[34] – in other words, intellectuals not accepted as

Intellectuals – could be compared to where the MTA were in the mid-70s, as could their emphasis on autonomy, though they are much more scathing about French ideological universalism. The signatories also included some with a longer history of involvement in immigrant-Left politics, such as Boumedienne-Thiery, Bouamama – who contributed to the debate by explicitly criticising a lack of memory about immigrant participation in 1968[35] – and CEDETIM veteran Bernard Dréano.

A concrete example of '68's legacy in the present is the Cité Nationale de l'Histoire de l'Immigration, France's first museum of immigration, which opened its doors in 2007 as a kind of French version of Ellis Island. The initiative for the museum came originally from an NGO, Génériques, founded by none other than the ex-MTA activists Saïd Bouziri and Driss El Yazami, with the aim of keeping the history of immigration from being forgotten.[36] It was El Yazami who wrote the crucial report for the then left-of-centre government of Lionel Jospin which ultimately led to the foundation of the CNHI. At one stage, it had been thought that the site of the Renault factory at Boulogne-Billancourt might make a suitable site for the CNHI. Inevitably, given that it was a right-wing government which finally gave the museum the go-ahead, and the unfortunate final choice of location (the ornate site of the 1931 Colonial Exhibition), Génériques' role in the CNHI attracted charges of sell-out and incorporation.[37] There is inescapably a certain irony that so many radical movements in French history end up in a museum. Yet the role of ex-MTAers in the CNHI could be seen as a paradigmatic example of the 'long march through the institutions', and of the necessary effort to remember past struggles for posterity. The 1968 poster, 'French and Immigrant Workers United', for example, features both in the museum's permanent exhibition and in the invitation for its opening launch. Bouziri also became treasurer of the Ligue des Droits de l'Homme which, founded during the Dreyfus Affair, was historically one of the most important human rights organisations in the world. I first met him at the European Social Forum in London in 2004. A bewilderingly eclectic and refreshingly chaotic range of international leftwing causes were represented, that gave the present-day historian something of a feel for what it must have been like at the Sorbonne in 1968. But this was no coincidence. The global justice movement, known in France as *altermondialisme*, owes much to a continuity in personnel with the struggles of the post-1968 era, a continuity often overlooked by those stressing the novelty of the movement.[38] Among the offerings at the ESF were a campaign to grant European citizenship, and therefore the right to vote in local and European elections, on a uniform basis to all residents of Europe, not only to nationals of EU states.

The utopian internationalism of the European Citizenship of Residence campaign is straight out of '68 – not surprisingly, since it was set up by Paul Oriol, formerly of the PSU's Commission Immigrés, and Pierre Gineste, a former *établi*. A memorable afternoon spent carrying the campaign's banner through the streets of London, laughing and joking with Saïd and Faouzia Bouziri, Gineste, Oriol and Anne Couteau, before sheltering from the rain in a Whitehall pub, brought that past joyously to life.[39]

Arguably, then, the '68 years' have left their mark beneath the surface. Ethnic minorities in contemporary France have actually been much more likely to participate in struggles about socio-economic issues, from the battle against selection on entry to university in 1986 to the movement against youth job insecurity of 2006, than ethno-cultural ones like the 'headscarf affairs' that periodically attract foreign TV crews. When ethnic minorities vote, most of them – 69 per cent in 2002 for example – still vote for the Left.[40] So a heritage from the '68 years is that class politics, and the universalist project of the Left, is not entirely dead in France, at least by comparison to the English-speaking world. One important legacy of the success of the first *sans-papiers* movement of 1972-73 is that on more than one subsequent occasion collective struggles have been able to force governments from below into amnesties for undocumented migrants, rather than these being dependent on the vagaries of top-down management of migration as in other European countries.[41]

There is of course still all too much injustice to drive present day campaigns. In the summer of 2005, for example, a series of fires uncovered the urgent state of unsafe and dilapidated housing Africans had to endure in northeastern Paris, and even one in the city centre in which seven people died, that was reminiscent of the Aubervilliers fire of 1970.[42] In recent years, shanty towns have once again appeared around the *banlieue*, this time inhabited by Roma from Bulgaria and Romania, and controversy has again surrounded attempts to demolish them. As in the 1960s, Europe is once again structurally dependent on the exploitation of cheap migrant labour. Yet because 'immigrant workers' are now just 'immigrants', it is as if the work they do has become taken for granted, invisible and underappreciated – people treated as a commodity to be removed when politically convenient, regardless of the impact on real lives. Since 2004 though, the Réseau Education Sans Frontière has mobilised thousands of parents and teachers to resist attempts to deport schoolchildren from France with their families. While most RESF parent-activists are not pre-existing militants, its non-hierarchical network approach is reminiscent of a certain sort of post-68 activism.[43] Indeed, as later generations grow up in a society ever more individualised, campaigns, meetings and demonstrations are often still highly dependent on the efforts of the massed ranks of sixty-somethings politicised in the era of 1968. This 'last generation of October' (in the words of Benjamin Stora) has many foibles in its past, but excels through its civic spirit and energetic activism.

Ends And Beginnings

Yet the onward passage of time threatens already to terminate this activist spirit. Tragically, on 23 June 2009, Saïd Bouziri died at the age of 62. Five days later, I went to Paris for an evening in his memory, organised by Génériques, the Ligue des Droits de l'Homme and the radio station Radio Soleil. Fittingly it took place in the very same building, the Salle Saint-Bruno in La Goutte d'Or, where Bouziri had gone on hunger strike 37 years before. The stairs leading up to the room were decorated with multiple tributes received from Tunisian militants and an Oxford professor, the rightwing patron of the CNHI and the leftwing mayor of Paris. This message from Bertrand Delanoë – himself born in Tunisia – stressed Bouziri's sense of generosity, that arguably typified the best side of the antiracist movement in France:

> I have learnt with great emotion of the passing of Saïd Bouziri. We will all miss this tireless, generous, ardent, disinterested militant of human dignity...I knew his immense qualities of intelligence and heart, his devotion, his intellectual and moral demand.[44]

Inside, the hall was decked out with posters from old campaigns as video images of Bouziri played. The crowd grew so large that that all the seats had to be removed to allow standing room only, and the room was so hot that water was brought round on trays to quench the crowd's thirst. They listened to MTA veterans alongside Armenians and Chinese, Socialists and Greens, reflecting the diverse origins and political allegiances of the causes Bouziri championed. The speeches continued in the sun outside, between the hall and the St Bernard church – best known to later generations for television images of riot police brutally evicting the *sans-papiers* of 1996 – as 68ers and younger campaigners alike paid homage to the departed activist. More than one speaker argued that the significance of Bouziri's militant career was that, unlike some champions of human rights, he remained rooted among a grassroots movement in the local area, not in an aloof elite leadership. On the one hand, the event reflected the resilient optimism characteristic of many of Bouziri's generation of activists. A poster had been produced of a smiling Bouziri in front of a poster bearing the apparently more contemporary words, in English, 'Yes We Can'. In fact this was an historically very appropriate choice, for Barack Obama's famous slogan was originally taken from another immigrant campaign of the very same earlier epoch: the 'Si, se puede' of Dolores Huerta and Cesar Chavez of the United Farm Workers – who, just like Bouziri, went on hunger strike in 1972.[45] But this optimism was inevitably overshadowed by the tragedy of Bouziri's untimely death. Some of the speeches gave the sense of an era ending, of nostalgia for the lost glory days of the secular Arab Left in France.

That evening, Tunisian activists also recalled Bouziri's active support over the years for opposition movements in the country of his birth. This now appears particularly poignant given that he did not live to see the 'Jasmine' Revolution that overthrew the Tunisian dictatorship only a year and a half later – opening up another international cycle of protest comparable to 1968, raising similarly broad issues of human dignity, and shattering many a cliché about the inevitability of oriental despotism. This was a popular revolt from below of a younger generation, reminding us of the importance of anonymous mass movements in history. Yet it also had the effect of returning to international visibility some previously marginalised older figures, who had been determined opponents of the regime ever since the post-68 era. At the height of the movement, just two days before President Zine El-Abidine Ben Ali fled the country – and as Ben Ali's supporters in the French government were desperately offering to export their expertise in riot control – Hamma Hammami, leader of the far Left Parti Communiste des Ouvriers de Tunisie, was arrested. But this had happened many times before, the first being in 1972 for his participation in the student movement, as Hammami later recounted in a book banned in Tunisia but distributed by Tunisian activists in France. And Saïd Bouziri was far from the only Tunisian leftist of his generation to have chosen the path of human rights organisations. The leadership of the Ligue Tunisienne des Droits de l'Homme, founded in 1976 as the first of its kind in the Arab world, produced at least two politicians prominent in the immediate aftermath of the 2011 Revolution, Abdeljelil Bedoui and Moncef Marzouki. Both men had studied in France in the 1970s, and Marzouki's most recent period there ended only when he joined the succession of returning exiles landing at Carthage International Airport immediately after the fall of Ben Ali.[46]

So once again, protest and migration were intimately bound up together. Eight thousand Tunisians celebrated the dictator's departure in Paris' Place de la République; an angry crowd forced two of his daughters to flee to Disneyland from the ambassador's residence in the exclusive 16th arrondissement; manifestos were issued in the name of the *banlieue*.[47] But like in the Portuguese Revolution of 1974, this was a complex relationship. The short-term economic disruption produced by the upheaval, as French tourists forsook Tunisia for the familiar comforts of the beaches of southern France, in turn led to a wave of Tunisian emigrants attempting to head for France via Italy. Back on the northern side of the Mediterranean, the mean-minded response of Nicolas Sarkozy's government to this historic turning point was to call into question one of the principal achievements of European integration, border-free travel within the Schengen area – sending police to systematically search trains for Tunisian passengers. Yet the pull of France as an ultimate migratory destination remains strong, for reasons rooted in history: 'My grandfather lives in Nantes, he fought for France, in Indochina. And Sarkozy doesn't want to let me in.'[48]

In defiance of the French government's refusal fully to accept the documents granted to the Tunisians by the Italian authorities, on 17 April 2011 a hundred Tunisians and three hundred Italian and French activists boarded a 'Train of Dignity' from Genoa, bound for Marseilles. But the French authorities sent some fifteen lorry-loads of riot police to the sleepy border resort of Menton, and blocked all trains from entering the country for six hours. Barred from proceeding beyond the frontier town of Ventimiglia, the demonstrators occupied the train tracks and marched through the streets shouting 'Liberty! Liberty!' and 'We are all illegals!'[49] This was a remarkable event. First, because the Ventimiglia-Menton train journey had, for the previous decade, from the partial perspective of many European travellers like myself, effectively been a curious non-border crossing, with no passport control, no currency exchange and no border post. The time when this narrow frontier between mountain and sea was a fiercely guarded site of national sovereignty, as in the 1930s when anti-fascist Italian refugees attempted to make it into France, had superficially appeared relegated to a forgotten past. Yet the border had now once more become a site of international dispute. And secondly because the real limits, from the perspective of non-European travellers, to today's apparent freedom were now being exposed – by an alliance of immigrants and intellectuals. Indeed among the voices denouncing Europe's complicity in dictatorship and exclusion of migrants was none other than Cohn-Bendit, refinding his passionate fervour: 'The problem is not them, it's us! It's our inability to show solidarity! It's our inability to open ourselves!'.[50]

Then in the heart of bourgeois-bohemian eastern Paris, in a street named after a Greek nationalist icon, some of the Tunisian migrants squatted a building formerly belonging to Ben Ali's party. They stumbled on archives and chequebook stubs that, so it was said, incriminated prominent French supporters of the old regime and documented its surveillance on French soil of Tunisian and French opponents, before being evicted and left to camp in the Napoleon III-era park below.[51] Weeks later, as people played table tennis on the pavement opposite, and the Tunisian flag flapped above in the evening sun, the only visible traces of the occupation were a flyposted proclamation of solidarity with the migrants, and painted-out graffiti to which had been added the words 'Wipe it off, we'll write it again'. Pro-migrant activism, and its ambivalent relationship with institutions, is a continued reality in a city where district town halls hang official banners denouncing deportations – and where in the winter of 2010-11 the Cité Nationale de l'Histoire de l'Immigration was itself occupied for months by five hundred mainly African *sans-papiers* supported by the CGT.[52]

Internationally, echoes of an earlier period of militancy are present, but sometimes hazy, subconscious, below the surface. In the summer of 2011, the Cairo-based theatre director Ahmed El Attar presented a performance based on his telephone conversations during the recent Egyptian Revolution, that ended with the poignant words 'It's only the beginning. It's only the beginning.' Given that El Attar had lived in Paris, studied at the Sorbonne, and during the performance compared protest in Egypt to protest in France – and that his analysis of the current situation was to me reminiscent of those who wanted to resist a 'return to normal' after May '68 – after the show I asked him whether his last line was a reference to the 1968 slogan 'Ce n'est qu'un début'. Yet it turned out that he had had no idea of this, but was fascinated to discover this link.[53] Meanwhile one of many significant developments of the Arab Spring had taken place, if relatively little noticed compared to the dramatic upheavals elsewhere. It was perhaps a sign of the Moroccan government's choice of a reformist alternative in response to mass demonstrations, and desire to avoid the fate of regimes elsewhere, that its former opponents were now being invited to participate. In March 2011 King Mohammed VI chose the former MTA activist Driss El Yazami to head the country's first independent human rights watchdog, the Conseil National des Droits de l'Homme. Some indication of how historic this was is that under Mohammed VI's father Hassan II, the Moroccan authorities had sentenced El Yazami to life imprisonment. But the events of 2011 propelled El Yazami – already president of the consultative body of Moroccans living abroad and who, like Bouziri, had been a senior figure in the French Ligue des Droits de l'Homme – onto a committee charged with revising the Moroccan constitution. Given the Moroccan monarchy's track record of trying to neutralise opposition by co-opting former dissidents, El Yazami is not without his critics. He was invited by Cohn-Bendit to address the French Green Party's summer school in Clermont-Ferrand, only to face a devastating denunciation from a younger Moroccan activist in the audience, Zineb El Ghazaoui.[54] But it is revealing that this debate took place in a milieu created by French *soixante-huitards*. Despite his choice to return home, El Yazami acknowledges the ambiguities of how much he learnt politically from French comrades during his activist years to the north of the Mediterranean: 'I never wanted to have French nationality. Friends had filled in the application for me, but I never applied. However I feel that I profoundly belong to the culture of this country.'[55]

68-era immigrant activism in France has left its mark, then, in more than one place and time. Half a century after decolonisation, the migrant solidarity movements of the years that followed have something to say to the present. But will there come a time when, like so many war veterans lining up for one last emotional reunion, the last survivors of '68 will stage a final march past down the Boulevard Saint-Germain – or Boulevard Barbès? And what will we do when they have gone?

Notes

Introduction

1 David Caute, *Sixty-Eight*, London: Paladin, 1988, p. 68.

2 I use these terms in their broadest sense to encompass all social movements and political currents on the Left that considered themselves radical alternatives to the existing forces of social democracy and orthodox pro-Moscow Communism. These include the Parti Socialiste Unifié (PSU) founded in 1960 to oppose the Algerian War; Maoists; Trotskyists; left-Catholics; anarchists and others.

3 Daniel Cohn-Bendit, speaking at Montreal University, 19 March 2008: Jean-Simon Gagné, 'L'ancien leader étudiant Daniel Cohn-Bendit: "Oublions mai 68!"', http://www.cerium.ca/L-ancien-leader-etudiant-Daniel.

4 Niall Ferguson, *Civilisation*, London: Allen Lane, 2011, p. 246.

5 André Gorz, 'Avant-propos', *Les Temps Modernes*, no. 196-197 (September-October 1962), pp. 384-402.

6 Luc Ferry and Alain Renaut, *La pensée 68*, Paris: Gallimard, 1985.

7 Kristin Ross, *May 68 and its Afterlives*, Chicago: Chicago University Press, 2002, p. 19; Michelle Zancarini-Fournel, *Le Moment 68*, Paris: Seuil, 2008, p. 67.

8 D.L.Raby, *Fascism and Resistance in Portugal*, Manchester: Manchester University Press, 1988, p. 234.

9 Eric Conan, *La gauche sans le peuple*, Paris: Fayard, 2004, pp. 27-58; Ross, *May '68 and its Afterlives*, pp. 3-4.

10 Colin Crouch and Alessandro Pizzorno, eds, *The Resurgence of Class Conflict in Western Europe Since 1968*, London: Macmillan, 1978; André Gorz, *Adieux au prolétariat*, Paris: Galilée, 1980, translated as *Farewell to the Working Class*, London: Pluto, 1997. Gorz did not mean, however that the proletariat had ended in quite the sense people assumed from this title.

11 Laurent Joffrin in *Le Nouvel Observateur*, 21-27 April 2011.

12 Stéphane Rozès, 'Anti-libéralisme idéologique et anti-capitalisme politique dans la France de 2005: discontinuité et perspectives', paper to Association for the Study of Modern and Contemporary France conference, Loughborough University, 8-10 September 2005.

13 See Keith Reader, *The May '68 Events in France*, Basingstoke: Macmillan, 1993, on this point. This is not to say that former participants cannot also produce solidly researched histories: see for example Marnix Dressen, *De l'amphi à l'établi*, Paris: Belin, 1999.

14 Earlier examples included Réné Mouriaux et al, eds, *1968 Exploration du mai*

français, 2 vols, Paris: L'Harmattan, 1992; the Institut d'Histoire du Temps Présent's programme on 'Les années 68', published in the journal *IHTP. Les années 68: événements, cultures politiques et modes de vie. Lettre d'information*, and in Geneviève Dreyfus-Armand et al, ed, *Les années 68*, Brussels: Complexe, 2000. A greater concentration of research appeared for the fortieth anniversary in 2008, reviewed in Daniel Gordon, 'History at last? 1968-2008', *Modern and Contemporary France*, vol. 17, no. 3 (August 2009), pp. 335-342.

15   Michael Seidman, *The Imaginary Revolution*, New York: Berghahn, 2004, p. 174.

16   Yvan Gastaut, *L'immigration et l'opinion en France sous la Ve République*, Paris: Seuil, 2000, pp. 37-51; Geneviève Dreyfus-Armand, 'L'arrivée des immigrés sur la scène politique', *IHTP. Les années 68*, no. 30 (June 1998), pp. 9-29.

17   Xavier Vigna, 'Une emancipation des invisibles? Les ouvriers immigrés dans les grèves de mai-juin 68' in Ahmed Boubeker and Abdellalli Hajjat, eds, *Histoire politique des immigrations (post)coloniales*, Paris: Amsterdam, 2008, pp. 85-94.

18   *Excess Baggage: Alternative Paris*, BBC Radio 4, 25 November 2000.

19   Richard Wolin, *Wind From the East*, Princeton: Princeton University Press, 2010, p. 87.

20   *Code 68* (2004), dir. Jean-Henri Roger.

21   Tony Judt, *Postwar*, London: Heinemann, 2005, p. 412.

22   Jeremy Harding, 'On Elias Khoury', *London Review of Books*, vol. 28, no. 22 (16 November 2006), p. 7.

23   Tony Judt, 'French Marxism 1945-1975', in *Marxism and the French Left*, Oxford: Clarendon, 1986, p. 237

24   Judt, 'French Marxism', p. 237.

25   CEDETIM, *Les immigrés*, Paris: Stock, 1975, p. 12.

26   Nicola Pizzolato, 'Workers and revolutionaries at the twilight of Fordism', *Labor History*, vol. 45, no. 4 (November 2004), pp. 419-443.

27   Stephen Spender, *The Year of the Young Rebels*, London: Weidenfeld & Nicolson, 1969, pp. 3-35.

28   Judt, *Postwar*, p. 413.

29   Etienne Balibar, 'De Charonne à Vitry', *Le Nouvel Observateur*, 9 March 1981, reprinted in *Les Frontières de la démocratie*, Paris: La Découverte, 1992, pp. 19-34.

30   The term *Beur* was popularised in the early 1980s to designate French people of North African heritage – essentially the sons and daughters of the immigrant workers of the 1950s, '60s and '70s. Hence the 1983 Marche pour l'Egalité et Contre le Racisme was referred to by the media as the 'Marche des Beurs'.

31   Philippe Artières and Michelle Zancarini-Fournel, eds, *68: une histoire collective [1962-1981]*, Paris: La Découverte, 2008.

32   '1970-1980: les années immigrés', *Sans Frontière*, 1 January 1980.

33   For example, Maryse Tripier, *L'immigration dans la classe ouvrière en France*, Paris: L'Harmattan, 1990, p. 174; Benjamin Stora, *Ils venaient d'Algérie*, Paris: Fayard, 1992, p. 429; Maxim Silverman, *Deconstructing the Nation*, London: Routledge, 1992, p. 49; Kursheed Wadia, 'France: from unwilling host to

bellicose gatekeeper', in Gareth Dale and Mike Cole, *The European Union and Migrant Labour*, Oxford: Berg, 1999, p. 189; Albert Levy and Caroline Andréani, *Chronique d'un combat inachevé*, Paris: MRAP, 1999, p. 50.

34 Jean-Marc Terrasse, *Génération Beur*, Paris: Plon, 1989, p. 11. For another example of the contrast, see Alec Hargreaves, *Multi-Ethnic France*, New York: Routledge, 2007, p. 1.

35 Martin O'Shaughnessy, *The New Face of Political Cinema*, New York: Berghahn, 2007, p. 76.

36 Roberto Dainotto, 'The discreet charm of the Arabist theory: Juan Andrés, historicism, and the decentring of Montesquieu's Europe', *European History Quarterly*, vol. 36, no. 1 (January 2006), p. 8.

37 'Un travailleur portugais', *Esprit*, vol. 34, no. 4 (April-June 1966), p. 806; Marianne Amar and Pierre Milza, *L'immigration en France au XXe siècle*, Paris: Armand Colin, 1990; Albano Cordeiro, 'Les Portugais, une population "invisible" ', in Philippe Dewitte, ed, *Immigration et intégration*, Paris: La Découverte, 1999, pp. 109-110.

38 See Laure Pitti's critique of this approach in ' "Travailleurs de France, voilà notre nom": les mobilisations des ouvriers étrangers dans les usines et les foyers durant les années 1970', *Migrance*, no. 25 (2005), pp. 50-71.

39 To avoid excessive repetition, I also sometimes use the terms 'migrant' and 'migrant worker', since every immigration is also an emigration. Because the majority of immigrants were foreign nationals, we shall also occasionally see the term 'foreign worker' used, but without forgetting that some migrant workers came from French overseas territories, and so were French citizens rather than 'foreigners'.

40 *Mémoires d'immigrés* (1997), dir. Yamina Benguigui; Laurent Gervereau et al, *Toute la France*, Paris: Somogny, 1998; *Le gone du Chaâba* (1997), dir. Christophe Ruggia, based on the autobiographical book by Azouz Begag, translated as *Shantytown Kid*, Lincoln, Nebraska: University of Nebraska Press, 2007; *Vivre au paradis* (1999), dir. Bourlem Guerdjou.

41 See Chapter Three.

42 Saïd Bouamama, *Dix ans de marche des Beurs*, Paris: Desclée de Brouwer, 1994, p. 30.

43 Saïd Bouamama et al, *Contribution à la mémoire des banlieues*, Paris: Volga, 1994, pp. 55-59; Cathie Lloyd, *Discourses of Anti-Racism in France*, Aldershot: Ashgate, 1998; Mogniss Abdallah, *J'y suis, j'y reste*, Paris: Reflex, 2000; Philippe Juhem, 'Entreprendre en politique de l'extrême gauche au PS: la professionalisation politique des fondateurs de SOS-Racisme', *Revue française de sciences politique*, vol. 51, nos 1-2 (February-April 2001), pp. 132-138; Laure Pitti, 'Grèves ouvrières versus luttes de l'immigration: une controverse entre historiens', *Ethnologie française*, vol. 31, no. 3 (Jul-Sep 2001), pp. 465-476; *Immigration et luttes sociales*, special issue of *Migrance*, no. 25 (2005); Abdellali Hajjat, ' "Les Arabes arrêtent la France!": retour sur les grèves générales contre le racisme de 1973', *Plein Droit*, no. 67, December 2005; *Postcolonialisme et immigration*, special issue of *Contretemps*, no 16 (January 2006); Jim House and Neil MacMaster, *Paris 1961*, Oxford: Oxford University Press, 2006;

Rabah Aissaoui, 'Political mobilisations of North African migrants in 1970s France: the case of the Movement des Travailleurs Arabes (MTA)', *Journal of Muslim Minority Affairs*, vol. 26, no. 2, August 2006, pp. 171-186; Boubeker and Hajjat, *Histoire politique*, pp. 81-174; Artières and Zancarini-Fournel, *68*, contributions by Vincent Lemire, 'Nanterre, les bidonvilles et les étudiants', pp. 137-143, Abdellali Hajjat, 'Alliances inattendues à la Goutte d'Or', pp. 521-527, Michelle Zancarini-Fournel, 'La construction d'une "problème national"': l'immigration', pp. 664-672 and Choukri Hmed, 'Les grèves de loyers dans les foyers Sonacotra: premier mouvement immigré?', pp. 725-728; Rabah Aissaoui, *Immigration and National Identity*, London: Tauris, 2009; Tangui Perron, *Histoire d'un film, mémoire d'une lutte: 2. Etrange étrangers*, Paris: Scope, 2009; Ed Naylor, 'The Politics of a Presence: Algerians in Marseille from independence to "immigration sauvage" (1962-1974)', PhD thesis, Queen Mary University of London, 2011, pp. 207-240, 261-267.

44 Abdellali Hajjat, 'Le Mouvement des travailleurs arabes: sociologie d'une nouvelle génération politique dans l'immigration postcoloniale', paper to *Mai 68: Forty Years On* conference, University of London Institute in Paris, 15-17 May 2008.

45 *Francais-immigrés, même patron, même combat*, La Petite Rockette, Paris, 22 May 2008.

46 Pitti, ' "Travailleurs de France" ', pp. 54-56.

47 Aissaoui, *Immigration and National Identity*, p. 202.

48 Ahmed Boubeker and Abdellali Hajjat, 'Introduction', in Boubeker and Hajjat, *Histoire politique*, p. 15.

49 Gérard Noiriel, *Immigration, antisémitisme et racisme en France (XIXe-XXe siècles)*, Paris: Fayard, 2007, describes the Tunisian Saïd Bouziri as 'Algerian' (p. 587), as well as dating the first far Left campaigns on immigrant housing to March 1969 (p. 563) when they had already existed during May 1968 and the foundation of the Comités Palestine to 1971 (p. 569, n. 2), when they had been active since 1969.

50 Maud Bracke, 'May 1968 and Algerian immigrants in France: trajectories of mobilization and encounter', in Gurminder Bhambra and Ipek Demir, eds, *1968 In Retrospect*, Basingstoke: Palgrave Macmillan, 2009, pp. 115-130. As stated on p. 123, the 1968 Renault strike involved African, Portuguese and Italian workers too; but it is not made clear that the leadership of the Mouvement des Travailleurs Arabes (pp. 125-126) were mainly Tunisian or Moroccan, or that the Renault worker Saddok Ben Mabrouk (p. 126) was Tunisian. There is also a tension between the accusation Bracke levels against leftists, even such thirdworldist groups as the Comité des Trois Continents, of 'a denial of socio-cultural specificity and a naive view that was both Eurocentric and universalist' (p. 121) and the positive approval she gives to immigrant workers' adoption of 'a *multinational* immigrant identity and the discovery of cross-national immigrant concerns' (p. 123). Arguably this reflected similar universalist ideals to those dismissed when coming from activists perceived as French.

51 Laure Pitti, 'Penarroya, 1971-1972: deux films, deux regards, une mobilisation'

in Perron, *Histoire d'un film*, p. 173.

52   Chapters Two and Three are revised versions of parts of 'Immigrants and the New Left in France, 1968-1971', DPhil thesis, University of Sussex, 2001, and one section of Chapter One includes revised material from 'The Paris Pogrom, 1961', MA dissertation, University of Sussex, 1998, but the whole of the rest of the book is based on more recent research. One section of Chapter Three was previously published in French as 'A Nanterre, ça bouge: immigrés et gauchistes à Nanterre, 1968 à 1971', *Historiens et Géographes*, no. 385 (January 2004), pp. 75-86, and one section of Chapter Five draws on part of 'Le PSU et les luttes de l'immigration: perspectives nationales et internationales' in Tudi Kernalegenn et al, eds, *Le PSU vu d'en bas*, Rennes: Presses Universitaires de Rennes, 2009, pp. 327-336, while the remainder of the book is previously unpublished. Parts of the thesis not included in this book were published as ' "Il est recommandé aux étrangers de ne pas participer": les étrangers expulsés en mai-juin 1968', *Migrations Société*, vol. 15, no. 87-88 (May-August 2003), pp. 45-65; 'Acteurs trans-méditerranéens dans un quartier cosmopolite. Juifs et musulmans à Belleville (Paris 20e), entre tolérance et conflit', *Cahiers de la Méditerrannée*, no. 67 (December 2003), pp. 287-298, http://cdlm.revues. org/index135.html; and 'Reaching out to immigrants in May '68: specific or universal appeals?', in Julian Jackson et al, eds, *May '68*, Basingstoke: Palgrave Macmillan, 2011. Related research not included here was published as 'Daniel Guérin et le mouvement des travailleurs immigrés en France après 68', in David Berry, ed, *Daniel Guérin, Dissidences*, vol 2, Paris: L'Harmattan, 2007, pp. 197-216; English version at http://www-staff.lboro.ac.uk/eudgb/DG_ conference_speakers.htm.

53   Eric Hobsbawm, *Age of Empire*, London: Pantheon, 1987, pp. 3, 5.

54   Sheila Rowbotham, 'The womens' movement and organising for socialism', in Sheila Rowbotham, Lynne Segal and Hilary Wainwright, *Beyond the Fragments*, London: Merlin, 1979, p. 40.

55   Timothy Garton Ash, *History of the Present*, London: Penguin, 2000, p. xviii.

56   Ranajit Guha, ed, *Subaltern Studies*, Delhi: Oxford University Press, 1982.

57   E.P.Thompson, *The Making of the English Working Class*, London: Pelican, 1968, p. 13.

Chapter 1

1   Abdelmalek Sayad, 'El Ghorba: le mécanisme de reproduction de l'émigration', *Actes de la recherche en sciences sociales*, no. 2 (March 1975), pp. 50-66, reproduced in Abdelmalek Sayad, *The Suffering of the Immigrant*, Cambridge: Polity, 2004, pp. 16-17.

2   Jean-François Sirinelli, *Les babyboomers*, Paris: Fayard, 2003; *Mourir à trente ans* (1982), dir. Romain Goupil.

3   Patrick Seale and Maureen McConville, *French Revolution 1968*, Harmondsworth: Penguin, 1968, p. 38.

4   Michel Lequenne, *Le trotskisme*, Paris: Syllepse, 2005, p. 317.

5   Hervé Hamon and Patrick Rotman, *Génération*, vol. 1, Paris: Seuil, 1987; Jean-

Paul Salles, *La Ligue communiste révolutionnaire (1968-1981)*, Rennes: Presses Universitaires de Rennes, 2005, pp. 46-52.

6   Mohammed Harbi, *Une vie debout*, Paris: La Découverte, 2001, p. 224.

7   Neil MacMaster, 'The role of European women and the question of mixed couples in the Algerian nationalist movement in France, circa 1918-1962', *French Historical Studies*, vol. 34, no. 2 (Spring 2011), p. 377; Pierre Brocheux, *Ho Chi Minh*, Cambridge: Cambridge University Press, 2007, pp. 11-22; Pascal Blanchard et al, *Le Paris Arabe*, Paris: La Découverte, 2003, pp. 100-179.

8   Bennetta Jules-Rosette, *Black Paris*, Urbana: University of Illinois Press, 1998, p. 42; Phillippe Dewitte, 'Les Africains en France de 1914 à 1960: naissance d'une élite moderne', in Laurent Gervereau et al, *Toute la France*, Paris: Somogny, 1998, pp. 172-174.

9   Sophie Bessis, '*Perspectives*: l'effervescence tunisienne des années 1960', in Philippe Artières and Michelle Zancarini-Fournel, eds, *68: une histoire collective [1962-1981]*, Paris: La Découverte, 2008, pp. 220-224; *Perspectives Tunisiennes*, January 1967 and December 1967; Abdellali Hajjat, 'Des Comités Palestine au Mouvement des travailleurs arabes (1970-1976)', in Ahmed Boubeker and Abdellali Hajjat, eds, *Histoire politique des immigrations (post)coloniales*, Paris: Amsterdam, 2008, pp. 146-147; Noureddine Ben Kheder, interview with Michel Camau and Vincent Geisser, Tunis, April 2002, transcript at http://lerenouveau.ettajdid.org/spip.php?article255, 20 July 2008.

10   Gisèle Halimi, *Le Lait de l'oranger*, Paris: Gallimard, 1988, translated as *Milk for the Orange Tree*, London: Quartet, 1990, pp. 2-11; Gisèle Halimi, *Le procès de Bobigny*, Paris: Gallimard, 2006; Albert Memmi, *Portrait du colonisé*, Paris: Corréa, 1957, translated as *The Colonizer and the Colonized*, London: Earthscan, 1990; Cathie Lloyd, *Discourses of Antiracism in France*, Aldershot: Ashgate, 1998, pp. 148-154; UNEF, Association Fédérative Générale des Etudiants de Strasbourg, *De la misère en milieu étudiant considérée sous ses aspects économique, politique, psychologique et notamment intellectuel, et de quelques moyens pour y remédier*, Strasbourg: Weibel, 1966, translated as 'On the poverty of student life', in Dark Star, ed, *Beneath the Paving Stones*, Edinburgh: AK Press, 2001, pp. 9-27.

11   Andy Merrifield, *Metromarxism*, New York: Routledge, 2002, p. 114; Manuel Castells, 'Citizen movements, information and analysis: an interview', *City*, no. 7 (May 1997), p. 141; Geneviève Dreyfus-Armand, *L'exil des républicains espagnols en France*, Paris: Albin Michel, 1999.

12   Cornelius Castoriadis, *Political and Social Writings*, vol. 1, Minneapolis: University of Minnesota Press, 1988, p. xxi; Arthur Hirsh, *The French Left*, Montreal: Black Rose, 1982, pp. 159-177, 221-233; Milza and Temime, *Toute la France*, p. 81; *Guardian*, 4 April 2009; Bob Jessop, *Nicos Poulantzas*, Basingstoke: Macmillan, 1985; Louis Soubise, *Le marxisme après Marx (1956-1965)*, Paris: Montaigne, 1967, p. 7; Michel Trebitsch, 'Voyages autour de la révolution: les circulations de la pensée critique de 1956 à 1968', in Geneviève Dreyfus-Armand et al, eds, *Les années 68*, Brussels: Complexe, 2000, p. 83.

13   Adrian Little, *The Political Thought of André Gorz*, London: Routledge, 1996, p. 1; *Independent*, 12 October 2007; Christophe Fourel, 'Itinéraire d'un penseur',

in Christophe Fourel, ed, *André Gorz*, Paris: La Découverte, 2009, pp. 13-35.

14   Herbert Marcuse, *Eros et civilisation*, Paris: Minuit, 1963; *Le Nouvel Observateur*, 10-22 September 1999; *Le Monde*, 5 June 2001; Guillaume Chérel, *Le fils caché de Trotsky*, Paris: Derrey, 2002; Boris Fraenkel, *Profession: révolutionnaire*, Latresne: Le Bord de l'Eau, 2004; Peter Lennon, *Foreign Correspondent*, London: Picador, 1994; *The Making of Rocky Road to Dublin* (2004), dir. Paul Duane; Peter Lennon, conversation with author, Liverpool, 31 October 2007; *Guardian*, 21 March 2011.

15   Sheila Rowbotham, *Promise of a Dream*, London: Allen Lane, 2000, p. 32.

16   Yaïr Auron. *Les juifs d'extrême gauche en mai 68*, Paris: Albin Michel, 1998; Pierre Goldman, *Souvenirs obscurs d'un juif polonais né en France*, Paris: Seuil, 1975.

17   Benjamin Stora, *La dernière génération d'octobre*, Paris: Stock, 2003, pp. 24, 38-39.

18   Elisabeth Salvaresi, *Mai en héritage*, Paris: Syros, 1988, pp. 148, 196; *Le Monde*, 29 May 1998; C.Favre, 'Mai 68 à Toulouse: le mouvement du 25 avril' in Geneviève Dreyfus-Armand and Laurent Gervereau, eds, *Mai 68*, Nanterre: BDIC, 1988, p. 200.

19   Daniel Cohn-Bendit, *Nous l'avons tant l'aimée, la révolution*, Paris: Bernard Barrault, 1986, p. 93.

20   Nicolas Sarkozy, *Témoignage*, Paris: XO, 2006, p. 8.

21   Kristin Ross, *May '68 and its Afterlives*, Chicago: Chicago University Press, 2002, p. 2.

22   Auron, *Juifs d'extrême gauche*, pp. 163-213.

23   Hervé Hamon and Patrick Rotman, *Les porteurs de valises*, Paris: Albin Michel, 1979; Martin Evans, *The Memory of Resistance*, Oxford: Berg, 1997; Jacques Charby, *Les porteurs d'espoir*, Paris: La Découverte, 2004.

24   Frantz Fanon, *Les damnés de la terre*, Paris: Maspero, 1961, translated as *The Wretched of the Earth*, New York: Grove, 2004.

25   See Robert Malley, *The Call from Algeria*, Berkeley: University of California Press, 1996.

26   Régis Debray, *Loués soient nos seigneurs*, Paris: Gallimard, 1996, translated as *Praised Be Our Lords*, London: Verso, 2007, p. 9.

27   Aimé Césaire, *Lettre à Maurice Thorez*, Paris: Présence Africaine, 1956, translated as *Letter to Maurice Thorez*, Paris: Présence Africaine, 1957.

28   *Le Monde*, 13 March 1987, cited in Alain Monchablon, 'Syndicalisme étudiant et génération algérienne', in Jean-Pierre Rioux and Jean-François Sirinelli, eds, *La guerre d'Algérie et les intellectuels français*, Brussels: Complexe, 1991, p. 183.

29   Heated controversies have raged over the exact number of deaths, with some claims ranging higher or lower than this, but the thorough investigation by Jim House and Neil MacMaster, *Paris 1961*, Oxford: Oxford University Press, 2006, p. 167, counted 'well over 120'.

30   Simone de Beauvoir, *La force des choses*, Paris: Gallimard, 1963, translated as *Force of Circumstance*, London: André Deutsch, 1965, p. 600.

31   Because of the focus on Papon, less attention has been paid to the roles of de

Gaulle and his prime minister Michel Debré, but House and MacMaster, *Paris 1961*, p. 143, suggests that there was 'secret state collusion' in which there was an informal understanding that Papon, like his men, would be 'covered' by superiors.

32 *Economist*, 4 November 1961.

33 Jean-Luc Einaudi, *La Bataille de Paris*, Paris: Seuil, 1991, p. 132.

34 Einaudi, *Bataille de Paris*, p. 166.

35 For this interpretation see House and MacMaster, *Paris 1961*, Part I.

36 *Vérité-Liberté*, November 1961.

37 Bibliothèque de Documentation International Contemporaine, Nanterre (BDIC), O PIECE 557 RES, République Algérienne, Ministère de l'Information, 'Les manifestations algériennes d'octobre 1961 et la répression colonialiste en France', December 1961, p. 20.

38 'Maurice' to 'Cher Frère', 17 and 21 October 1961, reproduced in Mohammed Harbi, ed, 'Dossier sur certains aspects occultés du FLN en France', *Sou'al*, no. 7 (September 1987), pp. 81, 85.

39 House and MacMaster, *Paris 1961*, pp. 216-241, gives a more nuanced analysis.

40 Michel Levine, *Les ratonnades d'octobre*, Paris: Ramsay, 1985, pp. 81, 120-126, 132; House and MacMaster, *Paris 1961*, pp. 219-222.

41 *Afrique-Action*, 25-31 October 1961; De Beauvoir, *Force of Circumstance*, pp. 599-600.

42 *La Tribune de l'Immigration*, October 1985.

43 Daniel Goldhagen, *Hitler's Willing Executioners*, New York: Alfred A. Knopf, 1996, created enormous controversy by emphasising the voluntary participation of ordinary Germans in the Holocaust.

44 *New York Times*, 18 October 1961.

45 'Les manifestations algériennes', pp. 10-12; Aouaouche Farhi, in Actualité de l'Emigration, *17 octobre 1961*, Paris: Amicale des Algériens en Europe, 1987, p. 57.

46 Pierre Vidal-Naquet, *Torture: Cancer of Democracy*, Harmondsworth: Penguin, 1963, p. 118; *Vérité-Liberté*, November 1961; BDIC Q PIECE 611 RES: Union Régionale Parisienne CFTC, 'Face à la répression', 30 October 1961; *L'Humanité*, 21 October 1961; Anne Tristan, *Le silence du fleuve*, Paris: Au Nom de la Mémoire, 1991, p. 80.

47 Linda Amiri, *La bataille de France*, Paris: Laffont, 2004, pp. 149-150.

48 *Le Travailleur Parisien*, 8 November 1961; Union Départementale CGT de la Seine, communiqué, 7 September 1961, reprinted in *Le Travailleur Parisien*, 8 November 1961; *La Tribune Socialiste*, 14 October 1961.

49 *Secret History: Drowning By Bullets*, first broadcast Channel 4, 13 July 1992; Jean-Philippe Renouard and Isabelle Saint-Saens, 'Festivals d'un film maudit: entretiens avec Jacques Panijel', *Vacarme*, no. 13 (Autumn 2000), pp. 20-22; House and MacMaster, *Paris 1961*, pp. 133, 222-226, 232; *Socialisme ou Barbarie*, December 1961-February 1962; Maurice Papon, *Les chevaux du pouvoir*, Paris: Plon, 1988, p. 222.

50 Hamon and Rotman, *Porteurs de valises*, p. 373; Benjamin Stora, *La gangrène et l'oubli*, Paris: La Découverte, 1992, p. 98; Ross, *May '68 and its Afterlives*, p.

    56.

51   See 'The Class Divide' below.

52   *L'Humanité*, 23 and 24 October 1961; Einaudi, *Bataille de Paris*, pp. 210, 225-226, 233-234, 238, 241; Levine, *Ratonnades d'octobre*, pp. 247, 274-276; *La Tribune Socialiste*, 28 October 1961; BDIC 4 DELTA 156 RES: 'Dossier sur les manifestations algériennes du 17 octobre 1961', no. 8: 'Pour la paix, contre les violences et le racisme', flyer for meeting; *Vérité-Liberté*, November 1961; *Pakistan Times*, 2 November 1961; *Times*, 2 November 1961; Marc Heurgon, *Histoire du PSU*, vol. 1, Paris: La Découverte, 1994, p. 337; Amiri, *Bataille de France*, pp. 178-180; MacMaster, 'European women', p. 376.

53   *La Tribune de l'Immigration*, October 1985.

54   *Le Travailleur Parisien*, 8 November 1961; *L'Humanité*, 18 and 31 October 1961; Michel Branciard, *Un syndicat face à la guerre d'Algérie*, Paris: Syros, 1984, p. 272; House and MacMaster, *Paris 1961*, pp. 226-230; *Quatrième Internationale*, November 1961.

55   Heurgon, *Histoire du PSU*, pp. 342-343; Henri Leclerc, *Un combat pour la justice*, Paris: La Découverte, 1994, p. 39; De Beauvoir, *Force of Circumstance*, p. 602.

56   *50 ans plus tard ... le réalisme c'est toujours l'utopie* conference, Issy-les-Moulineaux, 10 April 2010; Paul Oriol, conversation with author at this conference.

57   Hamon and Rotman, *Porteurs de valises*, p. 370; Evans, *Memory of Resistance*, p. 82. n. 21.

58   Jim House, 'Antiracism and antiracist discourse in France from 1900 to the present day', PhD thesis, University of Leeds, 1997, p. 283.

59   Jean-Luc Einaudi, *Franc-Tireur*, Paris: Sextant, 2004, p. 113.

60   *Libération*, 17 October 1980, reprinted in Olivier Le Cour Grandmaison, ed, *Le 17 octobre 1961*, Paris: La Dispute, 2001, pp. 27-30; Einaudi, *Franc-Tireur*, p. 115.

61   Einaudi, *Franc-Tireur*; Evans, *Memory of Resistance*, pp. 105-108; Jean-Paul Brunet, *Charonne*, Paris: Flammarion, 2003, pp. 56-59; Einaudi, *Bataille de Paris*, pp. 279, 280; Alain Dewerpe, *Charonne 8 fevrier 1962*, Paris: Gallimard, 2006.

62   De Beauvoir, *Force of Circumstance*, pp. 604-606; Heurgon, *Histoire du PSU*, p. 343; House and MacMaster, *Paris, 1961*, p. 244.

63   Etienne Balibar, 'De Charonne à Vitry', in *Les frontières de la démocratie*, Paris: La Découverte, 1992, p. 23.

64   Alain Monchablon, *Histoire de l'UNEF*, Paris: Presses Universitaires de France, 1983, pp. 115-120; *Pakistan Times*, 23 October 1961; House and MacMaster, *Paris 1961*, p. 89.

65   Archives Nationales, Paris 600 Mi 50, no. 597: Interior Minister and Information Minister to Prefects, 30 December 1960.

66   Norman Geras, *The Contract of Mutual Indifference*, London: Verso, 1998.

67   House and MacMaster, *Paris 1961*, p. 1.

68   *Secret History: Drowning By Bullets*.

69   Todd Shepard, 'After deaths, after-lives', *History Workshop Journal*, no. 66

(Autumn 2008), p. 251.

70   House and MacMaster, *Paris 1961*, pp. 231-232; Marie-Pierre Ulloa, *Francis Jeanson*, Paris: Berg International, 2001, translated as *Francis Jeanson*, Stanford: Stanford University Press, 2007, p. 179.

71   *New Statesman*, 27 October 1961.

72   David Schalk, *War and the Ivory Tower*, Lincoln, Nebraska: University of Nebraska Press, 2005, pp. 93-96.

73   *La Tribune Socialiste*, 6 July 1967; Frair Caraib, 'La Guadeloupe opprimée', *Les Temps Modernes*, no. 256 (September 1967), pp. 485-488; *La Commune*, 12 March 1968; *Class Struggle / Lutte de Classe*, March 1968; Sabine Rousseau, 'Frères du Monde et la guerre du Vietnam: du tiers-mondisme à l'anti-impérialisme (1965-1973)', *Le Mouvement Social*, no. 177 (October-December 1996), pp. 71-88; Ross, *May '68 and its Afterlives*, pp. 80-81, 90-95; Christophe Nick, *Les trotskistes*, Paris: Fayard, 2002, pp. 424-432; Michael Clemons and Charles Jones, 'Global solidarity: the BPP in the international arena', in Kathleen Cleaver and George Katsiaficas, eds, *Liberation, Imagination and the Black Panther Party*, New York: Routledge, 2001, pp. 36-37; Malley, *Call from Algeria*.

74   Hamon and Rotman, *Génération 1*, pp. 218-232; Donald Reid, 'Etablissment: working in the factory to make revolution in France', *Radical History Review*, no. 88 (Winter 2004), p. 85; Stany Grelet and Isabelle Saint-Saëns, 'Entretien avec Gus Massiah (CEDETIM)', *Vacarme*, June 2001; Bernard Dréano, 'Le Cedetim ou la continuité d'un combat', http://www.reseau-ipam.org/article-imprim-cedetim.php3?id_article=930, 14 April 2005; Anne Couteau and Paul Oriol, interview with author, Paris, 2 January 2006.

75   At different points in its history, CEDETIM was variously called the Centre d'Etudes sur les Problèmes du Tiers-Monde, the Centre Socialiste d'Etudes sur les Problèmes du Tiers-Monde and the Centre d'Etudes Anti-Impérialistes, the rather confusing name changes reflecting subtle shifts in emphasis.

76   *La Tribune Socialiste*, 28 September 1967.

77   Debray, *Praised Be Our Lords*, p. 24.

78   Marc Nacht, 'Les travailleurs noirs en France ou la misère organisée', *Les Temps Modernes*, July 1964, pp. 152-162; according to Duncan Thompson, *Pessimism of the Intellect?*, London: Merlin, 2007, p. 10, *Les Temps Modernes* was itself the template for the *New Left Review*; Maurienne, 'Un nouvel esclavage. Les travailleurs africains en France', *Partisans*, no. 9 (March-April 1963), pp. 137-152; Guy Desolre, 'Les travailleurs immigrés en Europe occidentale', *Partisans*, no. 28 (April 1966), pp. 9-19; Angel Villanueva, 'Causes et structures de l'émigration', *Partisans*, no. 34-35 (December 1966-January 1967); François Maspero, *Les passagers du Roissy-Express*, Paris: Seuil, 1990.

79   *La Tribune Socialiste*, 19 October 1967 and supplements to 19 January 1967 and 9 February 1967 issues; *Esprit*, vol. 34, no. 4 (April 1966): *Les étrangers en France*; *Hommes et Migrations* was founded as *Les Cahiers nord-africains* in 1950 before changing its name in 1965.

80   French for 'shanty town'.

81   R.W.Johnson, *The Long March of the French Left*, London: Macmillan, 1981, p.

x.

82   *Harkis* was the term applied to Algerians serving in the French army; some *harki* units were deployed to combat the FLN in metropolitan France.

83   *L'Humanité*, 19 and 26 October 1961; *Le Travailleur Parisien*, 8 November 1961; Tristan, *Silence du fleuve*, p. 110; Levine, *Ratonnades d'octobre*, p. 200; Einaudi, *Bataille de Paris*, p. 210; House and MacMaster, *Paris 1961*, pp. 232-235; *Socialisme ou Barbarie*, December 1961-February 1962.

84   House and MacMaster, *Paris 1961*, pp. 166, 233; BDIC 4 DELTA 156 RES, no. 6: 'Le Secours Populaire Français vous dit toute la vérité', December 1961; Amiri, *Bataille de France*, pp. 180-181. For a sample of Duclos' rhetoric in a different context, see the interview with him in the film *Le chagrin et la pitié* (1969), dir. Marcel Ophüls.

85   Balibar, 'De Charonne à Vitry', pp. 25-26.

86   Charby, *Les porteurs d'espoir*, p. 136; House and MacMaster, *Paris 1961*, p. 237.

87   Daniel Bensaïd, *Une lente impatience*, Paris: Stock, 2004, p. 56.

88   Ian Greig, *Today's Revolutionaries*, London: Foreign Affairs, 1970, p. 50; more rigorous research confirms that at least some of the LCR's leaders did come from a relatively comfortable background: Salles, *Ligue communiste révolutionnaire*, pp. 296-298.

89   Alain Krivine, *Ca te passera avec l'âge*, Paris: Flammarion, 2006, p. 93.

90   Bensaïd, *Lente impatience*, pp. 56, 58-60, 64; Krivine, *Ca te passera avec l'âge*, pp. 20-23; Salles, *Ligue communiste révolutionnaire*, p. 309.

91   Philippe Raynaud, *L'extrême gauche plurielle*, Paris: Autrement, 2006, p. 69.

92   The title of this section is taken from Bertrand Tavernier's 1998 film *De l'autre côté du périph*, a portrait of life in the *banlieue* made in response to a right-wing government minister's accusation that immigrant-supporting leftist intellectuals like Tavernier did not know anything about 'real life'.

93   Marianne Amar and Pierre Milza, *L'immigration en France au XXe siècle*, Paris: Armand Colin, 1990; Réné Gallissot, 'La guerre et l'immigration algérienne en France', in Jean-Pierre Rioux, eds, *La guerre d'Algérie et les Français*, Paris: Fayard, 1992, pp. 337-342.

94   Henri Bartolli, 'Les migrations de main-d'oeuvre', *Esprit*, vol. 34, no. 4 (April-June 1966), p. 903.

95   Natacha Lillo, tour attached to *Fins d'empire*, annual conference of the French Colonial History Society, Saint-Denis, 17-19 June 2010; Fanny Doumarou, 'Je suis un enfant des bidonvilles', in Tangui Perron, *Histoire d'un film, mémoire d'une lutte: 2. Etrange étrangers*, Paris: Scope, 2009, pp. 83-85.

96   Kristin Ross, *Fast Cars, Clean Bodies*, Cambridge, MA: MIT Press, 1996.

97   Bartolli, 'Migrations de main-d'oeuvre', pp. 902-903; Francette Vidal, 'Le bidonville de "La Campa"', *Esprit*, vol. 34, no. 4 (April-June 1966), pp. 651-661; Mehdi Lallaoui, *Du bidonville aux HLM*, Paris: Syros, 1993, pp. 44-57, 70-73; Vincent Lemire, 'Nanterre, les bidonvilles et les étudiants' in Artières and Zancarini-Fournel, eds, *68*, p. 140.

98   'Un travailleur portugais', *Esprit*, vol. 34, no. 4 (April-June 1966), p. 807.

99   *La Voix du 11è*, April 1968; François Manchuelle, *Willing Migrants*, Athens,

Ohio: Ohio University Press, 1997, pp. 213-215; Adrian Adams, 'Prisoners in exile: Senegalese workers in France' in Robin Cohen et al, eds, *Peasants and Proletarians*, London: Hutchinson, 1979, p. 319; Nacht, 'Travailleurs noirs', pp. 155-157; *Mémoires d'immigrés, l'héritage maghrébin* (1997), dir. Yamina Benguigi.

100 *Mémoires d'immigrés*, episode 1, *Les pères*.

101 Sayad, 'El Ghorba', pp. 16-17.

102 Herbert Marcuse, *One Dimensional Man*, Boston: Beacon, 1964.

103 Alec Hargreaves, *Multi-Ethnic France*, New York: Routledge, 2007, p. 166.

104 *Droit et Liberté*, September-October 1966 and March 1967; Frédéric Abadie and Jean-Pierre Corcelette, *Valéry Giscard d'Estaing*, Paris: Balland, 1997, p. 136; Gastaut, *L'immigration et l'opinion*, p. 193.

105 E.g. Centre d'Information et de Documentation sur l'Immigration et le Maghreb, Marseilles (CIDIM), Mouvement des Travailleurs Arabes, Comité de Solidarité aux Travailleurs Immigrés, 'Árrêtons le scandale!', c. November 1974.

106 Frank Georgi, *L'invention de la CFDT 1957-1970*, Paris: L'Atelier, 1995, pp. 112-114.

107 Here I am responding to the criticism of Michael Seidman, *The Imaginary Revolution: Parisian students and workers in 1968*, New York: Berghahn, 2004, p. 207, n. 104, who rightly suggests that 'a study of pre-1968 immigrant strike participation – which is still lacking given the period covered by his dissertation – is necessary to confirm' my argument that May 1968 gave rise to immigrant politicisation.

108 Desolre, 'Travailleurs immigrés', p. 17.

109 Stephen Castles and Godula Kosack, *Immigrant Workers and Class Structure in Western Europe*, Oxford: Oxford University Press, 1973, pp. 132-138; Juliette Minces, *Les travailleurs étrangers en France*, Paris: Seuil, 1973, p. 317; Stéphane Mourlane, 'Le Parti communiste français et l'immigration italienne dans les années soixante', *Studi emigrazione*, no. 146 (June 2002), pp. 415-427; Benoît Frachon, 'Prolétaires de tous les pays', *L'Humanité*, 15 April 1964, reproduced in Alain Ruscio, ed, *La question coloniale dans l'Humanité 1904-2004*, Paris: La Dispute, 2005, pp. 435-436; Laure Pitti, 'La main d'oeuvre algérienne dans l'industrie automobile (1945-1962), ou les oubliés de l'histoire', *Hommes et Migrations*, no. 1263 (September-October 2006), pp. 47-57.

110 Bibliothèque Nationale, Paris, *Document du secrétariat du comité central du Parti Communiste Français sur les tâches du parti parmis les travailleurs immigrés*, 5 May 1963.

111 Michel Branciard, *Histoire de la CFDT*, Paris: La Découverte, 1990, pp. 216-217; Castles and Kosack, *Immigrant Workers*, pp. 136-137; CFDT Archives Confédérales, Paris (CFDT), 7 H 735, Union Région Parisienne CFDT, 'Dépouillement du questionnaire "immigration"', 13 Februrary 1967; CFDT 7 H 734, CFDT to Anon, 17 January 1968; Minces, *Travailleurs étrangers*, p. 320.

112 P.Dubois, C.Durandsee and S.Erbès-Seguin, 'The contradictions of French trade unionism', in Colin Crouch and Alessandro Pizzorno, eds, *The Resurgence*

of *Class Conflict in Western Europe Since 1968*, vol. 1, London: Macmillan, 1978, pp. 64-67; Branciard, *Histoire de la CFDT*, p. 200; Georgi, *L'invention de la CFDT*, pp. 325-326; *Lavoro*, May 1966; Abadie and Corcelette, *Giscard*, p. 135; Gérard Lage, 'Le liaison étudiants-ouvriers à Caen', in René Mouriaux et al, eds, *1968, exploration du mai français*, vol. 1, Paris: L'Harmattan, 1992, pp. 217-236; *La Tribune du Travailleur Algérien*, December 1967; Marie-Christine Volovitch-Tavares, *Portugais à Champigny*, Paris: Autrement, 1995, p. 120.

113 Cited in Mark Miller, *Foreign Workers in Western Europe*, New York: Praeger, 1981, p. 3.

114 John Berger and Jean Mohr, *A Seventh Man*, Harmondsworth: Penguin, 1975, reprinted London: Verso, 2010, p. 68.

115 Castles and Kosack, *Immigrant Workers*; Stephen Castles and Godula Kosack, 'The function of labour migration in Western European capitalism', *New Left Review*, no. 73 (May-June 1972), pp. 3-21, reprinted in Stephen Castles, *Ethnicity and Globalization*, London: Sage, 2000, pp. 26-45.

116 Ulloa, *Jeanson*, pp. 178-179.

117 Parti Communiste Français (Marxiste-Léniniste), 'Contribution à l'analyse des classes en France', *L'Humanité nouvelle*, May 1966, reproduced in Patrick Kessel, ed, *Le mouvement <<maoiste>> en France*, vol. 1, Paris: Union Générale, 1972, p. 167.

118 'Conclusion', *Esprit*, no. 4 (April 1966), p. 912.

119 Gilles Bresson and Christian Lionet, *Le Pen*, Paris: Seuil, 1994, p. 292.

120 John Frears, *Political Parties and Electors in the French Fifth Republic*, London: Hurst, 1978, pp. 162-165; Nicholas Hewlett, *Modern French Politics*, Cambridge: Polity, 1998, p. 81; Edward Declair, *Politics on the Fringe*, Durham: Duke University Press, 1999, pp. 25-45; Frédéric Charpier, *Génération Occident*, Paris: Seuil, 2005; Daniel Gordon, 'Controlling the Streets in May 1968' in Jessica Wardhaugh, ed, *Paris and the Right in the Twentieth Century*, Newcastle: Cambridge Scholars, 2007, pp. 113-117.

121 John Ardagh, *The New French Revolution*, London: Secker & Warburg, 1968, p. 454.

122 Todd Shepard, *The Invention of Decolonization*, Ithaca: Cornell University Press, 2006, pp. 259-261; *Droit et Liberté*, 15 April-15 May 1964; Yvan Gastaut, *L'immigration et l'opinion en France sous la Ve République*, Paris: Seuil, 2000, pp. 109-117, 125.

123 *Droit et Liberté*, March 1967.

124 Jean-Pierre N'Diaye, *Négriers modernes*, Paris: Présence Africaine, 1970, p. 18; Gastaut, *L'immigration et l'opinion*, pp. 170-171, 184; Lallaoui, *Du bidonville au HLM*, p. 54; *Le Monde*, 29 August 2006; Gilles Verbunt, *L'intégration par l'autonomie*, Paris: CIEMM, 1980, pp. 285-286, 387; Philippe Bernard, *La crème des Beurs*, Paris: Seuil, 2004, pp. 36-41; Manuel Madeira, 'O Salto: synopsis/ observations', www.sudexpress.org, 2003; Volovitch-Tavares, *Portugais à Champigny*, p. 112.

125 *Droit et Liberté*, 15 Apr – 15 May 1964.

126 Lloyd, *Discourses of Antiracism in France*, pp. 49-53, 184-185.

127 Nicole de Maupeou-Abboud, *Les blousons bleus*, Paris: Armand Colin, 1968,

pp. 47-50; Philippe Gottraux, 'Autodissolution d'un collectif politique. Autour de Socialisme ou Barbarie', in Olivier Fillieule, ed, *Le désengagement militant*, Paris: Belin, 2005, p. 76.

128 Nacht, 'Travailleurs noirs', p. 153; Jean-Pierre N'Diaye, *Enquête sur les étudiants noirs en France* Paris: Réalités Africaines, 1962; Marie-Christine Volovitch-Tavares, 'Les incertitudes et les contradictions d'une "bonne intégration": les immigrants catholiques portugais en France, des années soixante aux années quatre-vingt', *Cahiers de la Méditerranée*, no. 78 (2009), pp. 158-176.

129 Sally N'Dongo, 'Itinéraire d'un militant africain', *Partisans*, no. 64 (March-April 1972), pp. 99-110; Sally N'Dongo, *Voyage forcé*, Paris: Maspero, 1975, pp. 9-10.

130 *Mémoires d'immigrés*, episode 1, *Les pères*.

131 Einaudi, *Bataille de Paris*, p. 300.

132 For example, the 1968 poster 'Non aux négriers du BUMIDOM'.

133 Sabrina Kassa, *Nos ancêtres les chibanis!*, Paris: Autrement, 2006, p. 51.

134 Archives Départementales du Val-de-Marne, Créteil, 6 J 96/13, *L'Evénement*, June 1968; *Témoignage Chrétien*, 18 July 1968; Patrick Hassenteufel, 'Citroën-Paris: une grève d'émancipation', in Mouriaux et al, *Exploration du mai français*, vol. 1, p. 35; *Le Nouvel Observateur*, 30 May 1968; *Economist*, 15 June 1968; Jean-Marie Leuwers, *Un peuple se dresse*, Paris: Editions Ouvrières, 1969, p. 184; Roger Gregoire and Fredy Perlman, *Worker-Student Action Committees*, Detroit: Black & Red, 1991, p. 15; *Rouge*, 29 October 1968; Seale and McConville, *French Revolution 1968*, p. 155; Angelo Quattrocchi and Tom Nairn, *The Beginning of the End*, London: Panther, 1968, p. 67; Ian Birchall, 'France 1968' in Colin Barker, ed, *Revolutionary Rehearsals*, London: Bookmarks, 1987, p. 22; Berger and Moir, *Seventh Man*, p. 142.

135 Manchuelle, *Willing Migrants*, pp. 1, 215-217, 225.

136 Caroline Brettell, 'Emigration and its implications for the revolution in northern Portugal', in Lawrence Graham and Harry Makler, eds, *Contemporary Portugal*, Austin: University of Texas Press, 1979, p. 294; Berger and Moir, *Seventh Man*, p. 218.

137 Françoise Gaspard, *Une petite ville en France*, Paris: Gallimard, 1990, translated as *A Small City in France*, Cambridge, MA: Harvard University Press, 1995, p. 48.

138 The title of an 1880 pamphlet by Karl Marx's son-in-law Paul Lafargue, foreshadowing the gradual reductions in the working week achieved by Left governments, notably in 1936, 1982 and 2000.

139 Extract from *Seize Millions de Jeunes*, broadcast 5 November 1964, in *La Saga des immigrés* (2007) dir. Edouard Mills-Affif and Anne Riegel.

140 Shepard, *Invention of Decolonization*, p. 260; Daniel Gordon, 'The back door of the nation state: expulsions of foreigners and continuity in twentieth-century France', *Past and Present*, no. 186 (February 2005), pp. 201-232. Even EEC nationals did not have voting rights in any French elections until the Maastricht Treaty of 1992.

141 Castles and Kosack, *Immigrant Workers and Class Structure*, p. 165.

142 Gastaut, *L'immigration et l'opinion*, p. 163; CFDT 7 H 734, Un groupe des

travailleurs maliens en France, 'Halte à l'exploitation des travailleurs maliens en France!', 15 June 1967.

143 Ralph Grillo, *Ideologies and Institutions in Urban France*, Cambridge: Cambridge University Press, 1985, p. 226.

144 Gilbert Meynier, *Histoire intérieure du FLN*, Paris: Fayard, 2004, pp. 531-545.

145 House and MacMaster, *Paris 1961*, p. 98.

146 House and MacMaster, *Paris 1961*, pp. 270-274.

147 House and MacMaster, *Paris 1961*, p. 259; Mohammed Harbi, 'Entre mémoire et histoire: un témoignage sur la politisation de l'immigration maghrébine en France', in Aïssa Kadri and Gerard Prévost, eds, *Mémoires algériennes*, Paris: Syllepse, 2004; Kassa, *Nos ancêtres les chibanis*, p. 26; Dewitte, 'Africains en France', p. 174; Jules-Rosette, *Black Paris*, p. 68.

148 Sayad, *Suffering of the Immigrant*, esp. Chapter 7, 'The Wrongs of the Absentee'; Ahmed Boubeker, *Les Mondes de l'ethnicité*, Paris: Balland, 2003, pp. 172-173.

149 *Mémoires d'immigrés*, episode 1, *Les pères*.

150 Rabah Aissaoui of Leicester University is currently researching the neglected history of Algerian exile politics in post-1962 France.

151 Nacht, 'Travailleurs noirs', p. 161; Centre des Archives Contemporaines, Fontainebleau, 19829599, article 41, Renseignements Généraux, 'Les travailleurs étrangers lors des événements de mai-juin', 28 June 1968.

152 Marie-Christine Volovitch-Tavares, 'L'Eglise de France et l'accueil des immigrés portugais', *Le Mouvement Social*, no. 188 (July-September 1999), pp. 89-102; Volovitch-Tavares, 'Incertitudes et contradictions'.

153 Rod Kedward, *French Roots*, Brighton: University of Sussex, 1995; Alun Howkins, *Poor Labouring Men*, London: Routledge, 1985; E.P. Thompson, *The Making of the English Working Class*, London: Victor Gollancz, 1963; Vladimir Andrlé, *A Social History of Twentieth Century Russia*, London: Hodder Arnold, 1994, pp. 95-104.

154 Catherine Wihtol de Wenden, 'Ethnic minority mobilisation against racism in France', in Alec Hargreaves, ed, *Racism, Ethnicity and Politics in Contemporary Europe*, Aldershot: Edward Elgar, 1995, p. 243.

155 'Un travailleur portugais', *Esprit*, no. 4 (April 1966), pp. 806-807.

156 CEDETIM, *Les immigrés*, Paris, 1975, p. 151; Minces, *Travailleurs étrangers*, pp. 13-25; Lillo, tour.

157 Pablo Carnicero, interviewed in Jean Anglade, *La vie quotidienne des immigrés en France de 1919 à nos jours*, Paris: Hachette, 1976, pp. 80-81.

158 *Esprit*, 'Conclusion', p. 915.

159 Christophe Bourseiller, *Les maoïstes*, Paris: Plon, 1996, pp. 33-39; Jacques Givet, *Le cas Vergès*, Paris: Lieu Commun, 1986; Jacques Vergès, *Le salaud lumineux*, Paris: Michel Lafon, 1990; *L'avocat de la terreur* (2007), dir. Barbet Schroeder.

160 Jean-Louis Brau, *Cours camarade, le vieux monde est derrière toi!*, Paris: Albin Michel, 1968, p. 178; Roland Biard, *Dictionnaire de l'extrême gauche*, Paris: Belfond, 1978; Kessel, *Maoïste*.

161 Sunil Khilnani, *Arguing Revolution*, New Haven: Yale University Press, 1993, pp. 142-145.

162 Bibliothèque Nationale, *Les tracts de mai 1968*, microfilm, Leiden, 1987, no. 4658: Comités de Défense Contre la Répression, 'Allons vers les travailleurs', [early May 1968].

163 Fausto Giudice, *Arabicides*, Paris: La Découverte, 1992, p. 118.

164 Gastaut, *L'immigration et l'opinion*, p. 155.

165 *Partisans*, no. 42 (May-June 1968), p. 84: Comité d'Action Maghrébin, 'Nous, travailleurs maghrébins', 20 May 1968; Bibliothèque Nationale, *Tracts de mai*, nos 3661: 'Université d'été "critique et populaire": commission "tiers monde" ', n.d. [before 5 July 1968], 4511: CLOTIF, 'Travailleurs émigrés/Trabajadores emigrantes/Trabalhadores emigrados', n.d. [before 22 December 1968], 4557: and 4896: *Luttes anti-racistes*, n.d. (March-April 1969); *Solidarité Anti-Impérialiste*, May 1969; Cahiers Révolution!, *Travailleurs français immigrés même combat*, Paris: Maspero, 1971, pp. 3-10.

166 Stéphane Courtois, et al, *Le sang de l'étranger*, Paris: Fayard, 1989.

167 Virginie Linhart, *Volontaires pour l'usine*, Paris: Seuil, 1994.

168 Those who did this were known as *établis*. Reid, 'Working in the factory', p. 85.

169 Ross, *May '68 and its Afterlives*, pp. 110-111.

Chapter 2

1 Henri le Boursicaud, 'Mai-juin 68 ... et trois millions d'étrangers', *Masses Ouvrières*, October 1968, pp. 40-41.

2 *Le Paria*, December 1969.

3 CFDT Archives Confédérales, Paris, (CFDT), 7 H 733, P.Manghetti to Commission Confédérale des Travailleurs Immigrés, 24 June 1968, P.Manghetti to R.Duvivier, R.Salanne, O.Ouhadj and P.Gonzalez, 27 June 1968, Sécrétariat des Travailleurs Immigrés to 'Cher Camarade', circular, 11 September 1968 and Sécrétariat des Travailleurs Immigrés, 'Session nationale des responsables, algériens du 11 octobre 1968, à Bierville'; *L'Ouvrier Algérien*, 7 September 1968; Archives Départementales des Hauts-de-Seine, Nanterre (ADHS), 44 J 227 ('JOC et immigrés: monographies – bilans 1968').

4 Alain Geismar et al, *Vers la guerre civile*, Paris: Premières, 1969, p. 342.

5 Le Boursicaud, 'Trois millions d'étrangers', p. 40.

6 CATE also used the alternative title Comité d'Action des Travailleurs Etrangers.

7 Roger Gregoire and Fredy Perlman, *Worker-Student Action Committees*, Detroit: Black & Red, 1991, pp. 15-16, 24-26; Bibliothèque Nationale, *Les tracts de mai 1968*, microfilm, Leiden, 1987, nos 4982-5026, leaflets by CATE; Angelo Quattrocchi and Tom Nairn, *The Beginning of the End: France, May 1968*, London: Panther, 1968, p. 68; Jacques Baynac, *Mai retrouvé*, Paris: Laffont, 1978, p. 137; Archives Départementales du Val-de-Marne, Créteil, 6 J 96/13, *L'Evénement*, June 1968, pp. 74-75.

8 Gregoire and Perlman, *Worker-Student Action Committees*, p. 16.

9 Quattrocchi and Nairn, *Beginning of the End*, p. 68; *L'Evénement*, June 1968, p. 75; David Caute, *Sixty-Eight*, London: Paladin, 1988, p. 206.

10 ADHS 44 J 227, Service Interdiocésan des Immigrés Paris, 'Groupe pastorale

"portugais" ', 20 May 1968 and R.Mossant, 'Travailleurs immigrés et événements: région parisienne mai juin 1968', June/July 1968; CFDT 7 H 730, 'Sessions de formation CFDT: Fiche de participation'.

11 Bibliothèque Nationale, *Tracts de mai*, no. 6080, strike committee leaflet, 26 May 1968

12 *La Cause du Peuple*, 23 May 1968; *L'Humanité*, 22 June 1968.

13 Bibliothèque Nationale, *Tracts de mai*, nos 4646, 5601, 5605-5608, 6080, 6085-88, 6707-08, 6710-11, 8339 and 8342; *L'Humanité*, 28 May 1968.

14 See below under 'Discussions and debates'.

15 Tangui Perron, *Histoire d'un film, mémoire d'une lutte. 2: Etrange étrangers*, Paris: Scope, 2009, p. 105.

16 Antoine Prost, 'Acteurs et terrains du mouvement social', in Réné Mouriaux et al, eds, *1968 Exploration du mai français*, vol. 2, Paris: L'Harmattan, 1992, p. 10; Baynac, *Mai retrouvé*, p. 141.

17 CFDT 7 H 735, CFDT Service des Travailleurs Immigrés, 'Note aux fédérations', 29 May 1968; Gregoire and Perlman, *Worker-Student Action Committees*, pp. 17-18.

18 Andrée Hoyles, *Imagination in Power*, Nottingham: Spokesman, 1973, pp. 19-20; Gregoire and Perlman, *Worker-Student Action Committees*, p. 30.

19 Jacques Fremontier, *La forteresse ouvrière*, Paris: Fayard, 1971.

20 This phrase, widely though wrongly attributed to Sartre, is emblematic of a period during the 1950s when intellectuals are held to have shown more deference towards the Communist beliefs of the French working class than to the truth about Eastern Europe.

21 See, however, Boris Gobille, *Mai 68*, Paris: La Découverte, 2008, pp. 54-57, for a critique of the overuse of this image.

22 Fremontier, *Forteresse ouvrière*, p. 84; *L'Humanité*, 18 May 1968.

23 Anon, *Paris: May 1968*, London: Solidarity, 1986, p. 12.

24 *Action*, 18 May 1968.

25 Fremontier, *Forteresse ouvrière*, p. 350; John Gretton, *Students and Workers*, London: Macdonald, 1968, p. 191; Pierre Andro et al, *Le mai de la révolution*, Paris: Julliard, 1968, p. 115; Anon, *Paris*, p. 12; *Témoignage Chrétien*, 23 May 1968. There were however, fewer multilingual leaflets than at Citroën, possibly because the many Algerians at Renault were more likely to know French than workers not from former French colonies.

26 The agreements became known under this name because they resulted from negotiations at the Ministry of Social Affairs in Rue de Grenelle.

27 Visible in the film *Le grand mouvement: la CGT en mai 1968* (Archives Départementales de la Seine-Saint-Denis, Bobigny, Archives audiovisuelles de la CGT, 2 AV 268/5256-5257); *Droit et Liberté*, June 1968; CFDT 4 W 86, CGT Syndicat des horaires, 'Exigeons: des logements à Billancourt'.

28 *La Tribune du Travailleur Algérien*, June 1968.

29 Xavier Vigna, 'Une émancipation des invisibles? Les ouvriers immigrés dans les grèves de mai-juin 68' in Ahmed Boubeker and Abdellali Hajjat, eds, *Histoire politique des immigrations (post)coloniales*, Paris: Amsterdam, 2008, pp. 90-92; Laure Pitti, "Travailleurs de France, voilà notre nom": les

mobilisations des ouvriers étrangers dans les usines et les foyers durant les années 1970', *Migrance*, no. 25 (2005), p. 55; Fremontier, *Forteresse ouvrière*, p. 108; Bibliothèque Nationale, *Tracts de mai*, no. 8233, Un Grupo de Jovenes Trabalhadores de Renault Billancourt, 'Para ler atentatmente' / 'Para leer con atención', c. 26 June 1968; CFDT 7 H 734, 'Réunion des Espagnols Bierville', 26-27 October 1968.

30   Réné Mouriaux, 'La CFDT' in Mark Kesselman and Guy Groux, eds, *1968-1982: le mouvement ouvrier français*, Paris: Éditions Ouvrières, 1984, pp. 95-96.

31   *Droit et Liberté*, February 1969.

32   Fremontier, *Forteresse ouvrière*, pp. 93, 100.

33   Jean-Philippe Talbo, *La grève à Flins*, Paris: Maspero, 1968; [Jean-Pierre Thorn], *Oser lutter, oser vaincre*, screenplay, Paris: Nouvelles Presses Parisiennes, 1972; Michel Mesaize, 'Renault-Flins, Aubergeville et les Mureaux', Masters dissertation, Université de Paris X, 1980, p. 183; Daniel Cohn-Bendit, *Nous l'avons tant l'aimée, la révolution*, Paris: Bernard Barrault, 1986, pp. 75-78.

34   Mesaize, 'Renault-Flins', p. 186; Hervé Hamon and Patrick Rotman, *Génération*, vol. 1, Paris, 1987, p. 561; Paul Rousselin, 'A Flins, les ouvriers n'en pouvaient plus', interview for *Libération*, http://www.libe.com/mai68/jour/jour0515b.html, 15 May 1998; Xavier Vigna, 'La figure ouvrière à Flins (1968-1973), in Geneviève Dreyfus-Armand et al, eds, *Les années 68*, Brussels: Complexe, 2000, p. 333.

35   Talbo, *Grève à Flins*, p. 17.

36   *Le Nouvel Observateur*, 12 and 26 June 1968; *Lutte Ouvrière*, 23 October 1968; Talbo, *Grève à Flins*, pp. 30, 79; *Oser lutter*, p. 210; Vigna, 'Emancipation des invisibles?', pp. 87, 92.

37   *L'Humanité*, 15 May 1968; *La Tribune du Travailleur Algérien*, June 1968; ADHS 44 J 227, 'La JOC immigré espagnole de Perpignan et les événements de mai 68'; Bibliothèque Nationale, *Tracts de mai*, nos 5397 and 5400; CFDT 7 H 48, *La Voix de la CFDT du Rhône, edition: Union syndicale de bâtiment, des travaux, du bois*, July 1968; CFDT 7 H 727, Service des Travailleurs Immigrés, 'Rétrospectives de l'activité du secrétariat pendant l'année 1968 et propositions pour l'avenir', January 1969; 'Réunion des Espagnols Bierville'; Centre des Archives Contemporaines, Fontainebleau (CAC), 19910194, article 13, liasse 4, P.Noirot-Cosson to J.Aubert, 11 October 1968; Institut Français d'Histoire Sociale, Paris, 14 AS 250/59, *Nous Les Immigrés: bulletin publié par l'association pour information sur la situation des étrangers en France*; University of Sussex Library, Mai 1968 Archive, folder 15, Comité d'Action des Ouvriers du Bâtiment, 'La pègre?', 25 May 1968; Corinne Hubert, ed, *1968 Un printemps val-de-marnais pas comme les autres*, Créteil: Conseil Général du Val-de-Marne, 1998, p. 70.

38   'JOC immigré espagnole de Perpignan'; ADHS 44 J 227, Fédération Vosges, '1- Face au racisme. L'accueil des immigrés'; Michèle Manceaux, *Les maos en France*, Paris: Gallimard, 1972, pp. 30-33.

39   CAC 19820599, article 41, 'Les travailleurs étrangers lors des événements de mai-juin', 28 June 1968.

40 Vigna, 'Emancipation des invisibles?', pp. 89-90.

41 ADHS 45 J 189, *Jeunesse Ouvrière*, May 1968; ADHS 44 J 227, R.Mossant, 'Travailleurs immigrés et événements: région parisienne mai juin 1968'; *L'Humanité*, 24 May 1968; Olivier Kourchid and C.Eckert, 'Les mineurs des houillères en grève: l'insertion dans un mouvement national', in Mouriaux, *Exploration du mai français*, vol. 1, p. 103.

42 Danièle Kergoat, *Bulledor*, Paris: Seuil, 1973, pp. 13, 32, 215-216.

43 Ngo Van, *In the Crossfire*, Edinburgh: AK Press, 2010, p. 213.

44 ADHS 45 J 595, Fédération Toulouse Immigrées, 'Reprise événements de mai 68'; Le Boursicaud, 'Trois millions d'étrangers'; 'Réunion des Espagnols Bierville'.

45 ADHS 44 J 227, 'Groupe pastorale "italiens"'; ADHS 44 J 227, 'Travailleurs immigrés et événements'.

46 ADHS 44 J 227, 'Les jeunes travailleurs portugais'.

47 *Bulletin de Liaison du CEDETIM*, November 1968; Stephen Castles and Godula Kosack, *Immigrant Workers and Class Structure in Western Europe*, Oxford: Oxford University Press, 1973, p. 171.

48 Bibliothèque de Documentation International Contemporaine, Nanterre (BDIC) F DELTA RES 813/7, Tribune du 22 mars, 'Premières remarques sur la commission permanente de mobilisation pour le soutien des entreprises occupées', 5 June 1968.

49 Jean-Marie Leuwers, *Un people se dresse*, Paris: Editions Ouvrières, 1969, p. 91.

50 Juliette Minces, *Les travailleurs étrangers en France*, Paris: Seuil, 1973, p. 159. The claim of Maud Bracke, 'May 1968 and Algerian immigrants in France: trajectories of mobilization and encounter', in Gurminder Bhambra and Ipek Demir, eds, *1968 In Retrospect*, Basingstoke: Palgrave Macmillan, 2009, pp. 122-123, that 'Relations between immigrant workers' organizations and the major trade unions deteriorated throughout May-June 1968, as immigrant workers became acutely aware of the persistence of racist attitudes' does not, therefore, appear to be supported by the primary evidence considered here.

51 Le Boursicaud, 'Trois millions d'étrangers', p. 40.

52 Jean Bertolino, *Les trublions*, Paris: Stock, 1969, pp. 130, 132-133; Roger Gascon, *La nuit du pouvoir*, Paris: Debresse, 1968, p. 48; CAC 19820599, article 41, 'Travailleurs étrangers lors des événements'; Le Boursicaud, 'Trois million d'étrangers', p. 37.

53 Bernard Hanrot, *Les sans-voix dans le pays de la liberté*, Paris: Editions Ouvrières, 1976, pp. 40-43.

54 CAC 19820599, article 41, 'Travailleurs étrangers lors des événements'; Commission Internationale de Juristes, 'Expulsions d'étrangers', *Migrations*, no. 13 (Autumn 1969), p. 41; Le Boursicaud, 'Trois million d'étrangers', p. 36; ADHS 44 J 227, 'Groupe pastorale "portugais"'.

55 Yvan Gastaut, *L'immigration et l'opinion en France sous la Ve République*, Paris: Seuil, 2000, pp. 38-39; Geneviève Dreyfus-Armand, 'L'arrivée des immigrés sur la scène politique', in *IHTP. Les années 68: événements, cultures politiques et modes de vie. Lettre d'information*, no. 30 (June 1998), p. 5; *Le Monde*, 15 June 1968. Vigna, 'Emancipation des invisibles', while generally placing more

emphasis on active participation, also chooses to foreground (pp. 86-87) the departure of the Portuguese.

56   Dreyfus-Armand, 'L'arrivée des immigrés', p. 5.

57   Based on 1968 census figure of 2,621,088 foreigners resident in France, from Marianne Amar and Pierre Milza, eds, *L'immigration en France au XXe siècle*, Paris: Armand Colin, 1990, p. 272.

58   Marie-Antoinette Hily and Michel Poinard, 'Entre France et Portugal, l'attrait du va-et-vient', *Hommes et Migrations*, no. 1210 (November-December 1997), pp. 63-72; Alexis Spire, *Etrangers à la carte*, Paris: Grasset, 2005, pp. 302-303.

59   ADHS 44 J 227, 'Témoignage d'un militant portugais'.

60   CAC 19820599, article 41, 'Travailleurs étrangers lors des événements'; Manceaux, *Maos*, p. 36.

61   Commission Internationale de Juristes, 'Expulsions d'étrangers', p. 41; Charles Posner, *Reflections on the Revolution in France*, Harmondsworth: Penguin, 1970, p. 90; Castles and Kosack, *Immigrant Workers and Class Structure*, p. 173; *Droit et Liberté*, June 1968; Jean Anglade, *La vie quotidienne des immigrés en France de 1919 à nos jours*, Paris: Hachette, 1976, pp. 190-191.

62   CAC 19820599, article 41, 'Travailleurs étrangers lors des événements'; CAC 19890519, article 10, liasse 3, Sécrétariat-Général pour la Police, 'Note', 4 June 1968; Robert Boissésson, 'Répercussions en Espagne des événements de France', 10 June 1968, reproduced in Maurice Vaïsse, ed, *Mai 68 vu de l'étranger*, Paris: CNRS, 2008, p. 59; *Le Figaro*, 22 May 1968; Office National d'Immigration, *Statistiques de l'Immigration*, 1968, p. 9.

63   Boissésson, 'Répercussions en Espagne', p. 59.

64   CAC 19820599, article 41, 'Travailleurs étrangers lors des événements'; ADHS 44 J 227, 'Témoignage d'un militant portugais'.

65   CAC 19820599, article 41, 'Travailleurs étrangers lors des événements'.

66   Office National d'Immigration, *Statistiques de l'Immigration*, 1971, p. 8.

67   *L'Aurore*, 19 June 1968.

68   *L'Express*, 23 October 2003; Manceaux, *Maos*, pp. 166-168; Denis Boutelier and Dilip Subramanian, *Mon Eldorado la France?*, Paris: Denoël, 1997, p. 110.

69   John Follain, *Jackal*, London: Weidenfeld & Nicolson, 1998, p. 12; *Le Figaro*, 20 May 1968; *Independent*, 16 May 1998.

70   Claude Paillat, *Archives secrètes*, Paris: Denoël, 1969, pp. 167-169.

71   ADHS 44 J 227, 'JOC – Belfort 68'; Kergoat, *Bulledor*, pp. 120, 126.

72   ADHS 45 J 331, P.Grangeon, 'Weekend – Nogent 26-27 octobre 1968: quelques aspects du dialogue avec les J.T. maghrébins'.

73   Le Boursicaud, 'Trois millions d'étrangers', p. 42.

74   ADHS 44 J 227, 'Travailleurs immigrés et événements'; CAC 19820599, article 41, Travailleurs étrangers lors des événements'.

75   Le Boursicaud, 'Trois millions d'étrangers', p. 37; ADHS 44 J 227, 'Groupe pastorale "portugais"'.

76   *Droit et Liberté*, June 1968. *Raton*, literally 'young rat', was a racist term for Algerians.

77   Gretton, *Students and Workers*, p. 221; Laurent Joffrin, *Mai 68*, Paris: Seuil, 1998, p. 162; Kristin Ross, *May '68 and its Afterlives*, Chicago: Chicago

University Press, 2002, p. 31; Bibliothèque Nationale, *Tracts de mai*, no. 8325: 'Qui est Monsieur Papon?', n.d. [June 1968].

78 Leuwers, *Un peuple se dresse*, p. 186. This report, from which Seidman, 'Workers in a repressive society of seductions', p. 268, generalises to claim Spanish workers as a whole were more active than North Africans in 1968, may however be subject to bias, since it was by a Catholic activist who portrayed North Africans as 'exacting' and 'crafty' when it came to receiving solidarity payments. Vigna, 'Emancipation invisible?', p. 89 also rushes to claim Spanish workers were the most mobilised, on the basis of one single workplace.

79 Paul Werner, 'David's basket: art and agency in the French Revolution', PhD thesis, City University of New York, 1997, p. 239.

80 Leaflets in CFDT 7 H 61; document in CFDT 7 H 43, P.Manghetti, 'Les camarades immigrés du Secrétariat', n.d. [May-June 1968].

81 *La Cause du Peuple*, 29 May 1968.

82 For more details, see Daniel Gordon, 'Reaching out to immigrants in May '68: specific or universal appeals?', in Julian Jackson et al, eds, *May '68*, Basingstoke: Palgrave Macmillan, 2011.

83 *Partisans*, no. 42 (May-June 1968), pp. 84-85, Comité d'Action Maghrébin, 'Nous, travailleurs maghrébins', 20 May 1968; Vladimir Fisera, *Writing on the Wall*, London: Alison & Busby, 1978, p. 25.

84 *La Tribune Socialiste*, 28 November 1968; Peter Fysh and Jim Wolfreys, *The Politics of Racism in France*, Basingstoke: Macmillan, 1998, p. 33.

85 *Droit et Liberté*, June 1968.

86 Atelier Populaire, *Mai 68*, London: Dobson, 1969, poster no. 151.

87 Génériques, *Les étrangers en France*, 3 vols, Paris: Génériques, 1999, p. 2326; Atelier Populaire, *Mai 68*, no. 154, claims that the second poster was 'asked for by Bidonville', but the work- rather than housing- related slogan suggests the Citroën explanation is more plausible, as does the use of Serbo-Croat, Italian, Greek and Spanish (alongside French, Portuguese and Arabic), since workers speaking all these languages worked at Citroën, while shanty-towns were predominantly North African or Portuguese.

88 *Igloos*, May-June-July-August-1968.

89 E.g. *Nous Les Immigrés*, n.d. [summer 1968].

90 ADHS 44 J 227, 'JOC et immigrés: monographies – bilans 1968' and 45 J 595, 'Réaction aux événements de mai 1968'; BDIC F DELTA RES 813/10, *Tricontinentale Sorbonne*.

91 Stephen Spender, *The Year of the Young Rebels*, London: Weidenfeld & Nicolson, 1969, p. 41.

92 *La Sorbonne par elle-même*, special issue of *Le Mouvement Social*, no. 64 (July-September 1968), pp. 244-246.

93 CAC 19890519, article 10, liasse 3, item in folder 'Agitateurs étrangers mai-juin 1968'; *Les travailleurs immigrés parlent*, special issue of *Cahiers du Centre d'études socialistes*, nos 94-98, (September-December 1969), p. 161.

94 Constantin Roman, *Continental Drift*, Bristol: Institute of Physics, 2000, pp. 36-37.

95 Kamal Salhi, 'Assia Djebar ... speaking' in Kamal Salhi, ed, *Francophone*

Voices, Exeter: Elm Bank, 1999, p. 75.

96   Patrick Seale and Maureen McConville, *French Revolution 1968*, London: Penguin, 1968, p. 104; CAC 19820599, 'Les meneurs expriment les motifs des étudiants', 14 May 1968; BDIC F DELTA RES 813/10, *Tricontinentale Sorbonne*; CAC 19890519, 'Agitateurs étrangers'.

97   *L'Aurore*, 16 May 1968.

98   Jill Lovecy, conversation with author, Liverpool, 31 October 2007.

99   Gamé Guilao, *France, terre d'acceuil, terre de rejet*, Paris: L'Harmattan, 1994, p. 44.

100 Robert Serrou, *Dieu n'est pas conservateur*, Paris: Laffont, 1968, p. 112; *L'Aurore*, 16 May 1968.

101 Patrick Ravignant, *La prise de l'Odéon*, Paris: Stock, 1968, pp. 95-97.

102 ADHS 44 J 227, 'Groupe pastorale "portugais"; Jean-Claude Kerbouc'h, *Le piéton de mai*, Paris: Julliard, 1968, p. 63.

103 *The Making of Rocky Road to Dublin* (2004), dir. Paul Duane, on DVD of *Rocky Road to Dublin*; conversation with Peter Lennon, Liverpool, 31 October 2007.

104 ADHS 45 J 594 Fédération Grand Quenilly, 'Rencontre des meneuses 14-17', May 1968.

105 *Le Figaro*, 9 May 1968.

106 Lucien Rioux and René Backman, *L'explosion de mai*, Paris: Laffont, 1968, p. 600; Paul Werner, email to author, 15 January 2002.

107 Paul Werner, email to author, 9 January 2002. Werner's recollection is supported by police figures showing that just over half of all the foreigners arrested in the Latin Quarter were from the Middle East or (mainly) North Africa, though sub-Saharan Africans were also arrested disproportionately to their size of the foreign population as a whole.

108 *L'Aurore*, 6 May 1968; *Paris-Presse L'Intransigeant*, 8, 9 and 10 May 1968; *France Soir*, 8 and 10 May 1968; *Le Figaro*, 8 and 9 May 1968; *Le Monde*, 9 May 1968; *L'Humanité*, 10 and 13 May 1968; *Témoignage Chrétien*, 16 May 1968; CAC 19910194, article 1, liasse 2, Préfecture de Police, 'A la suite de la manifestation du 6 mai...', 8 May 1968; CAC 19860146, Sous-direction des CRS, 'Manifestations de mai-juin 1968 à Paris et en province: l'action des manifestants à l'encontre des forces de police', 25 June 1968; Marc Kravetz et al, eds, *L'insurrection étudiante*, Paris: Union Générale, 1968, pp. 388, 501; UNEF / SNESUP Commission Témoignages et Assistance Juridique, *Ils accusent*, Paris: Seuil, 1968, pp. 92-93; Pierre Genève, *Histoire secrète de l'insurrection de mai*, Paris: Presses Noires, 1968, pp. 58-70; Bibliothèque Nationale, *Tracts de mai*, no. 7769, Doctor Le Guen, 'A Witness'.

109 Posner, *Reflections on the Revolution in France*, p. 72.

110 *Paris-Presse L'Intransigeant*, 12-13 May 1968; *L'Humanité Nouvelle*, 16-23 May 1968; CAC 19910194, article 13, liasse 4, letter to Raymond Marcellin from a Swiss national arrested that night; CAC 19890519, article 10, liasse 3, 'Notice de Renseignements', May 1968; Neal Ascherson, interview with author, London, 8 May 2001; Tariq Ali and Susan Watkins, *1968: marching in the streets*, London: Bloomsbury, 1998, p. 95; Réné Viénet, *Enragés et situationnistes dans le mouvement des occupations*, Paris: Gallimard, 1998, p.

59; Jan Willem Stutje, *Ernest Mandel*, London: Verso, 2009, p. 171.

111 Mavis Gallant, *Paris Notebooks*, London: Bloomsbury, 1988, p. 13.

112 CAC 19860146, Sous-direction des CRS, 'Manifestations de mai-juin 1968'; *L'Humanité Nouvelle*, 16-23 May 1968; Sabrina Kassa, *Nos ancêtres les chibanis!*, Paris: Autrement, 2006, p. 162.

113 *Lutte Ouvrière*, 11 December 1968

114 *L'Humanité*, 15 May 1968; ADHS 44 J 227, Mossant, 'Travailleurs immigrés et événements'; ADHS 44 J 227, 'Groupe pastorale "portugais" '; CAC 19820599, article 41, 'Travailleurs étrangers lors des événements'.

115 *Lutte Ouvrière*, 11 December 1968.

116 *Le grand mouvement.*

117 S.Yati, 'D'un désert à l'autre: le périple d'un jeune Algérien, du Sahara à Nanterre', *Preuves*, no. 214 (January 1969), p. 47.

118 'Down with the police state'.

119 Anon, *Paris*, p. 38; according to Ian Birchall, 'Seizing the time: Tony Cliff and 1968', *International Socialism*, no. 118 (Spring 2008), n. 17, the author's name was Chris Pallis, aka Maurice Brinton.

120 *L'Humanité*, 25 May 1968; *L'Aurore*, 25-26 May 1968; Posner, *Reflections on the Revolution in France*, p. 95; Andro, *Mai de la révolution*, pp. 149-161; Caute, *Sixty-Eight*, pp. 210-211; Danièle Tartakowsky, *Les manifestations de rue en France*, Paris: Sorbonne, 1997, p. 115-124; Seale and McConville, *French Revolution*, p. 172; Viénet, *Enragés et situationnistes*, p. 133.

121 CAC 19820599, article 41, 'Travailleurs étrangers lors des événements'.

122 *Paris-Presse L'Intransigeant*, 26-27 May 1968; *France-Soir*, 26-27 May 1968; Kergoat, *Bulledor*, pp. 130-131; *Le Nouvel Observateur*, 30 May 1968; University of Sussex, May 1968 Archive, Folder 17, 'Paris May 1968 Repression'; UNEF / SNESUP, *Ils accusent*, pp. 162, 168-175, Fisera, *Writing on the Wall*, pp. 30-31.

123 Ronald Fraser et al, *1968: a student generation in revolt*, London: Chatto & Windus, 1988, p. 198; *Le Journal du Rhône*, 25 and 26 May 1968; *L'Aurore*, 28 May 1968; *Dernière Heure Lyonnaise*, 8 June 1968; Laurent Burlet, 'Mai 68: mystères autour du commissaire Lacroix', www.lyoncapital.fr, 1 May 2008; Michelle Zancarini-Fournel, 'Jeux d'echelle: local-régional-national', paper to *Mai 68: Forty Years On* conference, University of London Institute in Paris, 15-17 May 2008.

124 CAC 19820599, article 43, 'Les non-étudiants dans l'action révolutionnaire', 21 August 1968.

125 *Le Journal du Rhône*, 26 May 1968.

126 Saïd Bouziri, interview with author, Paris, 6 November 2004; Bibliothèque Nationale, *Tracts de mai*, nos 9822, Mouvement de Soutien aux Luttes du Peuple, 'Non à la répression policière, 25 May 1968, 9823, 'Position du mouvement de soutien sur la manif de la nuit', 25 May 1968 and 9829, Mouvement du 22 mars, 'Exigeons la vérité'; *Le Journal du Rhône*, 27 and 31 May 1968; *L'Aurore*, 28 May 1968; *France-Soir*, 28 May 1968; CFDT 7 H 747, Secrétariat des Travailleurs Immigrés, 'Note aux fédérations, unions départmentales et syndicats de la région parisienne', 30 May 1968; *Le Figaro*, 27 May 1968.

127 CFDT 7 H 734, letter to Commission Immigrés, after 29 June 1968.

128 *L'Humanité*, 30 May 1968.

129 Daniel Gordon, 'Acteurs trans-méditerranéens dans un quartier cosmopolite. Juifs et musulmans à Belleville (Paris 20e), entre tolérance et conflit', *Cahiers de la Méditerranée*, no. 67 (December 2003), pp. 287-298, http://cdlm.revues. org/index135.html.

130 Daniel Gordon, " Il est recommandé aux étudiants de ne pas participer": les étrangers expulsés en mai-juin 1968', *Migrations Société*, no. 88 (May-August 2003), pp. 56-57.

131 Paul Werner, email to author, 9 January 2002.

132 *Paris-Presse L'Intransigeant*, 13 and 16-17 June 1968; *France-Soir*, 16-17 June 1968; *Le Monde*, 16-17 June and 30 June – 1 July 1968.

133 *France-Soir*, 14 June 1968; Bibliothèque Nationale, *Tracts de mai*, no. 9190, Mouvement du 25 Avril, 'Nous sommes tous des étrangers', n.d. [17 June 1968]; CAC 19910194, article 14, liasse 4, P.Noirot-Cosson to J.Aubert, 26 July 1968 and J.Aubert to J.Gouazé, 1 August 1968; Jean Dieuzaide, *Mai 68 à Toulouse*, Toulouse: Galerie Municipale du Château d'Eau, 1998, p. 24.

134 CAC 19820599, article 43, 'Non-étudiants'; CAC 19910194, article 11, liasse 1, 'Physionomie générale', n.d. [30 June 1968]; *Paris-Presse L'Intransigeant*, 7-8 July 1968; *L'Aurore*, 15 July 1968; *Le Figaro*, 18 July 1968.

135 *Rouge*, 24 December 1968; *Pour la Liberté*, January 1969.

136 This includes 51 of 596 on 3 May; 80 of 450 on 6 May; 61 of 468 on 10 May; 4 of 65 on 22 May; 46 of 186 on 23 May; 31 of 194 in Lyons on 24 May; 33 of 236 on 11 June; 13 of 36 on 29 June; 9 of 152 in early July; 52 of 218 on 13 July and 79 of 243 on 14 July. Figures taken from sources cited above for each demonstration; details in Daniel Gordon, 'Immigrants and the New Left in France 1968-1971', DPhil thesis, University of Sussex, 2001, pp. 111-132.

137 CAC 1980519, article 10, liasse 3, 'Manifestants étrangers expulsés, arrêtés du 18 juin 1968'; see Gordon, 'Il est recommandé', pp. 46-52 for further data and analysis.

138 Richard Evans, *The German Working Class 1888-1933*, London: Croom Helm, 1982, pp. 26-27.

139 Philip Converse and Roy Pierce, *Political Representation in France*, Cambridge, MA: Harvard University Press, 1986, pp. 422-424.

140 UNEF-SNESUP, *Ils accusent*, p. 197; Gordon, 'Il est recommandé', pp. 53-58.

141 CAC 19820599, article 40, 'Les séparatistes antillo-guyanais sont dans le mouvement', 27 May 1968; *Le Monde*, 31 May, 1 and 7 June 1968; *L'Humanité*, 31 May 1968; *Le Jounal du Dimanche Soir*, 2 June 1968; *Paris-Presse L'Intransigeant*, 7 June 1968; *Lutte Ouvrière*, 10 July 1968; Bibliothèque Nationale, *Tracts de mai*, tracts nos 4839-4846, by Comité d'Action des Travailleurs Etrangers et des Pays Sous Domination Coloniale Française; Laurent Farrugia, *Le fait national guadeloupéen*, Ivry: Laurent Farrugia, 1968, p. 138.

142 *Droit et Liberté*, June 1968; Bibliothèque Nationale, *Tracts de mai*, no. 6718, Mouvement de Soutien aux Luttes du Peuple, 'Le mouvement de mai n'est pas mort', n.d. [June 1968]; Castles and Kosack, *Immigrant Workers and Class*

Structure, p. 172.

143 *Le Monde*, 1 June 1968; *Paris-Presse L'Intransigeant*, 1 June 1968; *L'Humanité Nouvelle*, 6 June 1968; Guy de Bosschère, 'En Afrique, mai explose en juin', *Esprit*, nos 8-9 (August-September 1968), pp. 179-181; Charles Rousseau, 'Chronique des faits internationaux', *Revue de droit international public*, vol. 73, no. 1 (January – March 1969), p. 184; Abdoulaye Bathily, *Mai 68 à Dakar*, Paris: Chaka, 1992, p. 11; Kravetz et al, *L'insurrection étudiante*, p. 200; CAC 19820599, article 41, 'La FEANFF pendant la révolte estudiantine', 21 June 1968; CAC 19860146, article 3, 'Documentation no. 5/68: A/S, expulsion d'étudiants africains à la suite des événements de mai en France', 21 June 1968 and 'Documentation no. 6/68: Expulsion de France de ressortissants africains et malgaches (suite)', 2 July 1968.

144 *L'Humanité*, 12 June 1968; *Le Monde*, 13 June 1968; Rousseau, 'Chronique', p. 184.

145 Vaïsse, *Mai 68 vu de l'étranger*, pp. 11-19, 201-202; Paul Oriol, 'Alger en mai', http://pauloriol.over-blog.fr/article-18930235.html, 21 April 2008; Stéphane Hessel, *Indignez-vous!*, Montpellier: Indigène, 2010, translated as *Time for Outrage!*, London: Quartet, 2011; Stéphane Hessel, *Danse avec le siècle*, Paris: Points, 2011, pp. 219-232 mentions leftist *coopérants* in Algiers, though not this specific incident.

146 Bertrand Lemoine, *La Cité internationale universitaire de Paris*, Paris: Hervas, 1990, pp. 14-31; Seale and McConville, *French Revolution*, pp. 117-118; CFDT 4 W 85, 'Comité d'occupation du college d'Espagne', n.d. [after 18 May 1968]; Bibliothèque Nationale, *Tracts de mai*, nos 2387, Maison d'Afrique, 'Règlement intérieur', 21 May 1968, 2390, Le Comité d'Occupation du Pavillon d'Argentine, '1. Brûlures', 20 May 1968; 2401, Comité d'Occupation de la Maison du Brésil, 'La maison du Brésil occupée, n.d. [29 May 1968], 2403, Anon, 'Motion', 22 May 1968 and 2404, Anon, 'Maison des étudiants et travailleurs italiens', n.d. [after 9 June 1968]; Baynac, *Mai retrouvé*, p. 143; CAC 19910194, article 1, liasse 2, Préfecture de Police, 'Physionomie dans les facultés et les établisssments scolaires', 14 June 1968; CAC 19910194, article 1, liasse 2, Préfecture de Police, 'Etablissements universitaires encore occupé par des étudiants', 20 August 1968; CAC 19910194, article 1, liasse 2, Préfecture de Police, 'Physionomie du quartier latin au cours de la journée du 2 septembre', 2 September 1968.

147 Bibliothèque Nationale, *Tracts de mai*, nos. 2391, 2397, 2400 and 2409 by Comité d'Occupation de la Pavillion d'Argentine; *Le Monde*, 29 May 1968.

148 CAC 19890519, 'Agitateurs étrangers'; CAC 19820599, article 41, 'Travailleurs étrangers lors des événements'; Geneviève Dreyfus-Armand, *L'exil des espagnols républicains en France*, Paris, 1999, pp. 315-316.

149 Viénet, *Enragés et situationnistes*, p. 141.

150 Castoriadis wrote 'La révolution anticipée', in Edgar Morin et al, *Mai 1968, la brèche*, Paris: Fayard, 1968, pp. 89-142, only by using the pseudonym Jean-Marc Coudray; Arthur Hirsh, *The French Left*, Montreal: Black Rose, 1982, p. 147; Bob Jessop, *Nicos Poulantzas*, Basingstoke: Macmillan, 1985, pp. 7-13.

151 Yaïr Auron, *Les juifs d'extrême gauche en mai 68*, Paris: Albin Michel, 1998,

p. 192; Meïr Waintrater, ed, 'Benny Lévy, le passeur', *L'Arche*, no. 549-550 (November-December 2003), pp. 40-61; Michel Sarrasin, *Histoires de mai*, Choisy-le-Roi: Temps Présent, 1978, p. 188; Elisabeth Salvaresi, *Mai en héritage*, Paris: Syros, 1988, pp. 167, 181, 203; Jacques Tarnero, *Mai 68, la révolution fiction*, Toulouse: Milan, 1998, p. 58; Gilles de Staal, *Mamadou m'a dit*, Paris: Syllepse, 2008, pp. 90-91, 103; *Le Monde*, 6 May 1998; CAC 19910194, article 13, liasse 4, 'Révision des expulsions d'étrangers mai-juin 1968', August 1969.

152 ADHS 44 J 227, 'Groupe pastorale "portugais".

153 CAC 19890519, 'Agitateurs étrangers'; CAC 19910194, article 3, liasse 3, ' "Confédération nationale du travail" espagnole (Confederación national del trabajo)', December 1968.

154 *Economist*, 8 June 1968.

155 CAC 19890519, 'Agitateurs étrangers'; BDIC 9 PIECE 8078, 'Exposé de Monsieur Raymond Marcellin...', 14 November 1968; *Le Monde*, 11-12 and 15 August 1968; CAC 19910194, article 13, liasse 4, Corryell's wife to Raymond Marcellin, 22 March 1969; *Sydney Morning Herald*, 29 December 2010.

156 Hervé Hamon and Patrick Rotman, *Génération*, vol 1, Paris: Seuil, 1987, pp. 412-417, 430, 434-436; Ascherson, interview; reports on Ascherson and five German SDS activists in CAC 19890519, 'Agitateurs étrangers'; UNEF-SNESUP, *Ils accusent*, pp. 193-196; *Le Figaro*, 11 June 1968 and 12 June 1968; *Nice Matin*, 13 June 1968; *Paris-Presse L'Intransigeant*, 14 June 1968; *Le Nouvel Observateur*, 26 June 1968; *Droit et Liberté*, December 1968; *Pour la Liberté*, January 1969.

157 Raymond Marcellin, *L'ordre public et les groupes révolutionnaires*, Paris: Plon, 1969; Rioux and Backman, *Explosion de mai*, pp. 599-603.

158 CAC 19890519, 'Agitateurs étrangers', letters from Director of Renseignements Généraux, 30 and 31 May 1968 and Jean Gouzé, telegram to prefects, 10 June 1968; *Le Figaro*, 11-12 May 1968; CAC 19890519, article 10, liasse 3, J.Soyard to Renseignements Généraux, 7 May 1968 and Renseignements Généraux to Prefect of Bas-Rhin, 8 May 1968.

159 CAC 19890519, 'Agitateurs étrangers'; Ascherson, interview; Daniel Cohn-Bendit and Bernard Kouchner, *Quand tu seras président*, Paris: Laffont, 2004, p. 135; Stutje, *Mandel*, p. 172; Manus McGrogan, 'Vive la Révolution and the example of Lotta Continua: the circulation of ideas and practices between the left militant worlds of France and Italy following May '68', *Modern and Contemporary France*, vol. 18, no. 3 (August 2010), pp. 319-320.

160 Neal Ascherson, email to author, 8 July 2011.

161 Tony Judt, *The Memory Chalet*, London: Heinemann, 2010, p. 121.

162 Sheila Rowbotham, *Promise of a Dream*, London: Allen Lane, 2000, p. 179.

163 Tariq Ali, *Street Fighting Years*, London: Fontana, 1988, p. 197.

164 Murray Bookchin, '1960s: Myth and Reality', in *Anarchism, Marxism and the Future of the Left*, Edinburgh: AK Press, 1999, pp. 94-96; Jon Savage, *England's Dreaming*, London: Faber & Faber, 2001, p. 30.

165 Sally N'Dongo, 'Itinéraire d'un militant africain', *Partisans*, no. 64 (March-April 1972), p. 101.

166   Mogniss Abdallah, *J'y suis, j'y reste!*, Paris: Reflex, 2000, p. 18.
167   *Le Nouvel Observateur*, 15 May 1968.

Chapter 3

1   Céline Ackaouy, *Un nom de papier*, Paris: Clancier-Guénaud, 1981, p. 146.
2   Emmanuel Wallon, cited in Gilles de Staal, *Mamadou m'a dit*, Paris: Syllepse, 2008, p. 48.
3   Arthur Marwick, *The Sixties*, Oxford: Oxford University Press, 1998, p. 753.
4   *Le Figaro*, 14 June 1968 and 19 June 1968; *El Moudjahid*, 15 June 1968; *Le Monde*, 15 June 1968; *L'Aurore*, 19 June 1968; *Comité d'Action Révolutionnaire Odéon*, June 1968; *Droit et Liberté*, September-October 1968; *Pour la Liberté*, January 1969; Centre des Archives Contemporaines, Fontainebleau (CAC) 19890519, article 10, liasse 3, folder 'Manifestants étrangers expulsés, arrêtés du 18 juin 1968'; for a fuller analysis, see Daniel Gordon,"Il est recommandé aux étudiants de ne pas participer": les étrangers expulsés en mai-juin 1968', *Migrations Société*, no. 88 (May-August 2003), pp. 45-65.
5   *Le Journal du Rhône*, 27 May 1968; *Le Monde*, 15 June 1968; *Le Figaro*, 15-16 June 1968; *Droit et Liberté*, September-October 1968; CAC 19890519, article 10, liasse 3, 'Manifestants étrangers expulsés, arrêtés du 18 juin 1968'.
6   UNEF-SNESUP, Commission Témoigages et Assistance Juridique, *Ils accusent*, Paris: Seuil, 1968, pp. 191, 197-204; *Le Nouvel Observateur*, 12 June 1968 and 26 June 1968; *Paris-Presse L'Intransigeant*, 13 June 1968; *Jewish Chronicle*, 14 June 1968; *Le Monde*, 14 June 1968 and 27 June 1968; *Droit et Liberté*, September-October 1968; *Idiot International*, December 1969; Paul Werner, email to author, 9 January 2002.
7   UNEF-SNESUP, *Ils accusent*, pp. 193-196; CAC 19890519, article 10, liasse 3, 'Notice de renseignements', May 1968; *Le Figaro*, 11 June 1968 and 12 June 1968; *Nice Matin*, 13 June 1968; *Paris-Presse L'Intransigeant*, 14 June 1968; *Le Nouvel Observateur*, 26 June 1968; *Droit et Liberté*, December 1968; *Pour la Liberté*, January 1969; Neal Ascherson, interview with author, London, 8 May 2001.
8   Christine Fauré, 'Mai 68 à Toulouse: le movement du 25 avril', in Geneviève Dreyfus-Armand, and Laurent Gervereau, eds, *Mai 68*, Nanterre: BDIC, 1988, p. 203; *Le Figaro*, 14 June 1968; *France-Soir*, 14 June 1968; *Le Monde*, 14 June 1968 and 15 June 1968; CAC 19890519, article 10, liasse 3, 'Arrêtés d'expulsion pris contre des étrangers ayant participé aux manifestations de juin 1968. Province', n.d. [June 1968].
9   Daniel Gordon, 'The back door of the nation state: expulsions of foreigners and continuity in twentieth century France', *Past and Present*, no. 186 (January 2005), pp. 201-232.
10   UNEF-SNESUP, *Ils accusent*, pp. 194-195; MRAP Archives, Paris, box 'Travailleurs immigrés 1968-1978', folder 'Expulsions 1968', document 'Tribunal administratif de Paris: recours et mémoire. Pour Monsieur Frankel Boris…', n.d. [1968]; Boris Fraenkel, *Profession: révolutionnaire*, Latresne: Le Bord de l'Eau, 2004.

11   UNEF-SNESUP, *Ils accusent*, pp. 193, 209-210; *Le Figaro*, 13 June 1968; *Paris-Presse L'Intransigeant*, 14 June 1968; *Droit et Liberté*, September-October 1968 and December 1968; MRAP Archives, 'Expulsions 1968', 'Recours gracieux: Monsieur Pablo Paradès', n.d. [1968] and letters from N.Rein to R.Marcellin, n.d. [1968].

12   Maxim Silverman, *Deconstructing the Nation*, London: Routledge, 1992, p. 49.

13   Gary Freeman, *Immigrant Labor and Racial Conflict in Industrial Societies*, Princeton: Princeton University Press, 1979, pp. 86-87. Albert-Paul Lentin reached a similar conclusion in *Le Nouvel Observateur*, 26 June 1968.

14   CAC 19890519, article 10, liasse 3, Anon, 'Note', June 1968.

15   *Lutte Ouvrière*, 11 September 1968; *Rouge*, 16 October 1968; Jacques Frémontier, *La Forteresse ouvrière*, Paris: Fayard, 1971, p. 85; Maryse Tripier, *L'immigration dans la classe ouvrière en France*, Paris: L'Harmattan, 1990, p. 175; *Action*, 18 June 1968; Lucien Rioux and René Backmann, *L'explosion de mai*, Paris: Laffont, 1968, pp. 396-397; Michael Seidman, 'Workers in a repressive society of seductions: Parisian metallurgists in May-June 1968', *French Historical Studies*, vol. 18, no. 1 (Spring 1993), p. 275; Serge Ducrocq, *Histoire de la CGT à Nanterre*, Paris: Messidor, 1988, p. 113.

16   CFDT Archives Confédérales, Paris (CFDT), 7 H 43, Sécrétariat des Travailleurs Immigrés, 'Positions à défendre aux négociations de Grenelle', 29 May 1968 and 7 H 61, CFDT, 'Les positions syndicales respectives lors des negociations de "Grenelle" les 25, 26 et 17 mai 1968'.

17   CFDT 7 H 735, 'Réunion des Espagnols', October 1968.

18   Vasco Gasquet, *Les 500 affiches de mai 68*, Paris: Balland, 1978, pp. 26, 161.

19   *L'Aurore*, 13 June 1968; *Combat*, 13 June 1968; *Le Figaro*, 13 June 1968; *Action*, 13 June 1968; no. 241: Des Comités d'Action, Mouvement de Soutien aux Luttes du Peuple and Mouvement du 22 Mars, 'Communiqué', 12 June 1968.

20   Gasquet, *500 affiches*, p. 164; Atelier Populaire, *Mai 68*, London: Dobson, 1969, no. 59; Jean-Pierre Simon, ed, *La révolution par elle-même*, Paris: Albin Michel, 1969, p. 144: Coordination des Comités d'Action de la Région Parisienne, Mouvement de Soutien aux Luttes du Peuple, SNESUP and Mouvement des 22 Mars, 'Non à la discrimination', 11 June 1968.

21   *Le Monde*, 30 June - 1 July 1968; Bibliothèque Nationale, *Les tracts de mai 1968*, microfilm, Leiden, 1988, no. 2380: 'Le comité d'occupation de la Cité universitaire', n.d. [June 1968]; Jean-Jacques Lebel, conversation with author, London, 17 March 2000.

22   Hervé Hamon and Patrick Rotman, *Génération*, vol. 2, Paris: Seuil, 1988, pp. 141-142.

23   MRAP Archives, 'Expulsions 1968', letter from Georges Séguy to Daniel Mayer, n.d. [June 1968]; CFDT 7 H 43, letter from Daniel Mayer to Raymond Marcellin, 14 June 1968.

24   *Le Figaro*, 21 June 1968, 17 July 1968 and 14 October 1968; *Lutte Ouvrière*, 3 July 1968, 9 October 1968 and 16 October 1968.

25   Commission Internationale de Juristes, 'Expulsions d'étrangers', *Migrations*, no. 13 (Autumn 1969); Charles Rousseau, 'Chronique des faits internationaux', *Revue de droit international public*, vol. 73, no. 1 (January-March 1969), pp.

181-183.

26   *Lavoro*, October 1968 and December 1968; Serge Bonnet, 'Political alignment and religious attitudes within the Italian immigration to the metallurgical districts of Lorraine', *Journal of Social History*, vol. 2, no. 2 (Winter 1968), pp. 123-155. As late as 2002, 27 per cent of voters in Audun-le-Tiche voted Communist or Trotskyist: Didier Francfort, 'From the other side of the mirror: the French-German border in landscape and memory', in Henrice Altink and Sharif Gemie, eds, *At The Border*, Cardiff: University of Wales Press, 2008, p. 91.

27   Bibliothèque Nationale, *Tracts de mai*, no. 9428: Le Syndicat des Métaux CGT d'Usinor – Longwy, 'Avec la CGT pour le respect et l'élargissement des libertés syndicales et démocratiques'.

28   *Lavoro*, October 1968 and December 1968; *Droit et Liberté*, November 1968 and December 1968; Bibliothèque Nationale, *Tracts de mai*, no. 9450, Cartel de défense et d'extension des libertés syndicales et démocratiques, 'Appel à la population', 30 November 1968; European Court, 'Judgement of the Court of 28 October 1975: Roland Rutili vs Ministre de l'intérieur', http://eurlex. europa.eu/smartapi/cgi/sga_doc?smartapi!celexplus!prod!CELEXnumdoc&lg =en&numdoc=61975J0036.

29   UNEF-SNESUP, *Ils accusent*, pp. 204-205; *Rouge*, 26 November 1968; *Droit et Liberté*, December 1968; CAC 19910194, article 13, liasse 4, letter from P.Wacquet to R.Marcellin, 24 October 1968.

30   *Le Figaro*, 21 June 1968; *Le Monde*, 22 June 1968; *Le Nouvel Observateur*, 12 June 1968 and 26 June 1968; Yves Aupetitallot, *Groupe de recherche d'art visuel*, Grenoble: Centre National d'Art Contemporain, 1998, pp. 240, 254, 257; *Guardian*, 25 March 2011; *Le Monde*, 26 June 1968; *Le Monde*, 19 June 1968; *Action*, 27 June 1968.

31   *Le Monde*, 19 June 1968; *Combat*, 28 June 1968; *Pour la Liberté*, March-April 1969; UNEF/SNESUP, *Ils accusent*, pp. 196-197; Bibliothèque Nationale, *Tracts de mai*, no. 4675: Comité Pour la Liberté et Contre la Répression, 'Les étrangers en France', n.d. [c. March 1969]; Stephen Castles and Godula Kosack, *Immigrant Workers and Class Structure in Western Europe*, Oxford: Oxford University Press, 1985, p. 174.

32   *Le Monde*, 12 September 1968 and 3 March 1970; Michel Levine, *Affaires non classées*, Paris: Fayard, 1973, pp. 225-262; Jan Willem Stutje, *Ernest Mandel*, London: Verso, 2009, p. 185.

33   Letters in CAC 19910194, article 13, liasse 4.

34   Bibliothèque de Documentation International Contemporaine, Nanterre (BDIC), F DELTA RES 688/36, Colette Kay to Daniel Guérin, 19 September 1968, Guérin to Goutier, 24 September 1968, Kay to Guérin, 6 November and 10 December 1968 and 10 December 1969.

35   Ascherson, interview; CAC 19890519, article 10, liasse 3, item in folder 'Agitateurs étrangers mai-juin 1968'.

36   *La Tribune du Travailleur Algérien*, December 1968.

37   Bibliothèque Nationale, *Tracts de mai*, no. 8660, Rhône-Poulenc, Comité central de grève, 'Nous, travailleurs de Rhône-Poulenc Vitry', 28 May 1968;

Archives Départementales du Val-de-Marne, Créteil, 1 J 1192, Groupe "Lutte de Classe" Rhône-Poulenc, 'Des comités de lutte au pouvoir: mai-juin 1968 à Rhône-Poulenc/Vitry' [1968]; CFDT 7 H 44, *Syndicalisme*, 6 July 1968; Corinne Hubert, *1968 un printemps val-de-marnais pas comme les autres*, Créteil: Conseil Général du Val-de-Marne, 1998, pp. 73-74.

38   Jean-Paul Salles, *La Ligue communiste révolutionnaire (1968-1981)*, Rennes: Presses Universitaires de Rennes, 2005, pp. 164-166. Cf the analysis of the French May by the British Trotskyists Tony Cliff and Ian Birchall, *France: the struggle goes on*, London: Socialist Review, 1968, which mentioned immigrant workers only in terms of their isolation being a 'factor militating against involvement'.

39   Michèle Manceaux, *Les maos en France*, Paris: Gallimard, 1972, p. 200; Stephen Castles, 'Thirty Years of Research on Migration and Multicultural Societies', in *Ethnicity and Globalization: from migrant worker to transnational citizen*, London: Sage, 2000, p. 1.

40   Manceaux, *Les maos*, p. 136.

41   Robert Linhart, *L'Etabli*, Paris: Minuit, 1978, translated as *The Assembly Line*, London: Calder, 1981, pp. 19-64.

42   Linhart, *The Assembly Line*, p. 66.

43   Linhart, *The Assembly Line*, pp. 68-96.

44   Linhart, *The Assembly Line*, pp. 88-120.

45   Pierre Vermeren, *Histoire du Maroc depuis l'indépendance*, Paris: La Découverte, 2006, p. 49; Alain Geismar et al, *Vers la guerre civile*, Paris: Premières, 1969.

46   Gilbert Mury, *On leur fera la peau*, Paris: Cerf, 1973, pp. 79-85; Manceaux, *Les maos en France*, 204; Hamon and Rotman, *Génération*, vol. 2, pp. 99-101.

47   *Rouge*, 8 May 1969; *La Cause du Peuple*, 17 May 1969; Yvan Gastaut, *L'immigration et l'opinion en France sous la Ve République*, Paris: Seuil, 2000, p. 157; BDIC F DELTA RES 612/12, 'Texte de "Vive le communisme" – Mai 68 émergence des luttes / mai 1969 trahison révisionniste impréparation – erreurs / Vive le 1er mai 70'.

48   Ronald Fraser, *1968: a student generation in revolt*, London: Chatto & Windus, 1988, pp. 34, 85; Elisabeth Salvaresi, *Mai en héritage*, Paris: Syros, 1988, pp. 69-75; Hervé Hamon and Patrick Rotman, *Génération*, vol. 1, Paris: Seuil, 1987, p. 119; *La Cause du Peuple*, 23 May 1968 and 29 May 1968.

49   A. Belden Fields, *Trotskyism and Maoism*, New York: Praeger, 1988, pp. 100-101; Christophe Bourseiller, *Les maoïstes*, Paris: Plon, 1996, pp. 130-132; police report in CAC 19820599, article 76, 'Vive la révolution: groupement politique', 8 May 1971.

50   Roland Castro, *1989*, Paris: Bernard Barrault, 1984, unpaginated, under '1970'.

51   Castro, *1989*, under '1970'; Jean-Paul Sartre, *Critique de la raison dialectique*, vol 1, Paris: Gallimard, 1960, translated as *Critique of Dialectical Reason*, vol 1, London: Verso, 2004; *Vive la Révolution*, 15 November 1969; *Tout!*, 16 November 1970, Bourseiller, *Maoïstes*, p. 181.

52   Antoine Spire, *Profession permanent*, Paris: Seuil, 1980, pp. 163-210.

53   André Gorz and Philippe Gavi, 'La bataille d'Ivry', *Les Temps Modernes*, no. 284 (March 1970), pp. 1393-1416.

54 Gorz and Gavi, 'Bataille d'Ivry', p. 1398.
55 Gastaut, *L'immigration et l'opinion*, pp. 52-63; extract from *Les dossiers de l'écran*, TV broadcast, 14 January 1970, in the documentary *La saga des immigrés* (2007), dir. Edoaurd Mills-Affif and Anne Riegel; Maurice Clavel, *Combat de franc-tireur pour une libération*, Paris: Jean-Jacques Pauvert, 1968; *Le Paria*, supplement to December 1969 issue; Jean-Paul Sartre, 'Justice et Etat', in *Situations X*, Paris: Gallimard, 1976, pp. 69-71; Hamon and Rotman, *Génération*, vol. 2, pp. 125-126; Gorz and Gavi, 'Bataille d'Ivry', pp 1407-1411; Monique Bel, *Maurice Clavel*, Paris: Bayard, 1992, pp. 247-248; Henri Leclerc, *Un combat pour la justice*, Paris: La Découverte, 1994, pp. 66-71.
56 Maurice Rajsfus, *Mai 68*, Paris, 1998, p. 57; Gastaut, *L'immigration et l'opinion*, p. 160.
57 Gorz and Gavi, 'Bataille d'Ivry', p. 1398; *Rouge*, 22 September 1969; A. Belden Fields, 'French Maoism', in Sohnya Sayres et al, eds, *The 60s Without Apology*, Minneapolis: University of Minnesota Press, 1984.
58 *Rouge*, 27 November 1971.
59 *Le Monde*, 1-2 March 1970, 4 March 1970 and 5 March 1970; *L'Humanité*, 3 March 1970 and 4 March 1970; *Le Figaro*, 4 March 1970; *Le Nouvel Observateur*, 9 March 1970; Jean-François Lyotard, 'Nanterre, içi, maintenant', *Les Temps Modernes*, no. 285 (April 1970), pp. 1650-1665; Pierre Vidal-Naquet, 'Où en est le mouvement de mai?', *Raison Présente*, no. 17 (January-March 1971), p. 30.
60 *Tout!*, 25 April 1970 and 5 June 1970; BDIC F DELTA RES 813/12 ('Dossier France. Mouvement étudiant. Nanterre 1969-1970'), Anon, 'La crèche continue!', n.d. and Anon, 'Les crèches sauvages vers la révolution!', n.d. [before 14 February 1970].
61 *Tout!*, 5 June 1970.
62 John Gretton, *Students and Workers*, London: Macdonald, 1968, p. 119; Alain Delale and Gilles Ragache, *La France de 68*, Paris: Seuil, 1978, p. 172; Christian Bachmann and Nicole Le Guennec, *Violences urbaines*, Paris: Albin Michel, 1995, p. 235; BDIC F DELTA RES 612/16, *Information-Action du 5ème*, 16 November 1969; exhibition on the history of Vincennes at Université de Paris 8, June 2010.
63 BDIC F DELTA RES 813/12, *Base Ouvrière/Obrera*, 17 April 1970.
64 BDIC F DELTA RES 813/12, *Base Ouvrière/Obrera*, 17 April 1970.
65 Cf Eddy Cherki et al, 'Urban Protest in Western Europe', in Colin Crouch and Alessandro Pizzorno, eds, *The Resurgence of Class Conflict in Western Europe Since 1968*, vol. 2, London: Macmillan, 1978, pp. 247-275; John Ardagh, *France in the New Century*, London: Viking, 1999, pp. 212-213.
66 *Rouge*, 19 January 1970.
67 Ducrocq, *La CGT à Nanterre*, pp. 112-131; *Le Courrier Républicain de Seine et Seine-et-Oise (édition des Hauts-de-Seine)*, 22 May 1968, 5 June 1968 and 12 June 1968; *L'Eveil*, 24 May 1968 and 31 May 1968; reminiscences by participants at *Le mai des ouvriers de Nanterre*, public meeting, Agora Nanterre, 20 May 2008.
68 *Le Figaro*, 5 March 1970; *Le Monde*, 8-9 March 1970.

69   Roger Bourderon and Pierre de Perretti, eds, *Histoire de Saint-Denis*, Toulouse: Privat, 1988, p. 289; Gilbert Wasserman, *Nanterre: une histoire*, Paris: Temps Actuels, 1982, p. 163; CAC 19870056, article 7, Service d'Assistance Technique, 'Liste des points d'hébergement abritant des travailleurs migrants contactés par des responsables de mouvements extrémistes de gauche depuis 1967', 15 July 1970.

70   *Le Monde*, 1-2 March 1970; *Le Figaro*, 2 March 1970; BDIC F DELTA RES 813/12, Anon, 'Ricoeur tel qu'il est!', 27 February [1970].

71   Lyotard, 'Nanterre', p. 1658.

72   *Le Figaro*, 27 February 1970.

73   *Le Figaro*, 6 March 1970.

74   BDIC F DELTA RES 612/16, Les Etudiants Révolutionnaires de Nanterre, 'Les étudiants de Nanterre aux côtés du peuple dans la lutte pour la liberté!', n.d. [March 1970], F DELTA RES 813/13, Les Conseils de Gestion de la Faculté de Nanterre, 'Informations sur le restaurant universitaire de Nanterre', 2 November 1970 and F DELTA RES 612/16, *Nanterre Aujourd'hui*, supplement to *Tout!*, n.d. [1970].

75   BDIC F DELTA RES 813/9, Anon, 'Non l'esclavage n'est pas aboli à Nanterre!', n.d. [1969], F DELTA RES 813/10, Comité de Base Nanterre Lettres, 'Ultimatum', n.d. [c. 1969] and F DELTA RES 813/13, Anon, 'Après Darche le négrier, c'est Viallard le flic qui opprime les travailleurs', n.d. [c. 1970] and Centre Régional des Oeuvres Universitaires et Scolaires Paris, 'Décision', n.d. [June 1970].

76   *Le Monde*, 24-25 May 1970; *Tout!*, 16 November 1970; BDIC F DELTA RES 612/16, *Information action du 5e*, 24 May 1970.

77   *La Cause du Peuple*, 28 September 1970.

78   BDIC F DELTA RES 612/12, Anon, 'Projet de bilan du week-end sauvage', 1971.

79   BDIC F DELTA RES 612/12, Anon, 'Racisme et anti-racisme', 1971.

80   Daniel Gordon, 'Reaching out to immigrants in May '68: specific or universal appeals?', in Julian Jackson et al, eds, *May '68*, Basingstoke: Palgrave Macmillan, 2011.

81   Vive la Révolution, supplement no. 6: 'Changer la vie! Briser tous les obstacles!', n.d. [1970].

82   *Tout!*, 16 November 1970.

83   BDIC F DELTA RES 612/12, VLR, 'A propos du texte des camarades du "mai"', n.d.

84   Claire Brière-Blanchet, *Voyage au bout de la révolution*, Paris: Fayard, 2009, pp. 209-211.

85   Julian Bourg, *From Revolution to Ethics*, Montreal: McGill-Queen's University Press, 2007, p. 185.

86   Anne Couteau and Paul Oriol, interview with author, Paris, 2 January 2006.

87   Driss El Yazami, 'France's ethnic minority press' in Alec Hargreaves and Mark McKinney, eds, *Post-Colonial Cultures in France*, London: Routledge, 1997, p. 120.

88   *Résistance Populaire: bulletin du comité de soutien aux luttes de libération*

nationale des peuples arabes, 15 May 1968; *El Moudjahid*, 18 May 1968.

89   Gastaut, *L'immigration et l'opinion*, pp. 282-283.

90   Johanna Siméant, *La cause des sans-papiers*, Paris: Presses de Sciences Po, 1998, pp. 78, 85; Saïd Bouziri, interview with author, Paris, 6 November 2004; Abdellali Hajjat, 'Des Comités Palestine au Mouvement des Travailleurs Arabes', in Ahmed Boubeker and Abdellali Hajjat, eds, *Histoire politique des immigrations (post)coloniales*, Paris: Amsterdam, 2008, pp. 146-149.

91   BDIC Mfc 214/6, Fonds Saïd Bouziri, 'Declaration de Hamza Bouziri', n.d. [1971].

92   Mury, *On leur fera la peau*, pp. 85-88.

93   Mury, *On leur fera la peau*, p. 89-93; *Combat*, 23 June 1970 and 15-16 August 1970.

94   Mury, *On leur fera la peau*, p. 46; *Le Monde*, 4 June 1971; Raymond Casas, *Mémoires à nos petits-enfants*, vol. 2, Blois: Raymond Casas, 1998, p. 249.

95   Mury, *On leur fera la peau*, p. 70; *Le Monde*, 6-7 June 1971.

96   BDIC O PIECE 380 RES: 'Le Comité Maurice Audin et Verité Liberté présentent *Octobre à Paris*', [1962]; excerpt played in *Secret History: Drowning By Bullets*, first broadcast Channel 4, 13 July 1992.

97   Interview with Benny Lévy, *L'Evènement*, 6-12 May 1999. See also Yaïr Auron, *Les juifs d'extrême gauche en mai 68*, Paris: Albin Michel, 1998.

98   Rajsfus, *Mai 68*, pp. 60, 62, 183-187.

99   CEDETIM, *Les immigrés*, Paris, 1975, pp. 262-265; Agence Im'média, *Sans-papiers: chronique d'un mouvement*, Paris: Reflex, 1997, p. 9; Marie-Christine Volovitch-Tavares, 'Portugais de France, un siècle de présence', in Laurent Gervereau, et al, eds, *Toute la France*, Paris: Somogny, 1998, p. 148; Mogniss Abdallah, *J'y suis, j'y reste!*, Paris: Reflex, 2000, pp. 20-21; *Rouge*, 25 September and 30 October 1971.

100   Alfred Kastler, describing police intervention on 10 May 1968: Philippe Labro, *Ce n'est qu'un début*, Paris: Premières, 1968, p. 85.

101   Gastaut, *L'immigration et l'opinion*, p. 161; Claude Mauriac, *Et comme l'espérance est violente*, Paris: Grasset, 1976, pp. 282-283.

102   See Daniel Gordon, 'Daniel Guérin et le mouvement des travailleurs immigrés en France après 68', in David Berry, ed, *Daniel Guérin, Dissidences*, vol 2, Paris: L'Harmattan, 2007, pp. 197-216; English version at http://www-staff.lboro. ac.uk/eudgb/DG_conference_speakers.htm.

103   Paige Arthur, 'The persistence of colonialism: Sartre, the Left, and identity in postcolonial France, 1970-1974', in Jonathan Judaken, ed, *Race After Sartre*, Albany: State University of New York Press, 2008, p. 82.

104   It is to be hoped that this section, and the chapters that follow, answer the point made by Maud Bracke, 'May 1968 and Algerian immigrants in France: trajectories of mobilization and encounter', in Gurminder Bhambra and Ipek Demir, eds, *1968 In Retrospect*, Basingstoke: Palgrave Macmillan, 2009, p. 117, that earlier work on immigrants and 1968, including some of my own, 'continues to be limited by its focus on non-immigrant, white activists and their attitudes with regard to immigrants'. Arguably, this was in part a consequence of their chronological focus on the period before an autonomous

immigrant worker movement really got under way from 1971.

105 Alec Hargreaves, *Immigration and identity in Beur fiction*, Oxford: Berg, 1997, p. 86.

106 Mohammed Kenzi, *La menthe sauvage*, Lutry: Jean-Marie Bouchain, 1984, pp. 57-87; Nacer Kettane, *Le sourire de Brahim*, Paris: Denoël, 1985, pp. 53-55, 64-67, 74-77; Kassa Houari, *Confessions d'un immigré*, Paris: Lieu Commun, 1988, pp. 168-211; Brahim Benaïcha, *Vivre au paradis*, Paris: Desclée de Brouwer, 1992, pp. 225-251; Mogniss Abdallah, 'Autoportraits: Moha "l'antitransit" et Djamel d'Argenteuil', in Abdallah, ed, *Jeunes immigrés hors les murs*, special issue of *Questions Clefs*, no. 2 (March 1982), pp. 28-34; Ackaouy, *Nom de papier*, pp. 146-152; François Lefort, *Du bidonville à l'expulsion*, Paris: CIEMM, 1980, pp. 85-87; Tahar Ben Jelloun, *French Hospitality*, New York: Columbia University Press, 1999, pp. 92-94; Phillippe Bernard, *La crème des Beurs*, Paris: Seuil, 2004, pp. 297-313; Bruce Chatwin, 'The very sad story of Salah Bougrine' [1974], in *What Am I Doing Here*, London: Picador, 1990, p. 256. Both Lefort and Antoine Spire, to whom Roumi's story was told before being written down by Ackaouy, had worked with young people in the shanty towns of Nanterre for many years, while Abdallah is a journalist and political activist from Nanterre.

107 Hence the title of Hamon and Rotman, *Génération*.

108 Siméant, *La cause des sans-papiers*, p. 79.

109 Kenzi, *La menthe sauvage*, p. 59.

110 Kenzi, *La menthe sauvage*, pp. 59-60.

111 Richard Vinen, *France 1934-1970*, Basingstoke: Macmillan, 1996, back cover.

112 Ben Jelloun, *French Hospitality*, p. 92.

113 Ben Jelloun, *French Hospitality*, p. 92.

114 Benaïcha, *Vivre au paradis*, pp. 247-250, 232-234.

115 Benaïcha, *Vivre au paradis*, p. 226.

116 Benaïcha, *Vivre au paradis*, p. 227.

117 Abdallah, 'Autoportraits', p. 30.

118 Benaïcha, *Vivre au paradis*, p. 229; Lefort, *Du bidonville à l'expulsion*, p. 86.

119 See the novel by the Nanterre academic Robert Merle, *Derrière la vitre*, Paris: Gallimard, 1970, pp. 208-209.

120 Ackaouy, *Nom de papier*, p. 148.

121 Monique Hervo, diary entry, 16 March 1968, cited in Vincent Lemire, 'Nanterre, les bidonvilles et les étudiants' in Philippe Artières and Michelle Zancarini-Fournel, eds, *68: une histoire collective [1962-1981]*, Paris: La Découverte, 2008, p.141.

122 Lefort, *Du bidonville à l'expulsion*, p. 87.

123 Benaïcha, *Vivre au paradis*, p. 237.

124 Bernard, *Crème des Beurs*, p. 307.

125 'Réviso' (short for 'révisioniste') was a term of abuse by Maoists for orthodox pro-Moscow Communists

126 Houari, *Confessions d'un immigré*, p. 171. See also Kenzi, *La menthe sauvage*, p. 73

127 Ackaouy, *Nom de papier*, pp. 147-148.

128 Ackaouy, *Nom de papier,* pp. 147-148.
129 Kettane, *Le sourire de Brahim,* pp. 54-55.
130 Kenzi, *La menthe sauvage,* pp. 83-84.
131 Chatwin, 'Salah Bougrine', p. 256.
132 Houari, *Confessions d'un immigré,* pp. 170-188.
133 Houari, *Confessions d'un immigré,* p. 173, 183-185.
134 Houari, *Confessions d'un immigré,* pp. 198-208.
135 Steve Wright, *Storming Heaven,* London: Pluto, 2002, p. 121.

Chapter 4

1 Comité de Solidarité avec les Travailleurs Immigrés, *Vie et luttes des travailleurs immigrés,* Marseilles: Comité de Solidarité avec les Travailleurs Immigrés, 1973, p. 29.
2 This term was coined by the sociologist Pierre Bourdieu to refer to the domination exercised by those with more intellectual resources at their disposal.
3 Michèle Manceaux, *Les maos en France,* Paris: Gallimard, 1972, 178; Bibliothèque de Documentation International Contemporaine, Nanterre (BDIC), Fonds Saïd Bouziri, Mfc 214/6, 'Declaration de Hamza Bouziri', [1971]; Saïd Bouziri, interview with author, Paris, 6 November 2004.
4 And prior to that, a prominent place in the history of the French labour movement, for it was on the platform of Barbès metro station in 1941 that the famous Colonel Fabien, after whom the Communist Party's headquarters is named, had launched resistance to the German occupation by shooting a German officer as he boarded a train.
5 *L'Express,* 5-12 December 1971; *Le Monde,* 6 April 1972; Fausto Giudice, *Arabicides,* Paris: La Découverte, 1992, p. 60.
6 *Sans Frontière,* 30 September 1980.
7 MTA members cited in *Rouge,* 29 September 1973.
8 Saïd Bouziri, interview with author, Paris, 6 November 2004.
9 Rabah Aissaoui, *Immigration and National Identity,* London: Tauris, 2009, pp. 156-160.
10 Bouziri, interview; Johanna Siméant, *La cause des sans-papiers,* Paris: Presses de Sciences Po, 1998, pp. 78-79.
11 *Le Nouvel Observateur,* 15-21 November 1971; *Le Monde,* 17 November 1971; *Rouge,* 20 November 1971.
12 *Le Nouvel Observateur,* 15-21 November 1971 and 22-28 November 1971; *Rouge,* 20 November 1971; *Fedaï,* 25 November 1971; Claude Mauriac, *Et comme l'espérance est violente,* Paris: Grasset, 1976, pp. 291-292, 304; *Le Monde,* 23 June 1977; Didier Eribon, *Michel Foucault,* Paris: Flammarion, 1989, translated as *Michel Foucault,* Cambridge, MA: Harvard University Press, 1991, pp. 239-240; Giudice, *Arabicides,* p. 58; Yvan Gastaut, *L'immigration et l'opinion en France sous la Ve République,* Paris: Seuil, 2000, pp. 155-156; Bouziri, interview.
13 This is no longer exclusively the case today, but even now most middle-class

residents work outside the area. Maurice Goldring, *La Goutte d'Or, quartier de France*, Paris: Autrement, 2006, pp. 7-26.

14   Giudice, *Arabicides*, pp. 62-63; David Macey, *The Lives of Michel Foucault*, London: Hutchinson, 1993, pp. 293-294; Michelle Zancarini-Fournel, 'La question immigrée après 68', *Plein Droit*, no. 53-54 (March 2002). On the Jaubert affair, see Chapter 3.

15   Mauriac, *L'espérance est violente*, p. 281.

16   Mauriac, *L'espérance est violente*, p. 283.

17   Mauriac, *L'espérance est violente*, p. 288.

18   Mauriac, *L'espérance est violente*, pp. 289, 293, 301; Eribon, *Foucault*, p. 240; Macey, *Foucault*, p. 309.

19   *L'Express*, 5-12 December 1971; *Le Monde*, 6 April 1972; Mauriac, *L'espérance est violente*, pp. 290, 296, 326-329, 340-341; Claude Mauriac, *Une certaine rage*, Paris: Laffont, 1977; Eribon, *Foucault*, p. 240; Giudice, *Arabicides*, pp. 68-80; Gastaut, *L'immigration et l'opinion*, p. 156; Bouziri, interview.

20   See below for the 1972 murder; Eribon, *Foucault*, pp. 240, 260-261 for 1973 and 1984 references.

21   Fazia Ben Ali quoted in Catherine von Bülow, *La Goutte-d'Or ou le Mal des racines*, Paris: Stock, 1979, pp. 244-245.

22   Mauriac, *L'espérance est violente*, p. 293.

23   Von Bülow, *Goutte d'Or*, pp. 247, 243.

24   Cathie Lloyd, *Discourses of Anti-Racism in France*, Aldershot: Ashgate, 1998, pp. 202-203.

25   *Al Kadihoun*, February-March 1973.

26   Ralph Grillo, *Ideologies and Institutions in Urban France*, Cambridge: Cambridge University Press, 1985, p. 276.

27   Abdellali Hajjat, 'Alliances inattendues à la Goutte d'Or', in Philippe Artières and Michelle Zancarini-Fournel, eds, *68: une histoire collective [1962-1981]*, Paris: La Découverte, 2008, p. 524.

28   Bouziri, interview.

29   *La Tribune Socialiste*, 4 May 1972; CEDETIM, *Les immigrés*, Paris: Stock, 1975, pp. 265-269; Agence Im'média, *Sans-papiers: chronique d'un mouvement*, Paris: Reflex, 1997, p. 9; Siméant, *Cause des sans-papiers*, pp. 459-460; Mogniss Abdallah, *J'y suis, j'y reste!*, Paris: Reflex, 2000, pp. 21-22. The Lille hunger strike by a group of students also concerned the deportation of a political activist, as did that in Marseilles by members of the Secours Rouge. Michelle Zancarini-Fournel, 'La construction d'une "problème national": l'immigration', in Artières and Zancarini-Fournel, *68*, p. 666, refers to a hunger strike in April 1971 by 200 Senegalese students, but about repression in Senegal rather than their status in France.

30   Maurice Rajsfus, *Mai 68*, Paris: Cherche Midi, 1998; Daniel Gordon, ' "Il est recommandé aux étrangers de ne pas participer": les étrangers expulsés en mai-juin 1968', *Migrations Société*, no. 88 (May-August 2003), pp. 45-65.

31   Bouziri, interview; BDIC F DELTA 721/96/5, P.Denais to D.Guérin, 9 November 1972; BDIC F DELTA 721/96/5, tract by Comité de Défense de la Vie et des Droits des Travailleurs Immigrés, 27 November 1972; *Le Monde*, 16

and 21 November 1972; CEDETIM, *Les immigrés*, p. 270; Mauriac, *L'espérance est violente*, p. 391; Im'média, *Sans-papiers*, p. 10.

32　*La Tribune Socialiste*, 4 May 1972; Olivier Brillaut, 'L'expulsion des étrangers en France', doctoral thesis, University of Nice, 1982, p. 11.

33　Bouziri, interview; *Le Monde*, 16 November 1972.

34　Bouziri, interview; Abdellali Hajjat, 'Le MTA et la "grève générale" contre le racisme de 1973', *Plein Droit*, no. 67 (December 2005), pp. 36-40; Rabah Aissaoui, 'Political mobilisations of North African migrants in 1970s France: the case of the Movement des Travailleurs Arabes (MTA)', *Journal of Muslim Minority Affairs*, vol. 26, no. 2 (August 2006), p. 173; Abdellali Hajjat, 'Des Comités Palestine au Mouvement des travailleurs arabes (1970-1976)', in Ahmed Boubeker and Abdellali Hajjat, eds, *Histoire politique des immigrations (post)coloniales*, Paris: Amsterdam, 2008, p. 152. By contrast, Rabah Aissaoui, 'Le Mouvement des travailleurs arabes: un bref profile', *Migrance*, no. 25 (3rd trimester 2005), p. 13, dates the foundation of the MTA to late 1972 or early 1973, while Gastaut, *L'immigration et l'opinion*, p. 155, suggests that the 7 November 1971 Djellali Ben Ali demonstration was called by the MTA. These discrepancies may be accounted for by the dominance of spontaneity over formal organisation in this period, and the fact that the core group of militants in the MTA had campaigned together prior to its formation, since the time of the Comités Palestine in 1970-1971.

35　*Le Monde*, 21 November 1972.

36　Manuel Castells, 'Immigrant workers and class structures in advanced capitalism: the Western European experience', in Ida Susser, ed, *The Castells Reader on Cities and Social Theory*, Oxford: Blackwell, 2002, p. 101.

37　*La Tribune Socialiste*, 25 April and 6 June 1973; *Al Assifa*, May-June 1973; Centre d'Information et de Documentation sur l'Immigration et le Maghreb, Marseilles (CIDIM), yellow folder 'Revues Journaux, Periodiques', Les Travailleurs Immigrés, 'Pourquoi nous revendiquons la carte de travail', n.d. [after 8 May 1973]; Sylvie Lienart, 'Les circulaires Marcellin-Fontanet et les luttes des travailleurs immigrés', Masters thesis, Université de Paris VIII, 1975, p. 74; Mark Miller, *Foreign Workers in Western Europe*, New York: Praeger, 1981, p. 101; Catherine Wihtol de Wenden, *Les immigrés et la politique*, Paris: Presses de Sciences Po, 1988, pp. 158, 165-166; Johanna Siméant, 'Immigration et action collective: l'exemple des mobilisations d'étrangers en situation irrégulière', *Sociétés Contemporaines*, no. 20 (1994), p. 50; Johanna Siméant, *La Cause des sans-papiers*, Paris: Presses de Sciences Po, 1998, p. 460; Abdallah, *J'y suis, j'y reste!*, pp. 32-38; Gastaut, *L'immigration et l'opinion*, pp. 172-173; Alexis Spire, *Etrangers à la carte*, Paris: Grasset, 2005, pp. 244-246; Aissaoui, 'Political mobilisations', p. 175; Bouziri, interview.

38　Comité de Solidarité avec les Travailleurs Immigrés, *Travailleurs immigrés*, p. 29.

39　Catherine Polac, 'Quand "les immigrés" prennent la parole', in Pascal Perrineau, ed, *L'engagement politique*, Paris: Presses de Sciences Po, 1994, pp. 381-382; Siméant, *Cause des sans-papiers*; Abdallah, *J'y suis, j'y reste!*, pp. 35-38; Xavier Crettiez and Isabelle Sommier eds, *La France Rebelle*, Paris:

Michalon, 2006, pp. 363-376.

40   Olivier Piot, *La révolution tunisienne*, Paris: Les Petits Matins, 2011, p. 44.

41   Castells, 'Immigrant workers', p. 102; CEDETIM, *Les immigrés*, p. 120; Wihtol
      de Wenden, *Immigrés et la politique*, p. 176.

42   Bouziri, interview; *Le Monde*, 16 November 1972; *Sans Frontière*, 27 December
      1980; Gilles Verbunt, *L'intégration par l'autonomie*, Paris: CIEMM, 1980, pp.
      577-585; Hervé Hamon and Patrick Rotman, *Génération*, vol. 2, Paris: Seuil,
      1988, pp. 301-304; Macey, *Foucault*, p. 308; Abdallah, *J'y suis, j'y reste!*, p.
      22; Gastaut, *L'immigration et l'opinion*, pp. 171-174; Denis Pelletier, *La crise
      catholique*, Paris: Payot, 2005, p. 251-253; Goldring, *Goutte d'Or*, p. 157.

43   Bouziri, interview; Anne Couteau and Paul Oriol, interview with author, Paris,
      2 January 2006; Guy Phillippon, interview with author, Paris, 5 January 2006;
      Comité de Solidarité avec les Travailleurs Immigrés, *Travailleurs immigrés*,
      pp. 14-15; CEDETIM, *Les immigrés*, p. 281; Lienart, 'Circulaires Marcellin-
      Fontanet', p. 70; Siméant, *Cause des sans-papiers*, p. 85; Abdallah, *J'y suis, j'y
      reste!*, p. 36.

44   Alana Lentin, *Racism and Anti-Racism in Europe*, London: Pluto, 2004, p. 237.

45   CERES faction of Parti Socialiste, quoted in CEDETIM, *Les immigrés*, p. 355.

46   Jaubert, *France des luttes*, p. 419.

47   Maria Trindade, *Immigrés portugais*, Lisbon: Instituto Superior de Ciências
      Sociais e Política Ultramarina, 1973, p. 139.

48   *Le Monde*, 5 September 1973; Centre des Archives Contemporaines,
      Fontainebleau (CAC) 19900353, article 19, liasse 2, 'Note concernant le pasteur
      Andrew Parker', 1973, 'Note concernant le pasteur Perregaux Berthier', 1973;
      CIDIM, 'Meeting contre l'expulsion de Abounaim Courbage', August [1973];
      Wihtol de Wenden, *Immigrés et la politique*, p. 166; Siméant, *Cause des sans-
      papiers*, p. 85; Rajsfus, *Mai 68*, pp. 191, 193, 196; Gastaut, *L'immigration et
      l'opinion*, p. 164; Aissaoui, *Immigration and National Identity*, p. 189.

49   BDIC F DELTA 721/96/6, tract, Travailleurs Français Immigrés 11ème –
      19ème, 'Pourquoi nous quittons le Comité de Vie et des Droits des Immigrés',
      enclosed in D.Guérin to 'Chers Amis', 8 June 1973.

50   Abdallah, *J'y suis, j'y reste!*, pp. 36-37; Castells, 'Immigrant workers', pp. 102-
      103; CEDETIM, *Les immigrés*, pp. 278-284, 328; Fouad Lamine and Bernard
      Navacelles, 'De l'isolement vers l'unité', *Politique aujourd'hui*, March-April
      1975, pp. 75-86; CFDT Archives Confédérales, Paris (CFDT), 8 H 1763, 'Appel
      du Comité de Vigilance Anti-Raciste', n.d. [c. May 1973].

51   Ed Naylor, 'The Politics of a Presence: Algerians in Marseille from independence
      to "immigration sauvage" (1962-1974)', PhD thesis, Queen Mary University
      of London, 2011, p. 236.

52   Philipe Raynaud, *L'extrême gauche plurielle*, Paris: Autrement, 2006, p. 98.

53   Bouziri, interview.

54   Giudice, *Arabicides*, p. 120.

55   Jacqueline Costa-Lascoux and Emile Temime, *Les hommes de Renault-
      Billancourt*, Paris: Autrement, 2004, pp. 117-118, 121-123; Emile Temime, 'Les
      conditions de vie hors travail', in Renaud Sainsaulieu and Ahsène Zehraoui,
      eds, *Ouvriers specialisés à Billancourt*, Paris: L'Harmattan, 1995, p. 361.

56   Grillo, *Ideologies and Institutions*, p. 224.

57   Bouziri, interview; *Le Nouvel Observateur*, 15-21 November 1971; *Fedaï*, 25 November 1971 and 1 January 1972; *L'Express*, 5-12 December 1971; *Le Monde*, 6 April 1972; Macey, *Foucault*, p. 306. Bouziri emphasised, on the other hand, that the aim was to change the shopkeepers' attitude, rather than drive them from the area.

58   *Le Monde*, 23 June 1977.

59   *Le Monde*, 19-20, 21, 22 and 25 December 1971; Nonna Mayer, 'De Passy à Barbès: deux visages du vote Le Pen à Paris', *Revue française de sciences politiques*, vol. 37, no. 6 (December 1987), pp. 891-906.

60   The route was chosen so as to pass the Rex cinema where Algerians had been killed on 17 October 1961: Jim House and Neil Macmaster, *Paris 1961*, Oxford: Oxford University Press, 2006, p. 284.

61   Bouziri, interview; BDIC Mfc 214/6, 'Appel de Fatna, soeur de Mohamed Diab assassiné au commissariat de Versailles par un policier'; similar wording in BDIC Mfc 214/4, posters denouncing the murders of Ladj Lounès and Arezki Rezki; *Le Monde*, 1 December 1972 and 23 June 1977; Eribon, *Foucault*, p. 242; Macey, *Foucault*, p. 312; Rabah Aissaoui, 'Immigration, ethnicity and national identity: Maghrebis' socio-political mobilisation and discourse in the inter-war period and during the 1970s in France', PhD thesis, University of Leeds, 2001, pp. 220-228.

62   *Al Assifa*, August-September 1972; Comité de Solidarité avec les Travailleurs Immigrés, *Travailleurs immigrés*, pp. 18-19.

63   *Rouge*, 27 November and 31 December 1971; Jean-Paul Salles, *La Ligue Communiste Révolutionnaire (1968-1981)*, Rennes: Presses Universitaires de Rennes, 2005, pp. 165-166; Gilles de Staal, *Mamadou m'a dit*, Paris: Syllepse, 2008.

64   Zakya Daoud, *De l'immigration à la citoyenneté*, Casablanca: Mémoire de la Méditerranée, 2003, p. 37.

65   Alain Jaubert, *Guide de la France des luttes*, Paris: Stock, 1974, pp. 419-420; 'Les organisations des travailleurs immigrés', *PSU Documentation*, no. 141 (October 1980), pp. 8-9; Miller, *Foreign Workers*, p. 55; Wihtol de Wenden, *Immigrés et la politique*, pp. 169-171; Michel Fiévet, *Le livre blanc des travailleurs immigrés des foyers*, Paris: L'Harmattan, 1999, p. 87; Gastaut, *L'immigration et l'opinion*, pp. 163-164; Marie-Christine Volovitch-Tavares, 'Les immigrés portugais et la guerre coloniale portugaise (1961-1974)', paper to *Emigration politique en France et en Argentine* conference, Université de Paris 7, 24-25 March 2000, http://membres.lycos.fr/epoca/exil.html, p. 4; Pascal Blanchard et al, *Le Paris Arabe*, Paris: La Découverte, 2003, p. 184; Salles, *Ligue Communiste Révolutionnaire*, pp. 165-166; de Staal, *Mamadou*.

66   CFDT 8 H 1763, Un Groupe d'Immigrés pour une Initiative Autonome, 'La lutte contre la circulaire Fontanet: l'organisation des immigrés sur leurs objectifs autonomes', January-February 1973'; 'Organisations des travailleurs immigrés', p. 9; Wihtol de Wenden, *Immigrés et la politique*, p. 171-172; Grillo, *Ideologies and Institutions*, p. 230.

67   Mariarosa Dalla Costa and Selma James, *The Power of Women and the*

Subversion of the Community, Bristol: Falling Wall, 1972; Claire Duchen, *Feminism in France*, London: Routledge & Kegan Paul, 1986, pp. 8, 35; Steve Wright, *Storming Heaven*, London: Pluto, 2002; Maud Bracke, 'Our first discovery was our housework: 1970s feminist debate on women's work between Italy and Britain', paper to *The Limits of Transnationalism* conference, Exeter University, 30 March 2011; Nicola Pizzolato, 'Transnational radicals: labour dissent and political activism in Detroit and Turin (1950-1970)', *International Review of Social History*, vol. 56, no. 1 (April 2011), pp. 1-30.

68   Bouziri, interview.
69   CEDETIM, 'L'autonomie des immigrés: necessité et difficultés', *Politique aujourd'hui*, March-April 1975, pp. 99-101.
70   Bouziri, interview.
71   CFDT 8 H 1763, 'Lutte contre la circulaire Fontanet'.
72   Christian Chevandier, *Les tourments d'une génération*, Montreuil: Au Lieux d'Etre, 2008, pp. 198-199.
73   CIDIM, *Akhbar El-Baraka*, 2 July 1975.
74   Hajjat, 'MTA'; Couteau and Oriol, interview; de Staal, *Mamadou*, pp. 77-86, 112-114.
75   CEDETIM, *Les immigrés*, p. 221; Lienart, 'Circulaires Marcellin-Fontanet', p. 74; Aissaoui, 'Mobilisation and discourse', pp. 262-263; Yvan Gastaut, 'Marseille, epicentre de la problématique du racisme en 1973', *Migrance*, no. 25 (3rd trimester 2005), pp. 32-33.
76   *Travailleurs Français Immigrés Même Combat!: journal de lutte du comité pour l'abrogation de la circulaire Fontanet-Villeurbane*, May 1973.
77   Comité de Solidarité avec les Travailleurs Immigrés, *Travailleurs immigrés*.
78   CEDETIM, *Les immigrés*, 293-294.
79   PSU Paris 20th arrondissement branch, archives held by Guy Phillippon: Groupe d'Action Immigrés, 'Reunions avec les différents comités du 20e pendant le mois de décembre 1973'; 'Fete populaire', March 1974; 'Meeting du 10 avril 1974, 154, rue Saint Maur'.
80   Miller, *Foreign Workers*, p. 93.
81   CEDETIM, *Les immigrés*, pp. 288-322; Wihtol de Wenden, *Immigrés et la politique*, pp. 154-166; Zancarini-Fournel, 'Question immigrée'; Xavier Vigna, *L'insubordination ouvrière dans les années 68*, Rennes: Presses Universitaires de Rennes, 2007, pp. 122-131.
82   Algerian metal worker, cited in Grillo, *Ideologies and Institutions*, p. 226.
83   Laure Pitti, ' "Travailleurs de France, voilà notre nom": les mobilisations des ouvriers étrangers dans les usines et les foyers durant les années 1970', *Migrance*, no. 25 (3rd trimester 2005), pp. 50-71.
84   Laure Pitti, 'Filmer pour mobiliser: l'exemple de Penarroya', *Migrance*, no. 32 (4th quarter 2008), pp. 42-51; Laure Pitti, 'Penarroya, 1971-1972: deux films, deux regards, une mobilisation' in Tangui Perron, *Histoire d'un film, mémoire d'une lutte. 2: Etrange étrangers*, Paris: Scope, 2009, pp. 152-173; Phillippe Artières, 'Amor le Marocain et la grève de Penarroya-Gerland, Lyon, 1972' in Artières and Zancarini-Fournel, *68*, pp. 494-496; *Penarroya St Denis (Nouvelle société no. 8)* (1971), produced by the Cahiers de Mai group,

and *Dossier Penarroya: les deux visages du trust* (1972), dir. Daniel Anselme and Dominique Dubosc, both included on 2009 DVD of *Etrange étrangers*; Burleigh Hendrickson is researching Penarroya for a thesis at Northeastern University.

85 Michèle Manceaux and Jacques Donzelot, *Cours camarade, le P.C.F. est derrière toi*, Paris: Gallimard, 1974, pp. 13-44.

86 *Le Monde*, 14 November 1972.

87 Aissaoui, *Immigration and National Identity*, pp. 195-196.

88 *Al Assifa*, May 1972.

89 Vigna, *Insubordination ouvrière*, pp. 125, 129-130; Miller, *Foreign Workers*, pp. 94-95.

90 CEDETIM, *Les immigrés*, p. 318.

91 Miller, *Foreign Workers*, p. 92; CEDETIM, *Les immigrés*, pp. 288-322.

92 Laure Pitti, 'Différenciations ethniques et luttes ouvrières à Renault-Billancourt', *Contretemps*, no. 16 (January 2006), p. 74; Laure Pitti, 'Grèves ouvrières versus luttes de l'immigration: une controverse entre historiens', *Ethnologie française*, vol. 31, no. 3 (July-September 2001), pp. 465-476. Nevertheless, in suggesting that seeing these as 'immigration struggles' constitutes a retrospective imposition by researchers, Pitti does not really acknowledge how far militants at the time assimilated them into immigration struggles, while at the same time being aware of the worker dimension.

93 Manceaux and Donzelot, *Cours camarade*, 61-62.

94 The same year, Fonda starred in Jean-Luc Godard's *Tout va bien*, in which a gang of white leftist militants incite a crowd of shoppers to loot the shelves of a hypermarket (shades of the Fauchon raid perhaps) – but it is black shoppers who are bashed hardest over the head once the CRS arrive.

95 On violence, it is worth noting that Foucault's famous debate with the Maoists about the nature of justice and the courts system had originally been sparked by the death sentence passed, though not carried out, by the GP in autumn 1971 on one of its only black cadres, Moussa Fofana, for supposedly being a police informer. Immigrants could be the supposed beneficiaries as well as targets of the GP's penchant for 'people's justice', though, as in the summer 1972 case of Yugoslav squatters attacked, and one raped, by members of the 'scab' Citroën trade union Confédération Française du Travail in Issy-les-Moulineux, who were beaten and forced to parade the streets with placards detailing their crimes. Macey, *Foucault*, pp. 298-300, 305.

96 Hamon and Rotman, *Génération*, vol. 2, pp. 383-421; Giudice, *Arabicides*, p. 56; Kristin Ross, *Fast Cars, Clean Bodies*, Cambridge, MA: MIT Press, 1996, pp. 16-19; for a demolition of heroic views of the far Left's role in the affair, see Morgan Sportès, *Ils ont tué Pierre Overney*, Paris: Grasset, 2008.

97 *Fedaï*, 25 October 1971; Hamon and Rotman, *Génération*, vol. 2, pp. 385, 388-392; Ronald Hayman, *Writing Against*, London: Weidenfeld & Nicolson, 1986, p. 415; Simone Signoret, *Nostalgia Isn't What It Used To Be*, London: Grafton, 1986, pp. 401-404; Abdallah, *J'y suis, j'y reste!*, pp. 23-25; Sportès, *Overney*, pp. 59, 119, 159-165, 195-198.

98 De Gaulle's envoy Jean Moulin played a key role in linking together interior

Resistance groups before his death after torture by the Gestapo in 1943, while on Manouchian, see Chapter Five.

99   Sportès, *Overney*, pp. 198, 236-237, 280.

100 At this time the LC had close links to Latin American guerrillas, and even a clandestine armed wing preparing for the worst should France itself go down the Latin American path of a right-wing coup d'état. Accounts of the events of 21 June and their consequences can be found in Hamon and Rotman, *Génération*, vol. 2, pp. 493-514; Christophe Nick, *Les trotskistes*, Paris: Fayard, 2002, pp. 106-132. The party subsequently re-emerged as the Ligue Communiste Révolutionnaire (LCR).

101 Guidice, *Arabicides*, p. 126; Gastaut, *L'immigration et l'opinion*, pp. 288-290; Nick, *Les trotskistes*, pp. 110, 122-123.

102 *Politis*, 10 March 2011.

103 Giudice, *Arabicides*, p. 126.

104 CIDIM, *Le Méridional: grand quotidien d'information raciste*, supplement to several leftist newspapers, including *Libération*, 7 September 1973; CIDIM, *La Voix des Travailleurs Arabes*, October 1973; Bruce Chatwin, 'The very sad story of Salah Bougrine' [1974], in Bruce Chatwin, *What Am I Doing Here*, London: Picador, 1990, pp. 241-262; Giudice, *Arabicides*, pp. 93-103; Cathie Lloyd, 'Racist violence and anti-racist reactions: a view of France', in Tore Björgo and Rob Witte, eds, *Racist Violence in Europe*, Basingstoke: Macmillan, 1993, pp. 212-213; '1970-1980 Dix ans de luttes immigrées: esquisse d'une chronologie', *Migrance*, no. 25 (3rd trimester 2005), p. 126; photographs in Yvan Gastaut, 'Marseille, epicentre de la problématique du racisme en 1973', *Migrance*, no. 25, p. 20-35; Driss El Yazami, radio interview with Emmanuel Laurentin, *La Fabrique de l'Histoire: Histoire des étrangers*, episode 1, France Culture, 7 January 2008; see Naylor, 'Politics of a Presence', Chapter 6 for a fuller account of the events.

105 CIDIM, cutting from unidentified newspaper, 3 September 1973; *L'Aurore*, 4 September 1973; *Le Provençal*, 4 September 1973; CEDETIM, *Les immigrés*, pp. 274-276.

106 *Le Monde*, 5 September 1973.

107 Hajjat, 'MTA'. A strike was also held in Toulouse on 14 April: *Libération*, 18 September 1973 and 19 September 1973.

108 CIDIM, MTA, 'Appel à la grève dans la région parisienne', 10 September 1973; *L'Aurore*, 15 September 1973; *L'Humanité*, 15 September 1973; *Rouge*, 20 September 1973; Blanchard, *Paris Arabe*, p. 185; Abdallah, *J'y suis, j'y reste!*, pp. 30-31; Hajjat, 'MTA'. *Le Figaro*, 15 September 1973 put the turnout at the Mosque at two thousand.

109 Abdellalli Hajjat, 'L'expérience politique du Mouvement des travailleurs arabes', *Contretemps*, no. 16 (January 2006), pp. 76-85; Hajjat, 'Des Comités Palestine au Mouvement des travailleurs arabes', p. 115.

110 *La Marseillaise*, 4 September 1973, cited in Abdallah, *J'y suis, j'y reste!*, p. 31; *L'Humanité*, 15 September 1973. This development was similar to the CGT's attitude during May '68: when faced with a movement outside its control, the reflex response was condemnation, but this moved to one of incorporation

when faced with the size of such a movement.

111 CIDIM, *La Voix Des Travailleurs Arabes*, October 1973.

112 *Le Monde*, 4 September 1973.

113 CIDIM, *En souvenir de la rencontre du 11 septembre 1993: extraits de la revue de presse à propos des événements de septembre 1973*, Agence-France Press report, 7 September 1973; BDIC F DELTA 721/96/5, handwritten draft of D.Guérin to G.Belorgey, 4 September [1973]; Gastaut, *L'immigration et l'opinion*, p. 293.

114 CIDIM, *Le Méridional*, 7 September 1973.

115 Gastaut, *L'immigration et l'opinion*, p. 294.

116 *Le Monde*, 18 December 1973, cited in Miller, *Foreign Workers*, p. 99; Gastaut, *L'immigration et l'opinion*, p. 295; *Al Assifa*, December 1973, giving the high figure of 20,000, while CEDETIM, *Les immigrés*, p. 277, put it at 13,000. The police, known for seriously underestimating demonstration turnouts, put the figure at only 2300: *Le Monde*, 19 December 1973.

117 *Al Assifa*, December 1973.

118 Gastaut, *L'immigration et l'opinion*, pp. 282-288.

119 Chatwin, 'Salah Bougrine', p. 244.

120 CIDIM, Comité de Solidarité avec les Travailleurs Immigrés, *Bulletin d'Information et de Liaison*, 10 November 1973.

Chapter 5

1   Centre d'Information et de Documentation sur l'Immigration et le Maghreb, Marseilles (CIDIM), MTA, 'Appel à la grève dans la région parisienne', 10 September 1973.

2   Jacques Simon et al, *L'immigration algérienne en France*, Paris: L'Harmattan, 2002, pp. 147-148; Pascal Blanchard et al, *Le Paris Arabe*, Paris: La Découverte, 2003, p. 184.

3   Nikki Keddie, *Roots of Revolution*, New Haven: Yale University Press, 1981, p. 222.

4   Keddie, *Roots of Revolution*; Asef Bayat, 'Islamism and empire: the incongruous nature of Islamist anti-imperialism', *Socialist Register*, 2008, p. 42.

5   Gerd-Rainer Horn, *The Spirit of '68*, Oxford: Oxford University Press, 2007. In the Spanish case, this was apparent as early as 1967-1968, which was described as 'the first European student movement to achieve an organised, solidarity alliance with the workers': Fred Halliday, 'Students of the world unite' in Alexander Cockburn and Robin Blackburn, eds, *Student Power*, London: Penguin, 1969, p. 310.

6   George Kassimeris, 'Junta by another name? The 1974 *metapolitefsi* and the Greek extra-parliamentary Left', *Journal of Contemporary History*, vol. 40, no. 4 (October 2005), pp. 745-762. *La lutte finale* ['The Final Struggle'] is a phrase from the original French version of the *Internationale*.

7   Tony Judt, *Postwar*, London: Heinemann, 2005, p. 760.

8   Hugo Gil Ferreira and Michael Marshall, *Portugal's Revolution*, Cambridge: Cambridge University Press, 1986, p. 27.

9   Albert Calvalho and A.Monteiro, 'Press Censorship in Spain and Portugal',

Index on Censorship, vol. 1, no. 2 (Spring 1972), pp. 56-63; David Gilmour, *The Transformation of Spain*, London: Quartet, 1985, pp. 63-65; Jason Garner, 'A dissident voice that was quieted by self-interest', *Times Higher Education Supplement*, 15 October 2004.

10   'Spain: Indice: 20 years of censorship', *Index on Censorship*, vol. 1, nos 3/4 (Autumn 1972), pp. 197-210.

11   Antoine Spire, *Profession permanent*, Paris: Seuil, 1980, p. 213.

12   Gerd-Rainer Horn, 'The language of symbols and the barriers of language: foreigners' perceptions of social revolution (Barcelona 1936-1937)', *History Workshop Journal*, no. 29 (Spring 1990), p. 42.

13   Loukas Axelos, 'Publishing activity and the movement of ideas in Greece', *Journal of the Hellenic Diaspora*, vol. 11, no. 2 (Summer 1984), pp. 5-46; Kassimeris, 'Junta By Another Name', p. 745, 747; Alain Krivine, *Ca te passera avec l'âge*, Paris: Flammarion, 2006, pp. 262-263.

14   *Guardian*, 20 June 2011.

15   Raymond Carr and Juan Pablo Fusi Aizpurua, *Spain*, London: Allen & Unwin, 1989, pp. 123, 126, 132, 147, 151, 156; Victor Pérez-Diaz, *The Return of Civil Society*, Cambridge, MA: Harvard University Press, 1993, pp. 1-20; *Independent*, 5 January 2008.

16   José Maravall, *Dictatorship and Political Dissent*, London: Tavistock, 1978, pp. 137-138.

17   Daniel Bensaïd, *Une lente impatience*, Paris: Stock, 2004, pp. 144-148, 215-217; Jan Willem Stutje, *Ernest Mandel*, London: Verso, 2009, p. 196, which notes that 'the French comrades were nurturing the new sections – politically, materially and technically'; Edouard de Blaye, *Franco and the Politics of Spain*, Harmondsworth: Penguin, 1976, first published Paris, 1974, pp. 331, 494; Gilmour, *Transformation of Spain*, pp. 84-102, 213-214; Genevieve Dreyfus-Armand, *L'exil des républicains espagnols en France*, Paris: Albin Michel, 1999; Jean-Claude Duhourcq and Antoine Madrigal, *Mouvement ibérique de liberation*, Toulouse: CRAS, 2007; *Salvador* (2006), dir. Manuel Huelga.

18   *Lobo* (2004), dir. Miguel Courtois; review in *Sight and Sound*, June 2006 for confirmation of authenticity of period details.

19   Gisèle Halimi, *Le procès de Burgos*, prefaced by Jean-Paul Sartre, Paris: Gallimard, 1971; Robert Clark, *The Basque Insurgents*, Madison: University of Wisconsin Press, 1984, pp. 215-218; James Jacob, *Hills of Conflict*, Reno: University of Nevada Press, 1994. The influence worked both ways, with ETA spawning imitation, though more amateurish and less widely supported, attacks by Iparretarrak ('Those of ETA of the North') among an ultra-radical minority of young militants in the French Basque country from 1973 onwards: Jacob, *Hills of Conflict*, pp. 227-284.

20   *Le Monde*, 12-13 and 16 November 1972; de Blaye, *Franco*, pp. 329-332; Jacob, *Hills of Conflict*, p. 169; Bensaïd, *Lente impatience*, p. 145.

21   Carr and Aizpura, *Spain*, pp. 67, 99; Robin Blackburn, 'The test in Portugal', *New Left Review*, nos 87-88 (September-December 1974), p. 11; Tariq Ali, *1968 and After*, Colchester: Blond & Briggs, 1978, p. 91; Maravall, *Dictatorship*, p. 11; Horn, *Spirit of '68*; Pere Ysas, *Disidencia y subversión*, Barcelona:

Critica, 2004. Population figures from Carr and Aizpura, *Spain*, p. 58 and Marie-Christine Volovitch-Tavares, 'Les immigrés portugais en France et la "Révolution des oeillets" ', in M.H.Araujo Carreira, ed, *De la révolution des oeillets au 3è millenaire, Travaux et Documents*, no. 7 (2000), p. 49.

22   Ronald Fraser, 'Spain on the brink', *New Left Review*, no. 96 (March-April 1976), p. 19; Catherine Wihtol de Wenden, *Les immigrés et la politique*, Paris: Presses de Sciences Po, 1988, pp. 171-172; CEDETIM, *Les immigrés*, Paris: Stock, 1975, pp. 81-88.

23   Eusebio Mujal-León, *Communism and Political Change in Spain*, Bloomington: Indiana University Press, 1983, p. 126.

24   See Chapter Four.

25   R.W.Johnson, *The Long March of the French Left*, London: Macmillan, 1981, p. 247; Santiago Carillo, *Memorias*, Barcelona: Planeta, 1994, pp. 541-543; CEDETIM, *Les immigrés*, p. 87; Joe Foweraker, *Making Democracy in Spain*, Cambridge: Cambridge University Press, 1989, p. 55.

26   Though this policy, introduced in 1967 in contravention of previous bilateral agreements with France, was reversed in 1970, it still left most Portuguese living in France in a legally doubtful position: Volovitch-Tavares, 'Revolution des oeillets', p. 161.

27   Marie-Christine Volovitch-Tavares, 'Les immigrés portuguais et la guerre coloniale portuguaise (1961-1974)', paper to *Emigration politique en France et en Argentine* conference, Université de Paris 7, 24-25 March 2000, http://membres.lycos.fr/epoca/exil.html, p. 3; Volovitch-Tavares, 'Revolution des oeillets', pp. 152-153, 162.

28   Bill Lomax, 'Ideology and illusion in the Portuguese revolution: the role of the left', in Lawrence Graham and Douglas Wheeler, eds, *In Search of Modern Portugal*, Madison: Wisconsin University Press, 1983, pp. 109, 112-113; Martin Kayman, *Revolution and Counterrevolution in Portugal*, London: Merlin, 1987, pp. 56-58; D.L. Raby, *Fascism and Resistance in Portugal*, Manchester: Manchester University Press, 1988, pp. 223, 225, 240-244; Kenneth Maxwell, *The Making of Portuguese Democracy*, Cambridge: Cambridge University Press, 1995, pp. 73, 105. France was not the only arena for exile activity: Algeria and West Germany were also important.

29   Victor Perreira, 'Pélérinage au Portugal révolutionnaire: les intellectuels français et la révolution des oeillets', in Anne Dulphy and Yves Léonard, eds, *De la dictature à la démocratie*, Brussels: Peter Lang, 2003, p. 252; Maxwell, *Portuguese Democracy*, p. 181; Chris Harman, *The Fire Last Time*, London: Bookmarks, 1988, pp. 277-311. Twenty-five years later, I attended a seminar on the Portuguese Revolution at the Institute of Historical Research in London, at which a lively discussion took place as to whether the British Trotskyist organisation to which many present belonged had taken the 'right line' on Portugal, though participants were seemingly oblivious as to whether this would have been a matter of much concern for the people of Portugal.

30   Hans Janitschek, *Mario Soares*, London: Weidenfeld & Nicolson, 1985, pp. 42-43.

31   Caroline Brettell, 'Emigration and its implications for the revolution in

northern Portugal', in Lawrence Graham and Harry Makler, eds, *Contemporary Portugal*, Austin: University of Texas Press, 1979, pp. 281-298; Volovitch-Tavares, 'Revolution des oeillets', pp. 149-153.

32 Volovitch-Tavares, 'Revolution des oeillets', pp. 157-158; Maxwell, *Portuguese Democracy*, pp. 113-114, 132, 138, 141.

33 Antonio Cravo, *Les Portugais en France et leur mouvement associatif (1901-1986)*, Paris: L'Harmattan, 1995, pp. 104, 116-124; Volovitch-Tavares, 'Revolution des oeillets', p. 155-159.

34 Rabah Aissaoui, 'Immigration, ethnicity and national identity: Maghrebis' socio-political mobilisation and discourse in the inter-war period and during the 1970s in France', PhD thesis, University of Leeds, 2001, pp. 268-274.

35 Michèle Manceaux, *Les Maos en France*, Paris: Gallimard, 1972, p. 174.

36 Jacques Barou, *Travailleurs africains en France*, Grenoble: Presses Universitaires de Grenoble, 1978, p. 148; Salem Kacet, *Le droit à la France*, Paris: Belfond, 1991, pp. 36-43; Zakya Daoud, *De l'immigration à la citoyenneté*, Casablanca: Mémoire de la Méditerranée, 2003, pp. 38-40; John Berger and Jean Mohr, *A Seventh Man*, London: Verso, 2010, pp. 217-223; *Mémoires d'immigrés* (1997), dir. Yamina Benguigui, episode 1, *Les mères*.

37 Saïd Bouziri, interview with author, Paris, 6 November 2004.

38 Hervé Hamon and Patrick Rotman, *Génération*, vol. 2, Paris: Seuil, 1988, p. 32-33.

39 Bouziri, interview.

40 Aissaoui, 'Immigration, ethnicity and national identity', p. 242.

41 Abdellali Hajjat, 'Le MTA et la "grève générale" contre le racisme de 1973', *Plein Droit*, no. 67 (December 2005), pp. 36-40.

42 Catherine Polac, 'Quand "les immigrés" prennent la parole', in Pascal Perrineau, ed, *L'engagement politique*, Paris: Presses de Sciences Po, 1994, pp. 359-376.

43 Johanna Siméant, *La cause des sans-papiers*, Paris: Paris: Presses de Sciences Po, 1998, pp. 80, 85; 'Mémoires d'immigration: Driss El Yazami', *Le Courrier de l'Atlas*, September 2008.

44 Bouziri, interview; Saïd Bouziri, 'Itinéraire d'un militant dans l'immigration', *Migrance*, no. 25 (3rd trimester 2005), pp. 48-49.

45 Jim House, 'Antiracism and antiracist discourse in France from 1900 to the present day', PhD thesis, University of Leeds, 1997, p. 292.

46 Aïssa Kadri, 'L'histoire des bidonvilles', in Aïssa Kadri and Gérard Prévost, eds, *Mémoires algériennes*, Paris: Syllepse, 2004, pp. 38-39; Abelmalek Sayad, *The Suffering of the Immigrant*, Cambridge: Polity, 2004.

47 Laurent Gervereau et al, *Toute la France*, Paris: Somogny, 1998; Tahar Ben Jelloun, *French Hospitality*, New York: Columbia University Press, 1999, p. 1.

48 Kristin Ross, *May '68 and its Afterlives*, Chicago: Chicago University Press, 2002, p. 2.

49 Ahmed Boubeker, *Les mondes de l'ethnicité*, Paris: Balland, 2003, p. 211.

50 Siméant, *Sans-papiers*, p. 85.

51 Robert Lumley, *States of Emergency*, London: Verso, 1990, pp. 129-134. With French militants, this element of guilt may be linked to the distinct echoes of

Catholicism in the Maoist culture of the period: Donald Reid, 'Etablissement: working in the factory to make revolution in France', *Radical History Review*, no. 88 (Winter 2004), p. 100.

52　Siméant, *Sans-papiers*, p. 85.

53　Olivier Piot, *La révolution tunisienne*, Paris: Les Petits Matins, 2011, pp. 42-44, 91-93; as commentators on the 2006 movement against changes in youth employment law pointed out, the gap between students and workers in contemporary France is narrower than it was in 1968, because students come from more socially diverse backgrounds and more work at the same time as studying: Eric Zemmour, 'Pourquoi la mobilisation contre le CPE n'est pas un nouveau Mai 68', *Le Figaro*, 25 March 2006.

54　Siméant, *Sans-papiers*, p. 85; Ralph Schor, *L'opinion française et les étrangers en France 1919-1939*, Paris: Sorbonne, 1985, p. 157; George Orwell, *Down and Out in Paris and London*, London: Victor Gollancz, 1933, pp. 20-23.

55　Nicolas Hatzfeld et al, 'Mai 68: le débat continue', *Revue internationale des livres et des idées*, no. 6 (July-August 2008), pp. 54-57.

56　Bibliothèque Nationale, Paris, Union locale CFDT Chambéry, 'Travailler comme des Turcs', 22 August 1974, leaflet in dossier, Comité de Solidarité avec les Travailleurs Immigrés de Savoie, 'Le CSTIS pour quoi faire?', 1975; *La Tribune de Genève*, 15 September 1973.

57　CEDETIM, *Les immigrés*, p. 259.

58　CEDETIM, *Les immigrés*, p. 240.

59　Vincent Viet, *La France immigrée*, Paris: Fayard, 1998, pp. 348-356.

60　CAC 19870056, Groupe d'Information et de Soutien aux Travailleurs Immigrés, 'Etude GISTI: Les Logements-Foyers', n.d. [c. 1974].

61　Abdelmalek Sayad, 'Le Foyer des sans-famille', *Actes de la recherche en sciences sociales*, nos 32-33 (April-June 1980), pp. 89-103.

62　Tahar Ben Jelloun, *La Réclusion Solitaire*, Paris: Denoël, 1976, pp. 13-14, translated in Yehudit Ronen, 'Moroccan immigration in the Mediterranean region: reflections in Ben Jelloun's literary works', *Journal of North African Studies*, vol. 6, no. 4 (Winter 2001), pp. 5-6.

63　Alain Jaubert, *Guide de la France des luttes*, Paris: Stock, 1974, pp. 414-415 lists the following titles: *Travailleurs, français, immigrés, même combat*, 1971; Ahsène Zenraoui, *Les travailleurs algériens en France*, 1971; Monique Hervo and Marie-Ange Charras, *Bidonvilles*, 1971; FASTI, *Coopérants à rebours, les migrants en France*, 1971; Pierre and Paulette Calame, *Les travailleurs étrangers en France*, 1972; Léon Gani, *Syndicats et travailleurs immigrés*, 1972; Union Générale des Travailleurs Sénégalais en France, *Le livre des travailleurs africains en France*, 1972; Droit et Liberté, *Le Logement des Migrants*, 1973; Jean-Pierre Dumont, *La Fin des OS*, 1973; Juliette Minces, *Les travailleurs étrangers en France*, 1973; 'Mohammed', *Le Journal de Mohammed*, 1973; Françoise Pinot, *Les travailleurs immigrés dans la lutte des classes*, 1973; *Le petit livre juridique des travailleurs immigrés*, 1974.

64　Other examples of this genre include *Les travailleurs immigrés parlent*, special issue of *Cahiers du Centre d'études socialistes*, nos 94-98 (September-December 1969).

65 Maryse Tripier, *L'immigration dans la classe ouvrière en France*, Paris: L'Harmattan, 1990, p. 255.

66 Minces, *Travailleurs étrangers*, pp. 9-11, 223-225, 297-304.

67 Adrian Favell, 'Integration Policy and Integration Research in Europe: a review and a critique', in Alexander Aleinikoff and Doug Klusmeyer, eds, *Citizenship Today*, Washington: Carnegie Endowment, 2000, p. 353.

68 Stephen Castles, 'Thirty Years of Research on Migration and Multicultural Societies', in *Ethnicity and Globalization*, London: Sage, 2000, p. 1; Stephen Castles and Godula Kosack, *Immigrant Workers and Class Structure in Western Europe*, Oxford: Oxford University Press, 1973.

69 Manuel Castells, 'The Space of Flows' in Ida Susser, ed, *The Castells Reader on Cities and Social Theory*, Oxford: Blackwell, 2002, pp. 354-355; Alexis Spire, introductory talk to *Sciences sociales et l'immigration* seminar, Ecole Normale Superieure, Paris, 5 November 2004.

70 Berger and Mohr, *Seventh Man*, which was originally published in 1975.

71 Ralph Grillo, *Ideologies and Institutions in Urban France*, Cambridge: Cambridge University Press, 1985, p. 275.

72 André Gorz and Philippe Gavi, 'La bataille d'Ivry', *Les Temps Modernes*, no. 284 (March 1970), reproduced in Michel-Antoine Burrier and Bernard Kouchner, eds, *La France Sauvage*, Paris: Premières, 1970, p. 293.

73 Subtitle of Mark Miller, *Foreign Workers in Western Europe*, New York: Praeger, 1981.

74 Wihtol de Wenden, *Immigrés et la politique*, pp. 155-156; Miller, *Foreign Workers*, pp. 1-7, summarises the debate; Stephen Castles and Godula Kosack, *Immigrant Workers and Class Structure in Western Europe*, Oxford: Oxford University Press, 1985.

75 Manuel Castells, 'Immigrant workers and class structures in advanced capitalism: the Western European experience', in Susser, *Castells Reader*, pp. 92, 98-99.

76 Alison Smith, 'The problems of immigration as shown in the French cinema of the 1970s', *Modern and Contemporary France*, vol. 3, no. 1 (1995), pp. 41-50; Blanchard et al, *Paris Arabe*, p. 187; Ed Naylor, 'The Politics of a Presence: Algerians in Marseille from independence to "immigration sauvage" (1962-1974)', PhD thesis, Queen Mary University of London, 2011, p. 205, n. 170; *Les gens des baraques* (1995), dir. Robert Bozzi, in which he goes in search of the people depicted in his earlier film; *Est-ce ainsi que les hommes vivent* (1976), dir. Claude Dityvon, included on 2009 DVD of *Etranges étrangers* (1970), dir. Marcel Trillat and Frédéric Variot; Tangui Perron, *Histoire d'un film, mémoire d'une lutte. 1: Le Dos au mur*, Paris: Scope, 2007, p. 32.

77 CEDETIM, *Les immigrés*, p. 7.

78 *Le Monde*, 17 November 1971; David Macey, *The Lives of Michel Foucault*, London: Hutchinson, 1993, pp. 314-317. The worker's name was given as José, which may identify him as José Duarte (see Chapter Four).

79 *Le Nouvel Observateur*, 4 March 1974, cited in Michael Christofferson, *French Intellectuals Against The Left*, New York: Berghahn, 2004, 102.

80 Jaubert, *France des luttes*, pp. 418-419, 423; Grillo, *Ideologies and Institutions*,

pp. 190-192; Viet, *France immigrée*, pp. 314, 319.

81 Benjamin Stora, *La dernière génération d'octobre*, Paris: Stock, 2003, p. 146. Stora notes that this was not the case with Latin America, but then there were relatively few Latin American workers in France.

82 Anne Couteau and Paul Oriol, interview with author, Paris, 2 January 2006.

83 Driss El Yazami, radio interview with Emmanuel Laurentin, *La Fabrique de l'Histoire: Histoire des étrangers*, episode 1, France Culture, 7 January 2008.

84 BDIC Mfc 214/8, poster 'Djellali Kamal'.

85 CIDIM, 'Colloque MTA 20 et 21 avril 1974'.

86 Aissaoui, 'Immigration, ethnicity and national identity', pp. 176-178, 189, 228-235.

87 Bouziri interview; Aissaoui, 'Political mobilisations of North African migrants in 1970s France: the case of the Movement des Travailleurs Arabes (MTA)', *Journal of Muslim Minority Affairs*, vol. 26, no. 2 (August 2006), pp. 175-177.

88 CIDIM, 'Commission Information', n.d. [1974].

89 Wihtol de Wenden, *Immigrés et la politique*, p. 163.

90 'Jean-Marie Le Pen: candidat de salut public', in *Notes et études documentaires*, nos 4201-4203 (7 July 1974): *Textes et documents rélatifs à l'élection présidentielle des 5 et 19 mai 1974*, pp. 49-52; Viet, *France immigrée*, p. 360.

91 'Arlette Laguiller' and 'Krivine candidat du front communiste révolutionnaire', in *Textes et documents*, pp. 45-48, 41-44; Miller, *Foreign Workers*, pp. 103, 186; Gilles de Staal, *Mamadou m'a dit*, Paris: Syllepse, 2008, pp. 122-123; CIDIM, 'Colloque MTA 20 et 21 avril 1974'.

92 Blanchard, *Paris Arabe*, p. 185.

93 Yvan Gastaut, *L'immigration et l'opinion en France sous la Ve République*, Paris: Seuil, 2000, pp. 535-536.

94 E.g. Wihtol de Wenden, *Immigrés et la politique*, pp. 209-210.

95 Wihtol de Wenden, *Immigrés et la politique*, pp. 306-308.

96 Couteau and Oriol, interview; Guy Phillippon, interview with author, Paris, 5 January 2006.

97 Charles Hauss, *The New Left in France*, Westport: Greenwood, 1978, p. 47.

98 Wihtol de Wenden, *Immigrés et la politique*, pp. 195-200; Tripier, *L'immigration dans la classe ouvrière*, p. 80; Viet, *France immigrée*, 301-324; *Mémoires d'immigrés*, episode 2, *Les mères*; Patrick Weil, *La France et ses étrangers*, Paris: Gallimard, 1995, pp. 112-128; Brigitte Jelen, ' "Leur histoire est notre histoire": immigrant culture in France between visibility and invisibility', *French Politics, Culture and Society*, vol. 23, no. 2 (Summer 2005), pp. 102-106; Alec Hargreaves, *Multi-Ethnic France*, New York: Routledge, 2007, pp. 181-182; Stéphane Hessel, *Danse avec le siècle*, Paris: Points, 2011, pp. 283-288.

99 CIDIM, MTA, 'Unissons nous pour nos droits contre l'esclavage et pour la carte de travail', January 1975, *Journal du comité de soutien aux travailleurs immigrés de Montpeller*, 1974-75 and 'Soutenons les luttes des travailleurs immigrés', 1975; Hélène Trappo, 'De la clandestinité à la reconnaissance' (interview with Driss El Yazami), *Plein Droit*, no. 11 (July 1990); El Yazami, interview with Emmanuel Laurentin; Siméant, *Sans-papiers*, p. 462.

100 Fouad Lamine and Blanchard Navacelles, 'De l'isolement vers l'unité', *Politique*

aujourd'hui, March-April 1975, pp. 82-85; Trappo, 'Clandestinité'; Daoud, *Citoyenneté*, pp. 43-45; 'Mémoires d'immigration'; El Yazami, interview with Emmanuel Laurentin.

101 Alex Panzani, *Une prison clandestine de la police française (Arenc)*, Paris: Maspero, 1975, pp. 7-36; *Libération*, 30 April 1975; *La Marseillaise*, 30 April 1975. Subsequent research has confirmed that Arenc had been in operation since as early as 1964, representing an illegal form of administrative detention, used disproportionately more against Algerians than any other nationality, sometimes including families with children, and that there is some evidence suggesting detainees were beaten: Alexis Spire, 'L'héritage de l'expérience coloniale dans la réorganisation du traitement de l'immigration (1945-1974)', paper to Society for French Historical Studies Conference, Paris, 17-20 June 2004, pp. 12-13; Naylor, 'Politics of a Presence', pp. 82-85.

102 Panzani, *Arenc*, pp. 7, 29, 41, 59, 79-80.

103 Martin Evans, *The Memory of Resistance*, Oxford: Berg, 1997.

104 Olivier Clochard et al, 'Les camps d'étrangers depuis 1938: continuité et adaptations. Du "modèle" français à la construction de l'espace Schengen', *Revue européene des migrations internationales*, vol. 20, no. 2 (2004), pp. 57-85.

105 Naylor, 'Politics of a Presence', pp. 102-104.

106 *Le Monde*, 4 September 1973; Miller, *Foreign Workers*, pp. 180-186; Mogniss Abdallah, *J'y suis, j'y reste!*, Paris, 2000, p. 35.

107 Wihtol de Wenden, *Immigrés et la politique*, pp. 212-213, 256-264.

108 Miller, *Foreign Workers*, p. 65; Aissaoui, 'Immigration, ethnicity and national identity', pp. 260-261; Christian Chevandier, *Les tourments d'une génération*, Montreuil: Au Lieux d'Etre, 2008.

109 Viet, *France Immigrée*, pp. 321-322; cf Ambalavaner Sivanandan, *Race and Resistance*, London: Race Today, 1974.

110 Cathie Lloyd, *Discourses of Anti-Racism in France*, Aldershot: Ashgate, 1998, pp. 200-210, 161-175.

111 Jean-François Bizot, *Au parti des socialistes*, Paris: Grasset, 1975, pp. 199, 204-205.

112 Rémi Lefebvre and Frédéric Sawicki, *La société des socialistes*, Broisseux: Croquant, 2006, pp. 55-64.

113 Régis Debray, *Loués soient nos seigneurs*, Paris: Gallimard, 1996, translated as *Praised Be Our Lords*, London: Verso, 2007, p. 173.

114 François Mitterrand, *Changer la vie*, Paris: Flammarion, 1972, pp. 113, 144; Catherine Wihtol de Wenden and Rémy Leveau, *La beurgeoisie*, Paris: CNRS, 2001, pp. 27-28.

115 Neill Nugent and David Lowe, *The Left in France*, London: Macmillan, 1981, pp. 81-82.

116 'The Angry Ones', originally designating a radical faction from the French Revolution, and applied to far Left students in 1968.

117 See Hauss, *New Left*, based on a survey of PSU activists carried out in 1972-1973, in other words at the height of the interest in immigrant workers; Marc Heurgon, *Histoire du PSU*, Paris: La Découverte, 1994, the first volume of the PSU's official history; a second volume is being prepared by Bernard Ravenel,

a former party activist and later head of the Association France Palestine Solidarité; Horn, *Spirit of '68*, pp. 148-152; Tudi Kernalegenn et al, eds, *Le PSU vu d'en bas*, Rennes: Presses Universitaires de Rennes, 2009; Daniel Gordon, 'A "Mediterranean New Left"? Comparing and contrasting the French PSU and the Italian PSIUP', *Contemporary European History*, vol. 19, no. 4 (November 2010), pp. 309-330.

118 Nugent and Lowe, *Left in France*, p. 180.

119 Hauss, *New Left*, p. 43; Sylvie Lienart, 'Les circulaires Marcellin-Fontanet et les luttes des travailleurs immigrés', Masters thesis, Université de Paris VIII, 1975, p. 65; for more details, see Séverine Lacalmontie, 'De la recherche à l'invention d'une cause: les militants du PSU et le droit de vote des immigrés' and Daniel Gordon, 'Le PSU et les luttes de l'immigration: perspectives nationales et internationales', both in Kernalegenn et al, *PSU vu d'en bas*, pp. 317-326, 327-336.

120 Byron Criddle, 'The Parti Socialiste Unifié: an appraisal after ten years', *Parliamentary Affairs*, vol. 24, no. 2 (Spring 1971), p. 154; Hauss, *New Left*, p. 184; Jean Poperen, *L'Unité de la gauche 1965-1973*, Paris: Fayard, 1975, p. 410-411; Jean-François Kesler, *De la gauche dissidente au nouveau parti socialiste*, Paris: Privat, 1990, p. 409.

121 Couteau and Oriol, interview; Phillippon, interview; Guy Phillippon, private archives, Paris: PSU 20e archives, PSU, 'Texte annexe au texte sur les travailleurs immigrés du bureau national', undated [1973], Group d'action immigrés, notes, 23-24 February 1974 and 'Groupe d'action immigrés – débat sur les activités', n.d.; Centre d'Histoire du Travail, Nantes, Fonds PSU, box 46/1, *Les Pavés de la Commune: bulletin intérieur de la 20e section du PSU*, October 1978, 46/II/1, 'Rencontre nationale du secteur immigrés : compte-rendu de la réunion du 23 février 1980' and 46/III, PSU 20e, 'Les travailleurs immigrés : textes parus dans le bulletin intérieur de la 20e section du PSU', n.d. [c.1978].

122 Couteau and Oriol, interview; *PSU Documentation*, no. 154 (January 1983), p. 7.

123 'Les travailleurs immigrés', *PSU Documentation*, no. 16 (September 1970), cited in 'Les immigrés dans les textes "sacrés" ', *PSU Documentation*, no. 141 (October 1980), p. 13; *Contrôler aujourd'hui pour decider demain*, PSU party manifesto, Paris: TEMA, 1973, p. 211; Bizot, *Parti des socialistes*, pp. 156, 163; Gastaut, *L'immigration et l'opinion*, p. 166; Paul Oriol, *Les immigrés, métèques ou citoyens?*, Paris: Syros, 1985. The book states that Oriol had been a member of the Commission Immigrés for ten years (i.e. since 1975).

124 Vincent Duclert, 'La "deuxième gauche" ', in Jean-Jacques Becker and Gills Candar, eds, *Histoire des gauches en France*, vol 2, Paris: La Découverte, 2004, p. 177.

125 Couteau and Oriol, interview; PSU 20e archives, 'Bilan des Activités du Groupe d'Informations Immigrés Octobre 1974- Juin 1975'; conversations with other PSU activists at *Le PSU vu d'en bas* Conference, Rennes, 9-10 September 2008.

126 See Chapter One.

127 Stany Grelet and Isabelle Saint-Saëns, 'Entretien avec Gus Massiah

(CEDETIM)', *Vacarme*, June 2001; Catherine Simon, *Algérie, les années pieds-rouges*, Paris: La Découverte, 2009.

128 The GOP was the heir of the 'populist' faction of the PSU, led by Marc Heurgon and Abraham Behar, which had especially argued for the party to orientate itself towards immigrant workers as the most oppressed group in society: Hauss, *New Left in France*, p. 41.

129 Couteau and Oriol, interview; Grelet and Saint-Saëns, 'Gus Massiah'; Bernard Dréano, 'Le Cedetim ou la continuité d'un combat', http://www.reseau-ipam. org/article-imprim-cedetim.php3?id_article=930, 14 April 2005.

130 CEDETIM, *Les immigrés*.

131 The classic statement of this view was Balibar's 'De Charonne à Vitry', *Le Nouvel Observateur*, 9 March 1981. Examples of this influence are Evans, *Memory of Resistance*; Danièle Joly, *The French Communist Party and the Algerian War*, Basingstoke: Macmillan, 1991.

132 See Chapter Six.

133 Marcel Dufriche, 'Les travailleurs immigrés sont nos frères de classe', *L'Humanité*, 19 October 1964, reprinted in Alain Ruscio, ed, *La question coloniale dans* l'Humanité *1904-2004*, Paris: La Dispute, 2005, pp. 437-438; Gastaut, *L'immigration et l'opinion*, pp. 221-222, citing André Merlot, 'Immigrés, nos frères de classes', *Cahiers du communisme*, May 1972, pp. 62-70. The (not exhaustive) list compiled by Ruscio (pp. 569-570) shows that *L'Humanité* devoted at least 35 articles to the question of immigration between 1969 and 1976.

134 *Sans Frontière*, 24 January 1981; Miller, *Foreign Workers*, pp. 81, 183-185; Johnson, *Long March*, pp. 175-176, 313; Grillo, *Ideologies and Institutions*, p. 193.

135 Marius Apostolo, *Traces de luttes 1924-2007*, Paris: Autrement, 2008, pp. 152-160; Tangui Perron, *Histoire d'un film, mémoire d'une lutte. 2: Etrange étrangers*, Paris: Scope, 2009, pp. 118-121.

136 El Yazami, interview with Emmanuel Laurentin.

137 *La Marseillaise*, 4 September 1973.

138 Phillippon, interview; CFDT Archives Confédérales, Paris (CFDT) 8 H 1763, Réné Leschiera (CGT) to A.Amiral (CFDT), 23 February 1972; Amiral to Leschiera, 23 February 1972; PCF, 'Les travailleurs immigrés peuvent assurer le succès de leurs revendications', 25 February 1972; Amiral to J.Capievic (PCF), 1 March 1972; Michèle Manceaux and Jacques Donzelot, *Cours camarade, le P.C.F. est derrière toi*, Paris: Gallimard, 1974, pp. 78-88; Grillo, *Ideologies and Institutions*, p. 267.

139 André Vieuguet, *Français et immigrés*, Paris: Editions Sociales, 1975, p. 41.

140 Bouziri, interview; CFDT 8 H 1763, Union Locale CFDT du 20eme arrondissment, 'Soutenons les grévistes de la faim', 28 May 1973 and CFDT, 'Elements de réflexion pour une politique syndicale de l'immigration', 1973; Lienart, 'Circulaires Marcellin-Fontanet', 57; Grillo, *Ideologies and Institutions*, p. 231; Aissaoui, 'Political Mobilisations', p. 181.

141 *Journal Officiel*, 29 April 1970, reproduced in Editions Points, "*Vous frappez à tort et à travers*", Paris: Points, 2009, p. 35.

142 Yaïr Auron, *Les juifs d'extrême gauche en mai 68*, Paris: Albin Michel, 1998, pp. 145-162; Robert Linhart, *The Assembly Line*, London: Calder, 1981, p. 103.

143 René Gallissot, *Henri Curiel*, Paris: Riveneuve, 2009.

144 Apostolo, *Traces de luttes*, pp. 100, 175; Johnson, *Long March*, pp. 177-181; tables in Andrew Knapp, *Parties and Party Systems in France*, Basingstoke: Palgrave Macmillan, 2004, p. 97 show that in 1978 some 26% of 25-34 year olds voted PCF, and that despite subsequent decline this age cohort remained as late as 2002 more likely than any other to vote PCF.

145 Gino Raymond, *The French Communist Party during the Fifth Republic*, Basingstoke: Palgrave Macmillan, 2005, Chapter 7.

146 Marie-George Buffet, *Un peu de courage!*, Paris: Cherche Midi, 2004, pp. 13-16; 'L'école de mon enfance', video broadcast at www.mariegeorge2007. org, April 2007. Though there may be an element of retrospective rewriting of history here – the PCF under Buffet's leadership became more open to collaboration with other movements, even Trotskyists, for whom 1968 is an obvious reference point – the long term generational point is clear.

147 François Bachy, *François Hollande*, Paris: Plon, 2001, pp. 53-59.

148 General Secretary of the PCF between 1930 and 1964, Thorez typified the tendency of the PCF's historic leadership to both apparently impeccably proletarian credentials and a deeply uncritical attitude towards Stalinism.

149 Phillippe Bernard, *La crème des Beurs*, Paris: Seuil, 2004, pp. 94-100; Gérard Noiriel, *Penser avec, penser contre*, Paris: Belin, 2003, pp. 262-266; Daoud, *Citoyenneté*, pp. 52-55; Panzani, *Arenc*.

150 Tangui Perron, *Histoire d'un film, mémoire d'une lutte*, talk at Cité Nationale de l'Histoire de l'Immigration, Paris, 6 April 2010; Perron, *Histoire d'un film, 2*, p. 88; *Marcel Trillat, portrait* (2008), dir. Tangui Perron and Philippe Troyon, included on 2009 DVD of *Etranges étrangers*.

151 Yvan Gastaut, 'Marseille, epicentre de la problématique du racisme en 1973', *Migrance*, no. 25 (3rd trimester 2005), p. 23.

152 Phillippe Alfonsi and Patrick Pesnot, *Vivre à gauche*, Paris: Albin Michel, 1975, pp. 383-384.

153 Alfonsi and Pesnot, *Vivre à gauche*, p. 51.

154 Documentaries collected in the DVD *La saga des immigrés* (2007), dir. Edouard Mills-Affif and Anne Riegel.

155 *La Tribune Socialiste*, 7 January 1971.

156 Gérard Noiriel, *Immigration, antisémitisme et racisme en France (XIXe-XXe siècles)*, Paris: Fayard, 2007, pp. 675-676; Naylor, 'Politics of a Presence', while critical of Noiriel on other points, seems to concur with the idea that the far Left were only interested in ex-colonial migrants – perhaps because it is a local study of Marseilles, where Algerians were more dominant within the 'immigrant worker' category than was the case elsewhere.

157 Richard DeAngelis, *Blue-Collar Workers and Politics*, London: Croom Helm, 1982, pp. 125-127, 173.

158 Guy Michelat and Michel Simon, *Les ouvriers et la politique*, Paris: Presses de Sciences Po, 2004, pp. 51-52.

159 Stéphane Beaud and Michel Pialoux, 'Racisme ouvrier ou mépris de classe?

Retour sur une enquête de terrain', in Didier Fassin and Eric Fassin, eds, *De la question sociale à la question raciale?*, Paris: La Découverte, 2009, pp. 80-98.

160 Alfonsi and Pesnot, *Vivre à gauche*, p. 321.

161 *La Tribune Socialiste*, 27 May 1971.

162 Benjamin Stora, *Le transfert d'une mémoire*, Paris: La Découverte, 1999; Michelat and Simon, *Ouvriers et la politique*, p. 166.

163 Grillo, *Ideologies and Institutions*, p. 238.

164 André Harris and Alain de Sédouy, *Voyage à l'intérieur du Parti communiste*, Paris: Seuil, 1974, p. 117.

165 Neil MacMaster, 'The 'seuil de tolérance': the uses of a 'scientific' racist concept', in Maxim Silverman, ed, *Race, Discourse and Power in France*, Aldershot: Avebury, 1991, pp. 19-23; comments by mayor of Aubervilliers in *Etrange étrangers*.

166 Ralph Grillo, ' "Les chargeurs sont dans la rue!": racism and trade unions in Lyons', in Silverman, *Race, Discourse and Power*, pp. 40-54.

Chapter 6

1   Mogniss Abdallah, 'Autoportraits: Moha "l'antitransit" et Djamel d'Argenteuil', in Abdallah, ed, *Jeunes immigrés hors les murs*, special issue of *Questions Clefs*, no. 2 (March 1982), p. 32.

2   *Nice-Matin*, 17 March 1976, reproduced in Mehdi Lallaoui, *Du bidonville au HLM*, Paris: Syros, 1993, p. 74.

3   See Chapter Four. Louis Althusser, *The Future Lasts a Long Time*, London: Vintage, 1994, p. 232; Kristin Ross, *Fast Cars, Clean Bodies*, Cambridge, MA: MIT Press, 1996, pp. 17-19; David Macey, *The Lives of Michel Foucault*, London: Hutchinson, 1993, p. 315.

4   Nick Hewlett, *Modern French Politics*, Cambridge: Polity, 1998, p. 175.

5   Pascal Ory, *L'entre-deux-mai*, Paris: Seuil, 1983.

6   Robert Lumley, *States of Emergency*, London: Verso, 1990, p. 2.

7   Andrew Knapp, *Parties and the Party System in France*, Basingstoke: Palgrave Macmillan, 2004, pp. 149-152. The Common Programme for Government was the agreement signed in 1972 between Mitterrand and his Communist opposite number Georges Marchais, paving the way for the Union of the Left to come to power.

8   Sunil Khilnani, *Arguing Revolution*, New Haven: Yale University Press, 1993. Michael Christofferson, *French Intellectuals Against the Left*, New York: Berghahn, 2004, though contesting the conventional emphasis on Solzhenitsyn in favour of French domestic politics, underlines the extent of the change in intellectual climate. By 1976, Maurice Clavel, once a key intellectual patron of Maoist immigration activism, was enthusiastically touting the 'New Philosophers' with their somewhat hysterical insistence that the Common Programme would lead to the gulag (pp. 193-197). Julian Bourg, *From Revolution to Ethics*, Montreal: Queen's-McGill University Press, 2007, takes a more positive view of such developments as a turn to ethics, while Bent Boel, 'French support for Eastern European dissidents, 1968-1989:

approaches and controversies', in Poul Villaume and Odd Arne Westad, eds, *Perforating the Iron Curtain*, Copenhagen: Museum Tusculanum, 2010, pp. 215-241, emphasises broader grassroots contacts rather than the famous names. Interestingly, Driss El Yazami says he was given Solzhenitsyn to read by a Trotskyist schoolteacher in Morocco in 1967 or 1968, long before the Russian was loudly 'discovered' by the New Philosophers: radio interview with Emmanuel Laurentin, *La Fabrique de l'Histoire: Histoire des étrangers*, episode 1, France Culture, 7 January 2008.

9   Pierre Bourdieu and Jean-Claude Passeron, *Les héritiers*, Paris: Minuit, 1964; E.P. Thompson, 'The Poverty of Theory' in *The Poverty of Theory and other essays*, London: Merlin, 1978, p. 371. Bourdieu and Passeron's study of French students emphasised the class advantage perpetuated within the theoretically egalitarian republican education system by those students who had the most cultural capital, acquired from the upper-middle-class backgrounds that they were soon to rebel against.

10   Charles Hauss, *The New Left in France*, Westport: Greenwood, 1978, p. 11.

11   Chris Harman, *The Fire Last Time*, London: Bookmarks, 1988, pp. 346-347; Olivier Fillieule, ed, *Le désengagement militant*, Paris: Belin, 2005.

12 Daniel Gordon, 'Le PSU et les luttes de l'immigration: perspectives nationales et internationales', in Tudi Kernalegenn et al, eds, *Le PSU vu d'en bas*, Rennes: Presses Universitaires de Rennes, 2009, pp. 327-336.

13   Hervé Hamon and Patrick Rotman, *Génération*, vol. 2, Paris: Seuil, 1988, p. 577, 580-581; Yvan Gastaut, *L'immigration et l'opinion en France sous la Ve République*, Paris: Seuil, 2000, pp. 166-167.

14   Phillippe Juhem, 'Entreprendre en politique de l'extrême gauche au PS: la professionalisation politique des fondateurs de SOS Racisme', *Revue française de sciences politique*, vol. 51, nos 1-2 (Feb-Apr 2001), pp. 131-153; *Ils ont voulu le pouvoir*, broadcast LCP, 9 August 2011; Benjamin Stora, *La dernière génération d'octobre*, Paris: Stock, 2003, p. 249.

15   The account of the strike in the following paragraphs is based on an interview with Malik, a member of the strike's Coordinating Committee, *Sans Frontière*, 31 July 1979, unless otherwise stated.

16   Daniel Gordon, 'The back door of the nation state: expulsions of foreigners and continuity in twentieth century France', *Past and Present*, no. 186 (February 2005), pp. 214-215.

17   Vincent Viet, *La France immigrée*, Paris: Fayard, 1998, p. 350.

18   *Sans Frontière*, 31 July 1979; Cathie Lloyd, *Discourses of Antiracism in France*, Aldershot: Ashgate, 1998, p. 206.

19   Lloyd, *Discourses of Antiracism in France*, pp. 206-211.

20   Report to FASTI congress by Commission Immigrés, 1977, cited in Gilles Verbunt, *L'intégration par l'autonomie*, Paris: CIEMM, 1980, p. 166.

21   Sheila Rowbotham, Lynne Segal and Hilary Wainwright, *Beyond the Fragments*, London: Merlin, 1979; Harman, *Fire Last Time*, pp. 351-355.

22   Verbunt, *L'intégration par l'autonomie*, pp. 164, 166.

23   Verbunt, *L'intégration par l'autonomie*, p. 333; Pierre Turpin, *Les révolutionnaires dans la France social-démocrate*, Paris: L'Harmattan, 1997,

p. 57; Isabelle Saint-Saens et al, 'Vingt ans après (Assane Ba): le mouvement des foyers Sonacotra (1975-1980)', *Vacarme*, June 2001; Saïd Bouamama, 'Extrême gauche et luttes de l'immigration postcoloniale', in Ahmed Boubeker and Abdellali Hajjat, eds, *Histoire politique des immigrations (post)coloniales*, Paris: Amsterdam, 2008, p. 241; Choukri Hmed, 'Les grèves de loyers dans les foyers Sonacotra: premier mouvement immigré' in Philippe Artières and Michelle Zancarini-Fournel, eds, *68: une histoire collective [1962-1981]*, Paris: La Découverte, 2008, pp. 725-729; Nicola Cooper, *France in Indochina*, Oxford: Berg, 2001, pp. 195-199; *Sans Frontière*, 4 Sep and 20 Nov 1979. The UCFML also attempted to forge links between the strikers and other categories of excluded people like the disabled.

24 SONACOTRA strike coordinating committee, quoted in *Sans Frontière*, 4 Dec 1979.

25 *Assifa*, 11 May 1976; Saint-Saens, 'Vingt ans après'.

26 Viet, *France immigrée*, p. 350.

27 Hmed, 'Grèves de loyers', p. 728.

28 Jane Jenson and George Ross, *The View from Inside*, Berkeley: University of California Press, 1984, pp. 96-97; Catherine Wihtol de Wenden, *Les immigrés et la politique*, Paris: Presses de Sciences Po, 1988, pp. 270-272; Pascal Blanchard et al, *Le Paris Arabe*, Paris: La Découverte, 2003, p. 199.

29 Gérard Noiriel and Bennaceur Azzaoui, *Vivre et lutter à Longwy*, Paris: Maspero, 1980; Gérard Noiriel, *Longwy. Immigrés et prolétaires*, Paris: Presses Universitaires de France, 1984; Gérard Noiriel, *Penser avec, penser contre*, Paris: Belin, 2003, pp. 269-270.

30 Fouad Lamine and Blanchard Navacelles, 'De l'isolement vers l'unité', *Politique aujourd'hui*, March-April 1975, pp. 83-84.

31 *Al Assifa*, 11 May 1976; Blanchard, *Paris Arabe*, p. 187; Rabah Aissaoui, 'Immigration, ethnicity and national identity: Maghrebis' socio-political mobilisation and discourse in the inter-war period and during the 1970s in France', PhD thesis, University of Leeds, 2001, pp. 195-198; Ahmed Boubeker, *Les mondes de l'ethnicité*, Paris: Balland, 2003, pp. 213-217.

32 Xavier Crettiez and Isabelle Sommier eds, *La France Rebelle*, Paris: Michalon, 2006, p. 365; Michelle Zancarini-Fournel, 'La construction d'une "problème national": l'immigration', in Artières and Zancarini-Fournel, *68*, pp. 668-669.

33 *Sans Frontière*, 26 June 1979.

34 Abdellali Hajjat, 'L'expérience politique du Mouvement des travailleurs arabes', *Contretemps*, no. 16 (January 2006), pp. 84-85.

35 Driss El Yazami, 'France's ethnic minority press' in Alec Hargreaves and Mark McKinney, eds, *Post-Colonial Cultures in France*, London: Routledge, 1997, pp. 122, 124; Jacques Simon et al, *L'immigration algérienne en France*, Paris: L'Harmattan, 2002, p. 187; El Yazami, interview with Emmanuel Laurentin.

36 *Sans Frontière*, 24 January 1981.

37 *Sans Frontière*, 6 and 13 June 1981.

38 *Sans Frontière*, 7 February 1981.

39 *Sans Frontière*, 18 December 1979.

40 El Yazami, 'Ethnic minority press', pp. 123-124.

41   Pierre Goldman, *Souvenirs obscurs d'un juif polonais né en France*, Paris: Seuil, 1975.

42   Hamon and Rotman, *Génération*, vol. 2, pp. 601-602.

43   *Sans Frontière*, 2 October 1979.

44   *Sans Frontière*, 20 November 1979.

45   *Sans Frontière*, 1 May, 31 July and 2 October 1979, 20 November 1981.

46   In the sense used by Pierre Nora, *Les Lieux de mémoire*, 7 vols, Paris: Gallimard, 1984-1992, translated as *Realms of Memory*, 3 vols, New York: Columbia University Press, 1996-1998.

47   *Sans Frontière*, 1 January 1980.

48   For example, the story of an Algerian miner from northern France who was involved in early 1970s Maoism: *Sans Frontière* 29 January and 12 February 1980.

49   *Sans Frontière*, 27 December 1980, 3-9 January and 10 January 1981.

50   *Sans Frontière*, 24 June 1980.

51   *Sans Frontière*, 30 September 1980.

52   *Sans Frontière*, 27 March 1979.

53   *Sans Frontière*, 22 April 1980.

54   *Sans Frontière*, 7, 14, 21 and 18 February 1981.

55   *Sans Frontière*, 26 February 1980.

56   *Sans Frontière*, 20-26 December 1980.

57   Saïd Bouziri and Driss El Yazami, 'Prendre la peine', *Migrance*, no. 14 (1st trimester 1999), pp. 2-4.

58   Abdellali Hajjat, 'Le MTA et la "grève générale" contre le racisme de 1973', *Plein Droit*, no. 67 (December 2005), pp. 36-40.

59   *Sans Frontière*, 27 March 1979; Raghu Krishnan and Adrien Thomas, 'Resistance to neo-liberalism in France', *Socialist Register*, 2008, p. 306.

60   Peter Fysh and Jim Wolfreys, *The Politics of Racism in France*, Basingstoke: Macmillan, 2003, p. 163; Richard Derderian, *North Africans in Contemporary France*, New York: Palgrave Macmillan, 2004, p. 50.

61   Julien Dray, *SOS Génération*, Paris: Ramsay, 1987, p. 172.

62   *Sans Frontière*, 1 May 1979.

63   *Sans Frontière*, 4 September 1979; Simon, *L'immigration algérienne*, p. 188.

64   Ahmed Boubeker and Nicolas Beau, *Chroniques métissées*, Paris: Alain Moreau, 1986, pp. 122-124.

65   Georges Abou-Sada, 'Générations issues de l'immigration: problèmes de définition et aspects démographiques', in Georges Abou-Sada and Hélène Milet, eds, *Générations issues de l'immigration*, Paris: Arcantère, 1986, p. 25.

66   Turpin, *Révolutionnaires*, p. 95; figures from Abou-Sada, 'Générations', pp. 31-33.

67   *Le Monde*, 16-17 December 1984, cited in Serge Boulot and Danielle Boyzon-Fradet, 'Diversité de références des publics scolaires et réponses institutionelles', in Abou-Sada and Milet, *Générations issues de l'immigration*, p. 41.

68   Mogniss Abdallah, *J'y suis, j'y reste!*, Paris: Reflex, 2000, pp. 50-51.

69   Patrick Weil, *La France et ses étrangers*, Paris: Gallimard, 2004, pp. 144-192;

Abdelmalek Sayad, 'Le Foyer des sans-famille', *Actes de la recherche en sciences sociales*, nos 32-33 (April-June 1980), p. 93.

70 François Lefort, *Du bidonville à l'expulsion*, Paris: CIEMM, 1980, Fysh and Wolfreys, *Politics of Racism*, pp. 167-168; Gilles de Staal, *Mamadou m'a dit*, Paris: Syllepse, 2008, pp. 151-167.

71 Albert Levy, 'Insécurité et racisme de crise', *Le Monde Diplomatique*, September 1977, reproduced in *Manière de voir*, no. 89 (October-November 2006), *Banlieues: trente ans d'histoire et de révoltes*, pp. 86-88; Farid Aïchoune, *Nés en banlieue*, Paris: Ramsay, 1991, pp. 47-56; Derderian, *North Africans*, p. 26.

72 *Sans Frontière*, 21 March 1981; Boubeker and Beau, *Chroniques métissées*, pp. 55-57.

73 Andy Merrifield, *Metromarxism*, New York: Routledge, 2002, p. 198; Hamon and Rotman, *Génération*, vol. 2, pp. 558, 655-656; *Mourir à trente ans* (1982), dir. Romain Goupil.

74 *Sans Frontière*, 26 February 1980.

75 Saïd Bouziri, interview with author, Paris, 6 November 2004.

76 *Sans Frontière*, 30 May 1981.

77 *Sans Frontière*, 13 June 1981.

78 *Sans Frontière*, 2 October 1979.

79 Tarik Kawtari, 'Du Comité national contre la double peine au Mouvement de l'immigration et des banlieues', in Boubeker and Hajjat, *Histoire politique*, p. 208. *Bled*, referring to the home village of a North African emigrant, is sometimes used in a derogatory sense by those people of North African origin who consider themselves more at home in France.

80 Boubeker, *Mondes de l'ethnicité*, pp. 216-217.

81 Boubeker and Beau, *Chroniques métissées*, pp. 52-53.

82 Derderian, *North Africans*, p. 49.

83 Boubeker and Beau, *Chroniques métissées*, p. 54.

84 Saïd Bouamama, *Dix ans de marche des Beurs*, Paris, 1994, pp. 11-12.

85 Abdallah, *J'y suis, j'y reste!*, pp. 53-55.

86 Fysh and Wolfreys, *Politics of Racism*, p. 168; Bouamama, *Dix ans*, pp. 32-33.

87 Neil MacMaster, 'The 'seuil de tolérance': the uses of a 'scientific' racist concept', in Maxim Silverman, ed, *Race, Discourse and Power in France*, Aldershot: Avebury, 1991, p. 20.

88 Etienne Balibar, 'De Charonne à Vitry', *Le Nouvel Observateur*, 9 March 1981.

89 Marius Apostolo, *Traces de luttes 1924-2007*, Paris: Autrement, 2008, pp. 175-192.

90 David Bell and Byron Criddle, *The French Socialist Party*, Oxford: Clarendon, 1988, p. 140; Tangui Perron, *Histoire d'un film, mémoire d'une lutte*, talk at Cité Nationale de l'Histoire de l'Immigration, Paris, 6 April 2010; *Libération*, 25 January 2003; *L'armée de crime* (2009), dir. Robert Guédiguian.

91 Marius Apostolo, 'Syndicalisme de classe et immigrés in CGT, *Questions de l'immigration et syndicat*, Paris: CGT, 1981, pp. 57-82.

92 Catherine Polac, 'Quand "les immigrés" prennent la parole', in Pascal Perrineau, ed, *L'engagement politique*, Paris: Presses de Sciences Po, 1994, pp.

361-366; Nacer Kettane, *Droit de réponse à la démocratie française*, Paris: La Découverte, 1986, pp. 91-93.

93 Abdallah, 'Autoportraits', p. 32.

94 Bouamama, *Dix ans*, p. 36.

95 Fysh and Wolfreys, *Politics of Racism*, pp. 164-167; Boubeker and Beau, *Chroniques métissées*, pp. 54-55; Adil Jazouli, *Les années banlieues*, Paris: Seuil, 1992, p. 36; Bouamama, *Dix ans*, p. 38; Saïd Bouamama et al, *Contribution à la mémoire des banlieues*, Paris: Volga, 1994, pp. 45-57; Claudie Lesselier, 'Mouvements et initiatives des femmes des années 1970 au milieu des années 1980', in Boubeker and Hajjat, *Histoire politique*, pp. 157-166; Gill Alwood and Khursheed Wadia, *Refugee Women in Britain and France*, Manchester: Manchester University Press, 2010, pp. 137-138.

96 Bouamama, *Dix ans*, p. 37; Phillippe Bernard, *La crème des Beurs*, Paris: Seuil, 2004, pp. 143-148.

97 Bouamama, *Dix ans*, p. 51.

98 Mark Miller, *Foreign Workers in Western Europe*, New York: Praeger, 1981, p. 104. It is interesting to note that the CGT's first response on hearing of Stoléru's plan, in a period when it is often held to have lurched towards xenophobia, was to leak it and denounce it as racist. R.W. Johnson, *The Long March of the French Left*, London: Macmillan, 1981, p. 247.

99 Toby Abse, 'The professor in the balaclava: Toni Negri and autonomist politics', *What Next*, no. 22 (2002); Lumley, *States of Emergency*, pp. 295-312; David Moss, 'Autonomia' in Gino Moliterno, ed, *Encyclopedia of Contemporary Italian Culture*, London: Routledge, 2000, p. 41; Philip Edwards, 'Autonomia and the political: an Italian cycle of contention, 1972-1979', *Modern Italy*, vol. 11, no. 3 (November 2006), pp. 267-283.

100 Adil Jazouli, *L'action collective des jeunes maghrébins de France*, Paris: CIEMI, 1986, pp. 61-62; Jazouli, *Années banlieues*, pp. 29-30.

101 Phil Cerny, 'Non-terrorism and the politics of repressive tolerance', in Phil Cerny, ed, *Social Movements and Protest in France*, London: Pinter, 1982, pp. 94-124; Daniel Gordon, 'From May to October: reassessing the 1968 generation', *Modern and Contemporary France*, vol. 13, no. 2, May 2005, pp. 232-233.

102 Michael Dartnell, *Action Directe*, London: Frank Cass, 1995, pp. 92, 98.

103 Dartnell, *Action Directe*, pp. 99, 181.

104 See Chapter Three.

105 *Sans Frontière*, 16 May and 23 October 1981; Dartnell, *Action Directe*, p. 93, n. 24.

106 Christian Delorme, *Par amour et par colère*, Paris: Le Centurion, 1985, pp. 94-97; *Sans Frontière*, 18 and 25 April 1981; Polac, '"Les immigrés" prennent la parole', p. 365, citing *Sans Frontière*, 16-22 May 1981.

107 Jazouli, *Années banlieues*, pp. 37-41; Fysh and Wolfreys, *Politics of Racism*, p. 168.

108 Jazouli, *Années banlieues*, p. 41.

109 Wihtol de Wenden, *Les immigrés et la politique*, pp. 256-275; Yvan Gastaut, *L'immigration et l'opinion en France sous la Ve République*, Paris: Seuil, 2000,

pp. 536-537; 'Je m'appelle Huguette Bouchardeau' and 'François Mitterrand' in *Notes et études documentaires*, nos 4647-4648 (21 December 1981), *Textes et documents rélatifs à l'élection présidentielle des 26 avril et 10 mai 1981*, pp. 87-90, 95-98.

110 Didier Eribon, *D'une révolution conservatrice*, Paris: Leo Scheer, 2007, p. 36.

111 Abou-Sada, 'Générations', p. 23; Thomas Christofferson, *The French Socialists in Power, 1981-1986*, Newark: University of Delaware Press, 1991, p. 117; Fysh and Wolfreys, *Politics of Racism*, p. 169; Bouamama, *Dix ans*, p. 43; Cécile Laborde, *Critical Republicanism*, Oxford: Oxford University Press, 2008, p. 185; Turpin, *Révolutionnaires*, pp. 85-86; Boubeker and Beau, *Chroniques métissées*, pp. 57-58.

112 Aïchoune, *Nés en banlieue*, pp. 45-46, 49; Jazouli, *Années banlieues*, p. 17.

113 Jazouli, *Années banlieues*, pp. 17-24.

114 Jazouli, *Années banlieues*, p. 24.

115 Turpin, *Révolutionnaires*, p. 99.

116 Aïchoune, *Nés en banlieue*, p. 58; Hamon and Rotman, *Génération*, vol. 2, p. 624.

117 *Haya* (1982), dir. Claude Blanche, extract shown at *Les luttes de l'immigration dans les années 1970*, Cité Nationale de l'Histore de l'Immigration, 6 April 2010.

118 Aïchoune, *Nés en banlieue*, p. 60.

119 Hamon and Rotman, *Génération. 2.*, p. 548.

120 Aïchoune, *Nés en banlieue*, p. 58.

121 Television news footage broadcast Antenne 2, 5 January 1984, extract included in *Douce France* (1992), dir. Ken Fero and Mogniss Abdallah, also cited in Mogniss Abdallah, 'Le 17 octobre 1961 et les médias: de la couverture de l'histoire immediate au "travail de mémoire" ', *Hommes et Migrations*, no. 1228 (November-December 2000), p. 130.

122 *Sans Frontière*, 26 February 1980.

123 Noiriel, *Longwy*.

124 Lumley, *States of Emergency*, pp. 308-310; Alberto Asor Rosa, *La due società*, Turin: Einaudi, 1977.

125 Abse, 'Professor in the Balaclava'; Edwards, 'Autonomia', pp. 276-278.

126 Gastaut, *L'immigration et l'opinion*, p. 496; *Sans Frontière*, March 1983 and Summer 1983.

127 Simone Bonnafous, 'Où sont passé les "*immigrés*"?', *Cahiers de la Méditerrannée*, no. 54 (June 1997), pp. 97-107.

128 Gastaut, *L'immigration et l'opinion*, pp. 493-495, 498-502; Christofferson, *French Socialists in Power*, pp. 117-118.

129 Jonathan Marcus, *The National Front and French Politics*, Basingstoke: Macmillan, 1995, pp. 53-54; *Presse et Immigrés en France*, no. 104-105 (March-April 1983), *Insécurité et Immigration*.

130 Bouamama, *Dix ans*, pp. 54-55.

131 Marcus, *National Front*, p. 79.

132 Abou-Sada, 'Générations', p. 23; Christofferson, *French Socialists in Power*, p. 116; Bouamama, *Dix ans*, p. 44; Gastaut, *L'immigration et l'opinion*, p. 538-

544; Saïd Bouamama, *J'y suis, j'y vote*, Paris: L'Esprit Frappeur, 2000, p. 59.

133 Adrian Favell, *Philosophies of Integration*, Basingstoke: Macmillan, 1998, pp. 40-93; Laborde, *Critical Republicanism*; Emile Chabal, 'Writing the French national narrative in the twenty-first century', *Historical Journal*, vol. 53, no. 2 (June 2010), pp. 495-516. For a critique of the ideology behind 'integration', see Azouz Begag, *L'intégration*, Paris: Le Cavalier Bleu, 2003.

134 Hamon and Rotman, *Génération*, vol. 2, p. 688.

135 Aïchoune, *Nés en banlieue*, p. 56; *Sans Frontière*, April 1983.

136 Bouamama, *Dix ans*, p. 23; Blanchard, *Paris Arabe*, p. 213. Even *Sans Frontière* made only a passing comparison to the general strike of 1973: *Sans Frontière*, October 1983.

137 Turpin, *Révolutionnaires*, p. 99; Bouamama, *Dix ans*, pp. 57-61; Derderian, *North Africans*, pp. 29-30.

138 Paul Oriol, interview with author, Paris, 2 January 2006; Guy Philippon, 'Paul Oriol ou la tenacité à construire L'égalité des droits entre Français et Immigrés', http://www.philippon.org/psu/index.php?2010/11/23/96-paul-oriol-ou-la-tenacite-a-construire-legalite-des-droits-entre-francais-et-immigres, 23 November 2010.

139 Stora, *Dernière génération d'octobre*, pp. 248-251.

140 Boubeker, *Mondes de l'ethnicité*, p. 223.

141 Yamina Benguigui, *Mémoires d'immigrés*, Paris: Albin Michel, 1999, p. 207.

142 Ahmed Boubeker, ' "La petite histoire" d'une generation d'expérience. Du mouvement beur aux banlieues d'Islam', in Boubeker and Hajjat, *Histoire politique*, p. 181-182; testimony of Kaïssa Titous in the film *Douce France*.

Epilogue

1 *Guardian*, 12 February 2011.

2 Driss El Yazami, 'France's ethnic minority press' in Alec Hargreaves and Mark McKinney, eds, *Post-Colonial Cultures in France*, London: Routledge, 1997, p. 123; Alec Hargreaves, *Multi-Ethnic France*, New York: Routledge, 2007; Françoise Gaspard and Claude Servan-Schreiber, *La fin des immigrés*, Paris: Seuil, 1985.

3 A powerful mobilising myth on the French Left, denoting the 'great night' when the Revolution will finally come.

4 Tangui Perron, *Histoire d'une film, mémoire d'une lutte. 1: Le Dos au Mur*, Paris: Scope, 2007, pp. 106, 107.

5 Steve Jeffreys, *Liberté, Egalité and Fraternité at Work*, Basingstoke: Palgrave Macmillan, 2003, p. 238.

6 Douglas Holmes, *Integral Europe*, Princeton: Princeton University Press, 2000.

7 Gérard Noiriel, *Immigration, antisémitisme et racisme en France (XIX-XXe siècles)*, Paris: Fayard, 2007, pp. 575-612.

8 Morgan Sportès, *Ils ont tué Pierre Overney*, Paris: Grasset, 2008, p. 142; Abderrazak Bouazizi Horchani, 'Notre frère et ami Ali Majri alias Ali Clichy vient de nous quitter', http://www.atf-paris.fr/spip.php?article509, 28 February 2011.

9   Eric Conan, *La gauche sans le peuple*, Paris: Fayard, 2004; Rémi Lefebvre and
        Frédéric Sawicki, *La société des socialistes*, Broisseux: Croquant, 2006; Didier
        Eribon, *D'une révolution conservatrice*, Paris: Leo Scheer, 2007.

10   Ahmed Boubeker, *Les mondes de l'ethnicité*, Paris: Balland, 2003, p. 165.

11   Adil Jazouli, *L'action collective des jeunes maghrébins de France*, Paris: CIEMI,
        1986, p. 154.

12   Driss El Yazami, 'Les beurs entre la mémoire et le débat', in *La Beur génération*,
        1984, quoted in Catherine Polac, 'Quand "les immigrés" prennent la parole',
        in Pascal Perrineau, ed, *L'engagement politique*, Paris: Presses de Sciences Po,
        1994, p. 374, and in Richard Derderian, *North Africans in Contemporary France*,
        New York: Palgrave Macmillan, 2004, p. 40; Thomas Lacroix, 'L'engagement
        citoyen des Marocains de l'étranger', *Hommes et Migrations*, no. 1256 (July-
        August 2005), pp. 96-97.

13   Farid Aïchoune, *Nés en banlieue*, Paris: Ramsay, 1991, pp. 21, 13.

14   Aïchoune, *Nés en banlieue*, p. 24.

15   Mireille Rosello, *Postcolonial Hospitality*, Stanford: Stanford University Press,
        2001, p. 2.

16   Jim House and Neil MacMaster, *Paris 1961*, Oxford: Oxford University Press,
        2006, Part 2.

17   Centre d'Information et de Documentation sur l'Immigration et le Maghreb,
        Marseilles, invitation.

18   For example, Abdellali Hajjat, 'Mémoire des luttes de l'immigration, immigrés
        en lutte', *Origines Contrôlées*, no. 2 (October 2006), pp. 10-11.

19   *Immigration et luttes sociales: filiations et ruptures (1968-2003)*, special issue of
        Migrance, no. 25, (3rd trimester 2005).

20   Tangui Perron, 'Le territoire des images: pratique du cinema et luttes ouvrières
        en Seine-Saint-Denis (1968-1982)', *Le Mouvement Social*, no. 230 (January-
        March 2010), pp. 127-143; Tangui Perron, *Histoire d'un film, mémoire d'une
        lutte*, talk at Cité Nationale de l'Histoire de l'Immigration, Paris, 6 April 2010.

21   For example, Alain Krivine, *Ca te passera avec l'âge*, Paris: Flammarion, 2006.

22   Daniel Gordon, 'Controlling the streets in May 1968' in Jessica Wardhaugh, ed,
        Paris and the Right in the Twentieth Century, Newcastle: Cambridge Scholars,
        2007, pp. 104-121; Daniel Gordon, 'Liquidating May '68: generational
        trajectories of the 2007 presidential candidates', *Modern and Contemporary
        France*, vol. 16, no. 2 (May 2008), pp. 143-159; Serge Audier, *La pensée anti-68*,
        Paris: La Découverte, 2008.

23   Daniel Gordon, 'History At Last? 1968-2008', *Modern and Contemporary
        France*, vol. 17, no. 3 (August 2009), pp. 335-342; Daniel Gordon, 'Memories
        of 1968 in France: reflections on the fortieth anniversary', in Sarah Waters and
        Ingo Cornils, eds, *Memories of 1968*, Bern: Peter Lang, 2010, pp. 49-78.

24   Philippe Raynaud, *L'extrême gauche plurielle*, Paris: Autrement, 2006, pp. 69-
        70.

25   Pierre Juquin, *De battre mon coeur n'a jamais cessé*, Paris: Archipel, 2006, pp.
        284-285, 568-580; Marie-George Buffet, 'L'école de mon enfance' video, www.
        mariegeorge2007.org, April 2007, and campaign broadcast, France 2, 16 April
        2007.

26 House and McMaster, *Paris 1961*, p. 283; Phillippe Bernard, *La crème des Beurs*, Paris: Seuil, 2004, pp. 297-313; *Sans-Frontière*, 1 May 1979.

27 Xavier Crettiez and Isabelle Sommier eds, *La France Rebelle*, Paris: Michalon, 2006, p. 372.

28 Bernard, *Crème des Beurs*, pp. 137-156.

29 Alima Boumediene-Thiery, 'Ma vie telle que racontée souvent à la presse', http://alima-boumediene.org.spip.php?article11, 30 June 2003; Alima Boumediene-Thiery, 'Qui est Alima Boumediene-Thiery', http://alima-boumediene.org.spip.php?article35, 26 September 2004.

30 Saïd Bouziri, 'Une démocratie riche de voix', *Hommes et Libertés*, no. 136 (October-December 2006), p. 17; Séverine Lacalmontie, 'A l'avant-garde de la cause? Les militants du PSU et la cause du droit de vote des immigrés', in Tudi Kernalegenn and François Prigent, eds, *Le PSU vu d'en bas*, Rennes: Presses Universitaires de Rennes, 2009, pp. 317-326; Jean-Pierre Dacheux, 'A quand le suffrage universel?', *La Lettre de la Citoyenneté*, July-August 2011; Fédération des Tunisiens pour une Citoyenneté des deux Rives, 'Février 1974: Il y a 36 ans naissait l'UTIT (FTCR)', http://www.citoyensdesdeuxrives.eu, 18 February 2010.

31 Maurice Goldring, *La Goutte d'Or, quartier de France*, Paris: Autrement, 2006, pp. 28, 150-175.

32 Raynaud, *L'extrême gauche plurielle*, pp. 168, 173-174; Jonathan Ervine, 'French cinema's representation of enforced return migration', in Scott Soo and Sharif Gemie, eds, *Coming Home?*, vol 3, Newcastle: Cambridge Scholars, 2011; *L'Humanité*, 6 November 2007.

33 Abdellali Hajjat, 'Révolte des quartiers populaires, crise du militantisme et postcolonialisme', in Ahmed Boubeker and Abdellali Hajjat, eds, *Histoire politique des immigrations (post)coloniales*, Paris: Amsterdam, 2008, p. 258.

34 Sharif Gemie, *French Muslims*, Cardiff: University of Wales Press, 2010, p. 143.

35 Saïd Bouamama, 'Les indigènes de la république', http://www.indigenes-republique.org/spip.php?article37, 15 March 2006.

36 See Génériques' journal *Migrance*, and its website www.generiques.org.

37 Brigitte Jelen, ' "Leur histoire est notre histoire": immigrant culture in France between visibility and invisibility', *French Politics, Culture and Society*, vol. 23, no. 2 (Summer 2005), pp. 111-118; Hajjat, 'Mémoires'.

38 Eric Agrikoliansky et al, *L'altermondialisme en France*, Paris: Flammarion, 2005.

39 Daniel Gordon, 'The tower of Babel comes to north London', *The Voice of the Turtle*, http://www.voiceoftheturtle.org, October 2004.

40 Hargreaves, *Multi-Ethnic France*, pp. 133-135.

41 Alain Morice, 'Le mouvement des sans-papiers ou la difficile mobilisation collective des individualismes', in Boubeker and Hajjat, *Histoire politique*, pp. 132-133.

42 *Libération*, 31 August 2005.

43 Brigitte Wieser et al, 'Militer, un jeu d'enfant', *Projet*, no. 321 (April-May 2011), pp. 4-19.

44 Bertrand Delanoë, 'Réaction suite au décès de Saïd Bouziri', www.paris.fr/portail/acceuil/Portal.lut?page_id=8447&document_type_id=7&document_

id=70655&portlet_id=19708, 24 June 2009.

45   Randy Shaw, *Beyond the Fields*, Berkeley: University of California Press, 2008, p. 92.

46   Olivier Piot, *La révolution tunisienne*, Paris: Les Petits Matins, 2011, pp. 142-143; Hamma Hammami, *Le chemin de la dignité*, Paris: Comité National et Comité International de Soutien à Hamma Hammami et Ses Camarades, 2002; Myriam Marzouki, 'Curriculum Vitae: le médécin et le militant', http://moncefmarzouki.com/spip.php?article41, 21 July 2005; Pierre Puchot, *Tunisie, une révolution arabe*, Paris: Galaade, 2011, pp. 101-106; Fayçal Anseur, 'Interview exclusive du Président Abdel Jelil Bedoui: le PTT crée son parti travailliste en Tunisie', http://www.algerie-focus.com, 3 May 2011.

47   France 24 news, 15 January 2011; *Mail on Sunday*, 16 January 2011; *Sunday Telegraph*, 16 January 2011; Parti des Indigènes de la République, 'The Tunisian Revolution: a source of inspiration to our *quartiers*', in Clare Solomon and Tania Palmieri, eds, *Springtime*, London: Verso, 2011, pp. 250-251.

48   *Sud-Ouest*, 23 April 2011.

49   *Le Monde*, 19 April 2011; *Sud-Ouest*, 24 April 2011; Association Nationale d'Assistance aux Frontières pour les Etrangers and Groupe d'Information et de Soutien des Immigrés, *L'Europe vacille sous le fantasme de l'invasion tunisienne*, Paris: ANAFE/GISTI, 2011.

50   European Parliament footage, BBC Democracy Live, http://news.bbc.co.uk/democracylive, 17 January and 10 May 2011.

51   *Libération*, 17 June 2011; *Le Monde*, 22 June 2011; *L'Humanité*, 15 July 2011.

52   Aurore Chéry, 'La Cité Nationale de l'Histoire de l'Immigration ou le musée schizophrène', paper to Association for the Study of Modern and Contemporary France conference, Stirling University, 1-3 September 2011.

53   Ahmed El Attar, *On The Importance of Being An Arab*, Liverpool Arabic Arts Festival, 8 July 2011.

54   Ali Amar, *Mohammed VI*, Paris: Calmann-Lévy, 2009, pp. 204-219; Salah Elayoubi, 'Règlements de comptes à Clermont-Ferrand: El Ghazaoui contre El Yazami', http://solidmar.blogspot.com/2011/08/zineb-el-ghazoui-demasque-driss-el.html, 26 August 2011.

55   Nadia Rabbaa, 'Driss El Yazami: les différents visages des droits de l'homme', *Le Courrier de l'Atlas*, April 2011.

Bibliography

1. Archives

Archives Départementales de la Seine-Saint-Denis, Bobigny
2 AV 268/5256-5257

Archives Départementales des Hauts-de-Seine, Nanterre
44 J 227; 45 J 189, 331, 594-595

Archives Départementales du Val-de-Marne, Créteil
1 J 1192; 6 J 96/13, 96/16, 105/6

Archives Nationales, Paris
600 Mi 50, 75

Bibliothèque de Documentation International Contemporaine, Nanterre
4 DELTA 156 RES; 9 PIECE 8078; F DELTA 721/96; F DELTA RES 612, 688, 813; Mfc 214; O PIECE 380 RES, 557 RES; Q PIECE 611 RES

Bibliothèque Nationale, Paris
Document du secrétariat du comité central du Parti Communiste Français sur les tâches du parti parmis les travailleurs immigrés, 5 May 1963
Comité de Solidarité avec les Travailleurs Immigrés de Savoie, 'Le CSTIS pour quoi faire?', 1975

Centre des Archives Contemporaines, Fontainebleau
19820599, articles 40-41, 43, 76; 19860146, article 3; 19870056, articles 7, 12; 19890519, article 10, liasse 3; 19900353, article 19, liasse 2; 19910194, article 1, liasse 2, article 3, liasse 3, article 11, liasse 1, article 13, liasse 4 and article 14, liasse 4

Centre d'Histoire du Travail, Nantes
PSU 46-50

Centre d'Information et de Documentation sur l'Immigration et le Maghreb, Marseilles
Mouvement des Travailleurs Arabes archives, uncatalogued

CFDT Archives Confédérales, Paris
4 W 85-86; 7 H 43-44, 47-48, 61, 727, 730, 733-735, 747; 8 H 1763

Institut Français d'Histoire Sociale, Paris
14 AS 238, 250

MRAP Archives, Paris
'Travailleurs immigrés 1968-1978' box, uncatalogued

Guy Phillippon private archives, Paris
PSU 20th arrondissement branch archives, uncatalogued

University of Sussex Library
Mai 1968 Archive

2. Interviews and personal communications

Neal Ascherson, London, 8 May 2001, and email, 8 July 2011
Saïd Bouziri, Paris, 6 November 2004
Anne Couteau and Paul Oriol, Paris, 2 January 2006 and Issy-les-Moulineaux, 10 April 2010
Jean-Jacques Lebel, London, 17 March 2000
Peter Lennon, Liverpool, 31 October 2007
Jill Lovecy, Liverpool, 31 October 2007
Nanterre residents, Nanterre, 20 May 2008
Guy Phillippon, Paris, 5 January 2006
PSU activists, Rennes, 9-10 September 2008
Paul Werner, emails, 9 and 15 January 2002

3. Newspapers and magazines

Action
Afrique-Action
Al Assifa
L'Aurore
Bulletin de Liaison du CEDETIM

La Cause du Peuple
Class Struggle / Lutte de Classe
Combat
Comité d'Action Révolutionnaire Odéon
La Commune
Le Courrier de l'Atlas
Le Courrier Républicain de Seine et Seine-et-Oise
Droit et Liberté
Economist
L'Eveil
L'Evènement
L'Express
Fedaï
Le Figaro
France Soir
Guardian
L'Humanité
L'Humanité Nouvelle
Idiot International
Igloos
Independent
Index on Censorship
Jeunesse Ouvrière
Jewish Chronicle
Le Jounal du Dimanche Soir
Le Journal du Rhône
Al Kadihoun
Lavoro
La Lettre de la Citoyenneté
Libération
Lutte Ouvrière
Mail on Sunday
La Marseillaise
Masses Ouvrières
Le Monde
El Moudjahid
New Statesman
New York Times
Nice Matin
Nous Les Immigrés

Le Nouvel Observateur
L'Ouvrier Algérien
Pakistan Times
Le Paria
Paris-Presse L'Intransigeant
Perspectives Tunisiennes
Pour la Liberté
Le Provençal
PSU Documentation
Quatrième Internationale
Résistance Populaire
Rouge
Sans Frontière
Sight and Sound
Socialisme ou Barbarie
Solidarité Anti-Impérialiste
Statistiques de l'Immigration
Sud-Ouest
Sunday Telegraph
Sydney Morning Herald
Témoignage Chrétien
Times
Times Higher Education Supplement
Tout!
Travailleurs Français Immigrés Même Combat!
La Tribune de Genève
La Tribune de l'Immigration
La Tribune du Travailleur Algérien
La Tribune Socialiste
Le Travailleur Parisien
Vacarme
Vérité-Liberté
Vive la Révolution
La Voix du 11è

4. Books, articles and unpublished papers

Abadie, Frédéric and Corcelette, Jean-Pierre, *Valéry Giscard d'Estaing*, Paris: Balland, 1997
Abdallah, Mogniss, *J'y suis, j'y reste!*, Paris: Reflex, 2000

-, 'Le 17 octobre 1961 et les médias: de la couverture de l'histoire immediate au "travail de mémoire" ', *Hommes et Migrations*, no. 1228 (November-December 2000), p. 130

Abou-Sada, Georges and Milet, Hélène, eds, *Générations issues de l'immigration*, Paris: Arcantère, 1986

Abse, Toby, 'The professor in the balaclava: Toni Negri and autonomist politics', *What Next*, no. 22 (2002)

Ackaouy, Céline, *Un nom de papier*, Paris: Clancier-Guénaud, 1981

Actualité de l'Emigration, *17 octobre 1961*, Paris: Amicale des Algériens en Europe, 1987

Adams, Adrian, 'Prisoners in exile: Senegalese workers in France' in Robin Cohen et al, eds, *Peasants and Proletarians*, London: Hutchinson, 1979, pp. 307-330

Agence Im'média, *Sans-papiers: chronique d'un mouvement*, Paris: Reflex, 1997

Agrikoliansky, Eric, et al, *L'altermondialisme en France*, Paris: Flammarion, 2005

Aïchoune, Farid, *Nés en banlieue*, Paris: Ramsay, 1991

Aissaoui, Rabah, 'Immigration, ethnicity and national identity: Maghrebis' socio-political mobilisation and discourse in the inter-war period and during the 1970s in France', PhD thesis, University of Leeds, 2001

-, 'Political mobilisations of North African migrants in 1970s France: the case of the Movement des Travailleurs Arabes (MTA)', *Journal of Muslim Minority Affairs*, vol. 26, no. 2, August 2006, pp. 171-186

-, *Immigration and National Identity*, London: Tauris, 2009

Alfonsi, Phillippe and Pesnot, Patrick, *Vivre à gauche*, Paris: Albin Michel, 1975

Ali, Tariq, *1968 and After*, Colchester: Blond & Briggs, 1978

-, *Street Fighting Years*, London: Fontana, 1988

-, and Watkins, Susan, *1968: marching in the streets*, London: Bloomsbury, 1998

Allwood, Gill and Wadia, Khursheed, *Refugee Women in Britain and France*, Manchester: Manchester University Press, 2010

Althusser, Louis, *The Future Lasts a Long Time*, London: Vintage, 1994

Amar, Ali, *Mohammed VI*, Paris: Calmann-Lévy, 2009

Amar, Marianne and Milza, Pierre, *L'immigration en France au XXe siècle*, Paris: Armand Colin, 1990

Amiri, Linda, *La bataille de France*, Paris: Laffont, 2004

Andrlé, Vladimir, *A Social History of Twentieth Century Russia*, London: Hodder Arnold, 1994

Andro, Pierre, et al, *Le mai de la révolution*, Paris: Julliard, 1968

Anglade, Jean, *La vie quotidienne des immigrés en France de 1919 à nos jours*, Paris: Hachette, 1976

Anon, *Paris: May 1968*, London: Solidarity, 1986

Apostolo, Marius, *Traces de luttes 1924-2007*, Paris: Autrement, 2008

Ardagh, John, *The New French Revolution*, London: Secker & Warburg, 1968

-, *France in the New Century*, London: Viking, 1999

Arthur, Paige, 'The persistence of colonialism: Sartre, the Left, and identity in postcolonial France, 1970-1974', in Jonathan Judaken, ed, *Race After Sartre*, Albany: State University of New York Press, 2008, pp. 77-95

Artières, Philippe and Zancarini-Fournel, Michelle, eds, *68: une histoire collective [1962-1981]*, Paris: La Découverte, 2008

Asor Rosa, Alberto, *La due società*, Turin: Einaudi, 1977

Association Nationale d'Assistance aux Frontières pour les Etrangers and Groupe d'Information et de Soutien des Immigrés, *L'Europe vacille sous le fantasme de l'invasion tunisienne*, Paris: ANAFE/GISTI, 2011

Atelier Populaire, *Mai 68*, London: Dobson, 1969

Audier, Serge, *La pensée anti-68*, Paris: La Découverte, 2008

Aupetitallot, Yves, *Groupe de recherche d'art visuel*, Grenoble: Centre National d'Art Contemporain, 1998

Auron, Yaïr, *Les juifs d'extrême gauche en mai 68*, Paris: Albin Michel, 1998

Axelos, Loukas, 'Publishing activity and the movement of ideas in Greece', *Journal of the Hellenic Diaspora*, vol. 11, no. 2 (Summer 1984), pp. 5-46

Bachmann, Christian and Le Guennec, Nicole, *Violences urbaines*, Paris: Albin Michel, 1995

Bachy, François, *François Hollande*, Paris: Plon, 2001

Balibar, Etienne, 'De Charonne à Vitry', *Le Nouvel Observateur*, 9 March 1981, reprinted in *Les Frontières de la démocratie*, Paris: La Découverte, 1992, pp. 19-34

Barou, Jacques, *Travailleurs africains en France*, Grenoble: Presses Universitaires de Grenoble, 1978

Bathily, Aboulaye, *Mai 68 à Dakar*, Paris: Chaka, 1992

Bayat, Asef, 'Islamism and empire: the incongruous nature of Islamist anti-imperialism', *Socialist Register 2008*, pp. 38-54

Baynac, Jacques, *Mai retrouvé*, Paris: Laffont, 1978

Beaud, Stéphane and Pialoux, Michel, 'Racisme ouvrier ou mépris de classe? Retour sur une enquête de terrain', in Didier Fassin and Eric Fassin, eds, *De la question sociale à la question raciale?*, Paris: La Découverte, 2009, pp. 80-

98

Begag, Azouz, *L'intégration*, Paris: Le Cavalier Bleu, 2003

-, *Shantytown Kid*, Lincoln, Nebraska: University of Nebraska Press, 2007

Bel, Monique, *Maurice Clavel*, Paris: Bayard, 1992

Bell, David and Criddle, Byron, *The French Socialist Party*, Oxford: Clarendon, 1988

Benaïcha, Brahim, *Vivre au paradis*, Paris: Desclée de Brouwer, 1992

Benguigui, Yamina, *Mémoires d'immigrés*, Paris: Albin Michel, 1999

Ben Jelloun, Tahar, *French Hospitality*, New York: Columbia University Press, 1999

Bensaïd, Daniel, *Une lente impatience*, Paris: Stock, 2004

Berger, John and Mohr, Jean, *A Seventh Man*, London: Verso, 2010

Bernard, Philippe, *La crème des Beurs*, Paris: Seuil, 2004

Bertolino, Jean, *Les trublions*, Paris: Stock, 1969

Biard, Roland, *Dictionnaire de l'extrême gauche*, Paris: Belfond, 1978

Bibliothèque Nationale, *Les tracts de mai 1968*, microfilm, Leiden, 1987

Birchall, Ian, 'France 1968' in Colin Barker, ed, *Revolutionary Rehearsals*, London: Bookmarks, 1987, pp. 5-40

-, 'Seizing the time: Tony Cliff and 1968', *International Socialism*, no. 118 (Spring 2008)

Bizot, Jean-François, *Au parti des socialistes*, Paris: Grasset, 1975

Blackburn, Robin, 'The test in Portugal', *New Left Review*, nos 87-88 (September-December 1974), pp. 5-46

Blanchard, Pascal, et al, *Le Paris Arabe*, Paris: La Découverte, 2003

Boel, Bent, 'French support for Eastern European dissidents, 1968-1989: approaches and controversies', in Poul Villaume and Odd Arne Westad, eds, *Perforating the Iron Curtain*, Copenhagen: Museum Tusculanum, 2010, pp. 215-241

Bonnafous, Simone, 'Où sont passé les "*immigrés*"?', *Cahiers de la Méditerrannée*, no. 54 (June 1997), pp. 97-107

Bonnet, Serge, 'Political alignment and religious attitudes within the Italian immigration to the metallurgical districts of Lorraine', *Journal of Social History*, vol. 2, no. 2 (Winter 1968), pp. 123-155

Bookchin, Murray, '1960s: Myth and Reality', in *Anarchism, Marxism and the Future of the Left*, Edinburgh: AK Press, 1999, pp. 59-111

Bouamama, Saïd, *Dix ans de marche des Beurs*, Paris: Desclée de Brouwer, 1994

-, *J'y suis, j'y vote*, Paris: L'Esprit Frappeur, 2000

- et al, *Contribution à la mémoire des banlieues*, Paris: Volga, 1994

Boubeker, Ahmed, *Les mondes de l'ethnicité*, Paris: Balland, 2003

- and Beau, Nicolas, *Chroniques métissées*, Paris: Alain Moreau, 1986

- and Hajjat, Abdellali, eds, *Histoire politique des immigrations (post) coloniales*, Paris: Amsterdam, 2008

Bourderon, Roger and de Perretti, Pierre, eds, *Histoire de Saint-Denis*, Toulouse: Privat, 1988

Bourdieu, Pierre and Passeron, Jean-Claude, *Les héritiers*, Paris: Minuit, 1964

Bourg, Julian, *From Revolution to Ethics*, Montreal: McGill-Queen's University Press, 2007

Bourseiller, Christophe, *Les maoïstes*, Paris: Seuil, 1996

Boutelier, Denis and Subramanian, Dilip, *Mon Eldorado la France?*, Paris: Denoël, 1997

Bouziri, Saïd, 'Une démocratie riche de voix', *Hommes et Libertés*, no. 136 (October-December 2006)

- and El Yazami, Driss, 'Prendre la peine', *Migrance*, no. 14 (1st trimester 1999), pp. 2-4

Bracke, Maud, 'May 1968 and Algerian immigrants in France: trajectories of mobilization and encounter', in Gurminder Bhambra and Ipek Demir, eds, *1968 In Retrospect*, Basingstoke: Palgrave Macmillan, 2009, pp. 115-130

-, 'Our first discovery was our housework: 1970s feminist debate on women's work between Italy and Britain', paper to *The Limits of Transnationalism* conference, Exeter University, 30 March 2011

Branciard, Michel, *Un syndicat face à la guerre d'Algérie*, Paris: Syros, 1984

-, *Histoire de la CFDT*, Paris: La Découverte, 1990

Brau, Jean-Louis, *Cours camarade, le vieux monde est derrière toi!*, Paris: Albin Michel, 1968

Bresson, Gilles and Lionet, Christian, *Le Pen*, Paris: Seuil, 1994

Brettell, Caroline, 'Emigration and its implications for the revolution in northern Portugal', in Lawrence Graham and Harry Makler, eds, *Contemporary Portugal*, Austin: University of Texas Press, 1979, pp. 281-298

Brière-Blanchet, Claire, *Voyage au bout de la révolution*, Paris: Fayard, 2009

Brillaut, Olivier, 'L'expulsion des étrangers en France', doctoral thesis, University of Nice, 1982

Brocheux, Pierre, *Ho Chi Minh*, Cambridge: Cambridge University Press, 2007

Brunet, Jean-Paul, *Charonne*, Paris, 2003

Buffet, Marie-George, *Un peu de courage!*, Paris: Cherche Midi, 2004

Cahiers Révolution!, *Travailleurs français immigrés même combat*, Paris:

Maspero, 1971

Caraib, Frair, 'La Guadeloupe opprimée', *Les Temps Modernes*, no. 256 (September 1967), pp. 485-488

Carillo, Santiago, *Memorias*, Barcelona: Planeta, 1994

Carr, Raymond and Fusi Aizpurua, Juan Pablo, *Spain*, London: Allen & Unwin, 1989

Casas, Raymond, *Mémoires à nos petits-enfants*, vol. 2, Blois: Raymond Casas, 1998

Castells, Manuel, 'Citizen movements, information and analysis: an interview', *City*, no 7 (May 1997), pp. 140-155

Castles, Stephen, *Ethnicity and Globalization*, London: Sage, 2000

- and Kosack, Godula, *Immigrant Workers and Class Structure in Western Europe*, Oxford: Oxford University Press, 1973

Castoriadis, Cornelius, *Political and Social Writings*, vol. 1, Minneapolis: University of Minnesota Press, 1988

Castro, Roland, *1989*, Paris: Bernard Barrault, 1984

Caute, David, *Sixty-Eight*, London: Paladin, 1988

CEDETIM, *Les immigrés*, Paris: Stock, 1975

Cerny, Phil, ed, *Social Movements and Protest in France*, London: Pinter, 1982

Césaire, Aimé, *Letter to Maurice Thorez*, Paris: Présence Africaine, 1957

CGT, *Questions de l'immigration et syndicat*, Paris: CGT, 1981

Chabal, Emile, 'Writing the French national narrative in the twenty-first century', *Historical Journal*, vol. 53, no. 2 (June 2010), pp. 495-516

Charby, Jacques, *Les porteurs d'espoir*, Paris: La Découverte, 2004

Charpier, Frédéric, *Génération Occident*, Paris: Seuil, 2005

Chatwin, Bruce, *What Am I Doing Here*, London: Picador, 1990

Chérel, Guillaume, *Le fils caché de Trotsky*, Paris: Derrey, 2002

Chéry, Aurore, 'La Cité Nationale de l'Histoire de l'Immigration ou le musée schizophrène', paper to Association for the Study of Modern and Contemporary France conference, Stirling University, 1-3 September 2011

Chevandier, Christian, *Les tourments d'une génération*, Montreuil: Au Lieux d'Etre, 2008

Christofferson, Michael, *French Intellectuals Against The Left*, New York: Berghahn, 2004

Christofferson, Thomas, *The French Socialists in Power, 1981-1986*, Newark: University of Delaware Press, 1991

Clark, Robert, *The Basque Insurgents*, Madison: University of Wisconsin Press, 1984

Clavel, Maurice, *Combat de franc-tireur pour une libération*, Paris: Jean-

Jacques Pauvert, 1968

Clemons, Michael and Jones, Charles, 'Global solidarity: the BPP in the international arena', in Kathleen Cleaver and George Katsiaficas, eds, *Liberation, Imagination and the Black Panther Party*, New York: Routledge, 2001, pp. 20-39

Cliff, Tony and Birchall, Ian, *France: the struggle goes on*, London: Socialist Review, 1968

Clochardet, Olivier, et al, 'Les camps d'étrangers depuis 1938: continuité et adaptations. Du "modèle" français à la construction de l'espace Schengen', *Revue européene des migrations internationales*, vol. 20, no. 2 (2004), pp. 57-85

Cohn-Bendit, Daniel, *Nous l'avons tant l'aimée, la révolution*, Paris: Bernard Barrault, 1986

- and Kouchner, Bernard, *Quand tu seras président*, Paris: Laffont, 2004

Comité de Solidarité avec les Travailleurs Immigrés, *Vie et luttes des travailleurs immigrés*, Marseilles: Comité de Solidarité avec les Travailleurs Immigrés, 1973

Commission Internationale des Juristes, 'Expulsions d'étrangers', *Migrations*, no. 13 (Autumn 1969)

Conan, Eric, *La gauche sans le peuple*, Paris: Fayard, 2004

Converse, Philip and Pierce, Roy, *Political Representation in France*, Cambridge, MA: Harvard University Press, 1986

Cooper, Nicola, *France in Indochina*, Oxford: Berg, 2001

Cordeiro, Albano, 'Les Portugais, une population "invisible"', in Philippe Dewitte, ed, *Immigration et intégration*, Paris, 1999, pp. 106-112

Costa-Lascoux, Jacqueline, and Temime, Emile, *Les hommes de Renault-Billancourt*, Paris: Autrement, 2004

Coudray, Jean-Marc, 'La révolution anticipée', in Edgar Morin et al, *Mai 1968, la brèche*, Paris: Fayard, 1968, pp. 89-142

Courtois, Stéphane, et al, *Le sang de l'étranger*, Paris: Fayard, 1989

Cravo, Antonio, *Les Portugais en France et leur mouvement associatif (1901-1986)*, Paris: L'Harmattan, 1995

Crettiez, Xavier and Sommier, Isabelle, eds, *La France Rebelle*, Paris: Michalon, 2006

Criddle, Byron, 'The Parti Socialiste Unifié: an appraisal after ten years', *Parliamentary Affairs*, vol. 24, no. 2 (Spring 1971), pp. 140-163

Crouch, Colin and Pizzorno, Alessandro, eds, *The Resurgence of Class Conflict in Western Europe Since 1968*, 2 vols, London: Macmillan, 1978

Dainotto, Roberto, 'The discreet charm of the Arabist theory: Juan Andrés, historicism, and the decentring of Montesquieu's Europe', *European History Quarterly*, vol. 36, no. 1 (January 2006), pp. 7-29

Dalla Costa, Mariarosa and James, Selma, *The Power of Women and the Subversion of the Community*, Bristol: Falling Wall, 1972

Daoud, Zakya, *De l'immigration à la citoyenneté*, Casablanca: Mémoire de la Méditerranée, 2003

Dartnell, Michael, *Action Directe*, London: Frank Cass, 1995

DeAngelis, Richard, *Blue-Collar Workers and Politics*, London: Croom Helm, 1982

De Beauvoir, Simone, *Force of Circumstance*, London: André Deutsch, 1965

De Bosschère, Guy, 'En Afrique, mai explose en juin', *Esprit*, nos 8-9 (August-September 1968), pp. 179-181

De Blaye, Edouard, *Franco and the Politics of Spain*, Harmondsworth: Penguin, 1976

Debray, Régis, *Praised Be Our Lords*, London: Verso, 2007

Declair, Edward, *Politics on the Fringe*, Durham: Duke University Press, 1999

Delale, Alain and Ragache, Gilles, *La France de 68*, Paris: Seuil, 1978

Delorme, Christian, *Par amour et par colère*, Paris: Le Centurion, 1985

De Maupeou-Abboud, Nicole, *Les blousons bleus*, Paris: Armand Colin, 1968

Derderian, Richard, *North Africans in Contemporary France*, New York: Palgrave Macmillan, 2004

Desolre, Guy, 'Les travailleurs immigrés en Europe occidentale', *Partisans*, no. 28 (April 1966), pp. 9-19

De Staal, Gilles, *Mamadou m'a dit*, Paris: Syllepse, 2008

Dewerpe, Alain, *Charonne 8 fevrier 1962*, Paris: Gallimard, 2006

Dieuzaide, Jean, *Mai 68 à Toulouse*, Toulouse: Galerie Municipale du Château d'Eau, 1998

Dray, Julien, *SOS Génération*, Paris: Ramsay, 1987

Dressen, Marnix, *De l'amphi à l'établi*, Paris: Belin, 1999

Dreyfus-Armand, Geneviève, 'L'arrivée des immigrés sur la scène politique', *IHTP. Les années 68: événements, cultures politiques et modes de vie. Lettre d'information*, no. 30 (June 1998), pp. 9-29

-, *L'exil des républicains espagnols en France*, Paris: Albin Michel, 1999

- and Gervereau, Laurent, eds, *Mai 68*, Nanterre: BDIC, 1988

- et al, *Les années 68*, Brussels: Complexe, 2000

Duchen, Claire, *Feminism in France*, London: Routledge & Kegan Paul, 1986

Duclert, Vincent, 'La "deuxième gauche"' in Jean-Jacques Becker and Gilles

Candar, eds, *Histoire des gauches en France*, vol 2, Paris: La Découverte, 2004, pp. 175-196

Ducrocq, Serge, *Histoire de la CGT à Nanterre*, Paris: Messidor, 1988

Duhourcq, Jean-Claude and Madrigal, Antoine, *Mouvement ibérique de liberation*, Toulouse: CRAS, 2007

Editions Points, *"Vous frappez à tort et à travers"*, Paris: Points, 2009

Edwards, Philip, 'Autonomia and the political: an Italian cycle of contention, 1972-1979', *Modern Italy*, vol. 11, no. 3 (November 2006), pp. 267-283

Einaudi, Jean-Luc, *La Bataille de Paris*, Paris: Seuil, 1991

-, *Franc-Tireur*, Paris: Sextant, 2004

El Yazami, Driss, 'France's ethnic minority press' in Alec Hargreaves and Mark McKinney, eds, *Post-Colonial Cultures in France*, London: Routledge, 1997, pp. 115-130

Eribon, Didier, *Michel Foucault*, Cambridge, MA: Harvard University Press, 1991

-, *D'une révolution conservatrice*, Paris: Leo Scheer, 2007

Ervine, Jonathan, 'French cinema's representation of enforced return migration', in Scott Soo and Sharif Gemie, eds, *Coming Home?*, vol 3, Newcastle: Cambridge Scholars, 2011

Evans, Martin, *The Memory of Resistance*, Oxford: Berg, 1997

Evans, Richard, *The German Working Class 1888-1933*, London: Croom Helm, 1982

Fanon, Frantz, *The Wretched of the Earth*, New York: Grove, 2004

Farrugia, Laurent, *Le fait national guadeloupéen*, Ivry: Laurent Farrugia, 1968

Favell, Adrian, *Philosophies of Integration*, Basingstoke: Macmillan, 1998

-, 'Integration Policy and Integration Research in Europe: a review and a critique', in Alexander Aleinikoff and Doug Klusmeyer, eds, *Citizenship Today*, Washington: Carnegie Endowment, 2000, pp. 349-399

Ferguson, Niall, *Civilisation*, London: Allen Lane, 2011

Ferreira, Hugo Gil and Marshall, Michael, *Portugal's Revolution*, Cambridge: Cambridge University Press, 1986

Ferry, Luc and Renaut, Alain, *La pensée 68*, Paris: Gallimard, 1985

Fields, A. Belden, 'French Maoism', in Sohnya Sayres et al, eds, *The 60s Without Apology*, Minneapolis: University of Minnesota Press, 1984, pp. 148-177

-, *Trotskyism and Maoism*, New York: Praeger, 1988

Fiévet, Michel, *Le livre blanc des travailleurs immigrés des foyers*, Paris:

L'Harmattan, 1999

Fillieule, Olivier, ed, *Le désengagement militant*, Paris: Belin, 2005

Fisera, Vladimir, *Writing on the Wall*, London: Alison & Busby, 1978

Follain, John, *Jackal*, London: Weidenfeld & Nicolson, 1998

Fourel, Christophe, ed, *André Gorz*, Paris: La Découverte, 2009

Foweraker, Joe, *Making Democracy in Spain*, Cambridge: Cambridge University Press, 1989

Fraenkel, Boris, *Profession: révolutionnaire*, Latresne: Le Bord de l'Eau, 2004

Francfort, Didier, 'From the other side of the mirror: the French-German border in landscape and memory', in Henrice Altink and Sharif Gemie, eds, *At The Border*, Cardiff: University of Wales Press, 2008, pp. 79-95

Fraser, Ronald, 'Spain on the brink', *New Left Review*, no. 96 (March-April 1976), pp. 3-33

- et al, *1968: a student generation in revolt*, London: Chatto & Windus, 1988

Frears, John, *Political Parties and Electors in the French Fifth Republic*, London: Hurst, 1978

Freeman, Gary, *Immigrant Labor and Racial Conflict in Industrial Societies*, Princeton: Princeton University Press, 1979

Fremontier, Jacques, *La forteresse ouvrière*, Paris: Fayard, 1971

Fysh, Peter and Wolfreys, Jim, *The Politics of Racism in France*, Basingstoke: Macmillan, 1998

Gallant, Mavis, *Paris Notebooks*, London: Bloomsbury, 1988

Gallissot, Réné, 'La guerre et l'immigration algérienne en France', in Jean-Pierre Rioux, eds, *La Guerre d'Algérie et les Français*, Paris: Fayard, 1992, pp. 337-347

-, *Henri Curiel*, Paris: Riveneuve, 2009.

Garton Ash, Timothy, *History of the Present*, London: Penguin, 2000

Gascon, Roger, *La nuit du pouvoir*, Paris: Debresse, 1968

Gaspard, Françoise, *A Small City in France*, Cambridge, MA: Harvard University Press, 1995

- and Servan-Schreiber, Claude, *La fin des immigrés*, Paris: Seuil, 1985

Gasquet, Vasco, *Les 500 affiches de mai 68*, Paris: Balland, 1978

Gastaut, Yvan, *L'immigration et l'opinion en France sous la Ve République*, Paris: Seuil, 2000

Geismar, Alain, et al, *Vers la guerre civile*, Paris: Premières, 1969

Gemie, Sharif, *French Muslims*, Cardiff: University of Wales Press, 2010

Génériques, *Les étrangers en France*, 3 vols, Paris: Génériques, 1999

Genève, Pierre, *Histoire secrète de l'insurrection de mai*, Paris: Presses Noires, 1968

Georgi, Frank, *L'invention de la CFDT 1957-1970*, Paris: L'Atelier, 1995

Geras, Norman, *The Contract of Mutual Indifference*, London: Verso, 1998

Gervereau, Laurent, et al, *Toute la France*, Paris: Somogny, 1998

Gilmour, David, *The Transformation of Spain*, London: Quartet, 1985

Giudice, Fausto, *Arabicides*, Paris: La Découverte, 1992

Givet, Jacques, *Le cas Vergès*, Paris: Lieu Commun, 1986

Gobille, Boris, *Mai 68*, Paris: La Découverte, 2008

Goldhagen, Daniel *Hitler's Willing Executioners*, New York: Alfred A. Knopf, 1996

Goldman, Pierre, *Souvenirs obscurs d'un juif polonais né en France*, Paris: Seuil, 1975

Goldring, Maurice, *La Goutte d'Or, quartier de France*, Paris: Autrement, 2006

Gordon, Daniel, 'Immigrants and the New Left in France, 1968-1971', DPhil thesis, University of Sussex, 2001

-, ' "Il est recommandé aux étrangers de ne pas participer": les étrangers expulsés en mai-juin 1968', *Migrations Société*, vol. 15, no. 87-88 (May-August 2003), pp. 45-65

-, 'Acteurs trans-méditerranéens dans un quartier cosmopolite. Juifs et musulmans à Belleville (Paris 20e), entre tolérance et conflit', *Cahiers de la Méditerrannée*, no. 67 (December 2003), pp. 287-298

-, 'A Nanterre, ça bouge: immigrés et gauchistes à Nanterre, 1968 à 1971', *Historiens et Géographes*, no. 385 (January 2004), pp. 75-86

-, 'The tower of Babel comes to north London', *The Voice of the Turtle*, October 2004

-, 'The back door of the nation state: expulsions of foreigners and continuity in twentieth-century France', *Past and Present*, no. 186 (February 2005), pp. 201-232

-, 'From May to October: reassessing the 1968 generation', *Modern and Contemporary France*, vol. 13, no. 2, May 2005, pp. 229-233

-, 'Controlling the streets in May 1968' in Jessica Wardhaugh, ed, *Paris and the Right in the Twentieth Century*, Newcastle: Cambridge Scholars, 2007, pp. 104-121

-, 'Daniel Guérin et le mouvement des travailleurs immigrés en France après 68', in David Berry, ed, *Daniel Guérin, Dissidences*, vol 2, Paris: L'Harmattan, 2007, pp. 197-216

-, 'Liquidating May '68: generational trajectories of the 2007 presidential candidates', *Modern and Contemporary France*, vol. 16, no. 2 (May 2008), pp. 143-159

-, 'History at last? 1968-2008', *Modern and Contemporary France*, vol. 17, no. 3 (August 2009), pp. 335-342

-, 'Memories of 1968 in France: reflections on the fortieth anniversary', in Sarah Waters and Ingo Cornils, eds, *Memories of 1968*, Bern: Peter Lang, 2010, pp. 49-78

-, 'A "Mediterranean New Left"? Comparing and contrasting the French PSU and the Italian PSIUP', *Contemporary European History*, vol. 19, no. 4 (November 2010), pp. 309-330

-, 'Reaching out to immigrants in May '68: specific or universal appeals?', in Julian Jackson et al, eds, *May '68*, Basingstoke: Palgrave Macmillan, 2011

Gorz, André, 'Avant-propos', *Les Temps Modernes*, no. 196-197 (September-October 1962), pp. 384-402

-, *Farewell to the Proletariat*, London: Pluto, 1997

- and Gavi, Philippe, 'La bataille d'Ivry', *Les Temps Modernes*, no. 284 (March 1970), pp. 1393-1416

Gregoire, Roger and Perlman, Fredy, *Worker-Student Action Committees*, Detroit: Black & Red, 1991

Greig, Ian, *Today's Revolutionaries*, London: Foreign Affairs, 1970

Gretton, John, *Students and Workers*, London: Macdonald, 1968

Grillo, Ralph, *Ideologies and Institutions in Urban France*, Cambridge: Cambridge University Press, 1985

Guha, Ranajit, ed, *Subaltern Studies*, Delhi: Oxford University Press, 1982

Guilao, Gamé, *France, terre d'acceuil, terre de rejet*, Paris: L'Harmattan, 1994

Hajjat, Abdellali, 'Le MTA et la "grève générale" contre le racisme de 1973', *Plein Droit*, no. 67 (December 2005), pp. 36-40

-, 'Mémoire des luttes de l'immigration, immigrés en lutte', *Origines Contrôlées*, no. 2 (October 2006), pp. 10-11

-, 'Le Mouvement des travailleurs arabes: sociologie d'une nouvelle génération politique dans l'immigration postcoloniale', paper to *Mai 68: Forty Years On* conference, University of London Institute in Paris, 15-17 May 2008

Halimi, Gisèle, *Le procès de Burgos*, Paris: Gallimard, 1971

-, *Milk for the Orange Tree*, London: Quartet, 1990

-, *Le procès de Bobigny*, Paris: Gallimard, 2006

Halliday, Fred, 'Students of the world unite' in Alexander Cockburn and Robin Blackburn, eds, *Student Power*, London: Penguin, 1969, pp. 287-326

Hammami, Hamma, *Le chemin de la dignité*, Paris: Comité National et Comité International de Soutien à Hamma Hammami et Ses Camarades, 2002

Hamon, Hervé and Rotman, Patrick, *Les porteurs de valises*, Paris: Albin

Michel, 1979

-, *Génération*, 2 vols, Paris: Seuil, 1987-1988

Hanrot, Bernard, *Les sans-voix dans le pays de la liberté*, Paris: Editions Ouvrières, 1976

Harbi, Mohammed, 'Dossier sur certains aspects occultés du FLN en France', *Sou'al*, no. 7 (September 1987), pp. 19-110

-, *Une vie debout*, Paris: La Découverte, 2001

Harding, Jeremy, 'On Elias Khoury', *London Review of Books*, vol 28, no 22 (16 November 2006), pp. 7-11

Hargreaves, Alec, *Immigration and identity in Beur fiction*, Oxford: Berg, 1997

-, *Multi-Ethnic France*, New York: Routledge, 2007

Harman, Chris, *The Fire Last Time*, London: Bookmarks, 1988

Harris, André and De Sédouy, Alain, *Voyage à l'intérieur du Parti communiste*, Paris: Seuil, 1974

Hatzfeld, Nicolas, et al, 'Mai 68: le débat continue', *Revue internationale des livres et des idées*, no. 6 (July-August 2008), pp. 54-57

Hauss, Charles, *The New Left in France*, Westport: Greenwood, 1978

Hayman, Ronald, *Writing Against*, London: Weidenfeld & Nicolson, 1986

Hessel, Stéphane, *Time for Outrage!*, London: Quartet, 2011

-, *Danse avec le siècle*, Paris: Points, 2011

Heurgon, Marc, *Histoire du PSU*, vol. 1, Paris: La Découverte, 1994

Hewlett, Nicholas, *Modern French Politics*, Cambridge: Polity, 1998

Hily, Marie-Antoinette and Poinard, Michel, 'Entre France et Portugal, l'attrait du va-et-vient', *Hommes et Migrations*, no. 1210 (November-December 1997), pp. 63-72

Hirsh, Arthur, *The French Left*, Montreal: Black Rose, 1982

Hobsbawm, Eric, *Age of Empire*, London: Pantheon, 1987

Holmes, Douglas, *Integral Europe*, Princeton: Princeton University Press, 2000

Horn, Gerd-Rainer, 'The language of symbols and the barriers of language: foreigners' perceptions of social revolution (Barcelona 1936-1937)', *History Workshop Journal*, no 29 (Spring 1990), pp. 42-64

-, *The Spirit of '68*, Oxford: Oxford University Press, 2007

Houari, Kassa, *Confessions d'un immigré*, Paris: Lieu Commun, 1988

House, Jim, 'Antiracism and antiracist discourse in France from 1900 to the present day', PhD thesis, University of Leeds, 1997

-, and MacMaster, Neil, *Paris 1961*, Oxford: Oxford University Press, 2006

Howkins, Alun, *Poor Labouring Men*, London: Routledge, 1985

Hoyles, Andrée, *Imagination in Power*, Nottingham: Spokesman, 1973

Hubert, Corine, ed, *1968 Un printemps val-de-marnais pas comme les autres*, Créteil: Conseil Général du Val-de-Marne, 1998

Jacob, James, *Hills of Conflict*, Reno: University of Nevada Press, 1994

Janitschek, Hans, *Mario Soares*, London: Weidenfeld & Nicolson, 1985

Jaubert, Alain, *Guide de la France des luttes*, Paris: Stock, 1974

Jazouli, Adil, *L'action collective des jeunes maghrébins de France*, Paris: CIEMI, 1986

-, *Les années banlieues*, Paris, 1992

Jeffreys, Steve, *Liberté, Egalité and Fraternité at Work*, Basingstoke: Palgrave Macmillan, 2003

Jelen, Brigitte, ' "Leur histoire est notre histoire": immigrant culture in France between visibility and invisibility', *French Politics, Culture and Society*, vol. 23, no. 2 (Summer 2005), pp.

Jenson, Jane and Ross, George, *The View from Inside*, Berkeley: University of California Press, 1984

Jessop, Bob, *Nicos Poulantzas*, Basingstoke: Macmillan, 1985

Joffrin, Laurent, *Mai 68*, Paris: Seuil, 1998

Johnson, R.W., *The Long March of the French Left*, London: Macmillan, 1981

Joly, Danièle, *The French Communist Party and the Algerian War*, Basingstoke: Macmillan, 1991

Judt, Tony, 'French Marxism 1945-1975', in *Marxism and the French Left*, Oxford: Clarendon, 1986, pp. 169-238

-, *Postwar*, London: Heinemann, 2005

-, *The Memory Chalet*, London: Heinemann, 2010

Juhem, Philippe, 'Entreprendre en politique de l'extrême gauche au PS: la professionalisation politique des fondateurs de SOS-Racisme', *Revue française de sciences politique*, vol. 51, nos 1-2 (February-April 2001), pp. 132-138

Jules-Rosette, Bennetta, *Black Paris*, Urbana: University of Illinois Press, 1998

Juquin, Pierre, *De battre mon coeur n'a jamais cessé*, Paris: Archipel, 2006

Kacet, Salem, *Le droit à la France*, Paris: Belfond, 1991

Kadri, Aïssa and Gérard Prévost, eds, *Mémoires algériennes*, Paris: Syllepse, 2004

Kassa, Sabrina, *Nos ancêtres les chibanis!*, Paris: Autrement, 2006

Kassimeris, George, 'Junta by another name? The 1974 *metapolitefsi* and the Greek extra-parliamentary Left', *Journal of Contemporary History*, vol. 40, no. 4 (October 2005), pp. 745-762

Kayman, Martin, *Revolution and Counterrevolution in Portugal*, London: Merlin, 1987

Keddie, Nikki, *Roots of Revolution*, New Haven: Yale University Press, 1981

Kedward, Rod, *French Roots*, Brighton: University of Sussex, 1995

Kenzi, Mohammed, *La menthe sauvage*, Lutry: Jean-Marie Bouchain, 1984

Kerbouc'h, Jean-Claude, *Le piéton de mai*, Paris: Julliard, 1968

Kergoat, Danièle, *Bulledor*, Paris: Seuil, 1973

Kernalegenn, Tudi, et al, eds, *Le PSU vu d'en bas*, Rennes: Presses Universitaires de Rennes, 2009

Kesler, Jean-François, *De la gauche dissidente au nouveau parti socialiste*, Paris: Privat, 1990

Kessel, Patrick, ed, *Le mouvement <<maoiste>> en France*, vol. 1, Paris: Union Générale, 1972

Kesselman, Mark and Groux, Guy, eds, *1968-1982: le mouvement ouvrier français*, Paris: Editions Ouvrières, 1984

Kettane, Nacer, *Le sourire de Brahim*, Paris: Denoël, 1985

-, *Droit de réponse à la démocratie française*, Paris: La Découverte, 1986

[Khayati, Mustapha], 'On the poverty of student life', in Dark Star, ed, *Beneath the Paving Stones*, Edinburgh: AK Press, 2001, pp. 9-27

Khilnani, Sunil, *Arguing Revolution*, New Haven: Yale University Press, 1993

Knapp, Andrew, *Parties and Party Systems in France*, Basingstoke: Palgrave Macmillan, 2004

Kravetz, Marc, et al, eds, *L'insurrection étudiante*, Paris: Union Générale, 1968

Krishnan, Raghu and Thomas, Adrien, 'Resistance to neo-liberalism in France', *Socialist Register* 2008, pp. 295-314

Krivine, Alain, *Ca te passera avec l'âge*, Paris: Flammarion, 2006

Laborde, Cécile, *Critical Republicanism*, Oxford: Oxford University Press, 2008

Labro, Philippe, *Ce n'est qu'un début*, Paris: Premières, 1968

Lacroix, Thomas, 'L'engagement citoyen des Marocains de l'étranger', *Hommes et Migrations*, no. 1256 (July-August 2005), pp. 89-102

Lallaoui, Mehdi, *Du bidonville aux HLM*, Paris: Syros, 1993

Leclerc, Henri, *Un combat pour la justice*, Paris: La Découverte, 1994

Le Cour Grandmaison, Olivier, ed, *Le 17 octobre 1961*, Paris: La Dispute, 2001

Lefebvre, Rémi and Sawicki, Frédéric, *La société des socialistes*, Broisseux:

Croquant, 2006

Lefort, François, *Du bidonville à l'expulsion*, Paris: CIEMM, 1980

Lemoine, Bertrand, *La Cité internationale universitaire de Paris*, Paris: Hervas, 1990

Lennon, Peter, *Foreign Correspondent*, London: Picador, 1994

Lentin, Alana, *Racism and Anti-Racism in Europe*, London: Pluto, 2004

Lequenne, Michel, *Le trotskisme*, Paris: Syllepse, 2005

Leuwers, Jean-Marie, *Un peuple se dresse*, Paris: Editions Ouvrières, 1969

Levine, Michel, *Affaires non classées*, Paris: Fayard, 1973

-, *Les ratonnades d'octobre*, Paris: Ramsay, 1985

Levy, Albert and Andréani, Caroline, *Chronique d'un combat inachevé*, Paris: MRAP, 1999

Lienart, Sylvie, 'Les circulaires Marcellin-Fontanet et les luttes des travailleurs immigrés', Masters thesis, Université de Paris VIII, 1975

Linhart, Robert, *The Assembly Line*, London: Calder, 1981

Linhart, Virginie, *Volontaires pour l'usine*, Paris: Seuil, 1994

Little, Adrian, *The Political Thought of André Gorz*, London: Routledge, 1996

Lloyd, Cathie, 'Racist violence and anti-racist reactions: a view of France', in Tore Björgo and Rob Witte, eds, *Racist Violence in Europe*, Basingstoke: Macmillan, 1993, pp. 207-220

-, *Discourses of Anti-Racism in France*, Aldershot: Ashgate, 1998

Lomax, Bill, 'Ideology and illusion in the Portuguese revolution: the role of the left', in Lawrence Graham and Douglas Wheeler, eds, *In Search of Modern Portugal*, Madison: Wisconsin University Press, 1983

Lumley, Robert, *States of Emergency*, London: Verso, 1990

Lyotard, Jean-François, 'Nanterre, içi, maintenant', *Les Temps Modernes*, no. 285 (April 1970), pp. 1650-1665

Macey, David, *The Lives of Michel Foucault*, London: Hutchinson, 1993

MacMaster, Neil, 'The role of European women and the question of mixed couples in the Algerian nationalist movement in France, circa 1918-1962', *French Historical Studies*, vol 34, no 2 (Spring 2011), pp. 357-386

Malley, Robert, *The Call from Algeria*, Berkeley: University of California Press, 1996

Manceaux, Michèle, *Les maos en France*, Paris: Gallimard, 1972

- and Donzelot, Jacques, *Cours camarade, le P.C.F. est derrière toi*, Paris: Gallimard, 1974

Manchuelle, François, *Willing Migrants*, Athens, Ohio: Ohio University Press, 1997

Maravall, José, *Dictatorship and Political Dissent*, London: Tavistock, 1978

Marcellin, Raymond, *L'ordre public et les groupes révolutionnaires*, Paris: Plon, 1969

Marcus, Jonathan, *The National Front and French Politics*, Basingstoke: Macmillan, 1995

Marcuse, Herbert, *One Dimensional Man*, Boston: Beacon, 1964

-, *Eros et civilisation*, Paris: Minuit, 1963

Marwick, Arthur, *The Sixties*, Oxford: Oxford University Press, 1998

Maspero, François, *Les passagers du Roissy-Express*, Paris: Seuil, 1990

Mauriac, Claude, *Et comme l'espérance est violente*, Paris: Grasset, 1976

-, *Une certaine rage*, Paris: Laffont, 1977

Maurienne, 'Un nouvel esclavage. Les travailleurs africains en France', *Partisans*, no. 9 (March-April 1963), pp. 137-152

Maxwell, Kenneth, *The Making of Portuguese Democracy*, Cambridge: Cambridge University Press, 1995

Mayer, Nonna, 'De Passy à Barbès: deux visages du vote Le Pen à Paris', *Revue française de sciences politiques*, vol. 37, no. 6 (December 1987), pp. 891-906

McGrogan, Manus, 'Vive la Révolution and the example of Lotta Continua: the circulation of ideas and practices between the left militant worlds of France and Italy following May '68', *Modern and Contemporary France*, vol. 18, no. 3 (August 2010), pp. 309-328

Memmi, Albert, *The Colonizer and the Colonized*, London: Earthscan, 1990

Merle, Robert, *Derrière la vitre*, Paris: Gallimard, 1970

Merrifield, Andy, *Metromarxism*, New York: Routledge, 2002

Mesaize, Michel, 'Renault-Flins, Aubergeville et les Mureaux', Masters dissertation, Université de Paris X, 1980

Meynier, Gilbert, *Histoire intérieure du FLN*, Paris: Fayard, 2004

Michelat, Guy and Simon, Michel, *Les ouvriers et la politique*, Paris: Presses de Sciences Po, 2004

Miller, Mark, *Foreign Workers in Western Europe*, New York: Praeger, 1981

Minces, Juliette, *Les travailleurs étrangers en France*, Paris: Seuil, 1973

Mitterrand, François, *Changer la vie*, Paris: Flammarion, 1972

Monchablon, Alain, *Histoire de l'UNEF*, Paris: Presses Universitaires de France, 1983

-, 'Syndicalisme étudiant et génération algérienne', in Jean-Pierre Rioux and Jean-François Sirinelli, eds, *La guerre d'Algérie et les intellectuels français*, Brussels: Complexe, 1991, pp. 175-189

Moss, David, 'Autonomia' in Gino Moliterno, ed, *Encyclopedia of Contemporary Italian Culture*, London: Routledge, 2000

Mouriaux, Réné, et al, eds, *1968 Exploration du mai français*, 2 vols, Paris: L'Harmattan, 1992

Mourlane, Stéphane, 'Le Parti communiste français et l'immigration italienne dans les années soixante', *Studi emigrazione*, no. 146 (June 2002), pp. 415-427

Mujal-León, Eusebio, *Communism and Political Change in Spain*, Bloomington: Indiana University Press, 1983

Mury, Gilbert, *On leur fera la peau*, Paris: Cerf, 1973

Nacht, Marc, 'Les travailleurs noirs en France ou la misère organisée', *Les Temps Modernes*, July 1964, pp. 152-162

Naylor, Ed, 'The Politics of a Presence: Algerians in Marseille from independence to "immigration sauvage" (1962-1974)', PhD thesis, Queen Mary University of London, 2011

N'Diaye, Jean-Pierre, *Enquête sur les étudiants noirs en France*, Paris: Réalités Africaines, 1962

-, *Négriers modernes*, Paris: Présence Africaine, 1970

N'Dongo, Sally, 'Itinéraire d'un militant africain', *Partisans*, no. 64 (March-April 1972), pp. 99-110

-, *Voyage forcé*, Paris: Maspero, 1975

Nick, Christophe, *Les trotskistes*, Paris: Fayard, 2002

Noiriel, Gérard, *Longwy. Immigrés et prolétaires*, Paris: Presses Universitaires de France, 1984

-, *Penser avec, penser contre*, Paris: Belin, 2003

-, *Immigration, antisémitisme et racisme en France (XIXe-XXe siècles)*, Paris: Fayard, 2007

- and Azzaoui, Bennaceur, *Vivre et lutter à Longwy*, Paris: Maspero, 1980

Nora, Pierre, *Realms of Memory*, 3 vols, New York: Columbia University Press, 1996-1998

Nugent, Neill and Lowe, David, *The Left in France*, London: Macmillan, 1981

Oriol, Paul, *Les immigrés, métèques ou citoyens?*, Paris: Syros, 1985

Orwell, George, *Down and Out in Paris and London*, London: Victor Gollancz, 1933

Ory, Pascal, *L'entre-deux-mai*, Paris: Seuil, 1983

O'Shaughnessy, Martin, *The New Face of Political Cinema*, New York: Berghahn, 2007

Paillat, Claude, *Archives secrètes*, Paris: Denoël, 1969

Panzani, Alex *Une prison clandestine de la police française (Arenc)*, Paris: Maspero, 1975

Papon, Maurice, *Les chevaux du pouvoir*, Paris: Plon, 1988

Parti des Indigènes de la République, 'The Tunisian Revolution: a source of inspiration to our *quartiers*', in Clare Solomon and Tania Palmieri, eds, *Springtime*, London: Verso, 2011, pp. 250-251

Parti Socialiste Unifié, *Contrôler aujourd'hui pour decider demain*, Paris: TEMA, 1973

Pelletier, Denis, *La crise catholique*, Paris: Payot, 2005

Pérez-Diaz, Victor, *The Return of Civil Society*, Cambridge, MA: Harvard University Press, 1993

Perreira, Victor, 'Pélérinage au Portugal révolutionnaire: les intellectuels français et la révolution des oeillets', in Anne Dulphy and Yves Léonard, eds, *De la dictature à la démocratie*, Brussels: Peter Lang, 2003, pp. 241-255

Perron, Tangui, *Histoire d'un film, mémoire d'une lutte. 1: Le Dos au mur*, Paris: Scope, 2007

-, *Histoire d'un film, mémoire d'une lutte. 2: Etrange étrangers*, Paris: Scope, 2009

-, 'Le territoire des images: pratique du cinema et luttes ouvrières en Seine-Saint-Denis (1968-1982)', *Le Mouvement Social*, no. 230 (January-March 2010), pp. 127-143

-, *Histoire d'un film, mémoire d'une lutte*, talk at Cité Nationale de l'Histoire de l'Immigration, Paris, 6 April 2010

Piot, Olivier, *La révolution tunisienne*, Paris: Les Petits Matins, 2011

Pitti, Laure, 'Grèves ouvrières versus luttes de l'immigration: une controverse entre historiens', *Ethnologie française*, vol. 31, no. 3 (July-September 2001), pp. 465-476

-, 'La main d'oeuvre algérienne dans l'industrie automobile (1945-1962), ou les oubliés de l'histoire', *Hommes et Migrations*, no. 1263 (September-October 2006), pp. 47-57

-, 'Filmer pour mobiliser: l'exemple de Penarroya', *Migrance*, no. 32 (4th quarter 2008), pp. 42-51

Pizzolato, Nicola, 'Workers and revolutionaries at the twilight of Fordism', *Labor History*, vol. 45, no. 4 (November 2004), pp. 419-443

-, 'Transnational radicals: labour dissent and political activism in Detroit and Turin (1950-1970)', *International Review of Social History*, vol. 56, no. 1 (April 2011), pp. 1-30

Polac, Catherine, 'Quand "les immigrés" prennent la parole', in Pascal Perrineau, ed, *L'engagement politique*, Paris: Presses de Sciences Po, 1994, pp. 359-376

Poperen, Jean, *L'Unité de la gauche 1965-1973*, Paris: Fayard, 1975
Posner, Charles, *Reflections on the Revolution in France*, Harmondsworth: Penguin, 1970
Puchot, Pierre, *Tunisie, une révolution arabe*, Paris: Galaade, 2011

Quattrocchi, Angelo and Nairn, Tom, *The Beginning of the End*, London: Panther, 1968

Raby, D.L., *Fascism and Resistance in Portugal*, Manchester: Manchester University Press, 1988
Rajsfus, Maurice, *Mai 68*, Paris: Cherche Midi, 1998
Ravignant, Patrick, *La prise de l'Odéon*, Paris: Stock, 1968
Raymond, Gino, *The French Communist Party during the Fifth Republic*, Basingstoke: Palgrave Macmillan, 2005
Raynaud, Philippe, *L'extrême gauche plurielle*, Paris: Autrement, 2006
Reader, Keith, *The May '68 Events in France*, Basingstoke: Macmillan, 1993
Reid, Donald, 'Etablissment: working in the factory to make revolution in France', *Radical History Review*, no. 88 (Winter 2004), pp. 83-112
Rioux, Lucien and Backmann, René, *L'explosion de mai*, Paris: Laffont, 1968
Roman, Constantin, *Continental Drift*, Bristol: Institute of Physics, 2000
Ronen, Yehudit, 'Moroccan immigration in the Mediterranean region: reflections in Ben Jelloun's literary works', *Journal of North African Studies*, vol. 6, no. 4 (Winter 2001), pp. 1-14
Rosello, Mireille, *Postcolonial Hospitality*, Stanford: Stanford University Press, 2001
Ross, Kristin, *Fast Cars, Clean Bodies*, Cambridge, MA: MIT Press, 1996
-, *May 68 and its Afterlives*, Chicago: Chicago University Press, 2002
Rousseau, Charles, 'Chronique des faits internationaux', *Revue de droit international public*, vol. 73, no. 1 (January-March 1969), pp. 181-183
Rousseau, Sabine, 'Frères du Monde et la guerre du Vietnam: du tiers-mondisme à l'anti-impérialisme (1965-1973)', *Le Mouvement Social*, no. 177 (October-December 1996), pp. 71-88
Rowbotham, Sheila, *Promise of a Dream*, London: Allen Lane, 2000
-, Segal, Lynne and Wainwright, Hilary, *Beyond the Fragments*, London: Merlin, 1979
Rozès, Stéphane, 'Anti-libéralisme idéologique et anti-capitalisme politique dans la France de 2005: discontinuité et perspectives', paper to Association for the Study of Modern and Contemporary France conference, Loughborough University, 8-10 September 2005
Ruscio, Alain, ed, *La question coloniale dans l'Humanité 1904-2004*, Paris: La Dispute, 2005

Salhi, Kamal, ed, *Francophone Voices*, Exeter: Elm Bank, 1999

Salles, Jean-Paul, *La Ligue communiste révolutionnaire (1968-1981)*, Rennes: Presses Universitaires de Rennes, 2005

Salvaresi, Elisabeth, *Mai en héritage*, Paris: Syros, 1988

Sarkozy, Nicolas, *Témoignage*, Paris: XO, 2006

Sarrasin, Michel, *Histoires de mai*, Choisy-le-Roi: Temps Présent, 1978

Sartre, Jean-Paul, *Critique of Dialectical Reason*, vol 1, London: Verso, 2004

- 'Justice et Etat', in *Situations X*, Paris: Gallimard, 1976

Savage, Jon, *England's Dreaming*, London: Faber & Faber, 2001

Sayad, Abdelmalek, 'Le Foyer des sans-famille', *Actes de la recherche en sciences sociales*, nos 32-33 (April-June 1980), pp. 89-103

-, *The Suffering of the Immigrant*, Cambridge: Polity, 2004

Schalk, David, *War and the Ivory Tower*, Lincoln, Nebraska: Nebraska University Press, 2005

Schor, Ralph, *L'opinion française et les étrangers en France 1919-1939*, Paris: Sorbonne, 1985

Seale, Patrick and McConville, Maureen, *French Revolution 1968*, Harmondsworth: Penguin, 1968

Seidman, Michael, 'Workers in a repressive society of seductions: Parisian metallurgists in May-June 1968', *French Historical Studies*, vol. 18, no. 1 (Spring 1993), pp. 255-278

-, *The Imaginary Revolution*, New York, 2004

Serrou, Robert, *Dieu n'est pas conservateur*, Paris: Laffont, 1968

Shaw, Randy, *Beyond the Fields*, Berkeley: University of California Press, 2008

Shepard, Todd, *The Invention of Decolonization*, Ithaca: Cornell University Press, 2006

-, 'After deaths, after-lives', *History Workshop Journal*, no. 66 (Autumn 2008), pp. 242-252

Signoret, Simone, *Nostalgia Isn't What It Used To Be*, London: Grafton, 1986

Silverman, Maxim, ed, *Race, Discourse and Power in France*, Aldershot: Avebury, 1991

-, *Deconstructing the Nation*, London: Routledge, 1992

Siméant, Johanna, 'Immigration et action collective: l'exemple des mobilisations d'étrangers en situation irrégulière', *Sociétés Contemporaines*, no. 20 (1994), pp. 39-62

-, *La cause des sans-papiers*, Paris: Presses de Sciences Po, 1998

Simon, Catherine, *Algérie, les années pieds-rouges*, Paris: La Découverte, 2009

Simon, Jacques, et al, *L'immigration algérienne en France*, Paris: L'Harmattan, 2002

Simon, Jean-Pierre, ed, *La révolution par elle-même*, Paris: Albin Michel, 1969

Sirinelli, Jean-François, *Les babyboomers*, Paris: Fayard, 2003

Sivanandan, Ambalavaner, *Race and Resistance*, London: Race Today, 1974

Smith, Alison, 'The problems of immigration as shown in the French cinema of the 1970s', *Modern and Contemporary France*, vol. 3, no. 1 (1995), pp. 41-50

Soubise, Louis, *Le marxisme après Marx (1956-1965)*, Paris: Montaigne, 1967

Spender, Stephen, *The Year of the Young Rebels*, London: Weidenfeld & Nicolson, 1969

Spire, Alexis, 'L'héritage de l'expérience coloniale dans la réorganisation du traitement de l'immigration (1945-1974)', paper to Society for French Historical Studies Conference, Paris, 17-20 June 2004

-, *Etrangers à la carte*, Paris: Grasset, 2005

Spire, Antoine, *Profession permanent*, Paris: Seuil, 1980

Sportès, Morgan, *Ils ont tué Pierre Overney*, Paris: Grasset, 2008

Stora, Benjamin, *La gangrène et l'oubli*, Paris: La Découverte, 1992

-, *Ils venaient d'Algérie*, Paris: Fayard, 1992

-, *Le transfert d'une mémoire*, Paris: La Découverte, 1999

-, *La dernière génération d'octobre*, Paris: Stock, 2003

Stutje, Jan Willem, *Ernest Mandel*, London: Verso, 2009

Susser, Ida, ed, *The Castells Reader on Cities and Social Theory*, Oxford: Blackwell, 2002

Talbo, Jean-Philippe, *La grève à Flins*, Paris: Maspero, 1968

Tarnero, Jacques, *Mai 68, la révolution fiction*, Toulouse: Milan, 1998

Tartakowsky, Danièle, *Les manifestations de rue en France*, Paris: Sorbonne, 1997

Temime, Emile, 'Les conditions de vie hors travail', in Renaud Sainsaulieu and

Ahsène Zehraoui, eds, *Ouvriers specialisés à Billancourt*, Paris: L'Harmattan, 1995, pp. 351-365

Terrasse, Jean-Marc, *Génération Beur*, Paris: Plon, 1989

Thompson, Duncan, *Pessimism of the Intellect?*, London: Merlin, 2007

Thompson, E.P., *The Making of the English Working Class*, London: Pelican, 1968

-, 'The Poverty of Theory' in *The Poverty of Theory and other essays*, London:

Merlin, 1978, pp. 193-397

[Jean-Pierre Thorn], *Oser lutter, oser vaincre*, screenplay, Paris: Nouvelles Presses Parisiennes, 1972

Trappo, Hélène, 'De la clandestinité à la reconnaissance', *Plein Droit*, no. 11 (July 1990)

Trindade, Maria, *Immigrés portugais*, Lisbon: Instituto Superior de Ciências Sociais e Política Ultramarina, 1973

Tripier, Maryse, *L'immigration dans la classe ouvrière en France*, Paris: L'Harmattan, 1990

Tristan, Anne, *Le silence du fleuve*, Paris: Au Nom de la Mémoire, 1991

Turpin, Pierre, *Les révolutionnaires dans la France social-démocrate*, Paris: L'Harmattan, 1997

Ulloa, Marie-Pierre, *Francis Jeanson*, Stanford: Stanford University Press, 2007

UNEF / SNESUP Commission Témoignages et Assistance Juridique, *Ils accusent*, Paris: Seuil, 1968

Vaïsse, Maurice, ed, *Mai 68 vu de l'étranger*, Paris: CNRS, 2008

Van, Ngo, *In the Crossfire*, Edinburgh: AK Press, 2010

Verbunt, Gilles, *L'intégration par l'autonomie*, Paris: CIEMM, 1980

Vergès, Jacques, *Le salaud lumineux*, Paris: Michel Lafon, 1990

Vermeren, Pierre, *Histoire du Maroc depuis l'indépendance*, Paris: La Découverte, 2006

Vidal-Naquet, Pierre, *Torture: Cancer of Democracy*, Harmondsworth: Penguin, 1963

-, 'Où en est le mouvement de mai?', *Raison Présente*, no. 17 (January-March 1971)

Viénet, Réné, *Enragés et situationnistes dans le mouvement des occupations*, Paris: Gallimard, 1998

Viet, Vincent, *La France immigrée*, Paris: Fayard, 1998

Vieuguet, André, *Français et immigrés*, Paris: Editions Sociales, 1975

Vigna, Xavier, *L'insubordination ouvrière dans les années 68*, Rennes: Presses Universitaires de Rennes, 2007

Villanueva, Angel, 'Causes et structures de l'émigration', *Partisans*, no. 34-35 (December 1966-January 1967)

Vinen, Richard, *France 1934-1970*, Basingstoke: Macmillan, 1996

Volovitch-Tavares, Marie-Christine, *Portugais à Champigny*, Paris: Autrement, 1995

-, 'L'Eglise de France et l'accueil des immigrés portugais', *Le Mouvement Social*, no. 188 (July-September 1999), pp. 89-102

-, 'Les immigrés portugais en France et la "Révolution des oeillets" ', in Maria Helena Araujo Carreira, ed, *De la révolution des oeillets au 3è millenaire, Travaux et Documents,* no. 7 (2000), pp. 147-164
-, 'Les immigrés portuguais et la guerre coloniale portuguaise (1961-1974)', paper to *Emigration politique en France et en Argentine* conference, Université de Paris 7, 24-25 March 2000
-, 'Les incertitudes et les contradictions d'une "bonne intégration: les immigrants catholiques portugais en France, des années soixante aux années quatre-vingt', *Cahiers de la Méditerranée,* no. 78 (2009), pp. 158-176
Von Bülow, Catherine, *La Goutte-d'Or ou le Mal des racines,* Paris: Stock, 1979

Wadia, Kursheed, 'France: from unwilling host to bellicose gatekeeper', in Gareth Dale and Mike Cole, *The European Union and Migrant Labour,* Oxford: Berg, 1999
Waintrater, Meïr, ed, 'Benny Lévy, le passeur', *L'Arche,* no. 549-550 (November-December 2003), pp. 40-61
Wasserman, Gilbert, *Nanterre: une histoire,* Paris: Temps Actuels, 1982
Weil, Patrick, *La France et ses étrangers,* Paris: Gallimard, 1995
Werner, Paul, 'David's basket: art and agency in the French Revolution', PhD thesis, City University of New York, 1997
Wieser, Brigitte, et al, 'Militer, un jeu d'enfant', *Projet,* no. 321 (April-May 2011), pp. 4-19
Wihtol de Wenden, Catherine, *Les immigrés et la politique,* Paris: Presses de Sciences Po, 1988
-, 'Ethnic minority mobilisation against racism in France', in Alec Hargreaves, ed, *Racism, Ethnicity and Politics in Contemporary Europe,* Aldershot: Edward Elgar, 1995, pp. 240-252
- and Leveau, Rémy, *La beurgeoisie,* Paris: CNRS, 2001
Wolin, Richard, *Wind From the East,* Princeton: Princeton University Press, 2010
Wright, Steve, *Storming Heaven,* London: Pluto, 2002
Yati, S., 'D'un désert à l'autre: le périple d'un jeune Algérien, du Sahara à Nanterre', *Preuves,* no. 214 (January 1969)
Ysas, Pere, *Disidencia y subversión,* Barcelona: Critica, 2004
Zancarini-Fournel, Michelle, 'La question immigrée après 68', *Plein Droit,* no. 53-54 (March 2002)
-, *Le Moment 68,* Paris: Seuil, 2008
-, 'Jeux d'echelle: local-régional-national', paper to *Mai 68: Forty Years On* conference, University of London Institute in Paris, 15-17 May 2008

5. Journal special issues

Cahiers du Centre d'études socialistes, nos 94-98 (September-December 1969): *Les travailleurs immigrés parlent*
Contretemps, no 16 (January 2006): *Postcolonialisme et immigration*
Esprit, vol. 34, no. 4 (April-June 1966): *Les étrangers en France*
Manière de voir, no. 89 (October-November 2006): *Banlieues: trente ans d'histoire et de révoltes*
Migrance, no. 25 (3rd trimester 2005): *Immigration et luttes sociales*
Notes et études documentaires, nos 4201-4203 (7 July 1974): *Textes et documents rélatifs à l'élection présidentielle des 5 et 19 mai 1974* and 4647-4648 (21 December 1981): *Textes et documents rélatifs à l'élection présidentielle des 26 avril et 10 mai 1981*
Le Mouvement Social, no. 64 (July-September 1968): *La Sorbonne par elle-même*
Partisans, no. 42 (May-June 1968): *Ouvriers étudiants un seul combat*
Politique aujourd'hui, unnumbered (March-April 1975): *Immigrés, étrangers ou travailleurs*
Presse et Immigrés en France, no. 104-105 (March-April 1983): *Insécurité et immigration*
Questions Clefs, no. 2 (March 1982): *Jeunes immigrés hors les murs*

6. Film, television and radio

L'armée de crime (2009), dir. Robert Guédiguian
L'avocat de la terreur (2007), dir. Barbet Schroeder
Le chagrin et la pitié (1969), dir. Marcel Ophüls
Code 68 (2004), dir. Jean-Henri Roger
De l'autre côté du périph (1998), dir. Bertrand Tavernier
Dossier Penarroya: les deux visages du trust (1972), dir. Daniel Anselme and Dominique Dubosc
Douce France (1992), dir. Ken Fero and Mogniss Abdallah
The Edukators (2004), dir. Hans Weingartner
Est-ce ainsi que les hommes vivent? (1976), dir. Claude Dityvon
Etranges étrangers (1970), dir. Marcel Trillat and Frédéric Variot
Excess Baggage: Alternative Paris, BBC Radio 4, 25 November 2000
La Fabrique de l'Histoire: Histoire des étrangers, episode 1, France Culture, 7 January 2008
Les gens des baraques (1995), dir. Robert Bozzi
Le gone du Chaâba (1997), dir. Christophe Ruggia

Haya (1982), dir. Claude Blanche
Ils ont voulu le pouvoir, LCP, 9 August 2011
Lobo (2004) dir. Miguel Courtois
The Making of Rocky Road to Dublin (2004), dir. Paul Duane
Marie-George Buffet campaign broadcast, France 2, 16 April 2007
Mémoires d'immigrés (1997), dir. Yamina Benguigui
Mourir à trente ans (1982), dir. Romain Goupil
News broadcast, France 24, 15 January 2011
Penarroya St Denis (1971), dir. Cahiers de Mai
La saga des immigrés (2007) dir. Edouard Mills-Affif and Anne Riegel
Salvador (2006), dir. Manuel Huelga
Secret History: Drowning By Bullets, Channel 4, 13 July 1992
Tout va bien (1972), dir. Jean-Luc Godard and Jean-Pierre Gorin
Marcel Trillat, portrait (2008), dir. Tangui Perron and Philippe Troyon
Vivre au paradis (1999), dir. Bourlem Guerdjou

7. Websites

Anseur, Fayçal, 'Interview exclusive du Président Abdel Jelil Bedoui: le PTT crée son parti travailliste en Tunisie', http://www.algerie-focus.com, 3 May 2011
Bouamama, Saïd, 'Les indigènes de la république', http://www.indigenes-republique.org/spip.php?article37, 15 March 2006
Boumediene-Thiery, Alima, 'Ma vie telle que racontée souvent à la presse', http://alima-boumediene.org.spip.php?article11, 30 June 2003
-, 'Qui est Alima Boumediene-Thiery?', http://alima-boumediene.org.spip.php?article35, 26 September 2004
Buffet, Marie-George, 'L'école de mon enfance', video, www.mariegeorge2007.org, April 2007
Camau, Michel and Geisser, Vincent, 'Entretien avec M. Noureddine Ben Khedder', http://lerenouveau.ettajdid.org/spip.php?article255, 20 July 2008
Delanoë, Bertrand, 'Réaction suite au décès de Saïd Bouziri', www.paris.fr/portail/acceuil/Portal.lut?page_id=8447&document_type_id=7&document_id=70655&portlet_id=19708, 24 June 2009
Dréano, Bernard, 'Le Cedetim ou la continuité d'un combat', http://www.reseau-ipam.org/article-imprim-cedetim.php3?id_article=930, 14 April 2005
Elayoubi, Salah, 'Règlements de comptes à Clermont-Ferrand: El Ghazaoui contre El Yazami', http://solidmar.blogspot.com/2011/08/zineb-el-ghazoui-demasque-driss-el.html, 26 August 2011

European Court, 'Judgement of the Court of 28 October 1975: Roland Rutili vs Ministre de l'intérieur', http://eurlex.europa.eu/smartapi/cgi/sga_doc?s martapi!celexplus!prod!CELEXnumdoc&lg=en&numdoc=61975J0036.

European Parliament footage, BBC Democracy Live, http://news.bbc.co.uk/democracylive, 17 January and 10 May 2011

Fédération des Tunisiens pour une Citoyenneté des deux Rives, 'Février 1974: Il y a 36 ans naissait l'UTIT (FTCR)', http://www.citoyensdesdeuxrives.eu, 18 February 2010

Gagné, Jean-Simon, 'L'ancien leader étudiant Daniel Cohn-Bendit: "Oublions mai 68!" ', http://www.cerium.ca/L-ancien-leader-etudiant-Daniel, 19 March 2008

Génériques, www.generiques.org, 2008-2011

Horchani, Abderrazak Bouazizi, 'Notre frère et ami Ali Majri alias Ali Clichy vient de nous quitter', http://www.atf-paris.fr/spip.php?article509, 28 February 2011

Madeira, Manuel, 'O Salto: synopsis/observations', www.sudexpress.org, 2003

Marzouki, Myriam, 'Curriculum Vitae: le médécin et le militant', http://moncefmarzouki.com/spip.php?article41, 21 July 2005

Oriol, Paul, 'Alger en mai', http://pauloriol.over-blog.fr/article-18930235.html, 21 April 2008

Philippon, Guy, 'Paul Oriol ou la tenacité à construire L'égalité des droits entre Français et Immigrés', http://www.philippon.org/psu/index.php?2010/11/23/96-paul-oriol-ou-la-tenacite-a-construire-legalite-des-droits-entre-francais-et-immigres, 23 November 2010

Rousselin, Paul, 'A Flins, les ouvriers n'en pouvaient plus', http://www.libe.com/mai68/jour/jour0515b.html, 15 May 1998

Index

Also published by the Merlin Press

Anti-Apartheid: A History of the Movement in Britain, 1959-1994
Roger Fieldhouse

This is the first full length study drawing on AAM archives, a full and substantial history of the Anti-Apartheid Movement from birth to death and beyond. It shows how things happened, it assesses AAM's achievements and evaluates its impact and effectiveness.

"Fieldhouse provides all the facts that the serious students needs and does so in clear, careful, concise considered English. ...It will surely be the first reference book those with a serious interest in the subject turn to" New Statesman

Paperback, ISBN 978 0 85036549 8 £22.50

London Recruits: The Secret War against Apartheid
Compiled and edited by Ken Keable
with an introduction by Ronnie Kasrils and a foreword by Z. Pallo Jordan

The history of the Anti-Apartheid movement brings up images of boycotts and public campaigns in the UK. But another story went on behind the scenes, in secret, one that has been never told before. This is the story of the foreign volunteers and their activities in South Africa, how they acted in defiance of the Apartheid government and its police on the instructions of the African National Congress. It tells of: ANC Banners that unfurled, ANC speeches that sounded through public places, buckets that exploded and showered ANC leaflets the transportation of weapons, communications, logistics, aid for ANC fighters to enter South Africa, and more..... This is their untold story.

Spring 2012, Paperback, 362 pages, ISBN 978 0 85036 655 6 £15.95

European Revolutionaries and Algerian Independence, 1954-1962
Edited by Ian Birchall

The book considers the course of Algerian War 1954-1962, and the response of the French left. It offers the fullest account in English of the role of the revolutionary left in giving political and practical solidarity to the Algerian liberation struggle. It presents substantial extracts from Sylvain Pattieu's, Les camarades des frères (Paris 2002), and will gives the fullest account of the role of Trotskyists in this period, drawing on documents and interviews with participants.
An Appendix considers how the war has been reflected in fiction.
Revolutionary History, Vol. 10, No.4

Spring 2012, Paperback, ISBN 978 0 85036 665 5   £16.95

A History of Pan-African Revolt
C.L.R. James, with an introduction by Robin D.G. Kelley

Originally published in England in 1938 (the same year as his magnum opus The Black Jacobins), and expanded in 1969, this work remains the classic account of global Black Resistance. Robin D.G. Kelley's substantial introduction contextualizes the work in the history and ferment of the times, and explores its ongoing relevance today. "one of those rare books that continues to strike a chord of urgency, even half a century after it was first published. Time and time again, its lessons have proven to be valuable and relevant for understanding liberation movements in Africa and the diaspora. Each generation who has had the opportunity to read this small book finds new insights, new lessons, new visions for their own age…. "A mine of ideas advancing far ahead of its time." –Walter Rodney.

Autumn 2012, Paperback, About 160 pages, ISBN 978 0 85036 660 0
£12.99